William Cowper, 1731–1800

WILLIAM COWPER

❧ *A Critical Life* ❧

BY

MAURICE J. QUINLAN

THE UNIVERSITY OF MINNESOTA PRESS
Minneapolis

PUBLISHED IN GREAT BRITAIN, INDIA, AND PAKISTAN BY
GEOFFREY CUMBERLEGE: OXFORD UNIVERSITY PRESS, LONDON, BOMBAY, AND KARACHI

TO

Anna, Margaret, and Mary

Preface

THE eighteenth century has sometimes been called a static age. This term has a proper application if we mean that the century was an era that defined taste, formulated rules for poetry, architecture, and painting, adhered to certain formalities, and viewed with satisfaction the stage of civilization it had reached. In retrospect, however, it seems more logical to regard the second half of the century as a great transitional period that brought the Renaissance to its lingering close and set the stage for modern life. As the following anecdote illustrates, by the middle of the era new ideas were already stirring the complacency of the upper ranks of society.

Lord Chesterfield, the personification of grace and polish, once found himself in the company of Mrs. Macaulay and Lady Huntingdon. The first of these ladies, having embraced republican principles, was prone to seize every opportunity to express her belief in equality. The second was a disciple of Whitefield and one of the few wealthy converts among the first generation of Methodists. Having somehow cornered the fastidious and cynical Lord Chesterfield, the two ladies launched into a fervent discussion of their political and religious views. The famous aristocrat, though bored and uncomfortable, was much too courteous to reveal his true feelings. Instead he complimented Mrs. Macaulay on her learning and humanity, and then, turning to her companion, he started to commend her piety and zeal. But Lady

Huntingdon, who professed to believe in the utter depravity of human nature, interrupted him. "Oh!" she sighed. "It is for want of your Lordship's knowing me more perfectly that you speak in such flattering terms, for I am conscious that I am nothing better than a poor, vile, miserable, sinful creature."

This exercise in self-abasement gave the quick-witted Lord his opportunity to make a polite exit. Bowing to both ladies, he said, "My excellent Lady Huntingdon, I never yet was in any room where I could stay and hear your ladyship abused. I am therefore under the immediate necessity of bidding your ladyship good morrow."

This anecdote does more than illustrate Lord Chesterfield's wit. His withdrawal from a discussion of democracy and Evangelical religion was symbolic of impending changes. Eventually the whole social structure of which he was one of the brightest ornaments was destined to give way to Evangelicalism, democracy, and the industrial revolution. These forces would not completely triumph for several decades, but they were already starting to crowd out the old order. That is why the second half of the eighteenth century may aptly be called an age of transition.

William Cowper, the subject of this biography, played an important part in the transition, since he was the leading poet of the religious revival. A considerable body of writing, designed chiefly to win converts and to govern opinion and conduct, was produced by the Evangelicals. As propaganda it was extremely effective. It revived Sabbatarianism, it created new forms of censorship, it promoted a rigid code of conduct and morals — in short, it did much to establish the social standards of the Victorian era. But the literature itself, with the exception of several hymns and a few other works, was soon forgotten. W. H. Lecky, writing in 1878, observed that almost no one read William Romaine's *Life of Faith*, Thomas Scott's *Force of Truth*, James Hervey's *Meditations,* or a dozen other volumes that had once been best-sellers. Among the various Evangelical writers only

Cowper had survived — and still survives — the rigorous judgment of time.

What has kept the poetry of Cowper alive? Certainly there are few today who read him for his religious message. One reason for his appearance in anthologies, of course, is the fact that he is a transitional poet in a second and more obvious sense. During the last two decades of the eighteenth century a new group of poets broke with the critical rules of the age and, by introducing new subjects and writing in their own manner, helped to usher in the romantic movement. Among the precursors of this movement Cowper best represents the transition from the old to the new. Unlike Burns and Blake, he was a fine classical scholar who knew and admired the Ancients. Possessing neither the eccentric individualism of Blake nor the artistic provinciality of Burns, he was nonetheless something of an innovator. His interest in nature, his lyrical qualities, and especially his strong personal note link him with Wordsworth and the other romantics, just as his classical tastes, his moral satires, and certain traits of prosody bear the stamp of the eighteenth century.

Cowper's reputation as a writer, however, rests more firmly on his particular merits than upon his place in social or literary history. Readers admire him as a nature poet, as a poet of domestic life, or as a writer of occasional verse. They like the unaffected tone of his letters and his whimsical and often shrewd comments on men and manners. But the perennial charm that he holds for those who know him best is not so easy to explain. There have been greater poets and more informative letter-writers, yet there are times when one returns to Cowper in preference to these others. Part of his distinctive charm, I feel, is the rapprochement he establishes with his readers. To be sure, he wrote for an audience of a different age, with different manners and values. But one thing that does not change is the appeal of an author who can strike up a fireside intimacy with his readers. And somehow the fireside seems to be the most appropriate place for reading him. Certain poets may be better suited to other times and places — Byron at the seaside, for instance, or Wordsworth in the country. Cowper, because of his warm, intimate tone, is especially a poet for a quiet winter evening when one has and needs no other diversion.

Finally one must confess that the interest in Cowper has been kept alive partly by the strange circumstances of his life. Although he can be an extremely cheerful companion, the reader can never quite forget that during his productive years his mind was gripped by the harrowing obsession that he was irrevocably damned. This conviction and his periodic fits of insanity make him one of the most pathetic and puzzling figures in English biography. In this work I have been able, I feel, to shed some new light upon his obsession and to reveal some hitherto unobserved influences which it had upon his verse. I must admit, however, like everyone else who has studied his mental history, that certain baffling aspects of his insanity remain, and no doubt will always remain, unsolved.

My chief purpose in writing this critical biography has been to show the man in relation to his works and his works in relation to his life. This approach seems particularly rewarding since Cowper's letters and poetry give so clear a reflection of his personality. His works, in turn, though seldom obscure, become more meaningful when studied in relation to his life and milieu. My task has been the easier because of various specialized studies of Cowper that have appeared in the past twenty-five years. While no one of these seriously alters our conception of the poet, taken together they serve to deepen our knowledge of his life and works. Recent biographies of Cowper's friends have shed additional if somewhat indirect light on the man. I refer in particular to *Blake's Hayley,* by Morchard Bishop, and to *John Newton,* by Bernard Martin. I have also had the opportunity to consult unpublished letters and other manuscripts. This considerable body of material, much of which was not available to earlier biographers, makes possible a new appraisal of William Cowper, and that is what I have attempted in this volume.

I wish here to acknowledge the kind assistance I have had from various sources. Professor James L. Clifford has added to many past favors by reading the manuscript and giving me valuable criticism. Professor Hoxie N. Fairchild, who many years ago encouraged me to undertake this biography, has made available to me his transcript of a Diary by Cowper's cousin, John Johnson. I am especially indebted to my good friends Mr. and Mrs. Albert C. Coote for their cheerful assistance in putting this work into final form. I wish also to express my gratitude to the American Philosophical Society for a Penrose Fund Grant that enabled me to complete research in England.

M. J. Q.

November 1952
St. Paul, Minnesota

Table of Contents

WILLIAM COWPER
A Critical Life

Youth

How readily we wish time spent revoked,
That we might try the ground again, where once
(Through inexperience as we now perceive)
We missed the happiness we might have found!
TASK VI.25–28

T HE hero of an eighteenth-century novel was often a robustious, self-sufficient youth, able to fend for himself, without the help of family or friends. He wrestled with fortune, as he did with his adversaries, and no matter what trials he met, he triumphed in the end. The strong, independent man has always had his counterpart in life, but most mortals, lacking this degree of self-sufficiency, must rely on others for strength, encouragement, and solace. William Cowper belonged to this larger class of humanity. Even more than most men, he needed the comradeship, interest, and sympathy of friends. As Sainte-Beuve so sagely remarked, he especially needed a mother.

Cowper's mother died when he was six years old. Born Anne Donne, she could trace her lineage back to Henry III and numbered the seventeenth-century poet John Donne among her ancestors. During the ten years of her married life she bore seven children. All died in infancy or early childhood with the exception of William, born November 26, 1731, and John, born November 7, 1737, a few days before his mother's death.

John Cowper, the poet's father, was rector of St. Peter's Church at Great Berkhampstead, Hertfordshire, and chaplain to George

II. One of his progenitors, Sir William Cowper, Baronet, of Rat-
ling Court, Kent, had been a loyal supporter of Charles I, although the family later became Whigs. Two of the baronet's
grandsons rose to positions of particular eminence during the
first decades of the eighteenth century. The first, also named
William Cowper, became Lord High Chancellor of England in
1707. His younger brother, Spencer Cowper, served as Judge of
the Court of Common Pleas as well as Chief Justice of Chester.
He was the father of the rector of Great Berkhampstead and the
grandfather of the poet. The Reverend John Cowper remarried
after the death of his first wife. Although Cowper lived at the
vicarage much of the time when he was not at school, he seems
to have formed no great attachment to his stepmother. In later
life he customarily referred to his father with filial respect, and
upon one occasion he spoke of the "sweetness of his temper and
character," [1] but from what little we know of the Reverend Mr.
Cowper, it would appear that he did not give his elder son the
affection which he so much needed.

For a record of Cowper's childhood one must rely chiefly on
his *Memoir*. This account, written shortly after his conversion
to Evangelical religion, is an interesting and sometimes frank
biography of his spiritual life. Like most converts, he over-
stressed his sinfulness before his religious awakening, and he was
so much preoccupied with the story of his regeneration that he
omitted many details of his ordinary life. For the most part his
recollections of early childhood were painful. At the age of six
he was enrolled in Dr. Pitman's Boarding School in Bedfordshire.
His existence there was made miserable by one youth who took
pleasure in continually persecuting the small boy. "I well remember being afraid to lift my eyes upon him higher than his
knees," Cowper later wrote, "and that I knew him better by his
shoebuckles than by any other part of his dress." [2] He did not
indicate what specific shame or humiliation he endured at school,
but the *Memoir* reveals that childhood, for most people a
pleasant period in retrospect, was for him a painful and unhappy experience.

4

Later in life Cowper wrote a poem entitled *Tirocinium,* in which he praised private instruction and, by contrast, bitterly indicted the English public school system. One of the most satiric passages he ever composed describes the evil influence of these schools on youth:

> Would you your son should be a sot or dunce,
> Lascivious, headstrong, or all these at once;
> That in good time the stripling's finished taste
> For loose expense and fashionable waste
> Should prove your ruin, and his own at last;
> Train him in public with a mob of boys,
> Childish in mischief only and in noise,
> Else of a mannish growth, and five in ten
> In infidelity and lewdness men.
> There shall he learn, ere sixteen winters old,
> That authors are most useful pawned or sold;
> That pedantry is all that schools impart,
> But taverns teach the knowledge of the heart;
> There waiter Dick, with bacchanalian lays,
> Shall win his heart, and have his drunken praise,
> His counsellor and bosom friend shall prove,
> And some street-pacing harlot his first love.

Although *Tirocinium* contains a strong protest against public schools, too much autobiographical significance has been attached to it. From the *Memoir* one gathers that Cowper's difficulties at Dr. Pitman's were owing largely to the brutality of his schoolfellows, yet in this poem he scarcely mentions bullies. Furthermore, he observes that students of a past generation, presumably those of his own time, were fairly sober and studious youngsters by comparison with the rapscallions of later days. Thus Cowper was not writing a mere chronicle of his bitter experiences as a boy, even though he drew upon his memory for details of public school life.

Because he was troubled by weak eyesight, Cowper was removed from Dr. Pitman's after two years and sent to live with a Mr. and Mrs. Disney, both of whom were oculists. The poet makes no comment on the period he spent in this household except to mention, in the characteristically pious tone of the *Memoir*, that the family neither knew nor practiced religion.

In 1741, at the age of ten, he entered Westminster, where he was to pass the next eight years. This tradition-shrouded institution, dating from the reign of Henry VIII, had gained particular renown under the direction of Richard Busby, who became headmaster in 1638. Introducing various innovations, he had discarded time-honored works like Lyly's Latin Grammar and substituted books composed under his own supervision. His students learned to pronounce Latin more in the English manner, a practice that soon spread to other schools. Greek, Hebrew, and mathematics were also stressed — the last subject being taught through the medium of Latin. Students devoted two hours a week to music, not to acquire skill in that art, but, curiously enough, to help them become clear elocutionists.[3] In Cowper's day special attention was given to the teaching of Latin and Greek. If the curriculum neglected more modern subjects, instruction in the classics, at least, was thorough. Westminster graduates remembered the passages they had memorized in school and retained their ability to construe the works of Homer and Virgil. Ten years after he left Westminster Cowper occasionally wrote letters in Latin, and forty years later he translated the *Iliad* and *Odyssey* and the Latin poems of Milton for publication.

At a period when corporal punishment was the common method of discipline, Westminster was using more modern corrective measures. John Nicoll, the headmaster in Cowper's time, believed in appealing to his scholars' sense of honor. When they committed a disgraceful act, he tried to shame them before their fellows instead of flogging them. Such practices gave him the reputation among his students of being a fair-minded man. According to Lord Chesterfield, Westminster was "the scene of illiberal manners and brutal behaviour." [4] It was probably no worse than most schools, though, like every institution for boys, it had its share of pranksters. Once an elegantly attired lady alighted from a sedan chair and asked Nicoll to be shown over the school. As he led her from room to room, he was shocked by the rude laughter of the Westminster boys. He soon discovered that the hoops and petticoats were a disguise for one of his own students. Another time the future Lord Mansfield held a lighted candle to the locks of Vincent Bourne, master of the sixth form, and then smartly boxed the schoolmaster's ears to put the fire out. Occasionally there were more serious infractions of discipline. Charles Churchill, later the famous satirist, eloped while he was a Westminster boy, and another student, Timothy Brecknock, forged a draft on his father, and when detected fled from the school.

Since Westminster was situated in London, students were allowed to attend the theater and to spend weekends with families or friends. The school had a good reputation, and members of polite society often invited the boys to their homes. In the dormitory the older students had certain cherished privileges. They could appoint younger students to take care of fires and prepare tea, and if they grew thirsty over their studies, they could send out a servant to fetch a tankard of porter or half-and-half from an inn.[5]

Cowper found life at Westminster much pleasanter than it had been at Dr. Pitman's. The school had a reputation, common enough in our own day, as a place in which boys could make connections that would be helpful in later life. Nevertheless, it was not an institution for the sons of parvenus. Many students came from excellent English families, as did Cowper, who found his companions there a congenial group. Although he later expressed regret that his religious education had been neglected at Westminster, that was largely the statement of a fervent convert. What he meant, no doubt, was that the institution failed to instruct him in the teachings of the Evangelical revival. He confessed that Dr. Nicoll took great pains in preparing the boys for confirmation, conducting himself with such a degree of sincerity and reverence that he aroused in Cowper a temporary feeling of piety.[6]

During Nicoll's headmastership the number of students who

were to attain renown in later life was larger than at any other period. Cowper's associates included Warren Hastings, Lord Dartmouth, and two future dramatists, Richard Cumberland and George Colman. Charles Churchill, the satirist, Robert Lloyd, the poet, and Bonnell Thornton, the translator of Plautus, were also Westminster students in Cowper's time. Since it was a small school, he knew all the boys; his most intimate companion was Sir William Russell, who remained a friend until Russell's early death in 1757.

Cowper's *Memoir* provides a few glimpses of his inner life at this time. One night as he was crossing a cemetery a gravedigger, working by lantern light, threw up a skull which struck him in the leg. This incident made him mindful of man's mortality, but the thought remained with him only briefly. He then conceived the idea, certainly not a rare one for youth, that he might never die. At a later date he developed the delusion that he was suffering from a consumptive constitution, but he told no one about his fear. He did contract smallpox, but the disease, instead of causing permanent injury, was credited with having improved his weak eyesight.

Two favorite sports at Westminster were cricket, then just coming into vogue, and a variety of football played by any number of boys on a team. Because certain writers have intimated that Cowper was effeminate, others have stressed the fact that he played both sports. But these were the common games of schoolboys, and no doubt only an extremely frail child would be exempt from engaging in them. His generally good physical health is indicated by the fact that he had few bodily ailments throughout his existence. People who knew him later in life described him as ruddy-complexioned, of medium height, and compactly built.

Yet even in boyhood he was probably not well adjusted emotionally. The early death of his mother left a void in his life, as we know from the poignant references to that event in a poem he wrote fifty-two years later. An unusually sensitive person, he must have reacted more strongly to unpleasant situations at school than most boys. His vivid recollection, thirty years later, of the bully who plagued him at Dr. Pitman's indicates how terrifying each encounter with such a boy must have been. Finally, if we are to believe with Wordsworth and the modern psychologists that the child is father of the man, we may assume that the melancholia which was to become so deep-seated later in life already existed in an incipient form during Cowper's adolescence.

Having completed his studies at Westminster at the age of eighteen, Cowper passed the next nine months at home in Great Berkhampstead. How he occupied himself he does not state, but a frequent topic of conversation at the vicarage was the choice of a career for the young man. At length it was decided that he should prepare himself for the legal profession. By family tradition he was eminently designated for the law. His grandfather had been a famous judge, his granduncle, England's first lord chancellor; other members of the family had won distinction as barristers and attorneys. In temperament, however, he was completely unsuited to the profession. Besides an unnatural timidity, which made him fearful of appearing in public, he had no real interest in legal studies. The decision to pursue them was not of his making. Throughout his life he was inclined to falter whenever he had to decide on a course of action, and in the end someone else usually shaped his plans. This time his father made the choice for him. When he was well advanced in middle age, Cowper wrote, "I was bred to the law — a profession to which I was never much inclined, and in which I engaged rather because I was desirous to gratify a most indulgent father, than because I had any hopes of success in it myself." [7] Characteristically, he expressed no resentment toward his father for launching him upon a career for which he was lamentably unsuited. He never held anyone but himself accountable for his mistakes, a trait that sprang partly from his persistent sense of guilt, and partly from an inherent honesty that would not allow him to shift blame from himself to others.

Cowper returned to London in 1749 to begin his study of the

law with Mr. Chapman, a solicitor of Ely Place, Holborn. His fellow student and companion at Mr. Chapman's was Edward Thurlow, the future lord chancellor. Young Thurlow had arrived at this stage of his career after being expelled from a school at Canterbury. He had also attended Cambridge as a member of Gonville and Caius College, but his continued infractions of rules again led to his expulsion, and he left without a degree. Despite his unpromising school record, however, Thurlow proved to be a more assiduous law student than Cowper and during these years laid the groundwork for a distinguished public career.

The young men frequently visited at the home of Ashley Cowper, an uncle who lived in Southampton Row. There were three daughters in the family, Harriet, Theodora, and Elizabeth, in whose company the young law students spent much time, "giggling and making giggle," as Cowper later remarked. Harriet was to be his devoted friend in youth and middle age, but it was Theodora to whom he gave his heart. Finding her a sympathetic companion, he was soon entrusting his secrets to her and eventually avowed his love. The affair, which began when they were not yet twenty, was to run its course over the next several years. Eventually they would separate, never more to meet, but meanwhile Cowper was a constant visitor at Southampton Row and the devoted escort of Theodora and her sisters when they attended church or went to the theater and public gardens.

To be young, to be surrounded by gay friends and companions, to be in love — what more could one ask? Cowper was now, moreover, an independent young man, for at twenty-one he had given up his lodgings at Mr. Chapman's to take chambers in the Middle Temple. Referring to this change, he observed, "I became in a manner complete master of myself." What he meant, no doubt, was that he had come of age and was no longer governed by his father. Actually he was to attain even less self-mastery than most people. Despite his seemingly happy situation, the young man was sick at heart. Soon after he moved to the Middle Temple he was overcome by a fit of dejection. Although he did not become irrational, a lassitude of spirits caused him to lose all interest in the classics and other means of diversion. Worst of all, he was troubled by horrible thoughts and feelings of despair. Groping for a new interest that would help him to forget his suffering, he came upon the poems of George Herbert. "Gothic and uncouth as they were," he wrote, "I yet found in them a strain of piety which I could not but admire." Perhaps it was not simply the piety of the seventeenth century poet that attracted him. Herbert's resignation and Christian fortitude may have given him a measure of strength to face his own unhappiness. But Herbert afforded him no lasting solace, and at the advice of a "near and dear relation," who thought that reading this author might only increase his melancholy, he laid the volume aside. At length, seeking divine assistance, he composed a set of prayers, the recital of which seems to have brought him some relief.[8]

The melancholy was to last for nearly a year. Finally, in order to get a change of scene, Cowper went to Southampton with a group of friends, among whom were his cousin Harriet and her future husband, Thomas Hesketh. Cowper remained at the seaside resort for several months. Apparently he could at least simulate cheerfulness in the company of others, and his friends may not have been aware of his depression. From a letter he wrote much later in life we learn that he went sailing with Thomas Hesketh, strolled along the beach to neighboring towns, and engaged in the other pleasures of the resort. Within a short time his spirits greatly improved.

The change came about suddenly, almost miraculously, according to the account which he gives in his *Memoir*. Soon after their arrival at Southampton, he observes, he and his friends took a walk along the coast. It was a pleasant morning, and the sun shone brightly on the sea.

"We sat down upon an eminence at the end of the arm of the sea which is between Southampton and the New Forest. Here it was that on a sudden, as if another sun had been kindled that instant in the heavens on purpose to dispel sorrow and vexation of spirit, I felt the weight of all my misery taken off, my heart became light and joyful in a moment. I could have wept with transport, had I been alone. I must needs believe that nothing less than the

Almighty could have filled me with such an inexpressible delight;
not by a gradual dawning of peace, but, as it were, with a flash
of his life-giving countenance. I think I remember something like
a glow of gratitude to the Father of mercies for this unexpected
blessing, and that I ascribed it to his gracious acceptance of my
prayers. But Satan and my own wicked heart quickly persuaded
me that I was indebted for my deliverance to nothing but a
change of season, and the amusing varieties of the place. By this
means he turned the blessing into poison, teaching me to con-
clude that nothing but a continued circle of diversion, and indulgence of appetite, could secure me from a relapse." [9]

Cowper afterward attached great importance to this experience. Ten years later he was to feel that the sudden lifting of his
melancholy was a providential act of mercy. But at the time, although he momentarily reflected that his prayers had been answered, he attributed his deliverance to a change of scene and the
diversions of Southampton. When he returned to London, he
burned his prayers and — to use his own self-accusing expression
— plunged into "an uninterrupted course of sinful indulgence." [10]
This statement, made after his conversion, was no doubt a gross
exaggeration. Although he was to lead the life of a young man of
fashion for the next ten years, his scruples probably kept him
from indulging in excesses.

Cowper's biographers have too often given the impression that
his whole existence was blighted. Actually there were long
stretches when he enjoyed life rather fully. Even during his later
years, when his dejection seemed worst, a streak of gaiety would
momentarily predominate over his melancholy. At the Temple,
during the period 1753 to 1762, he read the classics, wrote occasional verses, and passed considerable time at taverns in the company of friends. This mode of living, for which he later blamed
himself, he pursued partly because he was trying to prevent a
recurrence of his depression, but chiefly because it was the normal
course for a young man of his social station. The Victorian
Walter Bagehot ascribes Cowper's dejection of spirits and later
insanity in part to his lack of a regular occupation. Bagehot, with
the Victorian gospel of work in mind, thinks that his indolence

was shameful and almost implies that his later breakdown was a punishment for the sin of sloth.[11] For different reasons a modern psychologist might agree that a regular occupation could have helped to save Cowper from disaster. To be sure, many people of his rank, but lacking his peculiarly sensitive temperament, pursued the same leisurely existence without its entailing insanity.

In many ways it was a pleasantly indolent age. Time clocks had not yet been invented, and watches were still regarded as ornamental luxuries more than as aids to punctuality. Although domestic servants, porters, spinners, and lacemakers worked a long day, even these members of the lowest rank of society could often steal a few minutes from labor. Greater freedom existed among the middle classes, and artisans and members of the petty professions could generally pause to gossip or to enjoy a mug of ale. Among the upper ranks, where leisure was the keynote of existence, it was the practice to remain in bed to receive guests at morning levees and to loll in clubs and coffeehouses, with a retinue of servants at hand to supply one's slightest wish.

As a bachelor Cowper could live modestly enough to maintain himself in the upper middle class to which he had been bred. When he was in London he spent much time in the company of his fellow Templars. An interesting description of these carefree idlers, who made a legal career the pretext for living indolently, appears in the *Connoisseur*. Although the account is lightly satirical, it portrays the dilettante existence of many who had chambers in this traditional residence of lawyers:

"The Temple is the barrier that divides the city and the suburbs; and the gentlemen who reside there seem influenced by the situation of the place they inhabit. *Templars* are, in general, a kind of citizen-courtiers. They aim at the air and mien of the drawing-room; but the holiday smartness of a prentice, heightened with some additional touches of the rake or coxcomb, betrays itself in everything they do. The *Temple*, however, is stocked with its peculiar beaux, wits, poets, critics, and every character in the gay world: and it is a thousand pities that so gay a society should be disgraced with a few dull fellows, who can submit to puzzle themselves with cases and reports, and have not taste enough to follow the genteel method of studying the law." [12]

From the variety of entertainment in mid-eighteenth century London Cowper could select the amusements that appealed most to his somewhat fastidious tastes. Lacking the gusto of Dr. Johnson, he probably found little pleasure in the spectacle of crowds pushing along the Strand, the sight of an overturned sedan chair, or the brawling disputes of hackney coachmen and slovenly porters. Assumably he was too humane to join the holiday throng waiting for the procession of carts that carried culprits to Tyburn for execution. Nor can one imagine him joining in the rout to catch a pickpocket, or finding pleasure in cockfights or bear-baitings, even though many gentlemen enjoyed these coarser pleasures quite as much as did their servants. For the first few years at the Temple his social life centered in his uncle's home in Southampton Row, with Theodora and her sisters as his companions. He later observed that he never attended a public assembly, but he danced, had no aversion to cards, and enjoyed witty conversation and the theatrical performances given at Covent Garden and Drury Lane. He also passed many pleasant hours in the more informal society of his men friends, dining with old companions of Westminster days, visiting other residents of the Temple, and drinking and conversing in taverns and coffeehouses. Although his *Memoir* mentions few details of this period, he once remarks that he sometimes employed himself defending Scripture against the arguments of deists while he was "half-intoxicated." It is interesting to observe his qualification of the term in a work so full of self-condemnation. His drinking seems to have been almost always temperate, even at a time when gentlemen boasted of being three- or four-bottle men.

Like most people of fashion, he customarily left London for the summer months. In 1752 he visited cousins of his mother in Norfolk, going to Catfield and Mundesley, where he was later to enact the last sad scenes of his life. He also took trips to seaside places, like Southampton, Brighton, and Margate. If no invitations were forthcoming or if he lacked funds, he could always pass several weeks of the summer at his father's vicarage. One of the most interesting letters of his youthful period is postmarked from there. Addressed to "Dear Toby" (presumably his Temple friend, Clotworthy Rowley), the letter reveals Cowper as a carefree young man, enjoying rural life. "I am in such a hurry," he writes, "I hardly know how to set one leg before t'other to get to the end of my letter, and God knows if I shall be able to do it tonight. Dancing all last night, in bed one half of the day, and shooting all the other half, and am now going to — what? to kill a boding screech owl perched upon a tree just by my window." [13] Was it an actual screech owl? Or was it an emblem of the melancholy thoughts that he had once shaken off but which would eventually return? Probably the offending bird was real, since his mood throughout the letter is sportive. A pleasant life for a young man, dancing all night and hunting half the day.

Placing a high value on friendship, Cowper had kept in touch with his Westminster friends who had gone up to Oxford and Cambridge. Several of them drifted back to London upon the completion of their studies to engage in writing or to try their fortunes at other occupations. They were a brilliant, lighthearted coterie, fond of playing jokes and gathering for an evening of fun at one of the London taverns. Cowper introduced them to some of his Temple friends, and they got on so well that they decided to form a club. It was a very informal organization. Like dozens of other groups in eighteenth-century London, the young men simply appointed one night of the week for their gatherings and engaged a room at a tavern or coffeehouse for their meetings. Since gaiety was to be the keynote of their little society, the members called it the Nonsense Club.

Although these friends were probably no more dissipated than most young men of their rank, they were a sophisticated lot, and a far different set of companions from the scrupulous professors of Evangelical religion with whom Cowper was later to associate. Besides Cowper there were six other members of the club. Two of them, Bonnell Thornton and George Colman, had already started their collaboration on the *Connoisseur* while they were still at Oxford. They were brilliant young men, with a flair for writing and a reputation for perpetrating hoaxes. One of Thornton's pranks was to hold a London exhibition of the works of sign-painters in imitation of the annual display of pictures by professional artists. His friend Colman was to have the most brilliant career of all members of the group. A successful dramatist, he wrote *The Jealous Wife*, collaborated with David Garrick on the much applauded *Clandestine Marriage*, and later became the influential manager and owner of the Haymarket Theatre. Another member of the Nonsense Club was a man named Bensley, of whom little is known. The fourth member was Robert Lloyd, the son of one of the masters at Westminster. Young Lloyd also tried teaching at Westminster, but gave up what seemed to be a life of drudgery to enter the equally precarious profession of writing. For a time he edited a periodical called the *St. James's Magazine*. When it went bankrupt he was sent to a debtors' prison. There, saddened by the early death of his close friend Charles Churchill, Lloyd himself died in 1764. The identity of the two remaining members of the club is uncertain. One was probably Joseph Hill, a lawyer of steady disposition and a friend of Cowper throughout life. The other may have been either Richard Cumberland or William De Grey.[14]

Wordsworth's remark that

> We Poets in our youth begin in gladness;
> But thereof come in the end despondency and madness

was particularly applicable to the members of the Nonsense Club. Thornton, Bensley, and Lloyd died young, the last under tragic circumstances, and Cowper and Colman both became insane. But no shadow clouded the merriment of the gay wassailers who dedicated themselves to Nonsense each Thursday evening. Youth was at the helm, gay spirits predominated, and the meetings rang with laughter.

Their talent for writing gave the friends a community of interest. Several of them, besides Colman and Lloyd, contributed occasional pieces to the *Connoisseur*, which was one of the most successful imitators of the *Tatler* and *Spectator* papers. Unlike

Dr. Johnson, who had loaded his *Rambler* with sober moralizing, the authors preserved a light touch. Their witty and often satirical essays were clearly the works of men of fashion, mildly disturbed by evidence of bad taste and constantly amused by the foibles of mankind.

Cowper probably contributed several issues, though only three of the *Connoisseur* essays, numbers 119, 134, and 138, have been definitely ascribed to him. The first discusses the folly of entrusting secrets. Although he treats the subject in a light vein, later in life he prided himself upon having never divulged a confidence since his youth.[15] Tale-bearing, he observes in the *Connoisseur*, is all too frequently encouraged by indulgent parents: "If the butler has been caught kissing the housekeeper in his pantry or the footman detected romping with the chambermaid, away flies little Tommy or Betsy with the news; the parents are lost in admiration of the pretty rogue's understanding, and reward such uncommon ingenuity with a kiss or a sugar-plum." The second essay, written after a visit to the country, is a caustic report on village churches. After observing that churches in many communities were falling into ruin, and that no provision was made for their repair, he adds, "In other churches I have observed that nothing unseemly or ruinous is to be found, except in the clergyman, and the appendages of his person." Addison was his model, but Cowper occasionally introduces a satirical innuendo of the sort his master never used. For instance, in describing bands of itinerant church singers, he writes, "As these new-fashioned psalmodists are necessarily made up of young men and maids, we may naturally suppose that there is a perfect concord and symphony between them; and indeed, I have known it to happen, that these sweet singers have more than once been brought into disgrace by too close unison between the thorough-bass and the treble." The last of the three essays satirizes the boors who spoil polite conversation. Included in the list are the constant babblers, the affected elocutionists, and the idle prattlers. Cowper also deplored the universal passion for card games as a pastime that had almost annihilated good conversation.

Cowper's mode of life was little affected by his being called to the bar in 1754. Although he was now qualified to practice law, he appears never to have taken a case, and he probably devoted even less time to legal studies than heretofore. The only advantage he gained by his admission to the bar was his appointment in 1759 as Commissioner of Bankrupts, a sinecure with an annual salary of sixty pounds. His fathed died in 1756, and his visits to Great Berkhampstead were infrequent thereafter. Apparently he received little or no addition to his income by his father's death. Having some capital, however, in 1759 he purchased a set of chambers in the Inner Temple and took up his residence there on a more permanent footing.

His training at Westminster had made him, not a scholar exactly, but a man of cultivated literary taste, with an especial interest in the classics. Although Homer was a particular favorite of his, he was a little annoyed at the extravagant praise accorded Pope's translation. As a test, Cowper and his friend Alston made a line-by-line comparison of the original with Pope's version. They discovered, just what they had suspected, that Pope is woefully lacking in fidelity to Homer. Years later Cowper would try to produce a more faithful text when he translated the *Iliad* and the *Odyssey*. Having ample leisure, he perused with a poet's appreciation the works of the more famous English writers of the past generation, the essays of Addison and Steele, the letters of Swift, and the poetry of Milton, Dryden, and Prior. He also acquainted himself with many of the literary works of his contemporaries, Johnson's *Rasselas* and the *Rambler* papers, Goldsmith's *Citizen of the World*, novels like *Tom Jones, Sir Charles Grandison*, and *Ferdinand Count Fathom*, the odes of Collins, the precisely written poems of Gray, and the mordant satires of his old Westminster schoolfellow Charles Churchill.

His contributions to the *Connoisseur* show that Cowper might have become a professional prose-writer in the tradition of Addison and Steele, but he was more interested in poetry. His father, his uncle, and his brother all wrote verse, and his own inclinations were encouraged by his association with literary friends. When he was only seventeen, he had composed lines at Bath *On*

Finding the Heel of a Shoe. Considered as a piece of juvenilia, the poem is no mean performance. Some of the verses he wrote at the Temple have not survived, but among them were several halfpenny ballads, "two or three of which had the honor to be popular," he later observed. It is interesting that street ballads were among his early productions. Most of them were crudely rhymed poems that circulated in halfpenny sheets and thus had a wide sale among the poor. Often the lines were set to popular tunes, a device that helped the illiterate to memorize the words. Cowper kept his admiration for the ballad stanza as a native and unaffected English form, and he later employed it in some of his most successful pieces.

Cowper also became an anonymous contributor to Smollett's 1762 edition of the works of Voltaire. According to the title page, the translations were made by Thomas Francklin, a clergyman and writer of miscellaneous works. Most of the material, however, seems to have been translated by hack writers whose services Francklin enlisted.[16] Cowper's brother John, who may have known Francklin at Cambridge, was commissioned to put eight books of Voltaire's *Henriade* into an English version. After translating the first four cantos, he asked his brother to assist him. Cowper thus, it would appear, became the translator of books five through eight of the *Henriade*.[17]

The original poems he wrote during his residence at the Temple are mediocre productions, but they reveal him as something more than just another composer of prosy essays in iambic pentameter couplets. Instead of following in the footsteps of Dryden and Pope, he was more inclined to imitate Matthew Prior. In an *Epistle to Robert Lloyd* he calls his old school friend

> sole heir and single
> Of dear Mat Prior's easy jingle.

Cowper then proceeds in this poem to try to emulate Prior's fluent rhymes and graceful compliments. He falls short of his master, but the time would come when he would excel all poets of his century, except Prior, as a writer of society verse. His admiration for Prior continued throughout life. When he read Dr. Johnson's criticism of his favorite light poet, he took issue with the critic for failing to understand and appreciate "an author who, with much labour indeed, but with admirable success, has embellished all his poems with the most charming ease."[18] The longer poems, *Solomon* and *Alma,* were special favorites with him, but Prior's shorter verses and love lyrics seem to have served Cowper as models for the poems which he addressed to "Delia," the poetic name he gave to his cousin Theodora.

These poems, published after both were dead, are interesting chiefly as a testament of their love. The story, pieced together, forms a romantic tale of more pathos than passion. A shy and lonely lad, he had probably known few girls until he began visiting his cousins. Of the three sisters Theodora seemed the most charming. She could pierce his shyness, engage him in easy conversation, and unlock his reserved fund of gaiety and humor. From taking pleasure in her company, he soon passed to the stage of being in love, and when he found his passion reciprocated she became his "dear antidote of every pain." According to a humorous though conceivably circumstantial poem entitled *Of Himself,* Theodora tried to convert him from an awkward youth to a poised and self-confident man of society. He starts off by remarking:

> William was once a bashful youth;
> His modesty was such,
> That one might say (to say the truth)
> He rather had too much.

> Some said it was a want of sense,
> And others want of spirit,
> (So blest a thing is impudence,)
> While others could not bear it.

With Theodora's coaching he learned to dress smartly, to give the appearance of gaiety, and now and then to produce a witty remark. The transformation was so thorough that

> At length improved from head to heel,
> 'Twere scarce too much to say,
> No dancing bear was so genteel,
> Or half so *dégagé.*

The village of Olney, with the church of the Reverend John Bull in the background

Cowper's parlor, Cowper Museum, Olney, Bucks

The young Templar seems to have been a rather naive lover. In one of the few letters preserved from this period he tells a friend that Theodora has cultivated the habit of calling him her coxcomb. A little puzzled by this term of endearment, he soberly observes, "I am willing to allow her the privilege of calling me so because I know she cannot in reality think me one and love me as she does." The same letter mentions a slight lovers' quarrel, which had already come to a blissful end. "All is comfortable and happy between us at present," Cowper writes, "and I doubt not will continue so for ever. Indeed, we had neither of us any great reason to be dissatisfied, and perhaps quarrelled merely for the sake of the reconciliation, which you may be sure made ample amends."[19]

Cowper had written thus in February 1754. Not long thereafter his hope that their happiness would be everlasting began to wane, and eventually the romance came to an end. Various reasons have been given for the termination of the love affair. James Croft, who edited the love poems addressed to Theodora, said that Ashley Cowper refused to let his daughter marry the poet because they were first cousins.[20] It has also been suggested that Ashley Cowper detected signs of emotional instability or incipient insanity in his nephew. Whatever the cause, Theodora's father forbade the marriage, and she submitted to his judgment. The break did not come suddenly; even after Cowper had heard his uncle's verdict, he continued to see her and still hoped to make her his wife.[21] The love affair was ended by 1757, however, for in that year Cowper wrote a poem lamenting the double loss of his friend Sir William Russell, who had been drowned, and of his beloved Theodora, who would no longer see him. The poem, called *Absence and Bereavement,* is one of the best of his early productions.

> Doomed, as I am, in solitude to waste
> The present moments, and regret the past;
> Deprived of every joy I valued most,
> My friend torn from me, and my mistress lost,
> Call not this gloom I wear, this anxious mien,
> The dull effect of humour, or of spleen!
> Still, still I mourn, with each returning day,

Him snatched by fate in early youth away,
And her, through tedious years of doubt and pain,
Fixed in her choice, and faithful, but in vain!
O prone to pity, generous, and sincere,
Whose eye ne'er yet refused the wretch a tear;
Whose heart the real claim of friendship knows,
Nor thinks a lover's are but fancied woes;
See me, ere yet my destined course half done,
Cast forth a wanderer on a world unknown!
See me neglected on the world's rude coast,
Each dear companion of my voyage lost,
Nor ask why clouds of sorrow shade my brow,
And ready tears wait only leave to flow,
Why all that soothes a heart from anguish free,
All that delights the happy, palls with me!

None of Cowper's earlier poems addressed to Delia is quite so moving as *Absence and Bereavement*, but it is unfair to judge the depth of his passion by the quality of his verse. Byron and Burns, after flirting with a strange girl for an hour or two, could write verses that glow with apparently sincere expressions of undying love. Cowper, composing rather conventional stanzas, may nevertheless have been profoundly stirred. Indeed, it is hard to think otherwise, for his temperament was such that he badly needed someone to love and to be loved by. Nevertheless, the loss of Theodora was responsible for only a small share of the agony he was fated to endure. Later in life he seldom referred to her, and his devotion to other women would indicate that the scars of his blighted romance had healed.

Of the pair Theodora was the more pitiable. In *Absence and Bereavement* he had referred to her as "faithful, but in vain," an apt description of her fidelity throughout life. Sitting like patience on a monument, she nourished the memory of her lover on the scraps of news she got from her relatives and the verses addressed to her in youth. One can imagine her untying the packet of letters and poems and pathetically poring over the yellowed leaves. She never married, and she never saw her lover after he left London, but she kept his verses until she learned that he was dead. Then she gave them to a friend, so that when she too was gone the world could read the early love lyrics of the man who had become one of England's foremost poets.

The loss of Theodora and the death of Sir William Russell made Cowper feel "neglected on the world's rude coast." Despite his friends, the gay meetings of the Nonsense Club, and his taste for the classics, his life at the Temple must always have been a bit lonely. Now, with his youth ebbing away, the repetitious calendar of amusements began to pall on him. There were also practical reasons that would make his existence as an idle Templar no longer possible. His allowance had stopped in 1756 upon the death of his father, and he had spent nearly all of his little estate. Still there seemed to be no serious cause for alarm. He had been trained to a profession. Though he was too shy to conduct a regular law practice, there were various offices for which he could qualify. As a member of a distinguished family he was not without connections, and the time had come for him to make use of them.

II

The Crisis

This of all maladies that man infest,
Claims most compassion, and receives the least.

RETIREMENT 301–302

IN THE first year of the reign of George I the poet's grandfather, Spencer Cowper, had purchased the patent of the Clerkship of the Parliaments, to be held in reversion by his sons.[1] This ancient office, dating from the fourteenth century, had an income of about seven thousand pounds a year, and the incumbent enjoyed the privilege of appointing all the clerks of the House of Lords. Furthermore, it was virtually a sinecure, since the duties could be delegated to the Clerk Assistant.[2] Spencer's oldest son, William Cowper, held this lucrative Clerkship until his death in 1740. Thereafter his brother Ashley served as titular Clerk of the Parliaments, though Major William Cowper, son of the deceased William, appears to have exercised the prerogatives of the office.*

One of the positions to which Major Cowper had the power of appointment was the Clerkship of the Journals in the House of Lords. Inasmuch as the work entailed could be "transacted in private,"[3] the poet thought of it for himself, though he knew

---

* According to the *Gentleman's Magazine* (X [February 1740], 92) William (Major) Cowper succeeded his father as Clerk of the Parliaments in 1740. Upon the death of Ashley Cowper in 1788, however, the same periodical (LVIII [June 1788], 564) observes that Ashley had been "above sixty years Clerk of the Parliaments." Apparently this was the situation: Ashley had to succeed to the title of the office to keep it in the family, inasmuch as Spencer Cowper had purchased the patent for the lifetime of his sons. But, through

that a Mr. Mackley held the office at the time. One day he remarked to a friend that he had some hope of obtaining the appointment should there be a vacancy. Thereupon the two friends expressed a wish, no doubt in a joking manner, that the present incumbent would soon die. Not long afterwards, in April 1763, the clerk did conveniently expire, leaving the way open for Cowper to succeed him. At the same time two other vacancies occurred, the Office of Reading Clerk and the Clerkship of the Committees. Because these positions paid a larger stipend, the Major offered them to the poet, reserving the Clerkship of the Journals for a friend.

Cowper promptly accepted. Almost immediately, however, he became dejected in spirits. He had never mingled in the world of affairs, and at thirty-two so great was his shyness that he dreaded accepting responsibilities and rubbing shoulders with other men. The more he thought about his predicament, the unhappier he became. For a week he suffered mental conflict, torn between a reluctance to abandon a good opportunity and the fear that he would be unable to fulfill the duties of office. Finally he wrote to Major Cowper, asking him to confer the two better appointments on his friend and to name him to the more modest position of Clerkship of the Journals. To this arrangement his cousin agreed, and the poet's anxieties temporarily subsided.

Then an unforeseen obstacle arose. A party in the House of Lords, wishing to appoint their own candidate, challenged Major Cowper's right of nomination. The Major held his ground, but told his cousin that the opposition would seek to disqualify him. To test his abilities, they would insist upon examining him before the bar of the House. Unacquainted with the business

a family arrangement, Major Cowper served as his deputy, perhaps holding the title of Clerk Assistant, and received the income of the Clerk of the Parliaments. Upon his death in 1769, his brother, General Spencer Cowper, enjoyed the stipend, though all this while Ashley was nominally the Clerk. After Ashley's death the poet wrote, "The profits of the very lucrative office which he held so long were not his but General Cowper's, whose interest in them determined on the death of Ashley" (To Clotworthy Rowley, August 31, 1789).

of the clerkship, he would have to prepare himself by visiting the office and studying past records.

The prospect of being involved in an altercation was insupportable to Cowper. He was particularly terrified at the thought of appearing before the bar of the House to be examined. What caused this terror? He had a good mind and, with a little study, could undoubtedly have qualified for the position. He had always been extremely shy, of course, but something more than timidity must have provoked his anxiety. In August 1763 he wrote a curious letter to Harriet, the sister of his beloved Theodora. "Oh, my good cousin!" he agonized, "If I was to open my heart to you, I could show you strange sights; nothing, I flatter myself, that would shock you, but a great deal that would make you wonder. I am of a very singular temper, and very unlike all the men I have ever conversed with. Certainly I am not an absolute fool; but I have more weaknesses than the greatest of all the fools I can recollect at present."[4]

Much as he dreaded taking the examination, he started to prepare for it by studying the Journals kept by earlier office-holders. He made daily visits to the bureau, but the under-clerks gave him no help because they favored the opposing political group. Even if they had offered to instruct him, he was too much distracted to concentrate on the business. Later he remarked that he felt like a man preparing for an execution. Nevertheless, he continued to visit the office during the next six months.

That summer he went to Margate with friends and tried to forget his troubles. One day when walking on the beach he nearly lost his life. Having forgotten that the tide was coming in, he was almost caught between the sea and a cliff. To escape he had to run back every step of the way. But there was no such retreat from his anxieties. Although the change of scene and the companionship of friends raised his spirits temporarily, whenever he thought of the approaching winter, he became wretched and regretted the passing of every moment that brought his ordeal nearer.

The Crisis

Upon his return to London in the fall of 1763, he resumed his visits to the Office of the Clerk of the Journals. Misery and despair again beset him. He thought of rejecting the appointment, but feared that his resignation at this late date might injure his benefactor. At the same time he dreaded the disgrace of being disqualified by the examination. This conflict produced a form of hysteria. "In this situation," he wrote, "such a fit of passion has sometimes seized me, when alone in my chambers, that I have cried out aloud, and cursed the hour of my birth; lifting up my eyes to heaven, at the same time, not as a suppliant, but in the hellish spirit of rancorous reproach and blasphemy against my Maker."[5]

Cowper was gradually going insane. What is more, he foresaw this condition as the likely outcome of his depression. At first it was only a premonition. Then, as he reflected upon it, he began to entertain the hope that madness would ensue. If he lost his reason, he would not have to take the examination. And if he had to resign because of illness, his cousin's reputation would not suffer. What he longed for was a complete and overpowering form of insanity that would relieve him of all responsibility. The wish itself was an indication that he was no longer in his right mind, but as yet there was no visible evidence of a mental collapse. Meanwhile the day set for the examination was fast approaching. Only one other escape from his dilemma seemed possible. He reflected on suicide and deemed that violent step his only solution.

Cowper's description of his attempts at suicide constitutes a rare record of a mind becoming progressively deranged. Because he lacked self-sufficiency, he seldom acted as a free agent. Later in life he was to depend on various people to determine his course of action. But even in his youth, before he became a Calvinist, he seemed to lack freedom of the will. In his descriptions of his several attempts at suicide he appears almost as a passive agent. An inner voice prompts him to try self-destruction by one method. Then some uncontrolled circumstance intervenes, another warning voice restrains him, or a paralysis stays his hand. Some of these urgings he interprets as coming from God; others, from Satan. Later, when he described these experiences, he felt certain which voice had directed him in each instance. In the *Memoir* it is always the devil who encourages the thought of self-murder, and God who intervenes to save him. But in his later attacks of insanity, and even in periods of recovery, his hallucinations were so vivid that they predominated over reason and the teachings of his religious faith. Hence he was ultimately led to believe that the voice of God pressed him to commit suicide, and when his attempts to put this supposed command into effect failed, he thought that he had offended the Deity by thwarting his purpose.

His lack of volition is emphasized in the *Memoir* by his frequent use of the passive voice and impersonal constructions. When he describes his growing conviction that he should destroy himself, he writes, "The ruin of my fortune, the contempt of my relations and acquaintances, the prejudice I should do my patron, were all urged on me with irresistible energy." Again he remarks, "This impulse, having served the present purpose, was withdrawn."[6]

As the day set for the examination approached, he shut himself up in his rooms, and isolated himself from his friends. Meditating on suicide, he tried to justify the act. Perhaps Scripture was wrong. Did not a man's life belong to himself, to do with what he pleased? As a boy he had read a vindication of suicide, and he remembered discussing the work with his father. When the Reverend Mr. Cowper had asked his opinion of the book, the boy had argued against the lawfulness of the act. He now recalled his father's silence upon the occasion and concluded that he must have tacitly sided with the author. At a chophouse Cowper met an elderly man with whom he discussed self-murder. They agreed that most people refrain from suicide only because they lack the fortitude to end a miserable existence. Another chance acquaintance at a tavern expressed the opinion that anyone is at liberty to do as he pleases with his life. "Thus," wrote Cowper, "were the emissaries of the throne of darkness let loose upon me."[7]

The Crisis

One evening in November 1763 he stopped at an apothecary shop and bought half an ounce of laudanum. A week remained before he was to take the examination; if nothing else intervened to save him from the ordeal, he determined to swallow the drug. As his mind became more harried, symptoms of a persecution complex appeared. He picked up a newspaper at a coffeehouse and read a letter that he believed to be a libel on himself. The author seemed to know his intention to commit suicide and wanted to hasten the act. Cowper rushed from the place, determined to end his life immediately. Walking in the fields for solitude, he was struck with the idea that by going to France and joining a monastery he could avoid the necessity for suicide. He returned to his chambers and started to pack, but changed his mind when, as he says, "self-murder was recommended to me once more in all its advantages."[8]

Because he feared someone might intrude upon an attempt to poison himself in his chamber, he took a coach to Tower-Wharf, where he left the vehicle, intending to leap into the river. But when he came to the quay the water was low and a porter was seated nearby. God, it appeared to him, had intervened to prevent the act. Again seated in the coach, he put the phial of laudanum to his mouth, but a paralysis kept him from emptying it. "It seemed to me," he remarked, "that an invisible hand swayed the bottle downwards, as I set it against my lips."[9]

When he returned to the Temple, he shut himself up in his apartment, poured the laudanum into a basin and put it by his bed. Partly undressed, and shuddering at the act he was about to commit, he crawled in between the blankets, only (as he relates) to hear a voice saying, "Think what you are doing! — Consider, and live."[10] This monition stayed him for a few minutes, but resolution returned, and he reached toward the basin. Then a sudden paralysis contracted his hands, making them useless. The phenomenon so astonished him that though his arms were unaffected and he might still have lifted the basin, he gave himself over to reflection. He wondered if the new obstacle was an act of divine interposition. While he was musing on this question, the husband of his laundress entered the apartment. Cowper rose and walked into his dining room. When the intruder left, his views on suicide changed. Filled with horror at what he had attempted, he snatched up and emptied the basin, and threw the phial out the window.

In the evening a friend called and they spoke about his position as Clerk of the Journals. This discussion brought back the horrible prospect of the examination, and when his caller left, he determined once more to commit suicide. The week had slipped by, and he was scheduled to appear before the bar of the House the next day. Going to bed, he pressed a penknife against his heart, but the point was broken. He lay awake until daybreak. The clock struck seven, a dismal reminder that in a few hours he was expected to stand before the bar of the House. He rose and, as he thought, bolted the door of his chamber, now filled with seeming resolution. Making a noose of his garter, he tried to hang himself from a hook on the bed post, but the iron bent under his weight. He next climbed on a chair, pushed the loop over a door, and kicked the chair from beneath him. As he hung there, he heard a voice say, " 'Tis over."[11] Then he lost consciousness.

When he came to, he at first thought he was in hell, but he soon realized that instead he was merely stretched out on the floor of his chamber. The garter had broken. Staggering to the mirror, he saw around his neck a red circle, sanguinary evidence of how near he had come to death. A noise in the next room startled him. He investigated and found that his laundress had entered the apartment through the unbolted door which he thought he had locked. He sent for a friend, told him what he had done, and asked him to get Major Cowper. When his patron arrived, Cowper showed him the broken garter and described his attempt at suicide. His amazed cousin, after listening to his story, told him that under the circumstances he must withdraw his candidacy for the Clerkship of the Journals, and asked for the deputation. The distraught candidate silently motioned to a drawer where he kept it. Thus, he observed, "ended all connection with the Parliament Office."[12]

In a way the distressed poet had achieved what he wanted. He had escaped standing the examination, and he had not had to pay the full price of sacrificing his life. The attempt had been enough. Throughout the period of his mental conflict, he did not really want to kill himself, and yet death seemed the only way to avert a terrifying examination. Psychologists have remarked on the unusual length of this period of conflict sustained at high tension. For months, since he had heard that he must appear before an examining committee, his nerves had been taut. During the final week, he seems to have been in a state of hysteria. It is no wonder that a complete mental breakdown was to follow.

Although he apparently never realized it, Cowper himself obviously had frustrated each attempt at suicide. The paralysis of his hands, the broken knife blade, even the hanging episode reveal that he could not bring himself fully to the point of killing himself. Although his final effort nearly succeeded, he admitted that he had left open the door he thought he had locked. Moreover, he did not make this last attempt until after the clock had struck seven, about the time, probably, that his laundress customarily appeared. Subconsciously, he had perhaps intended that she should find him before he perished. Actually, he was saved because the garter, hardly a hangman's noose, broke under his weight. His last attempt differed from the earlier ones, however, in that it left visible evidence of the desperate measure he had taken. Although previously he had apparently disclosed his dread of taking the examination to no one, as soon as he saw the scars on his neck and could show the broken garter, he exploited these proofs by sending for his friends and revealing to them his efforts to hang himself. In short, he promptly used the attempt at suicide to relieve him of the necessity of taking the dreaded examination.

In the *Memoir* Cowper states that it was not until after the thwarted hanging and his release from the examination that he felt a sense of guilt about trying to kill himself. Actually he had had moral qualms from the beginning. While he had tried to convince himself that suicide is permissible, he had never fully succeeded. All along, it would appear, his scruples had subconsciously, though urgently, fought his impulse to perpetrate the deed. Once this conflict had been resolved by the attempt at suicide getting him out of the dilemma, his conscience spoke with a louder voice, and a gnawing sense of guilt followed. He now felt he had committed a horrible sin. Although he had merely reflected upon suicide and tried, but never with the full consent of his will, to effect it, he refused to mitigate the offense. "Though I had failed in my design," he wrote, "yet I had all the guilt of that crime to answer for: a sense of God's wrath, and a deep despair of escaping it, instantly succeeded. The fear of death became much more prevalent in me now than even the desire of death had been."[13]

Cowper now experienced a physical reaction in the form of flashings like fire before his eyes and a painful pressure on his brain. At a friend's advice he sent for a physician and told him that he feared a stroke of apoplexy. The doctor reassured him that he was in no danger on that score, but urged him to go to the country for a rest. Instead of taking this advice, Cowper remained in his chambers, where, he remarked, "the solitude of the situation left me at full liberty to attend to my spiritual state."[14]

Solitude only allowed him leisure to dwell upon the enormity of his crime. His sense of guilt was now so strong that when he went into the street, he thought people were laughing at him and regarding him with contempt. He heard a balladmonger singing and bought a copy of the song, believing he was the subject of it. When he dined out he ate alone, hiding himself in the most obscure corner of the tavern. His sleep was disturbed by grotesque dreams, and when he awoke, he staggered about like a drunkard. Meditating on his sins, he reviewed his past life and was appalled by his ungodly existence. "There was never so abandoned a wretch," he told himself, "so great a sinner."[15]

Believing that he must be shut out from God's mercy, he began to reflect on the application of various Biblical passages to himself. He recalled the parable of the barren fig-tree and momentarily felt that when God had cursed the tree he had pointed his malediction directly at him. The thought so disturbed him that he went through all Archbishop Tillotson's sermons, hoping to find an interpretation of the matter. Why in the first place did his mind turn to this particular parable? We cannot be sure, but if he was sexually impotent, and there is some basis for this theory, he may have associated his barrenness with the tree that bore no fruit.

Despondent as he was, a worse condition was to follow. In testing the relation of Biblical passages to his own sins, he seemed to be searching for proof of the full measure of his iniquity. Finally he convinced himself that he had been guilty of a sin that excluded him completely from grace. "The capital engine in the artillery of Satan had not yet been employed against me," he wrote. "This was a fit season for the use of it. Accordingly I was set to inquire whether I had not been guilty of the unpardonable sin; and was presently persuaded that I had."[16] This conviction was the stroke that was to tear away the last shred of hope and that drove him completely mad.

Just what did Cowper believe when he accused himself of committing an offense so terrible that it was beyond forgiveness? That question has never been satisfactorily answered, despite the fact that the *Memoir* specifically refers to the occasion upon which he deemed he had transgressed. Biographers of the poet have been especially confused on one point. There were two distinct periods when Cowper believed he was totally excluded from mercy. The first, beginning at the Temple in 1763, after his attempts at suicide, lasted until his conversion at Dr. Cotton's asylum. The second period extended from his attack of insanity in 1773 until the end of his life. But — and this distinction has often been overlooked — in each period Cowper found a different basis for despairing of salvation. Though he twice believed that he was irrevocably damned, in each instance his interpretation of the nature of his sin was different. His reason for later thinking he was an outcast soul must await discussion; here we shall be concerned only with his earlier self-accusation, that he was guilty of the unpardonable sin of Scripture.

The chief references to the unforgivable sin, or the sin against the Holy Ghost, are found in Matthew 12:22–32, Mark 3:22–30, and Luke 11:14–23. In these passages Christ is described as casting devils out of a man with an unclean spirit. The Pharisees, seeing the miracle performed, could not deny Christ's power, but instead of ascribing it to God, they accused Christ of casting out devils by the power of Beelzebub. This ascribing of Christ's works to the devil is called the unforgivable sin. According to the Gospel of St. Matthew (12:31–32), "All manner of sin and blasphemy shall be forgiven unto men; but the blasphemy against the Holy Ghost shall not be forgiven unto men. And whosoever speaketh a word against the Son of man, it shall be forgiven him; but whosoever speaketh against the Holy Ghost, it shall not be forgiven him, neither in this world, neither in the world to come."

The Biblical references to the unpardonable sin had, from the early centuries of Christianity, been variously interpreted. Some authorities believed that it could mean only one thing, namely, the specific sin of the Pharisees when they attributed Christ's power to Satan. According to this interpretation only those who had lived during the time of Christ and had seen him perform miracles could possibly commit this sin. Other writers, holding that anyone at any time might be guilty of the offense, believed it to consist of final impenitency, despair of salvation, maliciously opposing the known truth, or any one of a dozen transgressions. Thus the interpretations of what constitutes the sin against the Holy Ghost ranged from the assertion that it was the specific act of the Pharisees to the broad statement that it might be almost any form of religious scepticism.[17]

Although early theologians had frequently discussed the subject, members of the laity were probably little concerned about this sin, if indeed they had ever heard of it, until the Puritan emphasis upon Scripture made Bible-reading a common practice among ordinary persons. Many thereafter were troubled by the references to the sin against the Holy Ghost, and some developed a conviction that they were guilty of this offense. Apparently the Puritan preachers tried to discourage the belief. According to M. M. Knappen, "Timorous Christians who feared they had committed the unpardonable sin were given the Augustinian explanation; this sin was that of persistent indifference, and therefore to be troubled about it was a sure sign of innocence."[18] Richard Baxter, the Puritan divine, wrote a long treatise on the subject in which he reviewed both Catholic and Protestant pronouncements. His own opinion was that no true believer could possibly commit the sin. Even those who had not yet attained sanctifying grace, according to Baxter, were not likely to be guilty of the offense, unless they ascribed to Satan works which were, by clear and objective evidence, manifestly those of God.[19]

In his *Memoir* Cowper clearly describes the occasion when he believed he had committed this great iniquity. "A neglect to improve the mercies of God at Southampton," he wrote, "was represented to me as the sin against the Holy Ghost."[20] Ten years earlier, the reader will recall, he had gone to Southampton after suffering from melancholy for a period of twelve months. Suddenly, while he was gazing out to sea, another sun seemed to be kindled in the skies, his misery ended, and in a moment his heart became light and joyful. Momentarily the thought occurred to him that this transformation could have been caused only by "the Almighty fiat," but Satan, he observed, soon convinced him that his deliverance from melancholy had been wrought simply by the change of scene and the worldly diversions of Southampton.

As a Protestant, Cowper did not believe in miracles, except those performed during the time of Christ. But he did believe that God frequently intervenes in the affairs of men to punish or reward them. Now, when he looked back on the incident at Southampton, he accused himself of failing to credit his deliverance to a merciful act of God. The sin of the Pharisees had consisted of ascribing to Satan a miracle performed by Christ before their eyes. Cowper's sin, as he saw it, consisted of willfully ascribing his recovery at Southampton to worldly diversions, when in reality it had occurred, as the sudden nature of the experience seemed to prove, because God had intervened to save him in answer to his prayers. Thus, in his half-demented state, he believed that he had sinned, as had the Pharisees, by obstinately refusing to credit a manifest act of God. It may even have occurred to him that God had merely repeated his miraculous deed of Scripture, for in the Bible, casting out devils often refers to curing a person of insanity, and the melancholy from which he was relieved was a form of dementia.

Cowper probably arrived at the conviction that he was guilty of the unpardonable sin by a process of association. Like many others, he may have come across the scriptural passages dealing with this offense. Since he does not mention reading the Bible at the time, however, he may have got the idea from a reference in another work. Just before the delusion became implanted in his mind, the thought had occurred to him that the parable of the barren fig-tree was pointed directly at him. In an effort to dispel this terrifying reflection, he had "turned over all Archbishop Tillotson's sermons,"[21] hoping to find an interpretation of the parable. Apparently he discovered nothing to satisfy him on this point, but in looking through Tillotson he must have come upon a sermon that arrested his attention and, possibly, diverted his thoughts from the parable of the fig tree. This sermon of the seventeenth-century divine is entitled *Of the Sin against the Holy Ghost.*

While Cowper does not specifically state that he read this discussion, he does reveal how impressionable his mind was at this period. Immediately after remarking that he read Tillotson, he observes, "In every book I opened I found something that struck me to the heart. I remember taking up a volume of Beaumont and Fletcher, which lay upon the table in my kinsman's lodgings, and the first sentence I saw was this: 'The justice of God is in it.' My heart answered immediately, 'It is of a truth'; and I cannot but observe, that as I found something in the book to condemn me, so it was, in general, the first sentence I fixed upon. Every thing preached to *me,* and every thing preached the curse of the *law.*"[22]

Under these circumstances, when Cowper turned over *all* the sermons of Archbishop Tillotson, a caption such as *Of the Sin against the Holy Ghost* would doubtless rivet his attention. It will be interesting, therefore, to consider Tillotson's discussion of the offense, especially since it has never heretofore been pointed out as a likely source for Cowper's curious delusion. Tillotson first states that although one may be forgiven for blaspheming Christ, speaking against the Holy Ghost is unforgivable, because such blasphemy reflects on the divine power by which Christ wrought miracles. The reason the sin of the Pharisees was unique, he remarks, is that it "did consist in a most malicious opposition to the utmost evidence that could be given to the truth of any religion." Because the Pharisees saw the miracles performed, they could not deny them; yet such was their opposition to Christ and his doctrine that "they most maliciously and unreasonably ascribed them to the power of the devil."[23]

Other writers, such as Grotius and Dr. Hammond, had stated that though this sin was harder to forgive than others, they nevertheless deemed it ultimately pardonable, provided there was sufficient repentance for it. With this opinion Tillotson does not agree. He believes that those guilty of the offense can never gain forgiveness. The sin is unpardonable, he argues, because men who oppose the evidence of miracles resist the last means God can employ to convince them of divine revelation. When they have so hardened their hearts as to refuse the clearest kind of evidence, God withdraws his grace from them. Therefore, he adds, "when our Saviour here says that they shall not be forgiven, it is reasonable to suppose that he means that when persons are come to the degree of obstinacy and malice, God will (as justly he may) withdraw his grace from them."[24]

Tillotson argues strongly for his interpretation, but at the end of his sermon he gives his readers the assurance that, since the offense consisted of resisting the evidence of miracles wrought by Christ before the eyes of men, it could be committed only during the life of Christ on earth. Nevertheless, Tillotson warns against an approach to this sin. That which comes nearest to the actual offense, he observes, is total apostasy from Christianity after one has once embraced it and believed in its truths. Other near commissions are "sinning against the clear convictions of our consciences" and "malicious opposing of the truth, when the arguments for it are very plain and evident to any impartial and unprejudiced mind, and when he that opposeth the truth hath no clear satisfaction in his own mind to the contrary, but suffers himself to be furiously and headily carried on in opposition to it."[25]

One can imagine the effect of this last paragraph on Cowper's overwrought mind. His sense of guilt was so urgent that he might easily disregard the statement that to commit the sin now is impossible. Was not the nature of his offense, obstinacy to evidence of God's grace, identical with that of the Pharisees? When he had seen the finger of God in the lifting of his melancholy at Southampton, had he not ascribed his sudden peace of mind to his surroundings? There must have been some link which caused him to associate his Southampton experience with the unpardonable sin of Scripture. The fact that Cowper had been reading the seventeenth-century divine just before developing his delusion makes Tillotson a likely source.

Curiously, once he had fastened upon the idea that he had committed the unpardonable sin, he seemed to forget his attempt at suicide. His sense of guilt on that score was apparently transferred now to guilt for a worse offense, the unforgivable sin. For some reason his unbalanced mind seemed determined to find a specific ground on which he could convict himself. Generally one sees little evidence of his legal training, but in this instance he resembled a judge who reviews the statutes in order to make sure of giving a culprit the harshest sentence possible. Acting as his own judge, Cowper had discovered a law that penalized him for all eternity.

Cowper continued to live in his chambers at the Temple until December 1763. He now had disturbing dreams that he interpreted as confirmations of his guilt. In one of these he thought that he was in Westminster Abbey. When others were called to prayer, he hastened to join them, but an iron gate was flung in his face. Upon another occasion, he rose from his bed, picked up his prayer book, and attempted to pray, but the words stuck in his throat. Then he resolved to repeat the Creed to prove whether or not he possessed faith. His memory failed him, and he could not recall the words. This inability to pray he interpreted as a supernatural interposition that proved that he had really sinned against the Holy Ghost.

When John Cowper heard of his brother's predicament, he hastened to London. From the lips of the prostrate man, the young clergyman learned the tragic story of his attempts at suicide and his present delusion. John tried to reason with the half-mad Templar, but succeeded only in exasperating him. Hoping for solace, however, Cowper thought of a cousin on his father's side of the family, the Reverend Martin Madan. Although he had previously been scornful of the religious enthusiasm of this Evangelical clergyman, he now sent for him. Madan came to the Temple, sat down at his bedside, and engaged him in a discussion of the principles of Evangelicalism. He reminded Cowper that, because of original sin, man is naturally corrupt; he quoted Scripture to show the efficacy of the atonement; and he urged the importance of having a lively, personal faith in Jesus Christ. The poet was consoled by the clergyman's conversation on the natural depravity of all mankind and the significance of the atonement, but he felt incapable of developing the strong measure of faith so necessary for salvation. Nevertheless, the visit did him so much apparent good that his brother, who was not himself an Evangelical, urged the sick man to consult with Madan again. Cowper experienced a degree of relief from the clergyman's second visit, but his kinsman could not cure him; at best he only forestalled a complete mental collapse.

Satan now intervened, Cowper later wrote, and persecuted him with various physical torments. He saw horrible visions, and heard even more horrible voices. A numbness seized his body, his hands and feet became cold and stiff, and a clammy sweat broke out on his forehead. Then, while his brother was with him, came the final stroke. He described it as follows: "While I traversed the apartment in the most horrible dismay of soul, expecting every moment that the earth would open and swallow me; my conscience scaring me, the avenger of blood pursuing me, and the city of refuge out of reach and out of sight, a strange and horrible darkness fell upon me. If it were possible that a heavy blow could light upon the brain, without touching the skull, such was the sensation I felt. I clapped my hand to my forehead, and cried aloud through the pain it gave me. At every stroke my thoughts and expressions became more wild and incoherent; all that remained to me clear was the sense of sin, and the expectation of punishment."[26]

After months of torture his mind had finally given way. His brother, seeing the change, realized he was mad. Friends and relatives were consulted, and it was decided to send him to Dr. Cotton's asylum at St. Albans.

What was the basic cause of Cowper's insanity? We shall probably never know with certainty, but before turning to later events of his life, let us consider the subject. In the eighteenth century his form of dementia would have been called hypochondriacal melancholy. That, at least, is what Dr. William Heberden would have designated it, and Heberden's views are of particular interest inasmuch as he was one of Cowper's doctors. Heberden was also the friend and physician of Samuel Johnson and a very distinguished scholar. Cowper first consulted him while he was preparing to be examined for the Clerkship of the Journals. "As Saul sought to the witch, so did I to the physician, Dr. Heberden," he wrote, "and was so diligent in the use of drugs, as if they would have healed my wounded spirit."[27] Although the *Memoir* does not again mention Heberden by name, he was probably the doctor Cowper saw after his attempted suicide, when flashings before his eyes made him fear he might have a stroke of apoplexy. The physician consulted on this occasion advised him to go to the country for a rest. Heberden must certainly have prescribed that remedy at some time, for many years later Cowper wrote of him:

> Virtuous and faithful Heberden, whose skill
> Attempts no task it cannot well fulfill,
> Gives melancholy up to nature's care,
> And sends the patient into purer air.
>
> RETIREMENT 279–282

Heberden's description of hypochondriacal melancholy agrees very closely with Cowper's own almost clinical account of his symptoms. In *Commentaries on the History and Cure of Diseases* the doctor writes, "A giddiness, confusion, stupidity, inattention, forgetfulness, and irresolution all show that the animal functions are no longer under proper command, and that the mind is controlled by some foreign power. The comforts of sleep are in great measure denied these patients; for they have but little, and in it they are harassed with terrifying dreams. Restlessness, wandering pains, sudden flushings, cold sweats, a constant terror, tremors, catchings, numbness, contribute to their misery; which sometimes so overpowers them that they either sink under it in a fainting fit, or it is with great efforts and struggling that they can keep from it."[28]

In recent years several attempts have been made to diagnose Cowper's insanity and to explain it in psychiatrical terms. Those who have studied the case have generally taken into account his subsequent attacks as well as the first seizure, which occurred while he was living at the Temple. Dr. James Hendrie Lloyd observes that Cowper's insanity has several very puzzling aspects, but concludes, "The case is probably best described as a form of circular insanity, with alternating phases of profound depression and mild hypomanic reaction, but without distinct intervals of complete sanity. . . . It was a constitutional psychosis, call it what one may."[29] Gilbert Thomas, one of Cowper's more recent biographers, believes that the poet suffered from a manic-depressive form of insanity. However, Thomas adds, "I doubt if Cowper's madness can adequately be explained in psychogenic terms.

I question that any interpretation that fails to allow for a physical element in his successive derangements can be tenable."[30] David Cecil, another biographer, contends that the "sufferings of childhood" and a possible "inherent physical defect" were probably important causes of his madness.[31]

It will be observed that all these writers suggest that there was a constitutional or physical basis for Cowper's insanity. Just what the condition was has never been made clear, but apparently it was a sexual abnormality. The basis for this theory is a letter that the Reverend John Newton, Cowper's friend of later life, wrote to a member of the Thornton family. The letter itself was probably destroyed, but a striking piece of information contained therein has been published in Charles Greville's *Memoirs*. Greville came upon the story when he was asked to frank a packet of letters which were being sent to Robert Southey, one of Cowper's early biographers. Having considerable curiosity, Greville read the material and made a note on it in his diary. Because of prudery, however, the editors of the *Memoirs* expurgated his comment, and all that the nineteenth-century editions said was that Cowper's failure to take the Clerkship of the House of Lords and his morbidity were related "to some defect in his physical conformation." [32]

Southey's life of Cowper did nothing to clarify this statement; in fact, Southey does not even mention a physical abnormality. Nevertheless, he had apparently read Newton's letter on the subject, for his friend James Spedding remarked that Southey had given him "some very strange and interesting information about Cowper which he had gathered out of certain letters from Newton to Thornton." "The strangest of all," Spedding adds, "will not be made public." [33] Apparently, then, Southey suppressed the story because he felt it was too delicate, or too indelicate, for Victorian readers.

Greville's full text appears, however, in a recent, unexpurgated edition of his *Memoirs*. What Greville originally wrote was: "There is one curious fact revealed in these letters which accounts for much of Cowper's morbid state of mind and fits of depression, as well as for the circumstance of his running away from his place in the H. of Lords. He was an Hermaphrodite; somebody knew his secret, and probably threatened its exposure." [34] This statement, while frank enough, leaves much unexplained. Did Greville borrow the term "hermaphrodite" from Newton's letter, or was it his own way of expressing what Newton had said on the subject? And in either event just what was meant by the term? Probably it was intended in a popular rather than in a strictly biological sense.

One can easily theorize about the nature of Cowper's supposed sexual abnormality. For instance, he may have suffered from undescended testicles. If such a condition existed from birth, one could readily understand his unhappiness at Dr. Pitman's boarding school, where a physical abnormality of that kind would be likely to provoke the taunts of schoolboys. On the other hand, if he had a deformity of this sort, the Westminster boys would have been just as prone to ridicule him, but we know that he was relatively happy at Westminster.*

To speculate further on the nature of Cowper's physical abnormality would be useless, since we do not have sufficient evidence to constitute proof. On the other hand, no biographer can

---

* In his discussion of hypochondriacal melancholy, Heberden remarks that the victims often act on strange impulses. To illustrate his point, the doctor provides the curious case history of one of his patients: "A gentleman about thirty years of age, without any obvious cause, fell into a great dejection of spirits, which lasted some time. At length, by some perversion of mind, he seized a razor and amputated his penis and scrotum. After the wound was healed, he said of himself, it appeared very strange to him that he should have the courage to perform the deed, since he was always at other times of so timid a disposition that he had great dread even of being bled with a lancet; and could not suffer such a trifling wound without much agitation." (*Commentaries on the History and Cure of Diseases*, London, 1802, pp. 226–227, note.) The general description of Heberden's patient—a gentleman about thirty, of a timid disposition, and in dejected spirits—fits Cowper rather well. It is at least conceivable that the poet might have emasculated himself if he felt guilty about sexual indulgence, for he was prone to act on impulses, such as those that drove him to attempt suicide. In the absence of additional evidence, however, it is safer to suppose that the misfortunate man described by Heberden was some other client of the doctor.

validly neglect the possibility that he was either psychologically or physically impotent. Such a condition could contribute to his failure to marry Theodora and account for his fear of taking an examination before the bar of the House, especially if, as Greville indicates, someone knew his secret and threatened to disclose it. Furthermore, as we shall see, sexual impotency would help to explain various aspects of his later life.

III

The Convert

Far from the world, O Lord, I flee,
From strife and tumult far;
From scenes where Satan wages still
His most successful war.

HYMN XLVII

Private asylums, such as Dr. Cotton's, were rare in the eighteenth century. Only the well-to-do could afford them. Poorer people who went insane were kept at home, or confined in places like Bedlam, where they were exhibited to curiosity-seekers. In his youth Cowper had visited this institution in the company of other holiday ramblers who wanted to see the strange antics of the madmen. Later in life he wrote of this experience: "Though a boy, I was not altogether insensible of the misery of the poor captives, nor destitute of feeling for them. But the madness of some of them had such a humorous air, and displayed itself in so many whimsical freaks, that it was impossible not to be entertained, at the same time that I was angry with myself for being so." [1]

At St. Albans Cowper was spared the laughter of curiosity-seekers. His relatives chose this asylum because of the doctor's reputation for helping the insane, and because of his "well-known humanity and sweetness of temper." [2] Nathaniel Cotton, after studying medicine at Leyden, began his career at St. Albans in 1740. In addition to supervising the asylum, he carried on a regular medical practice, wrote occasional verses, and composed sermons. A man of deep religious convictions, he is described as a mild Evangelical. Cowper, who had been slightly acquainted with Cotton, developed great admiration for the doctor. He later wrote:

"I was not only treated by him with the greatest tenderness while I was ill, and attended with the utmost diligence, but when my reason was restored to me, and I had so much need of a religious friend to converse with, to whom I could open my mind upon the subject without reserve, I could hardly have found a fitter person for the purpose. My eagerness and anxiety to settle my opinions upon that long neglected point made it necessary that, while my mind was yet weak, and my spirits uncertain, I should have some assistance. The Dr. was as ready to administer relief to me in this article likewise, and as well qualified to do it, as in that which was more immediately his province." [3]

For the first six months at St. Albans Cowper was filled with despair. "Conviction of sin and expectation of instant judgment never left me," he wrote.[4] His dreams were troubled by the recollection of long-forgotten sins, and his waking moments filled with self-accusations. At length it occurred to him that divine vengeance might be deferred, and that until his doom was pronounced he might as well put aside his horrible thoughts. In this mood he was able to simulate cheerfulness so well that Dr. Cotton began to think he was improving. But his mind remained clouded, so long as he continued to believe he was damned.

During this period it once occurred to him that because he was barred from salvation, he might just as well have taken every opportunity to engage in sin. He envied those who departed this life with the knowledge that they had at least earned in full measure their sentence of doom. Here was a kind of Antinomianism in reverse. In the seventeenth century certain Calvinists had been so certain of their election that they believed no transgression of the moral law could bar them from salvation. Convinced that they were saved, some had indulged their passions to the full. Cowper, feeling as certain of damnation as the Antinomians had of salvation, momentarily felt, like them, that there was no purpose in obeying moral laws. This, however, was only a passing thought which he recorded in his *Memoir* to show the extent of his iniquity.

The first signs of recovery, according to his own account, appeared in July 1764, during a visit of his brother. When John asked how he felt, the harassed patient replied, "As much better as despair can make me." [5] The young clergyman tried to convince him that he was needlessly despondent by assuring him that he could be saved just as readily as anyone. Cowper, after listening to him, felt a ray of hope; from that time he became more cheerful. Throughout his life he was to be subject to tormenting dreams, but on this occasion when he went to bed he dreamed "that the sweetest boy I ever saw came dancing up to my bedside." When he awoke, he experienced, for the first time in months, a sensation of delight.[6]

One more step and he was able to overcome despair. Dr. Cotton had left copies of the Bible about his establishment in the hope that his patient would pick up one and find solace in reading it. A few months before his recovery, Cowper had gained momentary relief from perusing a volume of Scripture he found on a bench in the garden. The morning following his pleasant dream, he sat down in his room and discovered the customary Bible near at hand. Opening it at random, he came upon a text of St. Paul's Epistle to the Romans: "Whom God has set forth to be a propitiation through faith in his blood, to declare his righteousness for the remission of sins that are past, through the forbearance of God." The reading of this passage marked his recovery from despair and, insofar as one can designate a particular moment for it, his return to sanity. It was also, as he clearly indicates, the point at which he was converted.

The restoration to sanity was accompanied by an almost hysterical form of happiness. After believing for months that he was a damned soul, he now felt so ecstatically happy that he could scarcely sleep. At the mention of Scripture or the name of Jesus, tears would flow from his eyes. Dr. Cotton, noting these signs of hypomania, became fearful "lest the sudden transition from despair to joy should terminate in a fatal frenzy." [7] But fortunately Cowper did not lose his reason again until many years had passed. At length the doctor pronounced him cured, but the poet remained with him for almost another year. Like many Evangelicals, he now found his chief pleasure in discussing his faith, and in Dr. Cotton he had a sympathetic companion.

Cowper needed little formal instruction in the principles of Evangelical religion. Martin Madan had already explained its chief precepts to him. At the asylum he read various Evangelical writers, including the works of the lugubrious James Hervey. If he had questions, Dr. Cotton could no doubt have answered them, for the distinctive doctrines of the revival were relatively easy to comprehend. They were to have a profound influence on him, however, just as they were destined to have a great impact upon the nation. It is important for our purpose, therefore, briefly to consider these doctrines.

At the time of Cowper's conversion, the Evangelical movement had not perceptibly influenced English national life. Only a few members of the upper ranks had as yet adopted the faith. To the majority its adherents appeared to be a group of fanatics, who deserved the ridicule accorded them on the stage and by the press. The largest group of converts came from the ranks of miners, shopkeepers, rural laborers, and indigent town dwellers, people who had fallen under the spell of Whitefield's eloquence or Wesley's persuasiveness. In London and in scattered communities throughout the country there were Methodist chapels and Evangelical incumbents of churches of the Establishment, but the largest congregations were those that gathered out of doors to hear Wesley or one of his itinerant preachers exhort them to seek salvation through an active, revitalizing faith.

Before it could make much progress the Evangelical movement had to overcome two great obstacles, the prevailing tone of religious indifference and the tacit eighteenth-century belief that good works counted far more than piety or faith. The indifference of the period, partly a result of the apathy that followed the bitter religious struggles of the previous century, had been furthered by the deistical views of the age of reason. To be sure, the earlier advocates of deism were dead by the middle of the eighteenth century, and none of them had been such active proselytes as Tom Paine would prove to be when he revived their doctrines. Nevertheless, deism had created many nominal Christians who paid lip service to religion but who did not believe very strongly in revelation.

There was a common assumption that, if an after life exists, one could best be assured of eternity by performing good works in this world. The acceptance of this doctrine of salvation through practical merit resulted in various expressions of benevolence and charity. A new, if somewhat condescending, attitude toward the unfortunate led the wealthy to contribute generously to the erection of charity schools, hospitals, homes for the indigent, and asylums for prostitutes. In tune with their age, many writers encouraged the performance of good works by praising benevolence and condemning avarice and greed. In their books the hero was generally a man with a good heart. He might also be a gambler or wastrel, but so long as he acted upon charitable principles, he eventually triumphed over his parsimonious and self-righteous adversaries. The cult of benevolence thus led to a form of sentimentalism in literature, just as it encouraged an easy-going tolerance in the realm of morals and manners.

The revival was strongly opposed to this subordination of faith to works. Although the Evangelicals stressed the importance of charity and took an active part in founding benevolent institutions, they insisted that good works counted for naught in securing one's salvation. Man, they firmly averred, could be saved only by a resolute and active faith. If one had faith, then he would naturally perform good works as part of his Christian duty. But good deeds merely gave testimony that one had been saved; they were in no sense aids to salvation. No matter how generous a person might be, he was damned, according to the Evangelicals, so long as he remained indifferent to the truths of revelation. In the eyes of these reformers, therefore, a nominal Christian was little better than a heathen, for the occasional observance of the Sabbath or a casual perusal of the Bible gave no assurance of sanctity. To achieve salvation, one must possess strong faith, grounded on a profound realization of the significance of the atonement. This realization usually dawned upon the convert suddenly. A strong inner conviction gave him assurance that Christ's sacrifice had atoned for his sins. The process of conscious conversion was usually called the new birth, and the inner feeling that one was in a state of grace was sometimes designated as the testament of the spirit.

Cowper's conversion followed a fairly common pattern. Many Evangelicals had been awakened to faith by reading a devotional book, such as William Law's *Serious Call*, by hearing a sermon of Wesley, Whitefield, or some other revivalist preacher, or, like Cowper, by turning the pages of Scripture. Whatever the stimulus to conversion, the occasion was distinguished by the sudden and profound conviction that personal salvation is assured through the sacrifice of Christ. Various biographers have questioned whether Cowper was really converted, but any doubt on the subject can arise only from different definitions of conversion. To Cowper himself, the experience was genuine, and so it would seem to any eighteenth-century Evangelical. In his *Memoir* he states that upon reading the passage from St. Paul's Epistle he was immediately enabled to believe that Christ had redeemed him: "I saw the sufficiency of the atonement he had made, my pardon sealed in his blood, and all the fullness and completeness of his justification." [8] These words clearly indicate that Cowper had not only experienced a vivid realization of the meaning of Christ's sacrifice, but that he had also gone through the related Evangelical step to conversion, namely, the witness of the spirit, or the assurance of being in a state of grace.

While all Evangelicals subscribed to these doctrines, they differed among themselves upon other points. The largest bone of contention was the subject of predestination. Early in the history of the movement their disagreement on this subject had led to a split in the ranks. Whitefield, holding the Calvinistic view of election, parted company with Wesley and became the leader of the Calvinistic Methodists. This group, although never very large or influential in England, had thousands of adherents in Wales and in America. In England the Calvinists developed their greatest strength among clergymen of the Established Church. Unlike Wesley's itinerant preachers, these ministers generally remained as incumbents of parish churches and preached the doctrines of the revival to their own congregations. Notable among these clergymen were Cowper's friends Martin Madan and John Newton, as well as such leaders of the revival as William Romaine, Thomas Scott, and Henry Venn.

The Calvinistic Evangelicals, whether followers of Whitefield or members of the Establishment, held that from the beginning of time God had elected certain persons to be saved by Christ's sacrifice, and that the rest of mankind are doomed as sinful creatures to eternal death. It was generally agreed that the number of the elect was relatively small. Coupled with this doctrine was the belief that man is completely depraved, a naturally wicked being who can do nothing for his own salvation because he lacks freedom of the will. With these particular views of the strict Calvinists, Wesley and his followers were in violent disagreement. According to the Arminians, Christ's atonement had made salvation possible to all believers, not just to the predestined few. Although man was naturally corrupt, he was not completely depraved. He possessed some merit through the grace of God, and because his will was free, he could help effect his own salvation. Like the Calvinists, Wesley and his followers believed that salvation could be attained only through an inner consciousness of the meaning of the atonement, but they recognized, as the Calvinists could not because of their belief in predestination, that after a man was converted he might again fall into sin through a weakening of faith. In that event his case was not hopeless; through repentance he might be restored to grace and regain assurance of salvation.

In the early decades of the revival the differences between the Evangelical parties often led to bitter clashes of opinion, but as time went on the two groups became better disposed toward each other, chiefly because the second-generation Calvinists adopted a more compromising position than their predecessors. Known as the mild Calvinists, they realized that they had more in common with the Wesleyans than with other Christians. While they continued to adhere to a belief in election, they gave less emphasis to the complementary doctrine of reprobation. Their view was that common grace was extended to all men, allowing them to work for their salvation, but that special grace was granted to the elect, giving these perfect security of salvation. This position made their proselyting appear more logical to nontheologians, for there seemed to be some purpose in appealing to sinners to reform when by doing so they had a chance to be saved.

Even more than their emphasis on particular doctrines, certain practices shared by all Evangelicals set the group apart from other Christians and led to their reputation as fanatics, especially among the social group to which Cowper belonged. The revivalists were particularly obnoxious to other Englishmen because of (1) their extreme devotional zeal, (2) their attempts to be guided by literal interpretations of Scripture, and (3) their eagerness to promote a national reformation of morals and manners.

The term *Methodists,* applied in derision to all Evangelicals, was symbolical of the contempt others had for their piety. The name had first been given to Wesley and a small group of Oxford associates many years before his conversion and before the actual beginning of the revival. In this early stage there was no special emphasis on justification by faith or on other Evangelical doctrines. The young men were simply more devout than most members of the Oxford student body. Under the direction of John Wesley, the little group, numbering not more than thirty, developed the custom of reciting the collect of the day at prime, tierce, sext, and none, the canonical hours observed by Catholic monks. The young men also fasted until three o'clock two days a week, held meetings to read the Bible and other religious works, frequently received communion, and exercised stern self-denial in order to provide for the poor. These practices seemed so rigidly righteous to other Oxford students that they derisively called Wesley and his friends "the Methodists."

The Convert

The real revival began ten years later, when Wesley was converted after a period of reflection following upon his association with the Moravians. The emphasis on justification by faith and the new birth led the Evangelicals to subordinate the former emphasis on the sacraments of baptism and communion and to discard the popish observance of canonical hours. But the Evangelicals, like the young Oxford students of Wesley's time, were ardent worshipers. They designated regular periods for reading the Bible in the family circle, they restored the practice of saying grace before meat, and they held frequent evening devotions. Furthermore they regularly attended services two or three times on Sunday. These strict practices so astonished nonbelievers that "Methodism" seemed an appropriate designation. Throughout the eighteenth century, therefore, the term was indiscriminately applied to all Evangelicals, regardless of whether they were Calvinists or Arminians, and regardless of whether they attended a church of the Establishment, a Methodist chapel, or a dissenters' house of worship.

A second distinguishing characteristic of the Evangelicals was their bibliolatry. It was not simply that they knew the Bible in the intimate way that Cowper did. To many it was a wellspring of inspiration. Hence they often made decisions by opening it at random, read it for consolation in times of grief or affliction, and believed that the very sight or touch of its sacred pages could confer a blessing. Some of them refused to read any other book. To one of these fanatics, a Reverend Mr. Cadogan, John Wesley once sent a complete set of his works. Instead of being grateful for the gift, the stern zealot tossed the volumes into the fire with the remark that he would seek instruction nowhere but in Scripture. This emphasis on Holy Writ was largely responsible for the strict Sabbatarianism of the Evangelicals. In the Old Testament they read injunctions against profaning the Lord's Day by cooking, baking, gathering firewood, and traveling. These precepts were often carried out with self-righteous exactness. Strict families baked on Saturday and served only cold fare on Sunday. In the beginning most of them were too poor to own equipages, but later, when wealthy adherents became more numerous, Sunday travel for purposes of pleasure was taboo. Thus for the horses the Sabbath was a day of rest, but it afforded little relaxation to a good Evangelical. If he followed the regular practice of the group, he attended two or three church services, besides joining in family worship, and spent the intervening time in perusal of the Sacred Text.

The Evangelicals were further distinguished by their determination to reform the country. John Wesley had been particularly concerned to improve the conduct of the masses since they, like their betters, had fallen into degenerate ways during the eighteenth century. And he had a notable success. Many of his followers, converted from habitual indolence, gin-drinking, and thievery, became self-respecting citizens. The Calvinists were equally vigilant about improving the morals of their adherents. Because the Evangelicals made little distinction between manners and morals, however, they did not limit themselves to outlawing obvious infractions of Christian morality. Most of them strongly censured such pastimes as card-playing, dancing, and engaging in public revels. They condemned the theater as sinful, banned most forms of light reading, and adopted sober dress in place of finery. What most irked others was the Evangelical insistence that the whole nation adopt the strict and often prudish standards that the faithful imposed upon themselves. To the unregenerate it was vexing to be told that they must change their conduct when, according to some of the reformers, their destination in any event was hell. But the Evangelicals knew that their own members could more easily tread the paths of righteousness if the rest of the nation kept within reasonable bounds. Furthermore, a campaign to raise the general level of conduct was an adroit means of gaining adherents to their religious principles.

It has been questioned whether Cowper's conversion to this form of Christianity was fortunate for him. In recent years many of his biographers have regretted that he did not become an Arminian Evangelical instead of a Calvinist. Certainly the religion of Wesley with its message that salvation is possible for all offered more hope than Calvinism with its doctrines of election and reprobation. Perhaps Wesleyan Methodism would have been more compatible with his own forgiving nature, but one must remember that when he again lost faith in salvation, he thought his case unique and was not troubled by the Calvinistic doctrine of reprobation so much as by a peculiar delusion. Because of his extremely sensitive conscience and his overscrupulous nature, what he chiefly needed was a religion that offered a large measure of solace. Although thousands of others had found this sovereign virtue in Evangelical faith, and although he was himself to gain peace from it for nearly seven years, a creed emphasizing that an inner voice gives one assurance of salvation was psychologically ill-suited to his temperamental nature. Cowper relied too much upon monitions. Throughout his life, and especially in periods of insanity, he heard supernatural voices, was driven by compulsions, or had dreams that appeared to be monitory. These phenomena he regarded as warnings of God or promptings of the devil. So long as he heard what he believed to be messages from heaven, he was happy in his Evangelical faith, but when he became confused about the source of the monitions, his chosen religion failed him.

The good effects of his conversion, on the other hand, should not be underestimated. Since his first attack of insanity was probably induced by his sense of guilt, his recovery was no doubt aided by a religion that dramatized the doctrine that, no matter what his sins had been, he could still be saved through faith. Better than any other evidence, the contrast between two of his poems shows the great remedial value of his conversion. The first, *Lines Written under the Influence of Delirium*, reveals in agonizing Sapphics the tortures he endured while he was insane:

> Hatred and vengeance, my eternal portion,
> Scarce can endure delay of execution,
> Wait with impatient readiness to seize my
> Soul in a moment.
>
> Damned below Judas; more abhorred than he was,
> Who for a few pence sold his holy Master!

Twice-betrayed Jesus me, the last delinquent,
    Deems the profanest.

Man disavows and deity disowns me,
Hell might afford my miseries a shelter;
Therefore Hell keeps her ever-hungry mouths all
    Bolted against me.

Hard lot! encompassed with a thousand dangers;
Weary, faint, trembling with a thousand terrors,
I'm called, if vanquished, to receive a sentence
    Worse than Abiram's.

Him the vindictive rod of angry Justice
Sent quick and howling to the center headlong;
I, fed with judgment, in a fleshly tomb, am
    Buried above ground.

This dirge of despair with its note of finality conveys the impression that its author was beyond hope of recovery. Yet, through the influence of Evangelical religion, Cowper was again to find pleasure in living. A year or two after his recovery at St. Albans, he wrote a second poem called *A Song of Mercy and of Judgment*. These verses, expressing the exultation of a soul reborn, show the great and happy change brought about by his conversion to Evangelicalism.

> *A Song of Mercy and of Judgment*
> (reproduced in part)
> Me thro' waves of deep affliction
> Dearest Saviour! Thou has brought,
> Fiery deeps of dark conviction
> Hard to bear and passing thought.
>   Sweet the sound of grace Divine,
>   Sweet the grace that makes me Thine.
>
> . . . .
>
> Bound and watched, lest, life abhorring,
> I should my own death procure,
> For to me the pit of roaring
> Seemed more easy to endure.
>   Grace divine, how sweet the sound!
>   Sweet the grace which I have found.
>
> . . . .

But at length a word of healing,
Sweeter than an angel's note,
From the Saviour's lips distilling,
Chased despair and changed my lot.
　　Sweet the sound, etc.

.　.　.　.　.　.　.　.　.　.　.　.　.

"I," He said, "have seen thee grieving,
Loved thee as I passed thee by,
Be not faithless, but believing,
Look and live, and never die.
　　Sweet the sound, etc.

.　.　.　.　.　.　.　.　.　.　.　.　.

"Take the bloody seal I give thee
Deep impressed upon thy soul;
God, thy God, will now receive thee,
Faith hath saved thee, thou art whole."
　　Grace divine, etc.

.　.　.　.　.　.　.　.　.　.　.　.　.

All at once my chains were broken,
From my feet my fetters fell,
And that word in pity spoken,
Snatched me from the gates of Hell.
　　Grace divine, etc.

As one of the most widely read of all Evangelical writers, Cowper was to play an important part in arousing the conscience of the country. His contributions to the revival were to come several years later, however. Meanwhile his conversion profoundly affected his personal habits and tastes. He decided not to return to London. That city, which had been the scene of so much pleasure and pain, he now regarded as a center of iniquity. He no longer wanted the company of gay companions or the amusements of the metropolis. The theater, Vauxhall, social gatherings of people of fashion, the witty conversation and pleasant tippling at the tavern, the busy stir of the coffeehouses — all these he determined to abandon in favor of life in a small town and the society of religious persons. Dr. Johnson had once remarked that "the man who is tired of London is tired of life." Cowper, in retreating from his former life, was indeed weary of the world and of worldly pleasures. Henceforth he could cast only an occasional, half-interested glance at the larger stage of human activity.

Having determined not to return to London, he resigned from his position as Commissioner of Bankrupts and thus lost the stipend of £60 a year. His expenses at the asylum were so great that his relatives had to make up a fund for his support. Cowper accepted their bounty, as throughout life he was to acknowledge the financial aid of friends, with gratitude, but with no thought that his indebtedness to others should cause him to economize. When he left St. Albans he took two dependents with him. Samuel Roberts, an attendant who had become attached to him, was to be his personal servant. His compassion had also led him to adopt a six-year-old boy named "Dick" Coleman, who had been ill treated by his father, a drunken cobbler. Providing for these two dependents seemed like a needless extravagance to the relatives who contributed to his support, but they merely grumbled about the situation and did not cut off their remittances.

Upon leaving St. Albans in June 1765, Cowper went to Cambridge, where his brother was a fellow of the university. The original plan was that they should live in the same town, but because suitable lodgings were unavailable at Cambridge, Cowper moved to Huntingdon, fifteen miles away. John was probably relieved when William settled at some distance from the university. Although the younger brother was a clergyman, he was not an Evangelical, and no doubt he would have been embarrassed before his friends by a brother who discoursed so enthusiastically on the still unpopular subject of the revival.

Huntingdon, the birthplace of Oliver Cromwell, was a neat little town of two thousand inhabitants. A thriving market center, fifty-eight miles from London, it was situated on the left bank of the Ouse River, which, Cowper observed, was the most attractive feature of the region. At that time small boats still plied up the stream from Lynn, and the tiny community bustled with commercial and social life. For one so disposed there was a variety of entertainment. "Here is a card-assembly, and a dancing-assembly, and a horse-race, and a club, and a bowling-green, so that

I am well off, you perceive, in point of diversions," Cowper wrote Joseph Hill. Then, lest his former companion should miss his irony, he added, "especially as I shall go to 'em just as much as I should if I lived a thousand miles off." [9]

Cowper was well contented with Huntingdon. He took pleasure in managing his little household and wrote amusing letters to Hill about his habit of overstocking his larder with quantities of meat and small beer. In good weather he bathed in the Ouse, and once a week he rode to Cambridge on a hired mount to visit his brother. Much of his time was occupied by attendance at church and performing private devotions. He also made a few acquaintances. One was the rector of St. Mary's, whom he described as a good preacher and a sensible man. Soon after his settling in the town he had a call from a local draper, a man of amiable disposition, who undertook to supply him with copies of the *St. James's Chronicle* and offered him a key to a cold bath which he had installed in a shed. Another acquaintance, a Mr. Nicholson, is described as a "north country divine," a humble man who read prayers twice a week at Huntingdon and served two churches in the neighborhood. The poet, who was an early riser, also met an old man who walked a mile out of town to a fountain at six every morning. "He drinks nothing but water, and eats no flesh," Cowper wrote, "partly (I believe) from a religious scruple (for he is very religious) and partly in the spirit of a valetudinarian." [10] The poet's descriptions of his neighbors showed that he was developing a healthy interest in his new surroundings, but his chief concern continued to be religion.

He briefly considered becoming a clergyman, but the memory of what he had suffered at the thought of appearing before the public convinced him that he was not designed for the ministry. Nevertheless he hoped to have a share in making known the principles of the revival. It was with this intention that he wrote his *Memoir* while living at Huntingdon. In composing a narrative of his conversion, he followed the precedent of various Evangelicals who had written accounts of their religious experiences with the purpose of arousing faith in others. These testaments usually stressed, in general terms, the early sinfulness of the author, in order to highlight the change that occurred when he experienced the new birth. Because it vividly describes his madness, Cowper's narrative is much more interesting than most of these pious works. Having written with candor about his affliction, he shrank, however, from the thought of letting scoffers read it. His intention was to show it only to those who had received some degree of religious enlightenment. After it had circulated among the Madans and a few others, his cousin Harriet, now Lady Hesketh, asked for permission to read it. Cowper hesitated about sending it to her but finally agreed to, with the understanding that no other person should be allowed to look at the manuscript while it was in her possession. After perusing the narrative, Lady Hesketh returned it with the comment that she could not understand how a merciful God could have destined him to so much suffering or why he did not take full credit for his repentance. This unspiritual reaction sorely disappointed Cowper. He felt she had missed the point, and he was grieved that his *Memoir* had failed to arouse his worldly cousin to a sense of her own sinfulness.[11]

Lady Hesketh was also more annoyed than edified by the religious enthusiasm of his letters. With the fanatical zeal of the new convert, he had got into the habit of writing about his happiness in Evangelical religion, and the superiority of Bible Christianity to other forms of religion. Such topics delighted Evangelicals, like Mrs. Madan, but they irked Lady Hesketh. As a result the cousins eventually discontinued their correspondence. Many years later, after it had been resumed, he recalled his Huntingdon period and confessed that he had been overzealous. "When I left St. Albans, I left it under impressions of the existence of a God, and of the truth of Scripture that I never felt before," he was to write (April 3, 1786). "I had unspeakable delight in the discovery, and was impatient to communicate a pleasure to others that I found so superior to every thing that bears the name. This eagerness of spirit, natural to persons newly informed, and the less to be wondered at in me who had just emerged from the horrors of despair, made me imprudent, and, I doubt not, troublesome to many." [12]

Gradually, and more the result of circumstance than of desire, the poet's links with the past were sundered. He corresponded with only a few of his relatives and with none of his former acquaintances except Joseph Hill. This faithful friend and manager of his little estate paid him one short visit at Huntingdon, but though they continued to exchange cordial letters for nearly thirty more years, they never saw each other again. Fortunately, since Cowper was particularly dependent on companionship, he was to make new friends among those whose religious views were more nearly akin to his own.

One Sunday when he was leaving church he fell into conversation with an agreeable young man of twenty-one. Attracted by his sensible observations, Cowper invited him to tea that afternoon. His new acquaintance was William Unwin, a Cambridge student who was preparing for the ministry. Through him the poet soon met the other members of the family. The elder Mr. Unwin, whom Cowper described as "a man of learning and good sense, and as simple as Parson Adams," [13] was a clergyman, though not an Evangelical. There was also a daughter of eighteen, a modest young lady of considerable beauty. But it was Mrs. Unwin for whom Cowper developed the greatest admiration. A well-read woman, with genteel manners and a cheerful disposition, she was several years younger than her husband. Although she entertained serious religious views, her piety did not smother cheerfulness and good breeding. A few weeks after he was introduced to her, Cowper wrote, "That woman is a blessing to me, and I never see her without being the better for her company. I am treated in the family as if I were a near relation, and have been repeatedly invited to call upon them at all times." [14]

His intimacy with the family ripened. When he went to Cambridge to visit his brother, he rode with Mr. Unwin in his chaise. Soon he was making daily visits to the household. Finally, on November 11, 1765, when a student who had lodged with the

Unwins left, Cowper gave up his own rooms and became a permanent paying guest of the family. He was now to enjoy one of the happiest periods of his life. For the first time since his childhood he could take an assigned place at a congenial domestic hearth. To many his existence would seem a dull routine, but he felt no need of worldly diversions or of other society.

A year after he had become a member of the household Cowper described his existence to one of his relatives. Because he and the Unwins never took part in local amusements, the townspeople called them "Methodists," he wrote. The poet was amused by the term, almost smugly so, for he felt that he had discovered a mode of life far more satisfying than any the town could offer.

"We breakfast commonly between eight and nine," he wrote; "till eleven we read either the Scripture, or the sermons of some faithful preachers of those holy mysteries; at eleven we attend divine service, which is performed here twice every day; and from twelve to three we separate and amuse ourselves as we please. During that interval I either read in my own apartment, or walk, or ride, or work in the garden. We seldom sit an hour after dinner, but, if the weather permits, we adjourn to the garden, where with Mrs. Unwin and her son I have generally the pleasure of religious conversation till tea-time. If it rains, or is too windy for walking, we either converse within doors, or sing hymns of Martin's collection . . . After tea we sally forth to walk in good earnest. Mrs. Unwin is a good walker, and we have generally travelled about four miles before we see home again. . . . At night we read and converse, as before, till supper, and commonly finish the evening either with hymns or a sermon; and last of all the family are called to prayers." [15]

The even tenor of this peaceful existence was interrupted on July 2, 1767, when Morley Unwin was thrown from his horse while riding to church to conduct a service. After lingering four days, the elderly clergyman died of his injuries. Describing the circumstance to his cousin, Mrs. Madan, Cowper revealed that the Reverend Mr. Unwin had at one point in his career come under the teachings of the Socinian Dr. Samuel Clarke. As a result Mr. Unwin had developed Unitarian views. He had affirmed his belief in the divinity of Christ upon his deathbed, however, and Cowper felt that his last-hour repentance may have secured his salvation.[16]

The other members of the household took for granted that the poet would continue to live with them, even though William Unwin was away at Cambridge a good part of the time. "I am a sort of adopted son in the family, where Mrs. Unwin has always treated me with parental tenderness," Cowper wrote. "Therefore by the Lord's leave I shall still continue a member of it." [17] His decision to stay was wise. All his life he had needed a mother, as Sainte-Beuve remarked; now when he had at last found one, to sacrifice the connection would have been foolhardy. Mrs. Unwin gave him the sympathy he needed in full and indulgent measure. If she was not a thoroughgoing Evangelical when they first met, she soon became one, and their religious views were in perfect accord. They saw eye to eye on all points. When he introduced new friends into their domestic circle, she accepted them because they were his friends. If he developed a dislike of someone, she shared his aversion. If he discovered a new interest, she encouraged it. And when his anxiety returned, she gave him the comfort and assurance of her abiding friendship. Not that she lacked a mind or will of her own, but she was so completely devoted to him that she came to feel a greater kinship with him than with her own daughter.

To outsiders who knew little of Cowper's past the relationship was difficult to understand, and the unconventional circumstance of their living together gave rise to gossip. A month after the death of Mr. Unwin, Cowper wrote with bitterness that neighbors at Huntingdon had been casting aspersions upon them.[18] The accusations must have been particularly painful to such a pious pair. Yet if another man had been in Cowper's position, the assumption that they were lovers would be natural, especially since Mrs. Unwin was only seven years his senior. But the poet was not the normal man. One psychologist has remarked, his "relations with women all through life seem to have been those of a child or ward rather than of a man." [19]

With Mr. Unwin dead, there was no reason for the family to remain at Huntingdon, and the knowledge that they were the subject of gossip made them eager to leave. Where they settled did not matter, so long as they could have the inspiration of a sincere Evangelical preacher. A new acquaintance was to help them make their decision. The Reverend John Newton of Olney, having heard of the exemplary family through a Dr. Richard Conyers, called on them the day after Mr. Unwin's funeral. During the visit Cowper mentioned their desire to leave Huntingdon, and Newton proposed that they move to Olney. He began house-hunting on his return, and on August 3 Cowper and Mrs. Unwin went to Olney to inspect a vacant residence in the neighboring village of Emberton and another dwelling in the center of Olney. Having decided to take the latter, since it was near the church, the family moved to Olney on September 14, 1767, to begin a new chapter in their lives.[20]

IV

A Disciple of Newton

Oh for a closer walk with God!
A calm and heavenly frame;
A light to shine upon the road
That leads me to the Lamb!
                                    HYMN I

OLNEY was a lace-making center, situated, like Huntingdon, on the Ouse River. It was an ancient town, with a tall-spired, fourteenth-century church and a few splendid buildings, the relics of former times. High Street, the main thoroughfare, opened into a triangular market place to the south. Here stood the Swan Inn, which the poet mentions, the Round House, where lawbreakers paid the penalty for their crimes, and the Shiel, a two-storied stone edifice that served as the Town Hall. Cowper's house, called Orchard Side, also faced on the market place. A cheerless ark of a building, it was designed to house two families. For nineteen years Cowper was to occupy the western half of this residence.

The countryside through which the Ouse twisted its course had an unspectacular kind of beauty, but Olney itself was hardly a picturesque English village. The squalid, thatch-roofed cottages that lined High Street and the adjoining lanes were a constant reminder of the poverty of the inhabitants. It was the time of cottage industries, when whole families, including small children, engaged in such household occupations as spinning, weaving, and lace-making. At Olney, where lace-making was the chief industry,

65

the poor toiled late into the evening to earn a few shillings a week. Wages were so small that many families had to depend for an extra shilling or two upon the parish rates, or upon a special fund provided by the wealthy Evangelical, John Thornton.

Cowper felt great compassion for his poor neighbors. He frequently visited their cottages and distributed money which he received from Thornton or from correspondents to whom he had described the plight of the lace-makers. The townspeople, on their part, held the poet in great respect. By comparison with them he was an exalted personage, and they soon formed the habit of calling him "Sir Cowper."

Except for these humble inhabitants, Olney afforded him almost no society. Besides his own household, which consisted of Mrs. Unwin, her daughter, Sam Roberts, and another servant, his only intimates were the Newtons. But Cowper demanded nothing more. His purpose in coming to Olney was to enjoy the companionship of the clergyman, and in that respect he was not disappointed. Shortly after his arrival he wrote Mrs. Madan, "Nothing can exceed the kindness and hospitality with which we are received here by his dear servant Newton: and to be brought under the ministry of so wise and faithful a steward of his Holy Mysteries is a blessing for which I can never be sufficiently thankfull." [1] Because Orchard Side needed extensive repairs, Newton had invited the Cowper-Unwin household to be his guests until their own home was ready for them. According to Thomas Wright, Cowper moved into Orchard Side on December 9, [2] but this date must be incorrect, for in one of his letters Newton states that Cowper and Mrs. Unwin remained his guests until February 15, 1768, or for a period of five months after their removal to Olney. The clergyman adds that during their sojourn under his roof Cowper's man-servant and Mrs. Unwin's maid had both been converted. [3]

Once established in his own home, Cowper continued to have easy access to Newton. Their gardens were separated only by an orchard, and the friends paid the owner a guinea for the right to use it as a short cut. Daily visits between Orchard Side and the vicarage were customary, and the poet seems never to have tired of the neighbor whose character and history were so different from his own.

John Newton was a robustious, self-sufficient man whose convictions were as tough as his sinews. If he had doubts, they did not trouble him for long, for he soon resolved his conflicts into steadfast convictions. In his *Authentic Narrative* he confessed that during his early life as a sailor he had been an extreme sinner. After his conversion he renounced his habit of blasphemy and, somewhat later, succeeded in overcoming the ever present temptation to seduce the Negro girls that formed part of his cargo on the run from Africa to the Colonies. But that there was anything wrong in slave-trafficking never occurred to him until years later. "During the time I was engaged in the slave-trade I never had the least scruple as to its lawfulness," he wrote. "I was, upon the whole, satisfied with it as the appointment Providence had marked out for me." [4] Even after his realization of the evils of slavery, he consoled himself with the thought that he had tried to treat his human cargoes with consideration, and he probably never lost an hour's sleep in remorse for his earlier life as captain of a slave ship. Whatever his sins, Christ had atoned for them, and his conversion gave him assurance of salvation. It was unfortunate for Cowper's peace of mind that he did not possess a little more of this *sang-froid*. Had his tender feelings ever allowed him to engage in anything so brutal as the slave trade, he could never later have forgiven himself. This fundamental difference between the two men made it impossible for Newton, sympathetic though he was, to understand Cowper's doubts and self-accusations.

No hero of a picaresque novel had crowded into life more stirring adventures than those Newton had experienced in his youth. When he described them, however, instead of writing an unvarnished tale of his escapades, he interspersed his account with incessant moralizing, frequent ejaculations upon his sinfulness, and numerous references to the Bible. Thus what might have been a spiced biography of a rash seafaring man, became, as he intended it should be, just one more Evangelical tract on a sinner's conversion.

Newton was born in London, on July 24, 1725, the son of a hardy sea captain of the merchant fleet. His mother, a pious woman of Nonconformist faith, died when her son was only seven. Upon the remarriage of his father, young Newton was sent to a boarding school in Essex, where he remained two years. When the boy was eleven, his father took him aboard his ship, and except for a few months passed in Spain with a merchant friend of the elder Newton, he sailed with his father until 1742. It was then decided that he should go to Jamaica to engage in trade. Traveling to board his ship, he stopped in Kent with the Catlett family, who were distant relatives of his mother. He fell in love with the older daughter, a girl of fourteen and, with typical resolution, decided that at some future time she should become his wife. The marriage took place seven years later.

By delaying with the Catletts, Newton missed the boat for Jamaica. Instead of going to the New World, he signed aboard a ship bound for Venice. Back in England after this voyage, he was impressed into the Navy on the H.M.S. *Harwich*. Within a month, through the influence of his father, he obtained an appointment as midshipman aboard the same vessel, but the young sinner was soon in trouble. After once overstaying his shore leave, he finally deserted the ship while it was lying at Plymouth. A group of soldiers caught him and returned him to the *Harwich,* where he was degraded and publicly whipped. The captain ordered the crew to have nothing to do with him, and the young man was left solitary and unhappy. When the ship arrived at Madeira, he obtained permission to transfer to a slave ship bound for Guinea. Although the captain of this vessel was a friend of his father, the young scamp soon gained his enmity by ridiculing him before the crew.

Several months later, while the slaver was in an African port, the captain died. Fearing that the first mate, who detested him, would put him aboard a British man-of-war, Newton resolved to remain in Africa. He found employment at the port town with a white merchant who was engaged in buying blacks from the interior and selling them to slave traders. Newton was dazzled by the prospect of becoming wealthy at this new occupation, but fate directed that he should become a kind of slave himself. While his master was away, Newton fell ill of a fever. There was no one to take care of him except the black mistress of the merchant, and she, instead of pitying him, only ridiculed his plight. When he began to recover, she deprived him of food, and he was forced to slip into the plantation at night to grub for roots. So bad was his lot that even the slaves in chains were occasionally moved to give him a portion of their food. The master eventually returned, but he had developed such an aversion for the young man that he refused to give him proper food and clothing. After enduring harsh treatment for a year, Newton was finally allowed to transfer his services to another merchant, who showed more consideration for him.

Meanwhile his father had instructed a sea captain bound for Africa to inquire for his son and to try to bring him home. When, by an odd set of circumstances, the captain happened upon Newton, he had to employ a ruse to get his assent to return to England. Although he was in a desolate land, with no companions except a few slave traders, the independent youth wished to stay to make his fortune.

The journey home took more than a year, for the vessel returned to England by way of Newfoundland. Although the captain at first treated Newton kindly, later, when misadventures befell the ship, he came to regard his mischief-exciting young passenger as a Jonah. Newton instigated a contest among the ship's company, for instance, to see who could hold out longest after drinking alternate drafts of gin and rum. The innovator of the game was the first to become intoxicated and nearly lost his life in a rash attempt to dive into the sea to recover his hat. Later in the voyage his conduct changed. During a frightful storm, which threatened to sink the ship and all on board, Newton reviewed his past life. He realized his sinfulness, and, when the ship survived, determined to reform and henceforth to follow Scripture. It was from this time, March 1748, that he dated his conversion.

Back in England, Newton married Miss Catlett in 1750. After making a voyage aboard a slaver as mate, he became the master of his own slave ship, and, for the next several years, he engaged in transporting human cargoes from Africa to America. Even during the days of his distress, he had studied a copy of Euclid, and he now continued his self-education. Having taught himself Latin, he read Virgil, Terence, Livy, and Erasmus. He also devoted himself to Scripture, and in pursuit of this subject he learned Greek, Hebrew, and a little Syriac. Meanwhile he had come under the influence of a ship's master who made him acquainted with Calvinistic theology. Converted to its doctrines, Newton remained wedded to them for the remainder of his life.

After suffering a brief attack of paralysis, he determined to give up the sea. He went to Liverpool and there procured the fairly lucrative position of Surveyor of the Tides, an appointment he held from 1750 to 1755. Meanwhile he continued his study of the Bible, read the works of various theologians and preachers, and became an ardent follower of Whitefield. At length he resolved to enter the ministry. He applied for orders to the Archbishop of York but was refused, either because he was not a university man or because of his Evangelical views. Undaunted, he engaged in independent preaching until he finally attracted the attention of Lord Dartmouth. Through his influence Newton was ordained by the Bishop of Lincoln and appointed to the curacy of Olney, where he began his new duties in May 1764.

As a Calvinist, Newton had a thoroughgoing belief in the doctrines of election, the total depravity of mankind, and justification by faith. "If we admit the total depravity of human nature," he wrote, "the only way we can account for the conversion of a soul to God is by the doctrine of election. It is impossible for the sinner to seek the Lord, for he is so steeped in sin he is at enmity against God. (Moreover, his will is depraved, probably, so he can't.) Since the sinner can't seek God, God seeks him and sheds grace upon him. But all do not come to a knowledge and love of God, for all do not receive grace; therefore only some are elected." [5] Such was the simple logic of the man to whom most things were simple. Only upon one point did he seem unsure — whether or not man's will is totally depraved. "Man by nature is still capable of great things," he wrote. "His understanding, reason, memory, imagination, etc. sufficiently proclaim that the hand that made him is divine." [6] Because Newton, though believing in the depravity of mankind, was not completely certain that man's will is equally corrupt, and because he regarded belief in election more as a matter of logic than a requirement for salvation, he considered himself a mild Calvinist.

He believed these to be the steps through which a convert should go: consciousness of sin, turning to God, realization of the significance of the atonement, a conviction that through Christ's sacrifice he was saved, and only then, after he had assurance of salvation, a knowledge that God had elected him as well as others to eternal life. Because a belief in predestination came last in this process, Newton confessed that when he preached he seldom insisted upon the doctrines of Calvinism. His first business, as he saw it, was to awaken his listeners to a sense of sin. This view explains the position he takes in one of his letters:

"I am an avowed Calvinist; the points which are usually comprised in that term seem to me so consonant with Scripture, reason (when enlightened), and experience, that I have not the shadow of a doubt about them. But I cannot dispute; I dare not speculate. What is by some called High Calvinism I dread. I feel much more union of spirit with some Arminians than I could with some Calvinists; and if I thought a person feared sin, loved the word of God, and was seeking after Jesus, I would not walk the length of my study to proselyte him to the Calvinist doctrines. Not because I think them mere opinions, or of little importance to a believer — I think the contrary; but because I believe these doctrines will do no one any good till he is taught them by God." [7]

Newton believed that unless man receives enlightenment from God, his chance of salvation is hopeless. Education could not avail to open the eyes of the spiritually blind, nor could charitable works serve to usher the Good Samaritan through the gates of heaven. Man was saved by faith alone, and faith was the gift of God. If these were the clergyman's beliefs, why did he bother to expostulate with sinners? The main reason was that God had commanded it, and for Newton that was reason enough.

As Adelaide Thein has pointed out, he was not an original nor even a profound thinker. Yet he had an almost egotistical assurance of his own salvation. Considering himself justified by faith, he felt no intellectual compulsion to justify his creed through arduous study or speculation. Although he professed that man has no will of his own, he demonstrated his own will to believe doctrines that suited his sanguine temperament. "The painful whys of life never punctuated his superb self-confidence," Miss Thein remarks, "and the Word of God, especially the summary he selected, furnished him with a scheme of salvation — comfortable, simple, complete, and consistent." [8]

Although Newton did not become a clergyman of the Established Church until he was forty, he was to have a long and distinguished career in the ministry. His chance to make a name for himself came chiefly after 1780, when he left the small parish at Olney to accept the living of St. Mary Woolnoth Church, London. There his vigorous preaching attracted large congregations, and his pulpit oratory and individual persuasiveness led to many conversions. Eventually, because of his vigor in promoting the principles of the revival, he was to become the recognized leader of the Evangelical party within the Establishment.

In addition to having a forceful personality, Newton must have possessed considerable charm. Other clergymen found him a warm advocate of their interests; his wife and Miss Catlett, a niece who lived with him, loved and revered him; and such prominent converts as Hannah More and William Wilberforce delighted in his society. Thus Cowper was not alone in feeling a strong attraction to the man. Never a self-sufficient person himself, the poet found in him a reserve of strength upon which he could draw. If Newton's manners occasionally reflected the roughness of his early life, his heartiness and persuasive charm atoned for his defects in the eyes of his more gently bred companion.

The question whether Newton's influence on Cowper was good has been long contested. Many writers have believed that the clergyman's Calvinism served to strengthen the poet's gloomy views of religion. But the doctrines that Cowper had derived from Martin Madan and from his own reading were, in theory at least, as strongly Calvinistic as Newton's beliefs. Certain authors have also maintained that the Evangelical preacher helped to reawaken in Cowper the idea that he was guilty of the unpardonable sin. This view is false for two reasons. In the first place, when Cowper returned to the idea that he was an outcast from God, he did not again believe that he had committed the unpardonable sin of the Bible. Secondly, if he had been troubled by the same delusion, Newton's interpretation of the sin against the Holy Ghost would have given him consolation rather than pain.

Like many Evangelical preachers of the eighteenth century, Newton realized that earnest souls were frequently troubled by the thought that they might have committed the sin of the Pharisees. But, narrow as the Evangelical preachers were in many of their views, they were generally too intelligent to encourage this particular conviction. Several of them, including Wesley, Thomas Scott, and Newton, preached sermons in which they assured their listeners that it was impossible for them to be guilty of this offense. If Cowper discussed the interpretation of the unpardonable sin with Newton, as he probably did, his friend would doubtless have repeated the message he gave to his congregation in a sermon entitled *Messiah Derided upon the Cross* "This sin," said Newton with customary assurance, "no one can have committed who is fearful lest he has committed it, for it essentially consists in a deliberate and wilful refusal of the only means of salvation. It is the sign of final, absolute impenitence." [9]

When Cowper was again harassed by the thought that he was damned, though not this time for committing the sin against the Holy Ghost, Newton tried to persuade him that he need not fear for his salvation. Even after he had removed to London, the clergyman kept reverting to his argument. In one letter he wrote,

"How wonderful is that tincture, the inexpressible something that gives your sentiments when you speak of yourself so gloomy a cast, while in all other respects it leaves your faculties in full bloom and vigour! How strange that your judgment should be clouded on one point only, and that a point so obvious and strikingly clear to everybody who knows you! . . . Though your comforts have been so long suspended, I know not that I ever saw you for a single day since your calamity came upon you in which I could not perceive as clear and satisfactory evidence that the grace of God was with you as I could in your brighter and happier times." [10]

As this letter indicates, the clergyman could not understand why his friend had doubts. To Newton it was clear that the poet was among the elect, and he kept assuring him on that point. If he erred, it was probably in reverting too frequently to the subject, for no appeal to reason could cure the poet's delusion.

But Newton was not a tactful person. Indeed his lack of tact and other personality traits probably did the poet more harm than the clergyman's views. Cowper would perhaps have been better off with a counselor less confident of his own convictions, someone who could have assured him that most men have doubts, but that doubt itself, as Browning remarks, is evidence that man is more than a clod. Newton's strong assurance on matters of faith may have caused Cowper to feel that to have any religious doubts was abnormal and therefore a sign that he was different from other men.

The clergyman's vigor and drive had an unfortunate influence on the shy poet. When he first settled in Olney, Cowper often accompanied Newton on visits to nearby towns.[11] Upon these occasions, one may be sure, the principal topic of conversation was religion. Much as Cowper liked to discourse on this subject, the out-of-pulpit sermons of his clerical friend no doubt led to a revival of his habit of self-examination and to a resurgence of his overdelicate scruples. He might better have satisfied his liking for gospel conversation in quiet chats with Mrs. Unwin. Again, as other writers have observed, the clergyman forced the poet too much into the public gaze. Cowper was so shy that when he had first led daily prayers for his own household, he had been abashed until he had conducted the simple service several times. Yet Newton encouraged him to take part in public prayer meetings and to address his Olney congregation.

In one other respect the Evangelical preacher seems certainly to have had a harmful psychological effect. He was a consistent believer in dreams, as several of his works show. In the narrative of his early life, for instance, he describes how, when he was a young sailor making a voyage to Venice, a person appeared to him in his dream and gave him a ring which he charged him to keep. Then another apparition came upon the scene and urged him to throw the ring away. When Newton followed this advice, a whole range of mountains burst into flames, and his tempter told him that the ring had contained God's mercy for him. Finally a third person appeared, recovered the ring, and promised to keep it safely for Newton. Many years later, the clergyman interpreted this dream as a contest for his soul between God and the devil.[12] Toward the end of his life he reiterated his belief in the significance of dreams at a meeting of a little organization of Evangelicals called the Eclectic Society. At one meeting the question for discussion was, "What Is the Morality of Dreams?" After listening to the opinion of others, Newton remarked, "The imagination is like a harpsichord — open when asleep. Dreams are monitory." [13] Newton's interest even led him to refer to the subject in a hymn in which he observes:

> But though our dreams are often wild,
>   Like clouds before the driving storm;
> Yet some important may be styl'd,
>   Sent to admonish or inform.
>
> What mighty agents have access,
>   What friends from heaven or foes from hell,
> Our minds to comfort or distress,
>   When we are sleeping, who can tell?
>
>   OLNEY HYMNS, ON DREAMING

Cowper, it will be recalled, also believed dreams to be monitory, but his dreams were not those of the normal person. In his sleep he frequently heard the voice of God or of the devil prompting him to some act, or warning him about the future. Never a resolute person, he too often relied upon these dreams to direct his acts instead of reasoning out his decisions. When he returned to the delusion that he was a damned soul, his conviction this time would remain unshakable, chiefly because in his sleep he had heard a voice pronounce his doom. Although Cowper's tendency to rely on dreams existed before he met Newton, it was unfortunate that his counselor shared his superstition. The preacher, who was able to weave pleasant parables from his own dreams, probably did not sufficiently realize that Cowper's dreams and voices were at once products and causes of his dementia. Believing so firmly in dreams himself, Newton must have unwittingly encouraged his friend's habit of interpreting his hallucinations as directives of heaven or hell.

By way of summary, then, if Newton had a harmful influence on his friend, it was not simply because of his religious views. More injurious to a person of Cowper's sensitivity was the man himself. Although he was cheerful and not without a sense of humor, Newton was a zealot with a maddening certainty about his own convictions. Like Horatio, he was a sympathetic friend, but one fundamentally incapable of understanding the more finely attuned character of his companion. Finally, despite his good intentions, his superstitious attachment to dreams probably helped to confirm Cowper in his delusions.

Even if Cowper had never met Newton, however, he probably would have had recurring attacks of insanity. His was an extremely guilt-ridden mind, so sceptical of his own merit that he could not maintain forever perfect assurance of salvation. And without at least strong hope for redemption, he was unable to shut out melancholia. Doubts had started to reappear before he became acquainted with Newton. Although still generally convinced of his salvation, he tortured himself with the reflection that such a miserable sinner as he hardly deserved Christ's mercy.

As a result he lost much of the ecstatic joy he had known in the first year or two following his conversion. A few months before moving from Huntingdon, he had written to his aunt, "Oh! that I had retained my first love, that it were with me, as when I first came from the furnace: when the name of Jesus was like honey and milk upon my tongue, and the very sound of it was sufficient to quicken and comfort me. But I am still what I ever was, a chief sinner, and shall be so, while I inhabit a body of death." [14]

While it was typical of the Evangelicals to beat their breasts and call themselves sinners, Cowper was not feigning self-abasement. The doubts that filled his mind were too painful to be willfully entertained. "Ingratitude to the Author of all my mercies is my continual burthen," he again wrote Mrs. Madan. "Yet I do not groan under it as I ought, and wish to do. My spirit is dull and heavy in prayer, slow in meditation, and I have but little sensible communication with my Almighty Redeemer." [15] This conflict persisted after his removal to Olney. It is revealed, for instance, in the well-known hymn *Oh for a Closer Walk with God*. Because of the circumstances under which he wrote this hymn, both his conscious and subconscious mind are reflected in these stanzas. "I began to compose them yesterday morning before daybreak," he wrote, "but fell asleep at the end of the two first lines; when I awakened again, the third and fourth were whispered to my heart in a way which I have often experienced." [16] The second and third stanzas especially express his sorrow at having lost the glowing rapture of the newly made convert:

> Where is the blessedness I knew
> When first I saw the Lord?
> Where is the soul-refreshing view
> Of Jesus and his word?

> What peaceful hours I once enjoyed!
> How sweet their memory still!
> But they have left an aching void
> The world can never fill.

His doubts, as we shall see, eventually led him to despair again, but his religious convictions were still strong enough to carry him through the crisis caused by his brother's illness and death. The Reverend John Cowper, having completed his courses at Cambridge, had remained at the university as a fellow of Benet (or Corpus Christi) College, at the same time serving as rector in the neighboring town of Foxton. A good scholar, he had mastered several ancient and modern languages, and besides making translations, he occasionally composed English verses. During Cowper's sojourn at Huntingdon the two brothers had seen each other weekly, but when Cowper moved to Olney, the greater distance from Cambridge confined them to an exchange of visits once a year. Because he was not an Evangelical, the young clergyman was not asked to occupy Newton's pulpit when he visited Olney, nor even called upon to conduct family prayers if Newton was present. The different religious views of the brothers seem indeed to have hindered very close ties until the younger one was dying. Cowper learned that he was ill in September 1769. He journeyed to Cambridge and remained there until the patient partly recovered, but the next February he was again summoned, this time to attend his brother in his last weeks of life.

Cowper later described the circumstances of his brother's death, in a narrative called *Adelphi*. Although he showed several friends this rather typical Evangelical account of a deathbed conversion, he would not allow it to be published. It remained in manuscript until two years after his death, when it was printed at Newton's direction, in order to provide further evidence of God's mercy in bringing scoffers to faith. Cowper wrote that when he had first visited the sick man, he had been shocked to find his bed strewn with plays which he had been reading for diversion. On his second visit the poet entered into a series of talks with his brother on the state of his soul. These efforts were crowned with success, for in the last week or two of his life the young clergyman attained an Evangelical conception of the atonement and, as a result, died a convert.

Certain writers have suggested that John's death contributed to Cowper's second attack of insanity, but this seems very doubtful. The poet himself observed that though the loss of his brother had been "a cause of sorrow," his deathbed conversion had given him "much more cause of joy." [17] What really troubled him was the inner conflict which kept him wavering between hope and uncertainty about his own salvation.

Newton, knowing his state of mind, apparently thought it would be helpful to keep him occupied. In 1768 the clergyman had obtained Lord Dartmouth's permission to use an empty mansion, called Great House, for religious services held at Olney during the week. At Newton's urging, Cowper attended the meetings and was eventually prevailed upon to conduct the services. While the poet's shyness had at first kept him from speaking to the congregation, Newton observes, "the ardency of his love to the Saviour and his desire of being useful to others broke through every other restraint." He spoke with humility, yet with "freedom and fervency, as if he saw the Lord whom he addressed face to face." [18]

In order to supply the parishioners with religious songs, both men had tried their hands at composing hymns. When they had written several, Newton proposed that they pursue this joint endeavor and eventually publish a hymn collection which would serve to commemorate their close friendship. Such was the origin of the familiar volume entitled *Olney Hymns*. Each of the friends was to contribute approximately the same number of selections, but because Cowper's second attack of insanity interfered, the collection, which was published in 1779, contained only 67 hymns by Cowper and 281 by Newton.

In his preface to *Olney Hymns*, Newton explained that he had divided the volume into three parts: "In the first I have classed those which are formed upon select passages of Scripture, and placed them in the order of the Books of the Old and New Testaments. The second contains occasional hymns, suited to particular seasons or suggested by particular events or subjects. The third book is a miscellaneous, comprising a variety of subjects relative to a life of faith." [19] This plan closely adhered to that of *Hymns and Spiritual Songs* by Isaac Watts, the best-known hymn-writer of the eighteenth century. Watts, too, had divided his collection into three parts. In the first he placed hymns that paraphrased or were suggested by Biblical texts. (Like those in the Olney collection, they were supplied with references to particular chapters and verses of the Bible.) The second book contained efforts of a more original character, and the third, hymns to celebrate the Lord's supper.

Book One of *Olney Hymns* includes 80 hymns based on Old Testament and 41 on New Testament texts, a proportion that reflected the Evangelical tendency to revere the Old Testament even more than the Gospels. Cowper contributed 21 of these Biblical hymns. According to Newton, the poet was one of the most diligent students of the Bible he had ever known. This statement is easy to credit, for not only Cowper's hymns but much of his other poetry is strongly infused with Biblical imagery.

Cowper's hymns are the most Evangelical of all his poems. Although several express conflicts and doubts, the prevailing tone is one of hope. A few contain a note of exultation seldom or never found in his later poems. The poet who had twice before entered the gulf of despair would all too soon return to that dark region, but while he was composing his hymns, he could still feel, for short intervals at least, in close communion with the deity. Thus he could write:

> That were a grief I could not bear
> Didst thou not hear and answer prayer;
> But a prayer-hearing, answering God
> Supports me under every load.
>
> HYMN XXXIX

Several of Cowper's hymns contain a strong personal note. Others, in themselves quite impersonal, take on special significance when they are related to the poet's history. For instance, although *Ephraim Repenting* closely follows the Biblical passage on which it is based, the hymn might be considered a parable of his own life. Like Ephraim, he had suffered many strokes, but he could regard his earlier misfortunes as trials imposed by a merciful God to test him. A personal note is easy to detect in stanzas that reflect his individual tastes. In *Retirement,* for instance, when he praises the country as a place where one can enjoy a closer walk with God, he was expressing a sentiment that he would repeat in later poems. His love of nature is especially apparent in *I Will Praise the Lord at All Times*:

> Winter has a joy for me,
> While the Saviour's charms I read,
> Lowly, meek, from blemish free,
> In the snowdrop's pensive head.

There is danger, however, in inferring too much in the way of personal references from these religious songs, especially if one fails to keep in mind the plan of the volume. In one section, for instance, Cowper has several hymns on spiritual conflicts, but these hymns form a part of a particular group captioned "Conflict." Both Cowper and Newton contributed to this section, as they did to other groups entitled "Cautions" and "Comforts." Perhaps Cowper's hymns concerned with conflict are more personal than Newton's, but of this one cannot always be certain.

What, if anything, is peculiarly Evangelical in the hymns? Not the references to the sacrifice of Christ, for the atonement is a likely theme for any hymn-writer. Nor is there anything necessarily Evangelical in celebrating faith and hope, in finding comfort in prayer, or in asking for grace. The particular beliefs of the authors are expressed rather in the tone of certain hymns and in the emphasis accorded certain doctrines. Thus when Cowper speaks of faith, he shows that by faith he means the strong assurance which, according to the Evangelicals, a convert should experience at the new birth. He writes:

> E'er since, by faith, I saw the stream
> Thy flowing wounds supply,
> Redeeming love has been my theme,
> And shall be till I die.
>
> HYMN XV

Perhaps Cowper was not here thinking of his own conversion, but he clearly had in mind the transformation that occurred

upon the Evangelical's sudden realization of the significance of
the atonement.

In his didactic *Not of Works* Cowper stresses the thought that
deeds of charity do not count toward salvation:

> Grace, triumphant in the throne,
> Scorns a rival, reigns alone;
> Come and bow beneath her sway,
> Cast your idol works away!
> Works of man, when made his plea,
> Never shall accepted be;
> Fruits of pride (vain-glorious worm!)
> Are the best he can perform.
>
> Self, the God his soul adores,
> Influences all his powers;
> Jesus is a slighted name,
> Self-advancement all his aim;
> But when God the Judge shall come
> To pronounce the final doom,
> Then for rocks and hills to hide
> All his works and all his pride!
>
> Still the boasting heart replies,
> "What! the worthy and the wise,
> Friends to temperance and peace,
> Have not these a righteousness?"
> Banish every vain pretence
> Built on human excellence;
> Perish everything in man,
> But the grace that never can.

Certain critics, among them Mr. Gilbert Thomas, have maintained that Cowper's hymns are more strongly Calvinistic than
Newton's. That may be true, but great discrimination is necessary to weigh and compare the degree of Calvinism in each
author. In his Preface Newton wrote that he did not intend "to
flatter or to offend any party." [20] He hoped that most of the
selections would be suitable for Christians of all denominations.
On the other hand, he confessed that his hymns expressed views

based on his own experiences and implied that he had not been at any pains to omit Calvinistic doctrines. His assertion describes equally well Cowper's contributions. Both composers include some Calvinism, but it is difficult to say which has the more.

Like Cowper, Newton maintains that works without faith will not avail for salvation. Both men affirm that only a few, the elect, will have eternal life. Newton writes on this theme in the *Barren Fig-Tree*, as does Cowper in a hymn called *Abuse of the Gospel*, in which he shows scant pity for those he considers damned for eternity:

> Ah Lord, we know the chosen few
> Are fed with heavenly fare;
> But these, the wretched husks they chew,
> Proclaim them what they are.

Better than Newton, Cowper adhered to the definition that a hymn is a song of praise. Ever the preacher, Newton liked to use timely and local references to make his lesson clear. In one of his contributions, entitled *On the Fire at Olney*, he explains that the conflagration had occurred because the inhabitants had failed to be grateful for years of safety. According to Newton, only the prayers of a few godly parishioners had saved the town from complete destruction. In another hymn his subject is the earthquake of 1775, a phenomenon which he interprets as a warning to sinners. The next quake, he observes, may be so severe that the earth will open and swallow up evil-doers. Cowper generally omits such fire and brimstone cautions. In fact, there is less moralizing in his hymns than in many of his later poems. When he does point a moral, he sometimes treats the theme very much in the manner of a typical eighteenth-century poet. His hymn entitled *Vanity of the World*, for instance, is not much more Evangelical than Dr. Johnson's *Vanity of Human Wishes*.

Although Cowper's diction occasionally reflects the eighteenth-century liking for abstract terms, on the whole it is simple, direct, and forceful. Fortunately the hymn was not subject to the current canons of restraint. It was the one type of verse that was supposed to appeal directly to the emotions. If it was turgid or pretentious, it failed its purpose. Furthermore Cowper had the talents and good taste of a truly great poet, and these qualities kept him from writing such pedestrian lines as some by his collaborator.

One of the best tests of the quality of his imagery, of which more will be said later, is to compare Cowper's hymns on Biblical themes with the passages in Scripture upon which he based them. Sometimes the hymn paraphrases the original; sometimes it merely uses the text as the starting point for an independent theme. Even where he keeps close to the sense of the scriptural passage, however, his diction and metrical arrangement occasionally give his verse a note of exultation, such as one finds in Blake. *Wisdom,* a hymn based on Proverbs 8:22–31, is a good example:

"Ere God had built the mountains,
　　Or raised the fruitful hills;
Before he filled the fountains
　　That feed the running rills;
In me, from everlasting,
　　That wonderful I am
Found pleasure never wasting,
　　And Wisdom is my name.

"When like a tent to dwell in,
　　He spread the skies abroad,
And swathed about the swelling
　　Of Ocean's mighty flood;
He wrought by weight and measure,
　　And I was with him then;
Myself the Father's pleasure,
　　And mine the sons of men."

Thus Wisdom's words discover
　　Thy glory and thy grace,
Thou everlasting Lover
　　Of our unworthy race!
Thy gracious eye surveyed us
　　Ere stars were seen above;
In wisdom thou hast made us,
　　And died for us in love.

84

And couldst thou be delighted
  With creatures such as we,
Who, when we saw thee, slighted,
  And nailed thee to a tree?
Unfathomable wonder,
  And mystery divine!
The Voice that speaks in thunder,
  Says, "Sinner, I am thine!"

The Olney hymnal was destined to have an important place in the Evangelical movement. Congregations found that it fittingly expressed their doctrinal views and their religious emotions. "It became," one writer remarks, "a people's manual of Evangelical doctrine and an instrument of spiritual discipline." [21] If it failed to celebrate the sacraments and the offices of the Prayer Book, these omissions were in keeping with the low-church beliefs of the Evangelicals. If the hymns, contrary to the traditions for this type of verse, contained a strong personal expression of private experience, that emphasis accorded with the revival practice of stressing individual testaments of faith as a means of bringing converts into the fold. As a collection, the Olney hymnal has gone out of use, but many of the individual hymns, such as Cowper's *God Moves in a Mysterious Way* and *Oh for a Closer Walk with God,* and Newton's *How Sweet the Name of Jesus Sounds,* remain among the most famous hymns in the English language.

❧ V ❧

The Olney Recluse

O happy shades! to me unblest!
Friendly to peace, but not to me!
How ill the scene that offers rest
And heart that cannot rest agree!
THE SHRUBBERY

Cowper's despondency increased during the composition of the
Olney hymns. In March 1771 he wrote Newton, who was visiting
in London, "If you find yourself hindered by an outside bustle, I
am equally hindered by a bustle within. The Lord, I trust, will
give peace of mind in his own time; but I can truly say for the
most part that my soul is among lions."[1] To this letter Newton
replied, "I pity your conflicts and I try not to envy your comforts.
You are in safe hands. All your conflicts and your victories are
already marked out for you."[2]

Peace of mind was not to return, however. Instead Cowper
became more harassed. In June 1772 he wrote Mrs. Madan: "I
have temptations that are almost ever present with me, and shed
a thick gloom over all my prospect. Sin is my burthen, a sure
token that I shall be delivered from its remaining power, but
while it remains, it will oppress me. The Lord, who chose me in
the furnace of affliction is pleased to afford that tempter a large
permission to try me: I think I may say I am tried to the utmost."[3] Newton probably knew what his temptation was. Two
days before the poet composed the above, the clergyman wrote to
his wife in London, "Dear Sir Cowper is in the depths as much
as ever. The manner of his prayer last night led me to speak from

86

Hebrews II, 18." [4] The text the clergyman chose reads: "For in that he himself hath suffered being tempted, he is able to succour them that are tempted." Whatever the temptation was, it seems doubtful that Cowper felt a compulsion to attempt suicide at this time; more likely he was beset by an urge to give way to despair.

Despite the worsening of his mental condition, in the fall of 1772 Cowper became engaged to marry Mrs. Unwin. This fact was not generally known during his lifetime, probably because his relatives enjoined silence on the subject in order to spare the feelings of his old love Theodora. But after Cowper died both Newton and Reverend William Bull, a later friend, testified that a wedding had been planned.[5] Under normal circumstances the proposed marriage would have been the most natural thing in the world. Though Mrs. Unwin was seven years his senior, this difference of age should have been no barrier to two such thoroughly sympathetic persons. Yet no plans for marriage had been made, it would appear, until 1772, when changes in the household raised the issue. William Unwin, having been ordained, departed for Stock, Essex, in July 1769, to take up his duties as a clergyman. A few years later Mrs. Unwin's daughter became engaged to the Reverend Matthew Powley of Huddersfield, Yorkshire. Her marriage, which eventually took place in May 1774, would leave Cowper and Mrs. Unwin alone. They knew that people had gossiped about them at Huntingdon, and they may have heard similar whisperings at Olney. Hence, to forestall scandal, if for no other reason, the two highly principled friends planned to be married before the daughter of the house left home.

Curiously, Robert Southey emphatically denied that such a marriage was even contemplated.[6] Apparently this early biographer of Cowper did not see the statements of Newton and Bull on this subject, but he had seen papers that no later biographer has been able to consult. Because these documents affirmed that Cowper had a sexual abnormality, Southey probably felt that it would be physically impossible for Cowper to consummate a union.

If Cowper was impotent, then the prospect of marriage might

very well have been an immediate cause of the 1773 attack of insanity. Once he was married, he would have to explain his condition to Mrs. Unwin, and the dread of disclosing his secret, even to her, was perhaps more than he could bear. As Professor Hoxie N. Fairchild has observed, "Their marriage — if indeed true marriage was a physical possibility — would have entailed discovery of his burdensome secret. If in 1763 the prospect of a routine examination had led him to attempt suicide, there was now a much stronger motive for hysterical evasion of the issue." [7]

Whatever the cause, Cowper's growing despondency developed into insanity before the date set for the wedding. On New Year's Day, 1773, he heard what was to be his last sermon. That afternoon he drank tea at the vicarage. The next day, according to Newton, "a violent storm overtook him." [8] What the symptoms were is not clear, except that his despondency was accompanied by hallucinations. Newton attended him every day, took him walking, and led family prayers at Orchard Side. The poet and his friends prayed for his restoration, but instead of recovering, on January 24 he was "plunged into a melancholy" that made him "almost an infant." [9]

His extreme shyness having returned, he refused to call at the vicarage. His excuse was that he would go nowhere until he could once more enter church for worship. He broke this resolution in April, when the noise of the annual fair at Olney drove him to seek refuge with the Newtons. Once he was lodged there, he refused to return to his own home, and Mrs. Unwin had to move to the vicarage to take care of him. There they were to remain for the next thirteen months. What quirk of mind made Cowper unwilling to return to Orchard Side? Whatever the reason, his refusal to leave the vicarage during this period of distress was a symbol of his pitiful reliance on the strong-willed clergyman.

Given the heavy and unexpected burden of supporting two guests, one of whom was in a dangerous condition, Newton met this severe test with commendable fortitude. His sympathy for his friend never wavered, and one feels certain that he did his best to assure Cowper that he need not fear for his salvation. Because his own convictions were so sturdy, however, the clergyman was somewhat puzzled by his friend's apparently sudden change from faith to despair. Describing the situation to Lord Dartmouth, who had been a schoolmate of Cowper at Westminster, Newton observed:

"He is perfectly sensible as to common things but is a continued prey to distressing and gloomy thoughts, which he has no power to resist. What a striking instance of the vanity and precariousness of all below the skies. He is now sitting by me, disconsolate. How brittle is the blessing of a fine understanding assisted by the advantage of education and literature. A slight alteration in the animal spirits or in the texture of the blood is sufficient to cloud the faculties, so that the gross illusions of the powers of darkness shall be received as if they were sealed to the mind with the indubitable impressions of truth. . . . I believe few people living have enjoyed more abounding consolation or given more unquestionable evidence of a heart truly devoted to God than my friend, yet he is now upon the brink of despair and our most earnest endeavours to comfort him seem but to add to his distress." [10]

Many years later Cowper described this attack as similar to his madness at St. Albans, but "covered with a still deeper shade of melancholy." "I did not indeed lose my senses," he wrote, "but I lost the power to exercise them. I could return a rational answer even to a difficult question, but a question was necessary, or I never spoke at all. This state of mind was accompanied . . . with misapprehension of things and persons that made me a very untractable patient. I believed that everyone hated me, and that Mrs. Unwin hated me most of all; was convinced that all my food was poisoned, together with a thousand megrims of the same stamp." [11] According to Newton, Cowper also had the delusion that butcher's meat was human flesh, and feeding him became a problem.[12] Despite his belief that Mrs. Unwin hated him, he would allow no one else to take care of him. She was called on to minister to his needs night and day, a task that she performed with cheerfulness and devotion.

Neither Mrs. Unwin nor Newton sought medical advice for their patient until several months had passed. No doubt they hoped from day to day that he would become better; besides there was not much doctors could do for him with their limited knowledge of mental diseases. Finally, in May, Newton rode over to St. Albans to consult Dr. Cotton. The little physician who had previously helped the poet recommended that he be bled and asked that a sample of the blood be sent to him for examination. After analyzing the specimen, the doctor, *in absentia*, prescribed various medicines. At first they seemed to agree with Cowper. During the summer he occasionally puttered about the yard, and his friends began to hope for a speedy recovery. But within a few weeks he complained that the medicines made him feel worse, and he stopped taking them.

No tonic or laxative, such as Dr. Cotton probably prescribed, could cure Cowper's deep-seated trouble. He had once more developed the delusion that he was a lost soul, with no hope of salvation. Again he sought desperate relief from his agony. In October, while the Newtons were away and while the poet was still at the vicarage, he again attempted to hang himself. Mrs. Unwin prevented his suicide, and when the Newtons returned his mental state had improved. From this time, however, he had to be watched to keep him from repeating the attempt.

The circumstances of the 1773 attack have never been made as clear as the details of his earlier insanity. This much is certain. In both instances Cowper lost all hope of salvation, and upon both occasions he tried to kill himself. But neither he nor his associates ever intimated that he returned to the idea that he had committed the unpardonable sin of Scripture. He continued to think that he had been renewed in holiness at St. Albans and seemingly never returned to the delusion that he had been guilty of the unpardonable sin at Southampton. The second seizure left him with the belief that he was shut out from God's mercy, but for a different reason. This time he thought he was barred from salvation, not by any text of Scripture, nor by any offense common to other men, but rather by a special ordinance of God.

He did not despair completely until February 1773. In that month he had what his biographer Thomas Wright calls a fatal

dream. It was fatal only because Cowper attached great importance to dreams. This particular one became the occasion for his
lasting despair, according to Wright. During the dream Cowper
heard a voice saying, "*Actum est de te, periisti,*" or, "It is all over
with thee; thou hast perished." [13] But Wright may have attached
too much importance to this dream. Simply to have heard a voice
pronouncing his doom would probably not in itself have had
such a lasting effect on Cowper. He had heard similar voices and
experienced like hallucinations at the Temple, but had later
been able to dismiss them as delusional.

Newton and Samuel Greatheed, a later friend of Cowper, both
gave a different reason for Cowper's despair — his failure to commit suicide. He had sought self-destruction this time, according
to Newton, because of "the power the enemy had of impressing
upon his disturbed imagination that it was the will of God, he
should, after the example of Abraham, perform an expensive act
of obedience, and offer, not a son, but himself." [14] When the attempt failed, he thought that he had so displeased God that his
Maker barred him from all hope of salvation. This conviction remained unshakable, even after he had recovered his senses. According to Greatheed, he "supposed that his involuntary failure
at the performance had incurred the irrevocable vengeance of
the Almighty! To this, and never to any other deficiency of
obedience has he been heard to ascribe his imaginary exclusion
from mercy." [15]

Thus two theories are offered for Cowper's lasting belief that
he was denied salvation — the dream, and the delusion that he
had offended God by failing to commit suicide. No doubt the two
were closely related in Cowper's mind. When he heard a voice
pronouncing his doom, he may at the same time or soon afterward have thought he received a command to commit suicide. He
passed the time from February until the following October, it
would appear, trying to steel himself to attempt the act. When
his effort was frustrated, he may have felt that he had closed the
one door by which, in his deluded mind, he thought he might
still escape perdition.

Cowper's later letters lend support to the idea that there was a close connection between his dream and the belief that he had disobeyed God's will. When he spoke of being excluded from mercy in later life, he sometimes dated the pronouncement of his doom from the dream of February 1773, but when he explained his inability to attend worship and to offer up private prayers, he asserted that the sin of disobedience barred him from these means of seeking grace. He referred to the dream, for instance, on January 13, 1784, when he commented, "Nature revives again; but a soul once slain lives no more . . . The latter end of next month will complete a period of eleven years in which I have spoken no other language." [16] Again on October 16, 1785, he wrote, "I had a dream twelve years ago, before the recollection of which all consolation vanishes, and, it seems to me, must always vanish." [17] On the other hand, when William Bull, a clergyman whom Cowper esteemed, attempted to reason with him about his despair, the poet replied with an allusion, not to his dream, but to his supposed sin of disobedience: "Prove to me that I have a right to pray, and I will pray without ceasing . . . But let me add, there is no encouragement in the Scriptures so comprehensive as to include my case, nor any consolation so effectual as to reach it. I do not relate it to you, because you could not believe it; you would agree with me if you could. And yet that sin by which I am excluded from the privileges I once enjoyed, you would account no sin, you would even tell me that it was a duty." [18] Here Cowper is apparently referring to his attempt to commit suicide. By frustrating that act, he felt that he had sinned, though his rational mind told him that Bull would have argued that averting self-destruction was a duty.

It would appear, then, that Cowper attributed his despair sometimes to the dream and at other times to his so-called sin of disobedience. Actually both explanations probably served to hide his basic sense of guilt. Once before, when he was at the Temple, he had sought to evade an issue by trying to take his life. Then, after a short period of blaming himself for attempting suicide, he had transferred his guilt to his supposed commission of the unpardonable sin of Scripture. In 1773, when faced by the prospect of marriage and the disclosure of his sexual abnormality, he again lost his mind and attempted suicide. But this time, instead of fastening upon the unpardonable sin of Scripture, he apparently transferred his guilt to a supposed act of disobedience in failing at self-destruction. Thus both the dream and the fiction that he had disobeyed God, though very real to him, were probably substitutions that allowed him to conceal from himself, as well as from others, the basic cause of his guilt.

At St. Albans Cowper's restoration to sanity had occurred almost simultaneously with his release from despair. This time, since he remained without hope of salvation, the restoration was to take years. During his sojourn at the vicarage he left the house only to work in the yard. No entreaty could make him return to Orchard Side. When Mrs. Unwin mentioned the subject, he would weep and beg to stay at the vicarage. He gradually grew better, however, and one day while he was feeding the chickens, Newton saw him smile at some little incident. Soon afterward, in May 1774, he surprised his friends by suddenly agreeing to return to his own home.

A few days after the departure of his long-implanted guest Newton wrote, "Upon the whole I have not been weary of my cross. Besides the submission I owe to the Lord, I think I can hardly do or suffer too much for such a friend, yet sometimes my heart has been impatient and rebellious." [19] Newton was probably put to another severe test by the seeming apostasy of his most eminent parishioner. After New Year's Day, 1773, Cowper never entered church. Believing he was an outcast, he felt that he was not permitted to engage in worship. He dared not even ask a blessing on his food, and only after many years did he resume private prayer. The parishioners of Olney were no doubt puzzled by this change, since heretofore Cowper had been one of the most regular and devout worshipers. What the Evangelical minister told his flock does not appear, but, to do him justice, he never allowed his embarrassment to interfere with his friendship for the poet.

Cowper's religious position from this time forth was curious
He thought, contrary to Calvinistic teachings, that God, afte
once extending his mercy to him, had apparently changed hi
mind and consigned him to hell. To those who regarded the doc
trine of election as a cardinal point, this view must have seemed
nothing short of heretical. Presumably God would not have al
lowed him to go through the process of the new birth if he had
not originally chosen him for salvation. Even worse was to thin
that the Deity, having once elected him, would whimsically alte
his decision. To be sure, Cowper considered his situation unique
He thought of himself as the only person in the world who, afte
being renewed in faith, had later been doomed to perdition
Meanwhile he continued to adhere to the general principles of
Evangelicalism. That is, he believed in their application to every
one but himself. And he still wholeheartedly wished to spread the
doctrines of the revival. In fact, it was not until after his indi
vidual apostasy that he became the great poet and propagandis
of the movement. In that respect his position was indeed unusual
for he was probably the only sincere Evangelical in England that
professed but did not personally practice the faith.

The conviction that he was irrevocably damned was to remain
with Cowper the rest of his life, despite all attempts to persuade
him that he was not barred from salvation. Newton, for instance
tried to convince him by describing the case of Simon Browne, a
clergyman who had also despaired of salvation. But Cowper re
fused to see the analogy. "I suppose no man would despair if he
did not apprehend something singular in the circumstances of
his own story," he replied, "something that discriminates it from
that of every other man, and that induces despair as an inevitable
consequence. You may encounter his unhappy persuasion with as
many instances as you please of persons who, like him, having
renounced all hope, were yet restored; and may thence infer that
he, like them, shall meet with a season of restoration — but it is
in vain. Every such individual accounts himself an exception to
all rules, and therefore the blessed reverse that others have experienced affords no ground of comfortable expectation to *him*." [20]

His conviction that he was a lost soul could probably have been removed by only one means. At St. Albans his recovery from despair had been effected by a comforting dream and by reading a hopeful passage in Scripture. The Bible could not again restore him to hope since there was no text in it, he felt, which could be related to his unique reason for being damned. But a strong monition in the form of a dream or a voice, serving as a sign that he was forgiven, might have succeeded. Such was the agency through which he had heard the pronouncement of his doom; such was the only measure, perhaps, that could have persuaded him that he might yet be saved.

Several times during his later years Cowper revealed that he lived in the hope of experiencing a happy monition of this sort. On June 25, 1785, he wrote, "I repine at my barrenness, and think it hard to be thus blighted; but when a glimpse of hope breaks in upon me, I am contented to be the sapless thing that I am, knowing that He who commanded me to wither, can command me to flourish again when He pleases." [21] Again, on October 26, 1790, he observed, "The only consolation left me on this subject is, that the voice of the Almighty can in one moment cure me of this mental infirmity. That He can, I know by experience; and there are reasons for which I ought to believe that He will." [22] At times he felt a promise of the longed-for monition. "I have now and then an intimation, though slight and transient, that God has not abandoned me for ever," he wrote on December 3, 1785. [23] Unfortunately these intimations were never strong enough, never of sufficient dramatic intensity to provide lasting hope. Frequently, especially toward the end of his life, he heard voices that seemed to be of a supernatural order, but instead of solacing him, they were generally so frightening that they only deepened his despair. Occasionally he had dreams that lent themselves to a pleasant interpretation, but they were not sufficiently vivid to furnish substantial comfort. For the most part, as he grew older, his dreams were horrible nightmares that only confirmed him, if confirmation were needed, in the belief that he was a lost soul, doomed to live in a frightful chaos of darkness until the day when the flames of hell would engulf him.

His friends, knowing that his release from despair depended upon his receiving a happy monition, flattered him in the hope that it would be forthcoming. Toward the end, as we shall see, his cousin John Johnson resorted to an absurd ruse to make him think that a supernatural voice was addressing words of comfort to him. About the same time William Hayley, another well-wisher, pretended that he had had a dream wherein, by proxy, the distraught poet was promised a happy life hereafter. These shams were to fail, but they show that Cowper's closest associates realized that nothing short of an apparent monition from God could convince him that he was not a lost soul.

When Cowper moved to Olney, he had chosen to live in a small world; that world became even more miniscule during his long convalescence. For a couple of years he wrote almost no letters. Previously he had taken trips with Newton to surrounding communities, where he could at least engage in sober conversations with other Evangelicals. Now he remained at Orchard Side, venturing out only for a visit at the vicarage, for a short walk, or to care for his garden. Where formerly the business of attending church services and prayer meetings had absorbed his time, he now had no religious occupation. Fortunately, however, he found new interests in the little island of Orchard Side. While he was still deeply immersed in melancholy, a local resident offered him a leveret that his children had grown weary of. The shy poet gratefully accepted the gift, feeling that the care of the animal would help divert his gloomy thoughts. Other neighbors, learning that he was pleased with it, offered him so many other hares that he might soon have "stocked a paddock." [24] Taking two others, he christened the three leverets Puss, Tiney, and Bess.

The animals proved to be a source of great diversion. Cowper carefully observed their feeding habits, their awareness of any slight change in their environment, and their mirth-provoking antics. In the evening, after supper, he would bring them into his little parlor and watch them frisk and gambol on the carpet. Each of them had its own distinctive character and disposition, he noted. Tiney was sulky and untractable; Bess was the drollest and most courageous; Puss, the tamest of the three. Cowper's tenderness toward animals and his hatred of the barbarities so often inflicted upon them in his day were admirably expressed in a charming prose piece on his leverets which appeared in the *Gentleman's Magazine.* Here he observed, "You will not wonder, Sir, that my intimate acquaintance with these specimens of the kind has taught me to hold the sportsman's amusements in abhorrence; he little knows what amiable creatures he persecutes, of what gratitude they are capable, how cheerful they are in spirits, what enjoyment they have of life, and that impressed as they seem with a peculiar dread of man it is only because man gives them peculiar cause for it." [25] His hares and the other animals he acquired also became the subject of several poems in which he appealed to his readers' sense of compassion for the brute creation. This appeal sounded a new note at a time when bearbaiting and cockfighting were favorite pastimes of the British public. Cowper was thus at the forefront of a movement to practice kindness to animals, and his verses no doubt did much to create the notably compassionate attitude of later times.

Adding to his animal kingdom, Cowper at one time or another owned several pairs of pigeons, a linnet, robins, a magpie, two goldfinches, a jay, a starling, and canaries, as well as guinea pigs, dogs, and cats. His desire to provide suitable shelter for them led to an interest in carpentry. He first constructed an elaborate little house for his leverets. He described it as consisting of three apartments into which they could retire for sleep and a common hall in which they could range in the daytime. As he acquired other pets he built cages or houses for them, too. His ability with hammer and saw also led him to construct a greenhouse, where he grew pineapples and other delicacies, and a summerhouse, where he later wrote several of his poems. Gardening, an occupation he had followed since his days at Huntingdon, continued to be an important means of distraction. An interest in freehand drawing became another hobby. His pictures won the admiration of James Andrews, a local artist who gave him instructions, but

Cowper never felt that he had any real talent for drawing. He regarded the occupation as a novelty, and when he found it injurious to his eyes he quickly abandoned it. Nevertheless, even this short-lived interest reflected his inherently romantic tastes. Although his was generally a chastened form of romanticism, occasionally it burst forth in rapturous utterance. After explaining to a correspondent that he drew scenes from nature, he exclaimed, "Oh! I could spend whole days and moonlight nights in feeding upon a lovely prospect! My eyes drink the rivers as they flow." [26]

When he resumed his correspondence with Joseph Hill, his letters were at first short epistles, frequently no more than an acknowledgment of a remittance. He never worried greatly about money matters, partly because more weighty concerns occupied his mind, partly because Hill's management of his little fortune relieved him of the burden. His income came from renting his Temple apartment, to which he still held title, and from certain other investments. He had received four hundred pounds from his brother's estate and a smaller inheritance upon the death of his old friend Thomas Hesketh. His total resources, however, were scarcely enough to provide for his needs, and for several years Mrs. Unwin contributed the larger amount to their joint household budget. Hill frequently assisted him by sending a remittance in advance and, occasionally, it would seem, by giving him money out of his own pocket.

Cowper's letters eventually became more cheerful — a sign that the cloud of melancholy was lifting. Partly because he wanted an additional source of income, he asked Hill in 1776 if he could find two students to instruct. His plan was to tutor them in Greek and Latin, according to the Westminster method, and to board them at Orchard Side. There were no applications, however, and he abandoned what probably would have proved an unfortunate project. "If it were to rain pupils, perhaps I might catch a tub full," he wrote cheerfully to Hill, "but till it does the fruitlessness of my inquiries makes me think I must keep my Greek and Latin to myself." [27] Hill, knowing that Cowper liked fish, dispatched to Olney consignments of oysters, plaice, herring, flounder, and lobster. In return Cowper and Mrs. Unwin sent the Hills an occasional haunch of venison, a brace of fowls, or produce from their garden. This exchange gave the poet an opportunity to make puns and to engage in pleasant sallies of wit. His letters now contained almost no references to religion. Instead they were filled with the trivia of his little world — a subject he treated so charmingly that one unacquainted with his past might think he was perfectly happy.

Cowper eventually resumed his correspondence with William Unwin. Besides touching on Olney gossip, the poet provided his young friend with discerning comments on books, for as he emerged from the depths of despair, reading again became one of his chief pleasures. He went through Gray's works and thought his poetry the best since Shakespeare, and his letters superior even to those of Dr. Swift. Curiously (or was it a natural interest for one who led such a secluded life?) travel literature especially attracted him. He would take up a volume by Cook, Forster, Byron, or some other voyager and, for an hour or two, escape from his delusions by sharing the author's adventures at sea or among the rarely visited islands of the Pacific. Unwin sent him the recently published edition of Samuel Johnson's *Lives of the Poets,* and Cowper found himself in agreement with many of the views of the great, unequivocating critic. He quarreled with Johnson, however, for failing to appreciate Milton's shorter poems and, interestingly, he felt that Johnson had passed too severe a moral judgment on Prior's *Henry and Emma.* The biographer had failed to consider the fashions in poetry that prevailed in Prior's day, Cowper observed, and being but a poor judge of verses dealing with the passions, Johnson had missed the charmingly "romantic turn" of Prior's poem.[28]

Cowper was now to be provided with another correspondent at the cost of losing his companion of the past twelve years. Newton was moving to London to become rector of St. Mary Woolnoth Church. When John Thornton had offered him the living, he had hesitated about accepting it. At Olney he had been the ruler as well as the preacher of his little congregation. "We are an

Ecclesia intra Ecclesium," he had written in a letter dated January 13, 1778. "I preach to many, but those whose hearts the Lord touches are the people of my particular charge. . . . I do not seem to rule them, but when my desire is known, it is seldom crossed, and I believe many of them could not sleep in their beds if they thought they had displeased me . . . my superiors in the church leave me a full liberty to preach and manage, within my own parish, as I please." [29] But all had not gone so serenely as this letter intimates. Shortly before writing it Newton had displeased the townspeople when he tried to stop the practice of illuminating houses on Guy Fawkes night. Several buildings had recently been destroyed in a serious fire, and he was eager to prevent another disaster. The Olney inhabitants, however, felt that he was meddling in a time-honored custom. When the evening of November 5 arrived, they defiantly put candles in their windows, and a drunken mob, after parading through the streets and breaking windows, besieged the vicarage. Newton escaped damage to his property and possible bodily harm only by sending a conciliatory message to the group and a bribe to the leader. These circumstances indicate that he was not a very popular figure in the community. When he received "a call" from London, he did not hesitate for long about leaving the town which, despite his efforts, persisted in the ways of evil.

Both Cowper and Mrs. Unwin had urged Newton to accept the London appointment, feeling that his promotion would serve the interests of the revival. When he was gone, however, the poet missed the company of the assertive clergyman. Since Cowper had moved to Olney expressly to be near him, there now seemed to be no reason for remaining, except that there was no other place to go. "If I were in a condition to leave Olney, too, I certainly would not stay in it," he wrote. "It is no attachment to the place that binds me here, but an unfitness for every other. I lived in it once, but now I am buried in it, and have no business with the world on the outside of my sepulchre." [30]

Newton, though absent, continued in the role of friend and counselor. When Cowper wrote to him about his mental distress, as he frequently did, the clergyman replied in a serious vein. But when he received one of the poet's whimsical letters, he tried to reply in kind, and he was not lacking a sense of humor. The gift of a brace of fowls caused him to remark, "The two five-toed, feathered inhabitants of Olney came safe to us, but had not long been in town before they went to pot." [31] Upon sending Cowper a basket of oysters, Newton playfully observed, "A small but (as I am told) a select company from Pyefleet will set out today by Roger's wagon for Olney . . . I hope they will not disturb you, for they are as mute as fishes, and though they will be as well at your house as anywhere, you will perceive, as soon as you see them, that they are not in their proper element. So far from being forward, a degree of violence will be necessary to make them open their mouths." [32]

Newton's successor at Olney, following a brief period in which the Reverend Mr. Page served as curate, was the Reverend Thomas Scott. Cowper had met him a few years before, when Scott was curate in the neighboring village of Weston. Like many men of his time, he had drifted into the clergy as an opportunity to enjoy a leisurely existence. After his ordination he had paid but casual attention to his duties. Then one day he learned that Newton had gone out of his way to visit two of his own parishioners who were on the point of death. Scott, who had neglected them himself, suffered a stab of conscience and resolved to be more observant of his duties. He got to know Newton, they corresponded, and before long the older man had converted Scott to Evangelical faith. Following a common practice, Scott wrote a description of his conversion, prefacing it with a narrative of his early life of sin. Unlike most confessions of this kind, however, *The Force of Truth* was not just another Evangelical thriller. It was a candid account of a man whose zeal burned through the rubbish of cant phraseology and produced a glowing declaration of faith. Some of its vitality may have been owing to Cowper, who revised the manuscript "as to style and externals." [33] How many changes the poet made we do not know, but one suspects that the book was almost entirely Scott's own.

Relations between Scott and Cowper were cordial enough, but the clergyman did not attempt to fill Newton's role of adviser and constant companion. Upon a couple of occasions Scott talked to the poet about his obsession, but perceiving that he was confirmed in his delusions, the clergyman wisely refrained from dwelling on the subject. Since Cowper felt that no one could understand the real nature of his difficulties, he was content to have a neighbor who tactfully directed his conversation to other topics.[34]

Before leaving, Newton had introduced Cowper to William Bull, an Independent clergyman of Newport Pagnell, a town five miles away. Bull formed the habit of riding over to Olney for weekly chats with the poet, who liked this amiable, pipe-smoking clergyman so well that he was eventually persuaded to return the visits. Bull seems to have possessed a warmer personality than Scott, and Cowper probably confided in him as much as he did in any friend of later life. It was probably through the Reverend Mr. Bull that Cowper became acquainted with Samuel Greatheed, a younger man who also became a cherished friend. Greatheed, having been converted while serving in the British army, had given up a military career to study for the ministry at an academy in Newport Pagnell. After his ordination he remained there as Bull's assistant until his appointment in 1789 as pastor to an Independent congregation in Woburn, Bedfordshire. A frequent visitor at Cowper's home for a period of ten or more years, Greatheed was able to supply many valuable biographical details after the poet's death.[35]

None of these new friends influenced Cowper as much as Newton had. In many ways this situation was fortunate, for Newton, well-intentioned though he was, had probably suppressed certain interests of the poet. The clergyman, for instance, was inclined to regard the composition of secular verse as a worldly, time-wasting occupation. With Newton out of the way, Cowper was free to devote his considerable talents to whatever subject he wished. The poems written during his youth had had a superficial charm and wit, but he had matured as a writer since that time. As Wordsworth was later to learn, a poet does not have to live

in a busy theater of activity to write well. In one respect the
confinement to a microcosm had made Cowper a better poet.
He had become a close observer of the habits of his birds and
animals, of the seasonal changes in trees and shrubs, of the daily
miracles of growth that occurred in his garden.

He had composed a few verses while still suffering from the
second attack of insanity. They are not pleasant poems, for they
describe a soul on the rack of despair. *Ode to Peace* is the agonizing lament of one from whom peace has departed, and his Latin
Die Ultimo expresses the hopelessness of one who feels he has
lost all his former happy associations. The most interesting of
the three compositions written during this period of distress is
The Shrubbery. Here he reveals his fairly consistent attitude
toward nature. Even though he found it one of the great sources
of pleasure when his mind was nearly normal, nature could not
serve as a refuge in his darkest moments. A pleasant landscape
or the sight of "alders quivering to the breeze" might stir a less
distraught being, he says in *The Shrubbery,* but for him all sights
of nature serve only to recall his lost happiness. Because nature
was never a completely satisfactory distraction for him, any no-
tion that he escaped into nature is false. It could arouse him to
rapture when he was not engulfed in melancholy, but it could
never lift him from the darkest abyss, as he himself attests in the
following poem which he later wrote, during a period of relative
happiness.

> When all within is peace
>   How nature seems to smile!
> Delights that never cease
>   The livelong day beguile.
> From morn to dewy eve,
>   With open hand she showers
> Fresh blessings, to deceive
>   And soothe the silent hours.
>
> It is a content heart
>   Gives nature power to please;
> The mind that feels no smart
>   Enlivens all it sees,

Can make a wintry sky
Seem bright as smiling May,
And evening's closing eye
As peep of early day.

The vast majestic globe,
So beauteously arrayed
In nature's various robe,
With wondrous skill displayed,
Is to a mourner's heart
A dreary wild at best;
It flutters to depart
And longs to be at rest.

SONG, WRITTEN ABOUT 1783

The pangs of the mourner's heart would return, but he was now sufficiently recovered from the second attack of insanity to be able to produce verses on more cheerful themes. He wrote several shorter pieces between 1777 and 1780. *The Winter Nosegay*, which celebrates gathering a bunch of hothouse pinks in midwinter, shows the pleasure he found in small domestic incidents at Orchard Side. Yet even in these stanzas, when he expresses gratitude to Mrs. Unwin, he cannot refrain from mentioning the shadow under which he lived:

See how they have safely survived
The frowns of a sky so severe;
Such Mary's true love, that has lived
Through many a turbulent year.
The charms of the late-blowing rose
Seem graced with a livelier hue,
And the winter of sorrow best shows
The truth of a friend such as you.

Cowper also composed two poems occasioned by observing a bee trying to light on some blooms under glass. From this incident he drew an analogy to Man's temptation to partake of forbidden joys. The moralizing here is not unpleasant, for it is in the tradition of the fable and not just a piece of Evangelical moroseness. Much in the same manner are his stanzas on *The Nightingale and the Glow-Worm* and his *Fable* of the raven.

Human Frailty is more Evangelical in theme, and his *Tale Founded on Fact* is nothing short of a tract in verse, in which he describes an example of providential interference. A hardened blasphemer who had been converted upon hearing a sermon expressed the wish that he might die rather than live and sin again. Hardly were the words out of his mouth when he dropped dead. Stories of this sort were in high favor among the Evangelicals, and possibly Newton had encouraged Cowper to render this tale in verse. Fortunately the poet's good taste kept him from writing many compositions of this kind.

In 1778 Cowper heard from the remote world of London that his old schoolfellow had been appointed Lord Chancellor of England. Upon taking this important office, Thurlow appointed Joseph Hill to a secretaryship. Cowper's friends hoped that he, too, might receive an appointment, though for him the office would have to be a sinecure. No offer was made, nor did he himself expect one. Nevertheless, he composed a poem praising the talents of his old companion. Although his verses addressed to various friends are among his best productions, the stanzas to Thurlow fall short of those he later addressed to Joseph Hill and to Mary Unwin.

It was this faithful sharer of his joys and sorrows who now started him on a new venture. Mrs. Unwin had observed the pleasure he found in writing, and thinking that a lengthy composition would serve as a more lasting distraction, she proposed that he write a reflective poem. Cowper felt that nothing but good could result from any suggestion she made. He was willing to try a more ambitious poem, but what should he write on? The good Evangelical lady pondered for a while and finally suggested "the progress of error" as a theme.

❧ VI ❧

The Progress of Error

At fifty years of age I commenced an author. It is a whim that has served me longest and best, and which will probably be my last.

LETTER TO THOMAS PARK, MARCH 10, 1792

THE PROGRESS OF ERROR must have seemed a singularly fitting title to Cowper. When Mrs. Unwin suggested the theme, she probably had in mind the persistence of evil among the unconverted, but to the middle-aged bachelor error seemed to be flourishing everywhere. The letters and newspapers he received at Orchard Side were filled with grim stories of protracted wars, of rebellious British subjects, of riots in London, of the corrupt practices of the upper ranks, of the pervading brutality of the poorer classes, and, occasionally, of the gross betrayal of principles by men of the chosen religion. This was the period of which Dickens was later to write, "It was the best of times, it was the worst of times, it was the age of wisdom, it was the age of foolishness, it was the epoch of belief, it was the epoch of incredulity, it was the season of Light, it was the season of Darkness, it was the spring of hope, it was the winter of despair." Cowper felt no such ambivalence about the age. In his judgment it was steeped in corruption and rapidly becoming engulfed in still worse sloughs of sin.

First there was the American Revolution. Cowper's family were Whigs, and he himself was ever a lover of liberty, but a liberty within the framework of traditional British institutions.

More conservative than Burke, he scarified that statesman for his defense of the Colonies. In a curious ballad entitled *The Modern Patriot,* he pictured Burke as a fomenter of rebellion, who had recklessly encouraged disrespect for the British constitution. When Cowper learned of the defeat of Cornwallis at Yorktown, he wrote Newton, "We are sorry to hear it, and should be more cast down than we are if we did not know that this catastrophe was ordained beforehand." [1] He had been particularly embittered when the Americans allied themselves with France against England. This act made them guilty of parricide, in his eyes, and he predicted that they would suffer for their perfidy by becoming enslaved to France.[2]

He admitted that England was partly to blame for its reverses. Poor leadership, luxury, a failing sense of responsibility had contributed, he felt, to lower national standards since his youth. When the war finally ended, he wrote to Hill, with a sigh for the good old days, "I am reconciled to the peace — and despair of my country. . . . A change of Ministry affords no hope. Where is the minister who can discharge our debt, eradicate corruption, and bind our generals to their duty? Till these ends are accomplished, whether we have peace or war, we are alike undone; more speedily perhaps by war, but by peace, by disadvantageous peace, as surely. How we are fallen since the year 6o!" [3]

Like most decent Englishmen, Cowper was shocked by the Gordon Riots of June 1780. A member of Parliament, the half-mad Lord Gordon was vehemently opposed to the removal of the disabilities imposed on Roman Catholics; in order to defeat the measure, he helped organize the Protestant Association. When antipapist sentiment had been sufficiently enflamed, he led a procession from St. George's Fields to the Houses of Parliament. The intention was to present a petition against the Acts granting relief to Catholics, but at Westminster the fury of the mob broke into riot. They put the torch to Catholic chapels, burned numerous houses, attacked the Bank of England and other public buildings, set fire to Newgate, and broke open other prisons. For days the London citizenry lived in terror of being pillaged and murdered, for the rioters, once they were aroused, did not stop with Catholics. When the militia finally restored the law, more than 450 persons had been killed or injured.

The nation had known nothing like the Gordon Riots in Cowper's lifetime. The outbreak seemed so far removed from the ordinarily placid temper of the Augustan Age that many believed that the riots had been instigated by the wicked French. Accepting this view, Cowper wrote a poem called *In Seditionem Horrendam,* in which he patriotically, though unjustly, charged France with employing the basest Englishmen to create civil disturbances. He must have learned that he had mistakenly accused the French, for in a later poem, *Cum Ratione Insanire,* he blames Lord Gordon. This poem, composed several years after the riots, satirically traces Gordon's strange career up to the time of his conversion to Judaism. For some reason Cowper never published these informal ballad stanzas with the formal Latin title, and they remained unknown until 1930, when they were first printed along with a few other newly discovered verses.

Cowper must have been further disturbed by the accounts of wickedness he read in Evangelical literature. A stream of religious periodicals, books, and tracts was beginning to flow from the presses at this time, and the poet, who occasionally contributed to the Evangelical magazines, seems to have been well supplied with these dreary literary productions. Aside from stories of conversion and providential interference, the favorite theme of the Evangelical writers was the evils of the age. In 1782, for instance, John Wesley published an article called *An Estimate of the Manners of the Present Time,* in which he named ungodliness as the predominating characteristic of the period. Although Wesley's view of the times was more temperate than that of many Evangelicals, he asserted that "a total ignorance of God is almost universal among us. The exceptions are exceedingly few, whether among the learned or the unlearned. High and low, cobblers, tinkers, hackney-coachmen, men and maid servants, tradesmen of all ranks, lawyers, physicians, gentlemen, Lords, are as ignorant of the creator of the world as Mo-

hametans or Pagans." Ignorance of God was coupled with a contempt of him, Wesley said, with the result that practicing Christians were relatively few. "A vast majority of the English," he
wrote, "live in the constant neglect of the worship of God. To
form a judgment of this you may take a specimen in the good
city of London. How few of the inhabitants worship God in
public, even one day in a week! Do not yet fewer of them make
a conscience of worshipping God in their families? And perhaps
they are still a smaller number that daily worship God in their
closets." [4]

A reader of such works might well think that England was at
its lowest ebb in religion and morals. Actually the tide had
turned. The great wave of the revival was sweeping across the
nation, bringing a noticeable improvement in religious and
moral standards. By 1781 there were ten Evangelical clergymen
of the Establishment in London, in addition to numerous Methodist, dissenting, and Moravian preachers of the revival. The
Methodist chapels alone, Newton estimated, held thirty thousand
worshipers, and they were always crowded for services.[5] Instead
of publicly recognizing their growing success, however, the Evangelicals continued to dwell on the unregeneracy of the age,
causing credulous readers, like Cowper, to shake their heads
over the wickedness of the times.

He was especially distressed when he learned that the Reverend Martin Madan, his cousin and first tutor in Evangelical
principles, had seemingly betrayed his faith. "Have you heard,"
he inquired of William Unwin, "that a certain kinsman of your
humble servant's has written a tract, now in the press, to prove
polygamy a divine institution!" [6] How appalling that Madan,
the son of his father's sister and a heretofore devout Evangelical,
should encourage such a barbarous and unchristian practice!
Cowper was not alone in being shocked. *Thelypthora* caused so
many sneers from the non-Evangelicals and created such a scandal that its author was forced to resign as chaplain of the Lock
Hospital and go into retirement.

Although Madan's book gained him the reputation of being

libidinous or insane, he had offered his plan in all sincerity. In London, where he served as chaplain of a charitable institution, he had seen and pitied the misery of unwed mothers and prostitutes. The laws, he observed, did not penalize seducers and adulterers; thus the victims of male licentiousness had no redress. To give women a greater degree of protection, he advocated reinstating the practice of allowing a husband to wed more than one wife. This modest proposal, expounded in a lengthy three-volume work, had the sanction of Holy Writ, according to Madan. Whereas the Bible generally condemns whoredom, fornication, and adultery, he observed, in the Old Testament men often had numerous wives. Furthermore the New Testament never forbids the law of the Old Testament.[7]

Ironically *Thelypthora* was itself a kind of abortive by-product of the revival. The Evangelicals had particularly emphasized the importance of the Old Testament and had restored a strict observance of the Sabbath and other practices enjoined by its text. Madan had simply advocated the restoration of one more institution. But his plan to cope with immorality seemed so highly immoral that in this case the precedent of the Old Testament carried no weight. In the eyes of the Evangelicals the formerly devout clergyman had suddenly become a stray sheep with certain goatish propensities.

Preserving his anonymity, Cowper attacked his cousin's book in a mock allegory entitled *Anti-Thelypthora*. In the poem an amorous witch called Hypothesis seduces a knight, Airy del Castro, and makes him the champion of her immoral purpose to promote free love. Airy del Castro, who represents Madan, tries to spread the views of his sinful mistress, but in the end, Sir Marmadan, a noble knight, who represents the critics of Madan,[8] overcomes the lascivious couple, and the votaries of Hymen rejoice in their defeat. Written in couplets and introducing some rather good Spenserian imagery, the poem was an experiment which Cowper never repeated. When he composed it he forgot his Evangelical restraints to such an extent that Newton seems to have felt that certain allusions in the poem were a trifle ribald. Actually there is nothing salacious in *Anti-The-*

lypthora, although it is a rather curious production for an Evangelical poet.

The glimpses that Cowper got of the world from his loopholes of retreat convinced him that it was a wicked place, more corrupt even than in the days of his youth. When he wrote his moral satires, therefore, the progress of error became the theme, not merely of the poem by that name, but of virtually the entire volume. On the other hand, his reflections upon the wickedness of the world did not entirely exclude cheerfulness from his poetry or cast a lasting shadow on his personal life. The existence of evil he could partly take for granted, since it only confirmed his religious belief that man is an utterly depraved creature. Furthermore, he was so obsessed with his own fate that the ways of other men, whom he deemed more fortunate than himself, could not seriously disturb him. Then, too, no matter how depressing his thoughts were, cheerfulness kept breaking in, as if nature were determined to prove that joy as well as sorrow has a part in the pattern of life. Even he was astonished by the arrival of one of his lighter moods. "I wonder that a sportive thought should ever knock at the door of my intellects, and still more that it should gain admittance," he wrote. "It is as if harlequin should intrude himself into the gloomy chamber where a corpse is deposited in state. . . . But the mind, long wearied with the sameness of a dull, dreary prospect, will fix its eyes on any thing that may make a little variety in its contemplations, though it were but a kitten playing with its tail." [9]

Happily, despite the provincial atmosphere of Olney, Cowper never entirely lost his urbanity. He could even joke about Madan's shocking advocacy of a system of plural wives when he reflected upon the probable results of such a system. In an impromptu quatrain on reading *Thelypthora* he wrote:

> If John marries Mary, and Mary alone,
> 'Tis a good match between Mary and John.
> Should John wed a score, oh, the claws and the scratches!
> It can't be a match — 'tis a bundle of matches.

His *Report of an Adjudged Case* is an even better example of his wit. Drawing upon his knowledge of the law, he mocked the pompous legal jargon of the courts in this description of the contending claims of nose and eyes for the ownership of a pair of spectacles.

Even when times seemed most out of joint, his letters to William Unwin and Joseph Hill are interspersed with humorous allusions and gay trifling. "The best wig," he remarks, "is that which most resembles the natural hair; why then should he that has hair enough of his own, have recourse to imitation? I have little doubt, but that if an arm or a leg could have been taken off with as little pain as attends the amputation of a curl or lock of hair, the natural limb would have been thought less becoming, or less convenient, by some men, than a wooden one, and been disposed of accordingly." [10] Flashes of gaiety sometimes appeared in his more serious letters to Newton. Upon hearing that the clergyman had safely received the manuscript of his long poem, he punned, "I am glad the Progress of Error did not Err in its progress, as I feared it had." [11]

Cowper had started writing *The Progress of Error* by December 1780. Previously he had composed verses when a thought struck him or when an impulse moved him. Now, working before a cheerful fire, he devoted several hours a day to his moral satires, while Mrs. Unwin hovered in the background, now and then giving him a word of encouragement or gently chiding a servant for disturbing Mr. Cowper while he was so busily engaged. He had completed the poem by January and immediately started work on two other moral satires. Among his correspondents, only Newton knew that he was seriously composing verse. He sent the clergyman a draft of *The Progress of Error,* and Newton was delighted with it. Shortly thereafter Newton approached his own publisher, Joseph Johnson, on the subject of bringing out an edition of the verse. Johnson agreed, insisting only that the volume appear with the poet's name on the title page. To this condition Cowper readily assented. You may tell Mr. Johnson, he wrote Newton, that he will, "if he pleases, announce me to the world by the style and title of

William Cowper, Esq.
Of the Inner Temple." [12]

How his memory clung to the old days! Although most of his former friends of the Inner Temple had forgotten the shy young man who had become mentally deranged and had retired into the country, they, as well as hundreds of others, were soon to learn that in a quiet corner of England there dwelt a middle-aged gentleman with a great talent for writing poetry. By February 1781 he had completed three moral satires and thought he would rest, but the urge to compose spurred him on to writing a fourth, called *Expostulation*. His incentive was something more than a creative impulse. He had found what for him was the most satisfactory of all diversions. "There is nothing but this," he wrote Newton, "no occupation within the compass of my small sphere, Poetry excepted — that can do much towards diverting the train of melancholy thoughts which, when I am not thus employed, are forever pouring themselves in upon me." [13]

Expecting his volume to appear in the summer of 1781, in May Cowper informed William Unwin that he was already "in the press." He did not have to tell Hill, for his old friend had picked up the news in London and had written to congratulate him on his forthcoming volume. Cowper was pleased to learn that he was already being referred to as an author in the great metropolis, but his pleasure was dimmed by Johnson's advice that publication be deferred, since summer was a poor season to introduce a book of verse.

The delay gave Cowper an opportunity to expand the collection. At first he had thought that his four long poems, together with a few shorter pieces, would make a respectable volume without resorting to the subterfuge of wide margins. During the summer of 1781, however, he had time to compose several additional selections. Chief among these were the four moral satires, *Hope, Charity, Conversation,* and *Retirement.* Each had its own didactic purpose. The intention in *Retirement,* for instance, was "to direct to the proper use of the opportunities it [retirement] affords for the cultivation of a man's best interests; to censure the vices and follies which people carry with them into their retreats," and to "enlarge upon the happiness of that state, when discreetly enjoyed and religiously improved." [14]

So serious was his purpose that he felt he must apologize for introducing even slight touches of levity. "I am merry that I may decoy people into my company, and grave that they may be the better for it," he explained to Newton. "Now and then I put on the garb of a philosopher, and take the opportunity that disguise procures me to drop a word in favour of religion. In short, there is some froth, and here and there a bit of sweetmeat, which seems to entitle it justly to the name of a certain dish the ladies called a trifle." [15] Almost anything short of a sermon would probably have seemed like froth to Newton, as Cowper probably knew. Nevertheless, the poet had no occasion to apologize, for his intention was sufficiently didactic. Although he was no longer a practicing Evangelical, he thoroughly believed in the revival and hoped that his verse would serve to further its principles. Thus his moral satires were essentially propaganda for the religious revival.

Cowper regarded publication as a bold venture. After years of retirement, he was about to thrust himself into public notice and challenge the judgment of professional critics. This prospect of appearing before the world alone and unprotected so abashed him that he turned to his old companion and asked him to contribute a preface for the volume. Newton willingly complied by writing a cheerless and egotistical introductory piece. With poor taste, he alluded to the poet's attack of insanity at the Temple, described his conversion, and even spoke of the derangement of 1773. He assured the public, though his statement was probably directed chiefly at the poet, that he believed the crisis in Cowper's life was "now nearly approaching." No doubt the blundering clergyman intended merely to use this opportunity to persuade his friend that his fear of damnation was illusory, but it was the wrong place to do it. The preface concluded with a neat little sermon for readers. This material was so ill-suited as an advertisement to the volume that the publisher, fearing that it would weigh down an already serious book, urged that the introduction be omitted. This suggestion caused some embarrassed discussion between Newton and Cowper, but they finally agreed that the public should be allowed to meet the poet face to face, without the vestibule counseling of his clerical friend. Johnson made another wise decision when he decided to give the strongly didactic *Progress of Error* second place and introduce the reader first to the more lively poem called *Table Talk*.

Cowper's volume of verse finally appeared in February 1782. Despite its strong Evangelical tone, it was not a particularly novel production. In choosing to write moral satires, he had followed in the tradition of Pope, Johnson, and various lesser poets, who had made the moral satire a vehicle for exposing the follies of the time, rebuking its vices, and, sometimes, pointing the way to reform. These authors assumed that the age was corrupt, and eighteenth-century readers, long accustomed to hearing that theirs were the most sinful of all ages, did not resent the charge, especially since the criticism was general and not personal in its application. In fact, most readers regarded good, sound moralizing as an almost necessary ingredient of literature.

The only fundamental difference in Cowper's moralizing was that, in addition to satirizing vice in the traditional manner, he introduced numerous passages in which he spoke with the admonishing voice of the Evangelical. To render these passages less offensive to a nonbeliever, however, he judiciously interspersed them among witty comments, interesting character portrayals, and occasional observations on nature. In a letter to his cousin Mrs. Cowper, he wrote, "My sole drift is to be useful; a point which, however, I knew I should in vain aim at unless I could be likewise entertaining. I have therefore fixed these two strings to my bow, and by the help of both have done my best to send my arrow to the mark. My readers will hardly have begun to laugh, before they will be called upon to correct that levity, and peruse me with a more serious air." [16] Having employed this artful method of introducing his readers to Evangelical principles, Cowper was not at all sure it would prove acceptable. Shortly after the publication of the volume, while he was waiting to hear what the critics would say, he wrote to

Unwin in nervous anticipation, "The Reviewers are such fiery Socinians that they have less charity for a man of my avowed principles than a Portuguese for a Jew. They may possibly find here and there somewhat to commend, but will undoubtedly reprobate the doctrines, pronounce me a Methodist, and by so doing probably check the sale of the volume, if not suppress it." [17]

Cowper's fears were for the most part unrealized. Only one of his critics, a writer for the *Critical Review*, commented on his preaching. He described the book as a "rather tedious volume, which is little better than a dull sermon, in very indifferent verse." Yet even this, the harshest of his critics, seemed unaware that he was reviewing a book closely linked with the religious revival. "He says what is incontrovertible," the writer complained, "and what has already been said over and over, with much gravity, but says nothing new, sprightly, or entertaining." [18] If the principles of the revival were "incontrovertible," then the Evangelicals were more firmly entrenched than even they realized. Actually, what had happened was that the reviewer had failed to distinguish Evangelical propaganda from the typical abstract moralizing of the eighteenth century.

Two other reviews, though brief, were kind enough. The *London Magazine* observed that Cowper's longer pieces were labored but that "the greatest part of the volume consists of lively sallies, called by the French *jeux d'esprit*." [19] This was hardly a true description of the emphasis of the book, but it was the sort of review that would attract readers. Another criticism, a short review in the *Gentleman's Magazine*, appears to have been written by John Duncombe, a former acquaintance of Cowper. After referring to the pleasure with which he had read the selections, the writer remarks, "The author we know to have been a keen sportsman in the classic fields of Westminster and was a coadjutor of the celebrated Mr. Town in *The Connoisseur*." [20]

Cowper awaited with particular eagerness the comments of the *Monthly Review*. Everyone in Olney — the watchmakers, the carpenter, the baker — read this periodical, he observed with a twinkle. "All these will set me down for a dunce if those terrible critics show them the example." [21] When it finally appeared, the criticism proved to be the most favorable he had received. While the *Critical Review* had complained of his lack of novelty, the *Monthly Review* described him as a remarkably original poet, whose "notes are peculiar to himself" and who "classes not with any species of bards that have preceded him." "Mr. Cowper's predominant turn of mind," the critic adds, "though serious and devotional, is at the same time dryly humorous and sarcastic. Hence his very religion has a smile that is arch, and his sallies of humor an air that is religious. . . . His versification is almost as singular as the materials upon which it is employed. Anxious only to give each image its due prominence and relief, he has wasted no unnecessary attention on grace and embellishment: his language, therefore, though neither strikingly harmonious nor elegant, is plain, forcible, and expressive." [22]

Comments on Cowper's diction and art of prosody are particularly interesting, since he is a transitional poet who reflects the tastes of two different periods. So far as language is concerned, he made no violent break with the past in his first volume. Though his verse contains less "poetic diction" than was common among his immediate predecessors, he, too, often favors the abstract and conventionally poetic word. Critics, however, were quick to detect his greater use of colloquial terms. The *Critical Review,* for instance, considered many of his expressions "coarse, vulgar, and unpoetical," citing his use of such words as "parrying," "pushing by," "spitting," and "abhorrence." A few years later, when he published his second volume of verse, the *Gentleman's Magazine* quarreled with his line

A serving maid was she, and fell in love.

According to the critic the last three words, "fell in love," constituted a colloquial "barbarism," for which Cowper should have substituted a more elegant expression, such as "enamored." [23]

Cowper himself realized the restrictions that had been put

upon verse by the habit of slavishly imitating Pope. In a well-known passage he observed:

> Then Pope, as harmony itself exact,
> In verse well-disciplined, complete, compact,
> Gave virtue and morality a grace,
> That, quite eclipsing pleasure's painted face,
> Levied a tax of wonder and applause,
> Even on the fools that trampled on their laws.
> But he (his musical finesse was such,
> So nice his ear, so delicate his touch)
> Made poetry a mere mechanic art,
> And every warbler has his tune by heart.
>
> TABLE TALK 646–655

Though Cowper's was no mere mechanic art, his satiric couplets displayed many of Pope's best qualities. Of the two, Pope had the advantage of caring less about what targets he chose. Cowper, on the other hand, felt that satire must always be used as a corrective measure. He says,

> Unless a love of virtue light the flame,
> Satire is, more than those he brands, to blame.

Nevertheless, though Cowper was never venomous, he could write with great acerbity. A few of his character sketches rank with Pope's portrayals of Atossa and Sporus. Perhaps Cowper's best achievement of this kind is his vivid representation of the ancient prude in *Truth*. Only a master satirist could have so deftly selected the details that contribute to the total effect, or have so nicely balanced the description of the prude's outward appearance with the revelation of her hypocritical character. His sketch of Lord Chesterfield, whom he calls Petronious, is equally astringent. To Cowper Chesterfield epitomized the evils of the fashionable world, and the poet's anger displayed itself when he described him as

> Thou polished and high-finished foe to truth,
> Grey-beard corrupter of our listening youth,
> To purge and skim away the filth of vice,
> That, so refined, it might the more entice,

Then pour it on the morals of thy son,
To taint *his* heart, was worthy of *thine own*.
PROGRESS OF ERROR 341–346

A judicious eighteenth-century reader must have observed that
Cowper's ear was not so good as Pope's, and that his skill as a
prosodist could not equal that of his predecessor. But where in
the eighteenth century was there a poet who wrote with a pen
so professionally disciplined as Pope's? Again, although Cowper's
verse does not contain so many glittering or memorable aphorisms
as the richly strewn lines of the *Essay on Criticism* or the *Essay
on Man*, nevertheless, many of his witty and compact couplets invite quotation. One admires the aptness of:

How much a dunce that has been sent to roam
Excels a dunce that has been kept at home.

The reader delights in the terseness of:

Men deal with life as children with their play,
Who first misuse, then cast their toys away.

And anyone familiar with the Biblical passage must recognize
Cowper's skill in paraphrasing Hebrews 6:19:

Hope, as an anchor firm and sure, holds fast
The Christian vessel, and defies the blast.

Even an eighteenth-century scoffer at religion could not miss the
stark forcefulness of certain subjective references such as:

I was a bondman on my native plain;
Sin forged, and ignorance made fast, the chain.

The discerning eighteenth-century reader might also observe
Cowper's appreciation of rural life and nature. In this respect
he invited comparison with James Thomson. Yet there is something different, a greater vividness, a markedly subjective tendency, a more fruitful harvest of a quiet eye than one finds in the
sometimes labored and prolix lines of *The Seasons*. Consider, for
instance, Cowper's description of the country lad in *Retirement*.
In this passage, to be sure, he had followed the custom of precisely balancing phrases and judiciously matching nouns with

adjectives, a studied device that generally destroys a sense of spontaneity. Nevertheless, Cowper's lines have a naturalness that was prophetic of a new era in poetry:

> Ask not the boy, who, when the breeze of morn
> First shakes the glittering drops from every thorn,
> Unfolds his flock, then under bank or bush
> Sits linking cherry-stones or platting rush,
> How fair is freedom? — He was always free:
> To carve his rustic name upon a tree,
> To snare the mole, or with ill-fashioned hook,
> To draw the incautious minnow from the brook,
> Are life's prime pleasures in his simple view.
>
> LL. 395–403

In this first volume, however, Cowper only occasionally strikes the familiar note of the major romanticists. For the most part he did not depart from eighteenth-century standards. His deft satire, his witty aphorisms, his sober moralizing are all in keeping with the predominant tendencies of the age. Thus there was nothing to shock the typical reader, unless a non-Evangelical suddenly realized that, for all its pleasantries, the volume was designed to indoctrinate him in the principles of the revival.

Almost every page of the moral satires, indeed, contains an Evangelical message. In *Table Talk* Cowper observed that England was no longer the strongly Christian nation that it once had been, and he hinted that unless it soon reformed it might suffer the fate of Nineveh, Babylon, and ancient Rome. He regretted that while writers wasted time on less worthy subjects, the nation had no truly religious poet. Curiously he was unable to see the similarity between Evangelicalism and Puritanism. While he had nothing but praise for the first, he condemned the fanaticism of the seventeenth century when he remarked:

> Religion, harsh, intolerant, austere,
> Parent of manners like herself severe,
> Drew a rough copy of the Christian's face
> Without the smile, the sweetness, or the grace.
>
> TABLE TALK 612–615

The Progress of Error is a handbook of Evangelical moral principles. Since any form of pleasure "admitted in undue degree enslaves the will," most pastimes were considered censurable. The "cassocked huntsman" and the "fiddling priest," those who break the Sabbath by playing the harpsichord or engaging in card games, and the wicked worldlings who dance their lives away were all severely lectured by Cowper. He particularly condemned the race of novelists because they too often set snares to corrupt the young and unwary, and he warned lady readers to avoid

> Whatever shocks or gives the least offence
> To virtue, delicacy, truth, or sense.

Truth, Hope, and *Charity* contain expositions in verse of the more important Evangelical doctrines. "Heaven's easy, artless, unencumbered plan," according to the poet who despaired of his own salvation, was "believe and live." Since faith alone could lead to eternal life, performing good deeds or doing one's best was no passport to heaven. Therefore, while hope was important, man must not expect to escape perdition by simply performing acts of charity. The poems also contain allusions to the natural depravity of mankind and to the importance of the atonement. Scripture is praised as the source of enlightenment and as "the only cure of woe." While personal references never obtrude, Cowper occasionally refers to himself and his experiences. One of the most touching of these subjective expressions concludes *Truth,* where he speaks with sincerity and humility of his own conversion.

Charity lauded the plan of the Maker who had created all men as brothers, and made their lands fruitful with goods they could exchange. Particular praise was accorded John Thornton, the charitable Evangelical who was Newton's patron, and Howard, the well-known prison reformer. In this poem Cowper also denounces slavery as an institution contrary to the natural and heaven-ordained brotherhood of man.

Expostulation repeated the exhortations found in the other poems. Chiefly it was an appeal for England to reform its morals and religion lest the nation perish. *Conversation,* containing fewer Evangelical precepts than the other moral satires, is a didactic poem which encouraged readers to engage in pious and cheerful discussions and to avoid pruriency, wrangling, blasphemy, gossip, and the practice of dwelling upon one's ailments. In *Retirement* there is a promise of the superior nature poetry which Cowper would write for *The Task,* but it is only a promise, since he did not dwell upon country living so much for its own sake. He praised it chiefly as an ideal situation for enjoying religious contemplation. In concluding the poem he remarked that religion does not censure all pleasures; among those that are justified are cultivating the soil, studying nature, or painting landscapes.

The fact that many readers, among them the reviewers, apparently failed to detect the persistent Evangelical tone of the moral satires may be explained by the truism that one sees in a book only what one wants to find. Converts easily recognized Cowper's purpose and acclaimed him their greatest poet. For the next few generations, in many Protestant religious groups his verse would rank second only to the Bible, despite the fact that a few years after he published his poetry such authoritative Evangelical periodicals as the *Christian Observer* and the *Eclectic Review* went on record as being opposed to *all* forms of satire.[24] Apparently regenerate readers forgot, or chose not to remember, that Cowper held a distinguished place in the long procession of eighteenth-century satirists. Little heeding his urbanity or his sharp sallies of wit, the Evangelicals esteemed him as a moral poet. Hence he was assured of an appreciative group of readers long after the popularity of the couplet and the taste for moral satire were eclipsed.

Upon the publication of the volume, Cowper had sent copies to his old friends George Colman and Chancellor Thurlow, hoping that the gift would provide an opportunity for a renewal of friendship. When neither of these former friends wrote acknowledgments, he was stung by their ungraciousness. He expressed his hurt feelings in a poem called *Valediction.* Fortunately he did not publish it, for both Colman and Thurlow later rallied to the support of their old companion of Temple days.

Cowper was much cheered by the praise of Benjamin Franklin, to whom John Thornton had sent a copy of the poems. "The relish for reading of poetry has long since left me," the American wrote; " but there is something so new in the manner, so easy and yet so correct in the language, so clear in the expression, yet concise, and so just in the sentiments that I have read the whole with great pleasure, and some of the pieces more than once." [25]

Later — in fact, more than two years after the publication date — Cowper heard that the great Dr. Johnson had also read and highly commended his verse. The circumstances are rather curious. As early as September 1781 Newton had suggested that a copy of the poetry be presented to the doctor. Cowper, who had read many of Johnson's critical views and did not always agree with them, was a bit frightened by the proposal. He felt that Johnson might disapprove his verse and spoil the sale by one of "his pointed sarcasms." Nevertheless, he finally agreed to the plan, with the understanding that Newton should arrange to provide Johnson with a copy. Something apparently changed Newton's mind, however, for he next informed Cowper that he had decided it would be wiser not to submit the verses to Johnson. Cowper quickly agreed.

Several months passed, and the subject was not again alluded to until the poet wrote Unwin that he was momentarily expecting Newton to relay Johnson's opinion. Apparently Newton had reverted to the original plan. Another long silence on the business; then, on May 22, 1784, Cowper sent a letter to the Evangelical clergyman, saying, "I am glad to have received at last an account of Dr. Johnson's favourable opinion of my book." It had been so long coming, he added, that he had feared Dr. Johnson's verdict was uncomplimentary and that Newton had therefore kept it from him.

Although none of Johnson's biographers indicate that he had ever read Cowper or even heard of him, the learned doctor probably did see the 1782 volume. Newton would hardly have deceived Cowper about the matter. Because Newton's letters on the subject have never been printed and have probably been destroyed, we cannot be sure of the reason for his long delay in procuring Johnson's opinion. Probably, however, being unacquainted with the doctor, he was endeavoring to find someone to serve as a mediator between him and Johnson. The person who finally served this end appears to have been Benjamin Latrobe, a Moravian minister who was acquainted with both Newton and Johnson. Evidence that Latrobe was the man exists in Cowper's letters. Upon receiving Johnson's favorable opinion, the poet asked Newton to give Latrobe his "thanks for the share he took in the patronage of the volume." He also enclosed a note of thanks to Johnson to be conveyed to the great critic by the Moravian clergyman.[26]

It is interesting to speculate on what Johnson might have said specifically about Cowper's verse. For, as G. B. Hill has observed in his essay *The Melancholy of Johnson and Cowper,* the two men had much in common. Both suffered from melancholy; both dreaded their future state. At times each was so overcome by fits of depression that nothing could rouse him from silent and gloomy contemplation. Furthermore they were both exceptionally pious Christians. One may conjecture that Johnson most certainly would have approved the moral and religious tone of the volume. Possibly he would have remarked on the occasional roughness of the poet's versification, but since Cowper had not violently departed from the critical canons of eighteenth-century verse, the great arbiter would no doubt have found much to praise and little to blame when he examined the compact couplets, the judiciously directed satire, and the whole conduct of the moral essays.

❧ VII ❧

Second Spring

This is just as it should be. We are all grown young
again, and the days that I thought I should see no more
are actually returned.

LETTER TO LADY HESKETH, OCTOBER 12, 1785

W<small>HEN</small> Newton moved from Olney, Cowper had felt that he
was left to end his days in a miserable sepulcher. Instead he was
entering upon one of his happiest periods. The recognition won
by his first volume encouraged him to proceed with a second and
much better book of verse. As his fame spread, old friends resumed their correspondence and visits. He also made several new
acquaintances who enlivened his routine existence and helped
him to forget, momentarily at least, that he was a damned soul.
Thus, instead of withering into senility, the middle-aged bachelor
was to enjoy a second spring.

The first of his new friends cast a sunset glow of romance upon
his retirement. In the summer of 1781, while he was writing the
last of his moral satires, he met a charming widow. Lady Austen
had recently come to the Olney region to visit her sister, the wife
of the Reverend Thomas Jones of Clifton. According to William
Hayley, Cowper's early biographer, the poet first saw Lady Austen
when she and Mrs. Jones called at a shop opposite his house in
the Market Place. Peering from his window, he was so taken by
her appearance that he asked Mrs. Unwin to invite the ladies to
tea. When they accepted, Cowper was overcome with shyness, and
Mrs. Unwin had to coax him to join the guests. His embarrass-

ment disappeared in the presence of Lady Austen, however, and when the visitors left, he escorted them to Clifton.[1]

Such, according to Hayley, was the romantic beginning of the most enriching of Cowper's friendships. Other writers have been inclined to accept this account, but Mr. Kenneth Povey has, with good reason, suggested that Hayley's sense of gallantry led him to invent the situation.[2] Cowper himself described his meeting with Lady Austen somewhat differently. Apparently the news that she was staying at Clifton had reached him before the first encounter. Furthermore, she and her sister appear to have paid a formal call at Orchard Side, for in a letter to Newton, Cowper wrote, "Lady Austen, waving all forms, has paid us the first visit; and not content with showing us that proof of her respect, made handsome apologies for the intrusion. We returned the visit yesterday."[3] Finally, in his *Epistle to Lady Austen* Cowper alludes to the friendship as growing out of a conventional meeting. He says,

> A transient visit intervening,
> And made almost without a meaning,
> (Hardly the effect of inclination,
> Much less of pleasing expectation,)
> Produced a friendship, then begun,
> That has cemented us in one.

Though the first encounter was probably more prosaic than Hayley indicates, nevertheless, it quickly led to an intimate friendship between the middle-aged poet and the charming widow. After a second meeting Cowper wrote Newton, "She is a lively, agreeable woman; has seen much of the world and accounts it a great simpleton, as it is. She laughs and makes laugh, and keeps up a conversation without seeming to labour at it."[4]

Compared with Cowper, Lady Austen had indeed seen much of the world. When she was eighteen or nineteen her father, John Richardson, had given her in marriage to Sir Robert Austen, Baronet. Her husband, who was much her elder, took her to France, where they lived for the next four years. During a visit to England, Lady Austen heard various Evangelical preachers and, as a result, became a convert. After Sir Robert's death in 1771, she lived for several years at Saucerre, France, but later took a house in London, where she mingled in polite society. Then, weary of the fashionable world, as she told Cowper, she came to Clifton to visit her sister.[5]

When the poet met her, she was a woman in her forties. Although her portrait, painted by Romney reveals a sensitive, almost pretty face, she was far from handsome. Sometimes she even referred to herself as "the ugliest of all women," according to the Reverend Samuel Greatheed. He hastens to add that she did herself an injustice by this remark but admits that "her conversation is certainly more fascinating than her features." [6] Like many women, she compensated for her plain appearance by cultivating her talents. Her witty remarks and gay laughter enlivened any company. She played the harpsichord, she sang, and she brightened her discourse by apt references to her long sojourn in France. In short, she was the kind of woman who could make a man forget her unattractive appearance. Like Cowper, the Reverend Mr. Greatheed was charmed by her company. Her talents for entertainment, he remarked, "are greater than any I had ever met with in another person of either sex." [7]

It would be a mistake, however, to think of Lady Austen as merely a gay woman of fashion. She had been an Evangelical for several years before she met Cowper, and no doubt their common religious interest helped form a bond between them. Probably she did not regard fashionable society so contemptuously as she intimated when she compared the world to a simpleton, but the observation had warmed Cowper's heart. Both of them, he felt, had learned from their experience in polite society to despise the tinsel trappings and to prefer a life of retirement. As a convert, she no doubt could speak with the solemnity of an Evangelical preacher when the conversation turned to graver topics. Fortunately for Cowper, however, her prevailing mood was one of gaiety.

Since his youth, he had not known a companion so full of spirits, and her animation served as an electric shock to rescue him from his torpor. His letters, reflecting a keener relish for life, became more playful, even when he was writing to the sober-minded John Newton. A few days after meeting the baronet's widow he sent the clergyman his famous hop-o'-my-thumb letter, a remarkably boyish epistle written in jingling rhyme. His next letters announce that the little group of friends have had a picnic, which, under the influence of the French-speaking Lady Austen, he refers to as a *fête champêtre*. Cowper, Mrs. Unwin, Lady Austen, and the Reverend Mr. and Mrs. Jones composed the party. The poet describes the outing with almost childish pleasure:

"Lady Austen's lackey, and a lad that waits on me in the garden, drove a wheelbarrow full of eatables and drinkables to the scene of our *Fête Champêtre*. A board laid over the top of the wheelbarrow served us for a table; our dining-room was a root-house lined with moss and ivy. At six o'clock the servants, who had dined under a great elm tree upon the ground, at a little distance, boiled the kettle and the said wheelbarrow served us for a tea-table. We then took a walk into the wilderness, about half a mile off, and were home again a little after eight, having spent the day together from noon till evening without one cross occurrence, or the least weariness of each other." [8]

Except for the obtrusive presence of the wheelbarrow, the friends had passed the day like a group of genteel shepherds in a French pastoral scene. For the rest of the summer Cowper and Lady Austen enacted the roles of characters in an Arcadian romance. The elegantly groomed widow was delighted with the tranquil existence of Olney. She was even more charmed to find in this rural setting a well-bred gentleman, with the courtly if rather old-fashioned manners of the previous generation, with a melancholy countenance that could nevertheless break into a gentle smile at one of her quips, with an observing eye for the beauties of nature and an engaging talent for writing about them. Cowper was equally pleased with his new companion. She had a taste for verse, she could discourse solemnly on religious and moral subjects or facetiously on the foibles of society. She knew not only the world to which he had been born but a fascinating

French civilization of which he had only read. The third actor in the *mise-en-scène* was perhaps not quite so happy in her role. Indeed, to an observer the aging Mrs. Unwin might well seem more like a lady in waiting to the younger and more scintillating Lady Austen.

To add to the pleasure of outdoor life, Cowper had converted a greenhouse in his garden into a "summer parlor" by spreading a carpet on the floor and hanging the sides with mats. There the three friends passed much of the day, conversing, reading, writing letters, or listening to "the sound of the wind in the trees and the singing of birds." [9] Their quiet retreat sheltered them from the noise of the brawling children in the Market Place, the sight of the dingy dwellings of the lacemakers, and the moral corruption of the greater world. Lady Austen was so much charmed by the rustic setting and the company of the romantically melancholy poet that she resolved to make Olney her permanent home. To Cowper, however, she discreetly mentioned other reasons for her decision. Naively he wrote Newton, "Lady Austen, very desirous of retirement, especially of a retirement near her sister, an admirer of Mr. Scott as a preacher, and of your two humble servants now in the greenhouse, as the most agreeable creatures in the world, is at present determined to settle here." [10]

Lady Austen planned to rent the other half of the house at Orchard Side. This dwelling was occupied by Richard Coleman, the protégé whom Cowper had adopted at St. Albans. Coleman, now married, was engaged off and on as a servant, but showing greater fidelity to the bottle than to his master, he had proved a disappointment to the poet.

Lady Austen's occupancy was to begin the following summer after renovations had been made. Meanwhile, having a house in the city, she returned to London for the winter months. During their separation, the friends corresponded, and in December Cowper wrote a *Poetical Epistle to Lady Austen*, in which he addresses her familiarly:

> Dear Anna — between friend and friend
> Prose answers every common end;

Serves, in a plain and homely way,
To express the occurrence of the day;
Our health, the weather, and the news;
What walks we take, what books we chuse;
And all the floating thoughts we find
Upon the surface of the mind.
   But when a poet takes the pen,
Far more alive than other men
He feels a gentle tingling come
Down to his finger and his thumb,
Derived from nature's noblest part,
The centre of a glowing heart;
And this is what the world, who knows
No flights above the pitch of prose,
His more sublime vagaries slighting,
Denominates an itch for writing.
No wonder I, who scribble rhyme
To catch the triflers of the time,
And tell them truths divine and clear
Which, couched in prose, they will not hear,
Who labour hard to allure and draw
The loiterers I never saw,
Should feel that itching and that tingling
With all my purpose intermingling,
To your intrinsic merit true,
When called to address myself to you.

These opening lines are particularly interesting because Cowper here places himself with later writers of the romantic school who thought of the poet as a man inspired above other men, gifted with special insight, and endowed with a rare ability to express the wisdom of the heart. In the remainder of the poem Cowper describes his friendship with Lady Austen as a special gift of Providence. He concludes with an affirmation that the fidelity of the three friends will be lasting because

A threefold cord is not soon broken.

Shortly afterward, however, the cord was strained almost to the breaking point. Something Lady Austen had written, perhaps a too ardent expression of her devotion, gave offense. The correspondence ceased abruptly, and for a time the vows of amity seemed to be forgotten. The friendship would probably have ended at this point but for Lady Austen's determination to preserve it. In an attempt to effect a reconciliation she sent Cowper several pairs of ruffles she had worked for him. In return, but in a spirit of cold courtesy, the poet ordered his publisher to present her a volume of his verse which was just about to appear. Meanwhile he professed to be indifferent about patching up the affair. In a letter to William Unwin he intimated that the friendship was permanently ruptured. He and Mrs. Unwin were quite happy in their retirement without the company of the fashionable Lady Austen, he explained in tones of offended pride. "She is exceedingly sensible, has great quickness of parts, and an uncommon fluency of expression, but her vivacity was sometimes too much for us." [11]

The return of warm weather brought a thaw in the glacier that had proved a barrier to reconciliation. Lady Austen sent a letter apologizing for her indiscretion, whatever it had been. Soon afterward the vivacious lady returned to Olney. Her presence soon dispelled whatever wintry mists remained. "We are reconciled," Cowper wrote William Unwin. "She seized the first opportunity to embrace your mother with tears of the tenderest affection, and I, of course, am satisfied. We were a little awkward at first, but now are as easy as ever. She stays at Clifton till after Christmas." [12] It would appear that the baronet's widow had particularly offended Mrs. Unwin, and that Cowper had supported his old companion, but the wound was healed for the time at least, and now there were to be more long summer days devoted to genteel and improving conversation, strolls through the garden, and cheerful laughter in the greenhouse.

The presence of Lady Austen gave a tinge of excitement to eventless Olney. Like a heroine of romance, she seemed destined to play the role of a lady in distress. One dismal evening Cowper heard a knock at his door. When he opened it he found her in a weakened condition, supported by the Reverend Thomas Scott. After riding from Clifton to attend Thursday evening service, she had been attacked by a bilious colic, which had caused her great suffering during the meeting. Scott released the stricken Lady to Cowper and Mrs. Unwin, who put her to bed at Orchard Side and called a doctor. By Saturday Lady Austen was able to get up. During the day she proved as sprightly as ever, but that night her friends had to go to her assistance when she was seized by convulsive fits. Not long afterward, while the Reverend Mr. Jones was away, burglars attempted to break into the vicarage at Clifton, and Lady Austen and Mrs. Jones fled to Orchard Side for refuge. Mrs. Jones went home when her husband returned, but Lady Austen remained a little longer. The earlier plan to renovate the other half of Orchard Side having been dropped, arrangements were now made for Lady Austen to occupy a part of Olney vicarage. Thus when her visit ended, she became a close neighbor of Cowper and Mrs. Unwin.

The passing of the second summer brought no abatement of pleasure, for the charming widow was to remain at Olney for the winter. During the next two years only an occasional visit to London took her away. Cowper saw nothing unusual in living so intimately with his two ladies. He wrote William Unwin, "From a scene of almost uninterrupted retirement, we have passed at once into a state of constant engagement; not that our society is much multiplied, — the addition of an individual has made all the difference. Lady Austen and we pass our days alternately at each other's *château*. In the morning I walk with one or other of the ladies, and in the afternoon wind thread. Thus did Hercules, and thus probably did Samson, and thus do I." [13] Cowper was probably happier than he had been for years; indeed, he seemed almost smug about his situation when he wrote Joseph Hill, "I see the winter approaching without much concern, though a passionate lover of fine weather and the pleasant scenes of summer; but the long evenings have their comforts too, and there is hardly to be found upon the earth, I suppose, so snug a creature as an Englishman by his fireside in the winter. I mean, however, an Englishman that lives in the country, for in London it is not very easy to avoid intrusion. I have two ladies to read to, sometimes more, but never less." [14]

The other ladies admitted to the cozy circle were probably Mrs. Scott, wife of the Olney clergyman, and Mrs. Jones. At rarer intervals Cowper enjoyed visits from the Reverend Thomas Scott and the Reverend William Bull. Although there was no change in the poet's conviction that he was damned, cheerful company helped to divert his melancholy thoughts. Furthermore, writing still served as an excellent distraction, and with Lady Austen at hand to suggest subjects and bolster his self-confidence, he produced some of his best verse during the years of their friendship.

Cowper owed a great deal to the sprightly widow. Besides serving as his muse, she had inspired many an otherwise gloomy day with merriment. Mrs. Unwin had helped him to accept his fate; Lady Austen served to make him forget it momentarily. He was deeply appreciative of his debt to her, but all he could offer in return was his companionship. Finally he had to deny her even that. In his poem to Lady Austen Cowper had asserted that "a threefold cord is not soon broken." But the metaphor hardly applies to a *ménage à trois*. The wonder is that the two ladies could live in seeming amity as long as they did. Compared with the traveled Lady Austen, Mrs. Unwin was a humble provincial, a brown little wren that must inevitably have suffered by contrast to her brightly plumed rival. Perceiving Cowper's devotion to the clergyman's widow, Lady Austen had at first treated her with proper deference, but as time went on she made the older woman the butt of her witticisms. "Her mind," Greatheed wrote, "afforded as great a contrast to Mrs. U's as can well be conceived; she entertained no small contempt and aversion for her; and frequently indulged her unequal turn for satire at Mrs. U's expense, sometimes in her company, but oftener in Mr. Cowper's." [15]

The poet was slow to perceive the growing hostility between the ladies. Under the spell of Lady Austen's charm, perhaps he even tolerated a few slights to Mrs. Unwin. He tried to keep his own relationship with the baronet's widow on a brother-and-sister basis, but sometimes a touch of gallantry betrayed him into playing the role of a lover. Upon one occasion he gave Lady Austen a lock of his hair. Responding to the romantic gesture, she entwined the strand in a diamond brooch and wore it upon her breast. Then, boldly capping the incident, Cowper wrote:

> The heart that beats beneath that breast
> Is William's well I know,
> A nobler prize and richer far
> Than India could bestow.
>
> TO A LADY

These lines might well be deemed an expression of devotion too ardent from a man engaged to another woman. No doubt Lady Austen did not know that Cowper and Mrs. Unwin were betrothed; the affair was kept secret from all but a few. But an engagement did exist. Though the 1773 attack of insanity had prevented their marriage, Cowper and Mrs. Unwin continued to think of themselves as pledged to each other. "Her fortune, her time, her health, her comfort, and (in some degree) her reputation were sacrificed to his safety and relief," Greatheed wrote. "His heart was deeply sensible of what he owed her; and he only waited for delivery from the distress of mind which unfitted him for every social engagement to complete that which he had formed with Mrs. Unwin. He has repeatedly said, that if he ever again entered a church, it would, in the first instance, be to marry her." [16]

What finally brought the threefold friendship to an end? According to one melodramatic version, Cowper had hired a chaise and was about to elope with Lady Austen when Mrs. Unwin discovered the plan and prevented its execution. This story, in which the poet is made to appear like a scheming fortune-hunter in a sentimental comedy, was no doubt a ridiculous fabrication. Greatheed's version of the affair seems much more reliable. According to him, Mrs. Unwin took the opportunity to speak to Cowper about Lady Austen while her rival was absent from Olney. Mrs. Unwin may have strengthened her cause by playing a trump card. Her daughter, Mrs. Powley, was visiting at Orchard Side in May 1784, and to her the aggrieved lady probably disclosed her situation. Mrs. Powley, who disliked Cowper and felt that her mother had wasted her property on him, possibly urged Mrs. Unwin to leave the poet and come to live with her in Yorkshire. With this refuge assured her, the distressed Mrs. Unwin may have threatened to leave Cowper. In any event she made him understand that she found living in a *ménage à trois* insupportable. He had probably not realized how much ill will existed between the two ladies; when he finally did, there was only one course open to him. He deeply appreciated the sacrifices Mrs. Unwin had made for him and he knew he could not allow her to suffer any longer. Consequently he wrote a farewell letter to Lady Austen, expressing his regret for the necessity of parting with one whose company he had so much enjoyed.[17]

Cowper and the lively widow never saw each other again. Although she returned to Clifton in 1785 and remained there for more than four years, no embarrassed meetings occurred between the former friends. The region probably seemed less romantic without the company of the well-bred poet, but she was too full of spirits to let a single rebuff cast a lasting shadow on her life. When the French Revolution began, she took a lively interest in the émigrés that fled to England. Among them she eventually found a husband in the person of a Monsieur de Tardiff, whom she married about 1796. When the Peace of Amiens brought a temporary lull in the hostilities between England and France, she went to Paris with her husband. There she died in 1802, two years after Cowper.[18]

During the years of Lady Austen's regnancy, Cowper wrote some of his best poetry. In the summer of 1782 the Reverend William Bull had given him three volumes of verse by the French Quietist Madame Guyon, and had asked him to translate a few of the poems. Finding the project congenial, Cowper produced translations of thirty-seven poems. Although he felt attracted by the piety of the French author, hers was a different sort of religious enthusiasm from that of the Evangelical school. Consequently, he remarked, he found it necessary to suppress a certain amount of her fanaticism. A recent study reveals that he deleted occasional stanzas which, he felt, failed to show proper reverence for the Deity or seemed overnaive in expressing religious emotion. Occasionally he injected into his translations typical Evangelical phrases. On the whole, however, his renditions reflected excellent taste and judgment. "Whether working upon the poem as a whole, or more often within the stanza," Dorothy L. Gilbert and Russell Pope remark, "Cowper's ingenuity is impressive and delightful. Always respecting the spirit of his original, he deftly transposes a word or a phrase, shifts lines or couplets, combining elements of these with others, and adding, if need be, the native idiom needed to reset the original in its proper light." [19]

Perhaps the French-speaking Lady Austen gave Cowper some slight assistance in the translations. In any event she was his chief influence during these few highly productive years. She saw that his muse needed prodding, and she had a happy flair for putting ideas into his mind. *John Gilpin,* the most popular of his poems, was composed after she told him the humorous incident of the draper whose horse ran away with him. Cowper, who had been depressed, was so amused by the story that when he went to bed he could not sleep until he had written out a first draft of his poem. He wisely chose the informal ballad stanza and used a happy admixture of old-fashioned colloquialisms to describe Gilpin's plight. After polishing the lines, he sent them to the *Public Advertiser,* which printed them as an anonymous contribution. Other newspapers copied the poem, and the famous actor Henderson popularized it by reciting it in public. Within a short time *John Gilpin* became a national favorite. At Lady Austen's urging Cowper also composed canzonettes to several tunes which she knew. Three of the lyrics produced under these circumstances are *No Longer I Follow a Sound, When All Within is Peace,* and the well-known *On the Loss of the Royal George.* If she did not suggest *The Colubriad* and *The Distressed Travellers,* the poems were at least written under the reflected glow of her good spirits. Furthermore, she seems to have put into his mind the idea of translating Homer. He sometimes read Pope's version aloud to the ladies, but he was irked by Pope's frequent departure from the original. When he expressed a wish that someone would produce a more faithful translation, Lady Austen is said to have prompted, "Why not do it yourself; who else is so capable of the undertaking?" [20]

As everyone knows, Lady Austen was chiefly responsible for getting Cowper started on *The Task*. When he was at a loss for a subject, she suggested that he write on "the sofa." Normally it would have been a prosy theme, but what Cowper chiefly needed was initial encouragement. Once he had a topic, he could improvise upon it with considerable imagination. It took what the eighteenth century called wit to compose the hundred lines describing the evolution of the sofa. The passage is still interesting as a *jeu d'esprit*, but we value it chiefly because it served to launch him on *The Task*. According to Samuel Greatheed, his decision to write the poem in blank verse was influenced by Lady Austen, who had a distinct preference for that form.[21] But blank verse was a perfectly natural choice for an ardent admirer of Milton. Furthermore, it was the medium traditionally employed in the English Georgic, and Cowper's didactic-descriptive poem was more or less in the tradition of James Thomson, "the English Virgil." [22]

His choice of blank verse might also be considered a symbol of the greater sense of freedom he now enjoyed when he composed poetry. In his earlier satires, he had felt constrained to moralize in a narrow, Evangelical manner. In *The Task*, though there was still much moralizing, he frequently stepped down from the pulpit to lead his readers through the pleasant Olney countryside. Nature, which he had previously touched upon, now became his frequent theme. Imitating no one, he dealt with the topic with a degree of originality that would be better appreciated today if the generation of romantic poets following him had not written so often and so well on the same subject.

Having completed *The Task* in October 1784, Cowper proceeded with plans for publishing his second volume. He decided to include in it the now famous, though as yet unacknowledged, *John Gilpin* and a second poem entitled *Tirocinium*. This last, a satire of some nine hundred lines, merits particular attention at this place. Although it has been customary to label *Tirocinium* an attack upon the public schools, it is much more than an indictment of an educational system. Written in iambic pentameter couplets, with few Evangelical allusions, *Tirocinium* is a curious blend of eighteenth-century satire, religious orthodoxy, and romantic philosophizing.

Cowper begins by asserting that it is not the body that gives man his dominion over the earth. Rather it is his soul, a soul that has at its command all the intellectual powers, including memory, fancy, and judgment. His description of the fancy or the imagination is particularly interesting, because of its transcendental note:

> For her [the soul] the fancy, roving unconfined,
> The present muse of every pensive mind,
> Works magic wonders, adds a brighter hue
> To nature's scenes than nature ever knew.
>
> LL. 21–24

Cowper proceeds to inquire why God made the sun and the earth, with its seasons and constituents. The explanation is that they were created for man, the summation of God's noble plan. The question next proposed is, Why did God make man? The answer, says Cowper, is clear, but it is one that may better be found in nature than in books:

> Truths that the learn'd pursue with eager thought
> Are not important always as dear-bought,
> Proving at last, though told in pompous strains,
> A childish waste of philosophic pains;
> But truths on which depend our main concern,
> That 'tis our shame and misery not to learn,
> Shine by the side of every path we tread
> With such a lustre he that runs may read.
>
> LL. 73–80

Man's purpose on earth is twofold, to praise God and to make "his Author's wisdom clear." Hence the chief purpose of education is to teach the young "heavenly truth." Although the child has a sharper conscience than the adult, he is naturally evil. This

138

tendency is encouraged when scoffing philosophy takes the place of religion, as so often happens when the child is educated in a public school. Other evils of this system result from letting a sensitive child mingle with older students who have already contracted bad habits. Cowper is particularly opposed to competition among boys, since he believes it often leads to permanently injured feelings.

According to Cowper, the teachers are partly responsible for the failure of the public schools. Motivated only by a love of money, most instructors neglect to train their students in morality:

> Much zeal in virtue's cause, all teachers boast,
> Though motives of mere lucre sway the most.

Even more at fault are the doting fathers who sentimentalize about their own school days, and send their children off to public institutions, not caring what they will learn so long as they make influential friends.

To avoid the evils of public schools, Cowper advocates home instruction. A father who can spare the time makes the best instructor, for he can direct a boy's feelings as well as his studies and will take more pains than a professional teacher. If the father is too busy, a tutor may take his place, but the tutor should be treated as one of the family, not as a menial. Finally, if the home environment is tainted, a boy may best be instructed by a humble clergyman, who does not have more than two boys to teach. Cowper concludes *Tirocinium* by saying that since the wealthy will not take his advice, he particularly urges people of the middle station to avoid the pitfall of placing their children in a public school.

Cowper's second volume of verse, which appeared in July 1785, won the admiration of the critics. The reviewer for the *Gentleman's Magazine* particularly liked the character sketches in *The Task,* such as that of Crazy Kate. He felt that Cowper's blank verse was superior to his couplets, and superior to the blank verse of any other author since Milton.[23] While the *Monthly*

Review objected slightly to the discursiveness of *The Task,* the writer immediately apologized for this defensible observation by adding that "an imagination like Mr. Cowper's is not to be controlled and confined within the bounds that criticism prescribes." What probably pleased the poet most was the observation that his verse is "always moral, yet never dull." [24]

The modern reader may not agree with this statement. Our taste and our values are such that many now read *The Task* only for the fine observations on nature that lie profusely scattered among Cowper's more didactic passages on ungodliness and corruption. The moralizing that the Augustans admired and the Victorians loved holds little charm for us. This change is partly the result of our finding many of the moral reflections banal and tediously repetitious. It is also owing, I think, to our different milieu. Modern readers live in a universe in which good and evil are likely to be weighed in terms of individual happiness, progress, or world peace, whereas the Augustans and Victorians generally tested good and evil by the standards of Protestant Christianity.

The eighteenth century did not think the worse of *The Task* because of its moralizing. The aged John Wesley, indeed, was disappointed that the poet had chosen so trifling a theme. "I think Cowper has done as much as is possible to be done with his lamentable story," he wrote. "I can only wish he had a better subject." [25] A more representative judgment was that of Burns. A sharp critic of hypocritical religious professions, he would have been the first to detect cant in another writer. Yet he has nothing but praise for Cowper, whom he calls "the best poet out of sight since Thomson." "How do you like Cowper?" he asks one of his correspondents. "Is not *The Task* a glorious poem? The Religion of *The Task,* bating a few scraps of Calvinistic Divinity, is the Religion of God & Nature; the religion that exalts, that ennobles man." [26]

The admiration of the critics would have sent another poet scurrying off to London to hear the plaudits of the literary world and to bask in the smiles of the famous. Cowper stayed at home,

little caring what the world at large thought, but delighted that
his poetry brought letters and visits from old friends. Meanwhile
his growing acquaintance with the Throckmortons gave him a
new interest. The estate of this distinguished Catholic family was
situated in the village of Weston, about a mile from Olney.
Several years earlier Cowper had received a key to their private
park, and he and Mrs. Unwin had formed the habit of going to
Weston almost daily to enjoy walking in the pleasure grounds.
But he had seen little of the owners until a son, John Courtenay
Throckmorton, took possession of the estate. Grandson of Sir
Robert Throckmorton, the young man, born July 27, 1753, had
been educated by the monks of Douay at a time when Catholics
were barred from English universities. Shortly before settling at
Weston, he had married Mary Catherine Gifford, a gracious
woman with a droll sense of humor. This young couple made the
first overture to become acquainted with the poet of their neighborhood when they invited him and Mrs. Unwin to witness a
balloon ascension on their estate.

It was the time when all western Europe was excited by the
new science of levitation, as it was called. The Montgolfier brothers of France had first introduced the new invention on June 5,
1783, when they sent aloft a balloon filled with preheated air. A
few months later their compatriots, the Robert brothers, successfully launched the first hydrogen balloon. Then, in October of
the same year, Jean Francois Pilâtre de Rozier made an ascent
and thus became the first man to fly. The news of these experi-
ments had spread through the Continent, inviting other scientists
to try to emulate if not surpass the amazing achievements of the
French. In England, when Vincent Lunardi announced that he
would make an ascension, thousands of Londoners gathered and
gazed with wonderment as the balloon left the ground and
soared over the roof tops.

Cowper had read the accounts of these flights. They had
aroused his curiosity and led him to make interesting speculations
upon the future of aviation. In a letter of December 15, 1783, he

wrote: "The invention of these new vehicles is yet in its infancy, yet already they seem to have attained a degree of perfection which navigation did not reach, till ages of experience had matured it, and science had exhausted both her industry and her skill, in its improvement." Having learned to keep aloft, Cowper added, man would probably next contrive wings and a tail to steer himself. "Should the point be carried," he continued,

"and man at last become as familiar with the air as he has long been with the ocean, will its consequences prove a mercy, or a judgement? I think, a judgement. First, because if a power to convey himself from place to place, like a bird, would have been good for him, his Maker would have formed him with such a capacity . . . Secondly, I think it will prove a judgement, because with the exercise of very little foresight, it is easy to prognosticate a thousand evils which the project must necessarily bring after it; amounting at last to the confusion of all order, the annihilation of all authority, with dangers both to property and person, and impunity to the offenders. Were I an absolute legislator, I would, therefore, make it death for a man to be convicted of flying, the moment he could be caught; and to bring him down from his altitudes by a bullet sent through his head or his carriage, should be no murder." [27]

Here, as elsewhere, Cowper illustrates his belief that advancement in science is contrary to nature and God's will. Nevertheless, he raises questions to which we, six generations later, can give but rueful answers.

Despite his opposition to the new science, Cowper and Mrs. Unwin accepted the Throckmorton invitation to watch a balloon ascension. When they arrived, they found a large assembly of eager spectators. For some reason the bag could not be filled, and the balloon failed to leave the ground. Cowper, sharing the disappointment of the other guests, wrote, "The endeavour was, I believe, very philosophically made, but such a process depends for its success upon such niceties as make it very precarious." [28] Socially, however, the visit was a great success. His hosts took particular notice of him and Mrs. Unwin, gave them chocolate, and asked them to stay to dinner. The guests from Orchard Side pleaded having a previous engagement, but a few days later, while walking in the park, they again met the Throckmortons. Bows and curtsies were exchanged, and Mrs. Throckmorton presented Cowper with a key to her private garden. Pleased by this sign that the young couple were eager to cultivate his acquaintance, Cowper wrote William Unwin, "They are Papists but much more amiable than many Protestants." Furthermore they were people of excellent breeding, a fact that counted heavily with the poet. The other local gentry, he observed, "are squires, merely such, purse-proud and sportsmen. But Mr. T. is altogether a man of fashion, and respectable on every account." [29] Although Cowper was eager to know his neighbors better, he felt he could not properly entertain these people of fashion in his humble home. But they were not purse-proud, as he remarked. Consequently he proceeded by degrees from taking chocolate with them, to dining at the Hall, and finally to entertaining them at Orchard Side.

Because the Throckmortons were Catholics, certain neighbors treated them with hostility. Cowper shared the common bias against Roman Catholicism, but he was enough the man of the world to be able to prize the Throckmortons for themselves. When he dined at the Hall, he often met George, a younger brother of Mr. Throckmorton, and Mr. Gregson, the Catholic chaplain. To dine in the company of a Catholic priest must at first have seemed strange to Cowper and Mrs. Unwin, but they found Mr. Gregson a quiet, well-bred man and came to esteem him. The hosts and their guests from Orchard Side scrupulously avoided religious discussion. After years of dwelling overmuch upon his religious difficulties, it was probably a healthy change for Cowper to turn to lighter subjects which brought out his more playful and witty disposition.

One of the happiest moments of his life occurred when he received a letter from his cousin Lady Hesketh. She had seen his poetry and, like the rest of England, had laughed over *John Gilpin*. If he could write with such whimsicality, he must be cured, she felt, of his morbid religious obsession. Consequently, after a lapse of seventeen years, she made an overture to renew their correspondence. He replied immediately: "It is no new thing with you to give pleasure; but I will venture to say that you do not often give more than you gave me this morning. When I came down to breakfast, and found upon the table a letter franked by my uncle, and when opening the frank I found it contained a letter from you, I said within myself—'This is just as it should be. We are all grown young again, and the days I thought I should see no more are actually returned.' " [30]

In his earlier years at Olney he had been willing to cut himself off from the past. But the tragic events of his youth — his disappointment in love, the abandonment of a career, the first painful period of insanity — were now distant events. His memory returned rather to the pleasurable hours he had spent with Harriet and Theodora, the evenings at Ranelagh, the holidays at the seaside, the flashing moments of gaiety and youthful laughter. The resumption of the tie with Lady Hesketh gave him an opportunity to engage in pleasant reminiscence. He also brought her up to date on the details of his life at Olney. He listed the virtues of Mrs. Unwin, gave a whimsical account of his own appearance in middle age, stated his preferences for tea, wine, and food, and explained his writing habits. When Lady Hesketh inquired about his finances, he told her that he and Mrs. Unwin shared expenses, and that they lived simply but adequately on their small joint income.

Soon afterward gifts began to arrive, a silver snuff box, a splendid pocketbook, a fine watch chain, and a writing desk that the poet described as "the most elegant, the compactest, and most commodious desk in the world." [31] Everything with the exception of the desk had been sent by Lady Hesketh. That handsome piece of furniture, she informed him, was a present from one who chose to remain anonymous. Soon afterward he received a letter from his mysterious benefactor, announcing that an annuity of fifty pounds was being settled on him. The unnamed and self-effacing friend was his old love Theodora. Cowper probably guessed as much, but Lady Hesketh told him she was pledged to secrecy, and he did not press his inquiries.

144

Subsequently his income was further increased by a second annuity of fifty pounds through the bounty of Lady Hesketh and other relatives.

When Lady Hesketh announced, after much urging, that she would pass the summer of 1786 at Olney, Cowper's joy reached the height of ecstasy. One problem weighed heavily on his mind, however. Orchard Side was much too small to accommodate his cousin and her servants. Consequently he and Mrs. Unwin spent weeks scurrying about Olney in search of lodgings. Nothing seemed quite suitable, until at last someone suggested the vicarage next door. Because the incumbent clergyman, the Reverend Mr. Postlethwaite, occupied only two rooms, the poet easily arranged for Harriet to have the rest of the commodious house. On the day set for her arrival he sent Kitchener, his gardener, to meet her coach at Newport and escort her suite to Olney. The townspeople had been appraised of the intended visit of the titled lady. When her coach appeared the church bells pealed out a welcome, the lacemakers and merchants stood gaping, and her middle-aged cousin rushed from his home to greet the most beloved of his living relatives.

Five years earlier Mrs. Thrale, the friend of Dr. Johnson, had set down in her diary an interesting though somewhat malicious description of Harriet:

"Dear Lady Hesketh! and how like a Naples washball she is: so round, so sweet, so plump, so polished, so red, so white — every Quality of a Naples washball. With more Beauty than almost anybody, so much Wit as many a body; and six times the Quantity of polite Literature — Belles Lettres as we call 'em; Lady Hesketh is wholly neglected by the men: — why is that? if it were Age that stopt her Progress — *Volontiere*, but many as old are caress'd, admired, and followed:

"I never can find out what that Woman does to keep people from adoring her." [32]

Cowper could have attested that one person adored her unfailingly. Her arrival satisfied his every expectation. He begrudged the time he spent from her company writing letters, and when he did write, he filled his pages with descriptions of her charm. Once more he could enjoy the devotion of two ladies. Once more Mrs. Unwin might have felt overshadowed by a younger and more beautiful woman, but this time she was better able to share the poet. Lady Hesketh was Cowper's cousin and the companion of his youth, not a fascinating stranger that had appeared out of nowhere. Besides, the parson's widow was no doubt much impressed by the fashionable Lady Hesketh, with her handsome coach, her train of servants, and her elegant manners.

Lady Hesketh, in turn, was favorably disposed toward her cousin's companion. Mrs. Unwin was a cheerful and accomplished woman, Harriet wrote her sister Theodora. "When she speaks upon grave subjects, she does express herself with a puritanical tone, and in puritanical expressions, but on all other subjects she seems to have a great disposition to cheerfulness and mirth; and indeed, had she not, she could not have gone through all she has. I must say, too, that she seems to be very well read in the English poets, as appears by several little quotations she makes from time to time, and has a true taste for what is excellent in that way. There is something very affectionate and sincere in her manner. No one can express more heartily than she does her joy to have me at Olney." [33]

In another letter Lady Hesketh provided a delightful sketch of Mrs. Unwin and Cowper in their domestic setting: "She sits knitting on one side of the table in her spectacles, and he on the other reading (when he is not employed in writing) in *his*. In winter, his morning studies are always carried on in a room by himself; but as his evenings are spent in the winter in transcribing he usually, I find, does this *vis-a-vis* Mrs. Unwin. At this time of year he writes always in the morning, in what he calls his *boudoir*; this is in the garden; it has a door and a window; just holds a small table with a desk and two chairs." [34]

The summer of 1786 was filled with business and pleasure. Shortly after Cowper had sent off his second volume to the printer, he began his translation of Homer. This time there was no secret about the project. Having decided to publish the work by subscription, he was eager for subscribers. When Hill told him his old friend George Colman had inquired about him, he forgave Colman's failure to acknowledge his gift copy of the earlier volume of verse, and sent Colman a cordial letter, asking him to help circulate his proposals for an edition of Homer. Walter Bagot, an old Westminster boy who had recently renewed his acquaintance with Cowper, also subscribed twenty pounds and promised to obtain further contributions among his acquaintances. With a considerable number of subscribers already on his list, Cowper felt compelled to keep at work. Unlike many poets, he maintained a schedule, setting apart an hour or two of the day for writing. He had done this when composing his own verse, and such regularity was still easier now that he was engaged in translation.

Before coming to Olney, Lady Hesketh had heard of the proposed edition of Homer. She had tried to further interest in it by bringing it to the attention of Paul Henry Maty, editor of the *New Review*. Accepting a copy of the prospectus, Maty told her he would review it in his periodical. When the review appeared, however, it greatly disappointed the lady and her cousin. Instead of lauding the sample translations provided in the prospectus, Maty had severely criticized them.[35] Undiscouraged, however, Cowper proceeded methodically with his translation, and Lady Hesketh spent part of the summer transcribing his work. Meanwhile the summer days afforded them leisure for long talks, for rides about the country in the Hesketh coach, and for pleasant visits at the Throckmortons.

Shortly before Lady Hesketh's arrival, Mr. Throckmorton had made an interesting proposal to Cowper. The young squire suggested that Cowper and Mrs. Unwin move into a fine house which he owned at Weston. The poet immediately thought of it as a permanent country home for Lady Hesketh and wrote her about it. When she arrived in Olney and saw Cowper's shabby residence, situated in the commercial section of the town, she urged him to move to Weston himself. Promising to visit him each year, she pointed out that the Weston Lodge was large enough to accom-

modate her suite as well as Cowper's household. Everything was
in favor of the move. The Throckmortons, eager to have Cowper
as a near neighbor, offered him the house at the same rental he
was paying at Orchard Side. Instead of being in dreary surroundings, the poet would be able to step out of his house into the
pleasure grounds of the Throckmorton estate at any time. Finally,
he had seen enough of his Catholic acquaintances to want to
strengthen his ties with them. After inspecting the house, Cowper
was easily prevailed upon to take it. The Lodge was a commodious two-and-a-half story residence, with double parlors, broad
windows, and a charming view. Here he would be able to have
his own study in addition to all the other advantages. To put the
house in repairs would take some time, but meanwhile he could
look forward with pleasure to a change from the place where he
had been confined for twenty years.

The translation of Homer, the preparations for moving, and
the company of Lady Hesketh, who had delayed her departure,
kept Cowper pleasantly occupied during the fall months. Only
one thing occurred to disturb him; that was a stern letter from
John Newton. Although the correspondence with his former
mentor had continued without interruption, relations of late
had been somewhat strained. Several incidents had contributed
to the situation. In the spring of 1784, Newton had asked Cowper
to write some prose pieces on religious subjects for the *Theological Miscellany*, a periodical in which the clergyman was interested. Cowper had declined, saying that he was seldom free from
despair, and "that a mind thus occupied is but indifferently qualified for the consideration of theological matters." He added,
"The most useful and delightful topics of that kind are to me
a forbidden fruit; — I tremble if I approach them." [36] When the
clergyman made his request, he did not know that Cowper was
busy writing *The Task*. For some reason Cowper had let William
Unwin negotiate with the publisher for its publication, and did
not inform Newton about the poem until it was in the hands of
the printer. This neglect irked the clergyman. "He was not
pleased that my manuscript was not first transmitted to him,"

Cowper wrote William Unwin, "and I have cause to suspect that he was even mortified at being informed that a certain inscribed poem was not inscribed to himself." [37]

Newton, of course, had heard about Lady Austen, but that affair had not seemed to disturb him, possibly because, at Cowper's request, the charming lady had dutifully called on the clergyman in London. But he was much displeased by the reports his former parishioners sent him during the summer of 1786. Apparently they had described Cowper's growing friendship with his Catholic neighbors, the visit of the fashionable Lady Hesketh, and the excursions in the coach. Fearful that his former disciple was becoming a worldly sinner, Newton addressed a stern letter to Mrs. Unwin, criticizing her conduct as well as Cowper's and observing that their friends in London were much grieved to hear of their lapse from grace.

Cowper, as he indicates in a letter to William Unwin, was extremely offended by Newton's reproach. Although he suppressed his anger in his reply, he treated the matter with firmness and with much more sense than the clergyman had. "Your letter to Mrs. Unwin," he wrote,

"concerning our conduct and the offence taken at it in our neighborhood, gave us both a great deal of concern; and she is still deeply affected by it. Of this you may assure yourself, that if our friends in London have been grieved, they have been misinformed; which is the more probable, because the bearers of the intelligence hence to London are not always very scrupulous concerning the truth of their reports. . . . They often see us get into Lady Hesketh's carriage, and rather uncharitably suppose that it always carries us into a scene of dissipation, which, in fact, it never does. We visit, indeed, at Mr. Throckmorton's and at Gayhurst; rarely, however, at Gayhurst, on account of the greater distance; more frequently, though not very frequently at Weston, both because it is nearer, and because our business in the house that is making ready for us often calls us that way. The rest of our journeys are to Bozeat Turnpike and back again; or perhaps to the cabinet-maker's at Newport. . . . What good we can get or can do in these visits, is another question, — which they, I am sure, are not at all qualified to solve. Of this we are both sure, that under the guidance of Providence we have formed these connections; that we should have hurt the Christian cause, rather than have served it, by a prudish abstinence from them." [38]

Such a letter, especially to Newton, Cowper could not have written ten years earlier. His views had undergone a profound change since those days. Although he still believed in the principles of Evangelicalism, he had shaken off much of the somberness of the earlier period. Cheerfulness had returned; he was now a famous poet, with friends of the sort he had enjoyed in his youth. But, in the midst of this second spring, just when things seemed brightest, the dark cloud of despair again descended upon him.

❧ VIII ❧

At Weston

It is a sort of April-weather life we lead in this world. A little sunshine is generally the prelude to a storm.

LETTER TO WALTER BAGOT, JANUARY 3, 1787

LADY HESKETH's visit to Olney lasted until mid-November, 1786. The day after her departure Cowper turned the key on Orchard Side and, with Mrs. Unwin, took possession of their more elegant residence. The poet left his "old prison" with a sigh. He recalled that he had once been happy there, in those first years following his conversion. Later Orchard Side had been a refuge from the stormy world. Once settled in the comfortable Lodge at Weston, however, he admitted that he had gained much by the exchange. "I find myself here situated exactly to my mind," he wrote Joseph Hill. "Weston is one of the prettiest villages in England, and the walks about it at all seasons of the year delightful. I know that you will rejoice with me in the change that we have made, and for which I am altogether indebted to Lady Hesketh. It is a change as great as (to compare metropolitan things with rural) from St. Giles's to Grosvenor Square." [1]

The middle-aged couple were hardly settled in their new home when they received sad tidings. William Unwin, who had been traveling in the west of England with his Evangelical friend Henry Thornton, had fallen ill of a putrid fever at Winchester. At first he seemed to be recovering; then a turn for the worse occurred, and he died November 29, 1786. The loss of her only

151

son was a bitter blow to Mrs. Unwin, but she had her sturdy faith to console her. Cowper, to whom the clergyman was almost a son, was less well prepared to cope with the sad event. It brought his melancholy to the surface and awakened a train of gloomy reflections on his own unhappy lot. "The mind does not perfectly recover its tone after a shock like that which has been felt so lately," he wrote Lady Hesketh.[2]

In order to shut out his melancholy thoughts he devoted more time to his Homer. He had started the translation, "hunted into it" as a diversion from misery. Now that his anguish had increased, he plunged into the work with the desperation of a sick man seeking an anodyne. But his efforts were to no avail. Perhaps he fatigued himself with overwork. In any event, by January he was suffering from a nervous fever and restless nights, which were again filled with horrible dreams. When he wrote Lady Hesketh about them, she tried to persuade him that dreams are no more than a normal operation of the fancy. But Cowper's experiences had led him to other conclusions. He had, he replied, a mind as free from superstition as anyone, and did not consider dreams generally as "predictive." Yet everyone must admit that in ancient times God had employed dreams to communicate with men. Since he had later made his will clear in Scripture, he no longer had occasion to speak so often through the medium of dreams, the poet reasoned. Nevertheless, God still used them at times to warn blind and fallible man of dangers man could not see. "As to my own peculiar experience in the dreaming way I have only this to observe," Cowper continued. "I have not believed that I shall perish, because in my dreams I have been told it, but because I have had hardly any but terrible dreams for thirteen years, and therefore I have spent the greatest part of that time most unhappily. They have either tinged my mind with melancholy or filled it with terrors, and the effect has been unavoidable."[3]

Every year since his attack of insanity in January 1773, Cowper had dreaded the approach of winter. Now, during his first January at Weston, he became so disturbed in mind that he was finally forced to stop work on his Homer. His letter to Lady Hesketh was the last he wrote for several months, for his nervous fever became so bad that before the month was out his mind once more became clouded with insanity.

We know relatively little about the attack of 1787. Although of briefer duration, it was apparently a worse fit of derangement than the two earlier ones. According to Thomas Wright, who does not cite sources for his information, Cowper again tried to commit suicide. He was stopped once from hanging himself when Mrs. Unwin entered the room and cut him down. Upon another occasion "he was prevented from taking his life in an even more dreadful manner by the sudden entrance of Mr. Bull." [4] Because of these attempts he may have been confined part of the time by a straitjacket. There are vague allusions to such a device in his letters. Furthermore, James Boswell, with his ear for curious facts, had heard that the poet had "been woefully deranged — in a strait waistcoat — and now is sometimes so ill that they take away his shoebuckles, that he may have nothing within his reach with which he can hurt himself." [5]

When he resumed letter-writing Cowper told Newton, "My indisposition could not be of a worse kind. . . . The sight of any face except Mrs. Unwin's was to me an insupportable grievance; and when it has happened that by *forcing* himself into my hiding-place, some friend has found me out, he has had no great cause to exult in his success, as Mr. Bull can tell you. From this dreadful condition of mind I emerged suddenly; so suddenly that Mrs. Unwin, having no notice of such a change herself, could give none to any body." [6]

By August he had recovered sufficiently to resume dining with the Throckmortons. Unlike his earlier attacks, this one did not cause any important change in his outlook. He continued to believe that by a special decree of Providence he was damned for eternity. But, as heretofore, he was able to hope that some singular manifestation might yet reveal that God had removed his sentence. He alludes to this hope in a letter to Mrs. King, one of his correspondents of later life. After explaining that his "singularities" of mind would not allow him to promise to visit her, he observes, "But all this may vanish in a moment; and if it please God, it shall." [7] Again, in a letter to Bull, he remarks, "I would I were a Hottentot, or even a dissenter, so that my views of a hereafter were more comfortable. But such as I am, hope, if it please God, may visit even me, and should we ever meet again, possibly we may part no more." [8] The only change, if indeed it were a change, concerned his relationship with Newton. After the attack he wrote the clergyman that he could now recognize and cherish him as his old and beloved friend. Yet for the past thirteen years, Cowper maintained, he had had such an unreal sense of Newton's identity that when he had written him during that period he had had to act a part and practice dissimulation.[9] This observation is the more curious since there seems to be no evidence in the earlier correspondence that he regarded the clergyman as a stranger. One wonders if the poet had really held this curious delusion for so long a time or if, writing so soon after his recent attack, he was still not entirely in his right mind.

Upon his recovery Cowper resumed work on his Homer and, except for the abiding fear of damnation, passed a relatively happy period of four years. Living at the Lodge contributed much to his enjoyment. For his daily walks he had merely to step out of doors into the beautiful park of the Throckmortons, where the land was so well drained, he said, that even in winter a lady could stroll through the grounds without wetting her slipper. The new residence was spacious enough to accommodate several guests, and Cowper frequently played host to Lady Hesketh and other relatives and friends. Then, too, he was now so situated that he could see the Throckmortons almost every day, and the more he encountered his Catholic neighbors, the more he esteemed them.

Mr. Throckmorton and his brother George were the finest gentlemen in England, Cowper declared, and there was no one who could better bring out his lighter side than Mrs. Frog, as he playfully called the mistress of the Hall. Their friendship, which was now extended to him in full measure, was one of the best restoratives he could have had after the recent attack of insanity. In September he wrote Lady Hesketh, "They have generally drunk tea with us twice a week, and all the other days we have either dined or drunk tea with them." [10] During his Olney years few books had been available, with the result that he had read little, but after his illness, the Throckmortons gave him free access to their well-stocked library. No favor seemed to be too irksome for them to perform. Mrs. Frog, having volunteered to act as Cowper's amanuensis, spent long hours making transcripts of his Homer, and when she left the Hall on a visit, George Throckmorton and Mr. Gregson, the Catholic chaplain, supplied their services as copyists. Cowper's regard for the priest increased upon closer acquaintance. In company the clergyman was likely to be as silent as himself, the poet remarked, but when they were alone they found abundant topics for conversation. They did not discuss religion, however. This omission was perhaps wise, inasmuch as Cowper's mental disturbance was so closely related to his religious obsessions. On the other hand, Catholicism with its strong consolation for the believer might have served to restore the poet's peace of mind.

Cowper's life at Weston was further enlivened by the visits of two young men whose friendship he made late in life. His acquaintance with Samuel Rose began when the young man, then a student at Glasgow, stopped at Weston to pay his respects to the poet whose works he had read and admired. The call was made in January 1787, just a few days before Cowper's lapse from sanity, but the poet remembered his young visitor, and when he began to recover he wrote his first letter to Rose. The correspondence continued, and Rose made several other visits to Weston, staying for several days at a time. Later, when he became an attorney in London, he performed various commissions for Cowper. It was Rose who first brought the poems of Burns to his attention. Cowper's comment is well-known — "though they be written in a language that is new to me, and many of them on subjects inferior to the author's ability, I think them on the whole a very extraordinary production." [11] Cowper further qualified his praise of Burns, however, in a letter to Lady Hesketh. "I think him an extraordinary genius, and the facility with which he rhymes and versifies in a kind of measure not in itself very easy to execute, appears to me remarkable," he said. "But at the same time both his measure and his language are so terribly barbarous, that though he has some humour, and more good sense, he is not a pleasing poet to an English reader, nor do I think him worth your purchasing." [12]

Cowper's second young friend was John Johnson, a cousin on his mother's side of the family. For several years Cowper had heard nothing of the Donnes. He was delighted therefore when young Johnson, a grandson of his mother's brother, Roger Donne, visited him in January 1790. This shy youth, then a student at Cambridge, quickly won his affection. The bachelor poet had always enjoyed the company of younger people, and his youthful cousin, whom he nicknamed Johnny of Norfolk, became almost a foster son. In June 1791 Johnny brought his sister Catharine and his aunt Mrs. Balls to Weston for a visit. Cowper found his three cousins such good company that he urged them to settle permanently in the neighborhood. They were agreeable to the idea, but failing to find a suitable residence, they returned to Norfolk. Johnny continued to pay the poet frequent visits, however, and the family tie, reforged after so many years, would never again be broken.

Shortly after Johnson's first visit, another cousin, Mrs. Anne Bodham of Norfolk, sent the poet a portrait of his mother. This bitter-sweet reminder of his childhood profoundly moved him. "I had rather possess it than the richest jewel in the British crown," he said, "for I loved her with an affection that her death, fifty-two years since, has not in the least abated." [13] The memories called up by the picture led him to compose one of his best poems. Although he excelled at writing occasional verse, no occasion had hitherto so strongly affected him, and his lines on his mother's picture represent an almost perfect example of the spontaneous overflow of powerful feeling. He himself observed that, with the exception of his verses to Mrs. Unwin, he found more pleasure in writing this poem than any other he ever composed.[14]

Meanwhile, though busily engaged in translating Homer, Cowper snatched time to write to a growing list of correspondents. After a silence of twenty-five years he heard from his old Temple friend, Clotworthy Rowley, now an attorney in Ireland. Though they were never to see each other again, they exchanged letters, and Rowley secured several Irish subscribers to the edition of Homer. Another correspondent of later days was Mrs. King, wife of the Reverend John King of Pertenhall, Bedfordshire. Cowper accepted her invitation to become a pen friend because she had known his deceased brother. He saw her only once, in June 1790, when she and Mr. King stopped briefly at Weston. Like most of his correspondents, she sent him delicacies and other gifts which he acknowledged with his customary warmth and graciousness.

Generally he allotted the hour between rising and breakfast to his correspondence, so that he could devote the rest of the day to the business of translation. He attached no literary importance to his letters; they were simply the means by which he kept in touch with a half-dozen friends and relatives. To have labored over his correspondence would have seemed an affectation. "I never aim at any thing above the pitch of every day's scribble, when I write to those I love," he remarked.[15] Yet these letters, written in haste, with no thought of their preservation, have secured him a permanent place in English literature. As a translator of Homer, he is almost forgotten; as a poet, he shares honors with his contemporaries Burns and Blake; but as a writer of personal letters he gives place to none.

If the letters of Horace Walpole are better known, that is because they provide incisive comments on the passing scene, witty remarks on current fashions, and discerning estimates of men in public office. Walpole is the chronicler of high life, the unofficial columnist of the fashionable world. His letters reflect the fastidious, sharply satirical, and often snobbish tastes of a man of society. Above everything else he is an eighteenth-century sophisticate. Cowper, by contrast, is a mere provincial. His world is a tiny corner of England, a stage on which no great events occur, and where the actors are usually of no consequence in public affairs. Rowland E. Prothers aptly contrasts the different worlds of these two letter-writers when he observes, "Walpole composes in the blaze of the lamps that lit the Pantheon, of the torches that waited on coaches and sedans, or of the wax tapers that illuminated the faro tables. Cowper writes, as it were, in the low-ceiled room of a lace-maker's cottage at Olney, by the light of a solitary farthing candle." [16] Living in two different worlds, each writer captured the spirit of his own milieu, but the world of Cowper, partly because it is the sort of microcosm that most people inhabit, seems more real.

Cowper's vivid pictures of English country life have often been compared to those in Jane Austen's novels. But another comparison, made by a French writer, seems even more apt. English literature, wrote T. De Wyzewa, possesses two great works, infinitely original, that permit us to penetrate with the most familiar intimacy into human life. One is the letters of Cowper. The other is that strange and marvelous biography of Samuel Johnson.[17] This is an interesting analogy. Johnson's world is a larger one, to be sure, but the genius of Boswell brings it to life and helps us to see its central figure as clearly, though perhaps not so accurately, as we see Cowper and his little world through his letters.

It is one of the many ironies of English literature that the joys of domestic life have been best celebrated by unmarried authors, like Herrick, Jane Austen, Lamb, and Cowper. The letters of Cowper are especially helpful, Sainte-Beuve has remarked, in aiding us to understand the wellspring of his fine poems of domestic life.[18] What is more, he has the ability to make his reader almost as much interested in the minor events of his *ménage* as in the trivia of one's own household. The reader admires Mrs. Unwin's thoughtfulness in fattening turkeys and ducks to send to Joseph Hill in return for untold favors, her forethought in brewing an extra quantity of small beer for Lady Hesketh's servants, her industry in knitting Cowper's woolen stockings, a chore reserved for the evening when she can sit by the fire with her busy needles while he reads aloud from the Bible or a book of travels. One rejoices with the inmates over the arrival of a gift from Hill, Lady Hesketh, or Mrs. King, whether it be a barrel of oysters, a basket of mackerel, a dozen bottles of wine, or a hand-made quilt. There is a satisfaction in watching the relationship with the Throckmortons develop from rare and rather formal meetings to the stage of almost daily visits and easy intimacy. And one almost shares Mrs. Unwin's admiring interest when the poet tries on his new wig, appears resplendent with new buttons on his coat, or reads a complimentary notice in the *Gentleman's Magazine*.

The well-nigh perfect picture of retirement may particularly attract older readers. Most of us have two strong and antithetical desires — on the one hand, a longing for activity, adventure, and a full life, and on the other, a desire for peace, freedom from social ties, and a quiet existence. While these conflicting passions seem to abide with us forever, the joys of retirement have a greater appeal as we reach middle life. As a young man Cowper had enjoyed a life of social activity in the busy metropolis, but at an earlier age than most he had sought and found a quiet corner of England. Thereafter, if he ever felt a desire to cut a figure on the larger stage, he satisfied the whim by sending his poems into the world while he continued to hug his fireside. No one can regret his decision. Indeed, his life of retirement seems so tranquil, so undisturbed by petty annoyances, so pleasant withal, that one may momentarily envy his existence. But not for long. The reader need only encounter one of the letters in which Cowper describes his mental anguish to be sharply reminded that this gentle soul, far from being an enviable creature, was one of the most unhappy of men.

Various brief collections of the letters have appeared in which the editor has selected chiefly those epistles that demonstrate Cowper's playful wit and his ability to write charmingly about trivial events. Such volumes, while they reveal his art as a letter-writer, fail to give a complete picture of the man. They have also led certain critics to the false opinion that the correspondence consists of a pleasant froth but lacks substance. Lytton Strachey, for instance, remarks, "Cowper had nothing to say, and he said it beautifully . . . His letters are stricken with sterility; they are dried up; they lack the juices of life." [19] This statement is exaggerated to the point of inaccuracy. Although Cowper surveyed the larger world through the loopholes of retreat, his letters contain much material on the great religious revival, interesting and often shrewd observations on nature and man, and comments on such current topics as the war with America, the French Revolution, and the English reaction to it. As Lodwick C. Hartley has so well demonstrated, the letters are also an important source of information on Cowper's keen interest in the Sunday School Movement, the abolitionist cause, and the awakening English conscience on the treatment of animals.[20] Thus while Cowper is not a social historian in the sense that Walpole is, his letters provide many illuminating side lights on the eighteenth century.

The tone and substance of the letters depend largely upon the particular correspondent addressed. Cowper can be frolicsome with the youthful Johnny Johnson, formal and respectful to his old schoolfellow, Lord Chancellor Thurlow, firm but polite with Walter Churchey, an undistinguished poet who sought to climb to prominence on his shoulders. Perhaps his best letters are addressed to Lady Hesketh. With her he is always affectionate and candid. Besides giving her a history of local events, he describes his state of mind, omitting the worst details only because he knows she will suffer with him. He makes no such reservations with Newton. Indeed, his letters to the clergyman form a chronicle of his terrible mental agony. Yet he is not always so frank upon other subjects when writing to the censorious clergyman. He withholds, for instance, details of his association with the Throckmortons, and when he describes his writing activity, he feels he must apologize to the strict Calvinist for translating a pagan classic instead of contributing further literary material to the Evangelical cause.

With the Reverend William Bull, who was equally well acquainted with his religious mania, Cowper can be more at ease. He can even jest with Bull on the subject of religion, something he would not dare do with Newton. "As for me," he wrote Bull on one occasion, "I go on at the old rate, giving all my time to Homer, who I suppose was a Presbyterian too, for I understand the Church of England will by no means acknowledge him as one of hers . . . if Presbyterians ever find the way to heaven, you and I may know each other in that better world, and rejoice in the recital of the terrible things that we endured in this. I will wager sixpence with you now, that when that day comes, you shall acknowledge my story a more wonderful one than yours: — only order your executors to put sixpence in your mouth when they bury you, that you may have the wherewithal to pay me." [21]

Many critics have commented on Cowper's humor and whimsicality, but perhaps the best treatment of the subject is by E. V. Lucas. He observes that whimsicality is essentially a modern form of humor. Touches of it appear in Gray and Walpole, but Cowper was the real father of whimsical writing, since Lamb, who popularized it, comes after him. The chief ingredient of this form of literary fun is an autobiographical quality, a playful but unaffected egotism that turns the trivialities of daily existence into amusing incidents.[22] For example, when Cowper thanks Rose for sending him Pope's translation of Homer, he describes a slight mishap with mock gravity and ends by making a sly allusion to Pope and himself as rival translators. He writes:

"Your very handsome present of Pope's Homer has arrived safe, notwithstanding an accident that befel him by the way. The Hall servant brought the parcel from Olney, resting it on the pommel of the saddle, and his horse fell with him. Pope was in consequence rolled in the dirt, but being well coated got no damage. If augurs and soothsayers were not out of fashion, I should have consulted one or two of that order in hope of learning from

them that this fall was ominous. I have found a place for him
on the chiffonier in the parlour, where he makes a splendid
appearance, and where he shall not long want a neighbour, one
who if less popular than himself, shall at least look as big
as he." [23]

Another quality that adds charm to the letters is Cowper's
ability to dramatize small events. He and Mrs. Unwin will be
sitting quietly in the parlor when the servant announces a caller,
or there will be a sudden commotion in the kitchen followed by
the appearance of a bustling electioneering candidate. Or Cowper will describe setting out for his morning walk in the park.
Suddenly he and Mrs. Unwin hear voices and laughter and then
perceive the Throckmortons approaching from an adjoining
field. Thus he makes a commonplace meeting with his nearest
neighbors seem as unusual as a chance encounter in the heart
of London.

To savor the full delight of the letters, one should read them
consecutively, as they appear in large collections, such as that
by Thomas Wright. The effect is similar to that produced by a
good novel, except that, in lieu of a plot, the reader will find
his satisfaction in the hundreds of little episodes, the vividly
described setting, and, above all, in the delightful characters.
The story has no villains, and its heroine is an aging widow who
never marries the hero. Yet it is a love story of a kind, with a
central character possessed of a strong sense of chivalry. It is also
a tale of an heroic struggle, not against a visible adversary, but
with a dragon that is no less real because it exists only in the
hero's mind.

Although Homer absorbed most of Cowper's poetic energies
from 1785 to 1791, duty, the desire to pay a compliment, or the
inspiration of the moment led him to write occasionally on
other subjects. One day a Mr. Cox, Clerk of All-Saints Church
in Northampton, knocked at the Lodge. A servant showed him
into the parlor, where Mr. Cox awkwardly stated his business.
He had walked a long distance to request Cowper to write some

appropriate verses to be printed with the yearly list of the deceased in his parish. The poet, half-flattered and half-amused by the earnest gentleman, agreed to accept the assignment. Describing the incident to Lady Hesketh, he joked in his whimsical manner, "A fig for poets who write epitaphs upon individuals! I have written *one* that serves *two hundred* persons." [24] Despite his jesting, he took the task seriously and for six years produced mortuary verses for All-Saints parish. The poems, all on the brevity of life, reflect both the skill and the elegiac mood of the poet who had often mused on man's mortality.

Humorous verses also flowed from his pen — *On the Death of Mrs. Throckmorton's Bullfinch, On a Mischievous Bull,* and the delightfully amusing *Retired Cat.* Complimentary verses were addressed to Lady Hesketh, Mrs. Throckmorton, and Miss Stapleton, the fiancée of George Throckmorton. In a more serious vein, and remembered among his best productions, were *The Dog and the Water Lily* and *Yardley Oak.* In 1789, upon the recovery of George III from a period of insanity, Cowper wrote his *Annus Mirabilis* and two other poems that tactfully celebrated the King's restoration to mental health. His only motive was to congratulate one who, like himself, had suffered the loss of his senses. It happened, however, that in the following year, upon the death of Thomas Warton, the poet laureateship became vacant. Lady Hesketh, feeling that the congratulatory verses could be put to good purpose, offered to use her influence to have Cowper appointed to the position. No one at the time could have given more distinction to the laureateship than the man Coleridge was soon to describe as the best of living poets, but Cowper did not want the office. "It would make me miserable," he wrote Lady Hesketh,[25] and that ended the matter.

Much as he liked to be obliging, he could not return to writing hymns, even though a request came from his esteemed friend, William Bull. "Ask possibilities and they shall be performed," he replied, "but ask not hymns from a man suffering by despair as I do. I could not sing the Lord's song were it to save my life, banished as I am, not to a strange land, but to a remoteness from

His presence." [26] A sense of gratitude, however, caused him to comply with John Newton's request that he translate a series of letters that the clergyman had received. The letters, written in Latin, described the sinful life and eventual conversion of Helperus Van Lier, a Dutch minister. The turning point in the clergyman's career had occurred upon his reading Newton's *Cardiphonia,* a set of lessons in Evangelical principles. No doubt Newton wanted the letters translated for publication in order to provide still another testimonial of an Evangelical conversion, though incidentally the correspondence gave testimony to Newton's persuasiveness. Cowper translated the letters during the summer of 1790. They were published under the title *The Power of Grace Illustrated,* with due credit given to the translator. [27]

Previously, in *Charity* and in *The Task,* Cowper had denounced the institution of slavery. He had needed no urging to write on this subject, for his humane and Christian character was sufficient to place him on the side of the reformers. It happened, however, that the strongest group of abolitionists were the Evangelicals. During the 1780's they were vigorously campaigning to end trafficking in blacks and to destroy the institution of slavery in the Colonies. In 1787 William Wilberforce, the most prominent layman among the Evangelicals, announced that he would lead the abolitionist fight in Parliament. The same year a committee was formed in London to work for the prohibition of the slave trade. To further their purpose the members asked for tracts and ballads to serve as propaganda. John Newton, now as ardent an abolitionist as he had once been a conscienceless slave captain, contributed *Thoughts upon the African Slave Trade.* Cowper, perhaps through Newton, was also asked to write for the great cause. Whether or not he was told specifically what kind of poems were wanted does not appear, but his colloquially expressed ballads, designed to be sung to popular tunes, were admirably suited to the purpose. At a time when only a minority of the people could read, a ballad, sung to a familiar tune, was one of the best means of circulating an opinion. Illiterates could quickly learn the simple words from others, and the repetition of the song drove home the views expressed. All ranks enjoyed the broadside ballads, which were sung in the streets, at the coffeehouses and taverns, and wherever the masses congregated. Of the four ballads that Cowper is known to have composed *The Negro's Complaint* enjoyed the greatest popularity. Thousands of copies were printed by the London abolitionists.

Cowper's feelings for the slaves were deep-seated. Doubtless he had learned of their condition from Newton and from reading the accounts of travelers. So great was his compassion for these poor, benighted creatures that for once doubts arose in his mind about the validity of Evangelical teachings. One could endure the thought of enslavement, he wrote, if that situation were to be followed by salvation. But because the Negroes were religiously unenlightened, according to most Evangelicals they were destined for hell. How could this double penalty accord with divine justice? He knew the answer one got from the theologians, he wrote Newton. "What passes upon this grain of sand which we call the earth is trivial considered with reference to those purposes that have the universe for their object. And lastly — All these things will be accounted for and explained hereafter." But Cowper could no longer be content with such reasoning. "An answer like this would have satisfied me once," he said, "when I was myself happy; — for I have frequently thought that the happy are easily reconciled to the woes of the miserable. But in the school of affliction I have learned to cavil and to question; and finding myself in my own case reduced frequently to the necessity of accounting for my own lot by the means of an uncontrollable sovereignty which gives no account of its matters, am apt to discover, what appear to me, tremendous effects of the same sovereignty in the case of others. Then I feel — I will not tell you what — and yet I must — a wish that I had never been, a wonder that I am, and an ardent but hopeless desire not to be." [28] Such reflections caused him to return with a sense of relief to the more congenial task of writing about ancient Greece and Troy.

Cowper had clearly in mind what he wished to do in his version of Homer. Above everything else he wanted to produce a text that would preserve the letter and the spirit of the original. He felt that Pope's translation had failed in both respects. His views on this subject appeared in an article which he wrote for the *Gentleman's Magazine* under the name "Alethes." He granted that Pope's original works excelled in "every species of poetical merit," but the translations, he felt, suffered from being made in rhymed verse. Ordinarily Pope had possessed "the happiest talent at accommodating his sense to his rhyming occasions," but such accommodation is not easy to achieve in translation, because "the sense is already determined." Thus the use of rhyme had frequently forced Pope to depart from "the meaning of the original." His couplets were unfortunate in the second place because rhyme does not permit "sufficient variety in the pause and cadence" and the ear becomes fatigued with repetition. Cowper further observed that while the original is second only to the Bible in simplicity, "Pope is nowhere more figurative in his own pieces than in his translation of Homer." Finally, although Homer nicely discriminates among his characters, Pope made them "speak all one language: they are all alike, stately, pompous, and stiff . . . He is often turgid, often tame, often careless, and, to what cause it was owing, I will not even surmise, upon many occasions has given an interpretation of whole passages utterly beside their meaning." [29]

In producing his *Iliad,* Cowper had the assistance of a silent partner. Upon receiving early drafts of the translation, the publisher Johnson had submitted several specimens to Henry Fuseli, a Swiss painter who had settled in London. Fuseli made several corrections which, Cowper realized, improved his text. He therefore encouraged Johnson to continue to employ Fuseli's editorial assistance. All negotiations were carried on through the publisher, and apparently not even a letter passed between the poet and Fuseli. At length the painter grew weary of performing this gratuitous labor. He wrote a friend, "I heartily wish with you that Cowper had trusted to his own legs, instead of a pair of stilts to lift him to fame." [30] When the translation of the *Iliad* was completed, the Swiss told Johnson that he could not spare the time to work on the *Odyssey*. He did, however, suggest certain revisions on the second epic while it was going through the press.[31] Despite his annoyance with the work, Fuseli considered Cowper the best poet of the age,[32] and when the translation finally appeared he wrote a lengthy and favorable criticism of it for the *Analytical Review*.

At last, in August 1790, after nearly six years of labor, Cowper completed his version of the *Iliad* and the *Odyssey*. Johnny Johnson brought the manuscript to London, where it was published July 1, 1791. During the interval Cowper corrected proof, added last-minute subscribers to the list, and waited impatiently to hear the verdict of the critics. His reputation by this time was so high that anything he wrote was bound to attract attention. The eighteenth-century reverence for the classics was a further guarantee that a translation of Homer would command the careful consideration of the critics, but hardly one of them praised the work without reservation. Most were able to collate the translation with the original, and a line-by-line comparison inevitably revealed certain deficiencies in Cowper's text. Nevertheless, the work as a whole won admiration and respect. The *Monthly Review* observed that Cowper sometimes departed from fidelity to the original by mistaking Homer's meaning and that he occasionally added material not found in the Greek text. On the other hand, the critic quoted passages which, he affirmed, surpassed the same lines in Pope. It was conceded, moreover, that anyone who attempted to translate such a great work was bound to fall short of the matchless original.[33] A few years later, when the *Monthly Review* carried a criticism of Gilbert Wakefield's edition of Pope's Homer, it accorded Cowper even higher praise, observing that "the true sense of Homer and the character of his phraseology may be seen in Mr. Cowper's version to more advantage beyond all comparison than in any other translation." [34]

The *Gentleman's Magazine* published a lengthy commentary that ran through several issues. While the writer asserted that

Cowper sometimes failed to give a close interpretation of Homer, he spoke in admiring terms of the poet's talents and judgment and called the translation "an ornament to our country." [35] The author of "A List of Living Poets," which also appeared in the *Gentleman's*, was even more flattering. In a brief summary of Cowper as a poet, the writer remarked, "As I am one of those who judge of a composition rather by its general fascination than an examination of its parts, and think a work excellent in proportion as it hurries me on by its powers of interesting, I am delighted with Cowper, because I cannot take him up without wishing to read him through; whereas I could never, by any exertion, get through one book of the translation of Pope." [36]

The most discerning judgment of Cowper's Homer was written by Fuseli for the *Analytical Review*. Inasmuch as Johnson edited this periodical and Fuseli had advised Cowper on the translation, this review might well appear to be an example of collusion. Actually the situation was not so much contrived as it seemed. In the first place Fuseli was relatively objective. While his criticism contains more praise than censure, he called attention to shortcomings that other critics had not stressed. He particularly observed that Cowper was often verbose where Homer was concise and that Cowper, by using many awkward inversions, had departed from the natural simplicity of the original. Furthermore, although Fuseli had helped chiefly with the *Iliad*, he asserted that the translation of the *Odyssey* was more successful.[37] Ironically, Cowper did not know that Fuseli was the author of the article in the *Analytical Review*. Upon reading it, he wrote Samuel Rose that he was "happy to have fallen into the hands of a critic, rigorous enough indeed, but a scholar, and a man of sense." Nevertheless, he disagreed with certain points raised by the reviewer. "With respect to inversions in particular," he remarked, "I know they do not abound. Once they did, and I had Milton's example for it, not disapproved by Addison. But on Fuseli's remonstrance against them, I expunged the most, and in my new edition have fewer still." [38] This statement clearly shows that Cowper did not suspect that the critic was his erstwhile collaborator. Had he known, he might have been angry with both Fuseli and his publisher, but the latter apparently kept the secret from him.

One of the first letters he received on his translation came from his onetime schoolfellow, Lord Chancellor Thurlow. Confessing to a partiality for rhyme, the noble lord remarked that he would have been pleased with a still more literal rendition of Homer. Nevertheless, he commended the poet for having succeeded so well in rendering a great classic into English. While this was not exactly high praise, it came from a high source, and Cowper felt complimented by his old friend's belated attention.

Cowper's Homer was the only one of his publications that returned him a substantial sum of money. During the preceding years his relatives and friends had secured about five hundred subscribers to the work at three guineas a subscription. Since Johnson took just enough to pay for the costs of publication, Cowper received a clear profit of a thousand pounds. The publisher's generosity is understandable in view of the considerable sums he made from Cowper's original poems. Because the 1782 edition did not sell well, the poet had given the publisher all profits that might accrue from *The Task*. When this second work proved extremely popular, Johnson hit upon the device of printing it along with the earlier material in a two-volume set. By 1794 he had brought out six such editions, besides selling several others in the years that followed. Altogether, according to Henry Crabb Robinson, Cowper's poems netted his publisher at least ten thousand pounds.[39]

Even before he had an opportunity to read the critics, Cowper began, at Johnson's suggestion, to revise his Homer with a view to a second edition. The revisions were to occupy him on and off for the remainder of his life. Like the original translation, the correcting of the text helped to divert him from his melancholy thoughts, especially during the last years when nothing else could serve to bring him relief. As a palliative, Homer served him well. But Cowper's version has not stood the test of time, and today other translations are more highly esteemed.

Cowper felt relieved upon completing his Homer, but he could not enjoy the same sense of freedom that another might have experienced upon finishing such a Herculean labor. Idleness, he had learned, was a door through which stalked the specter of despair. To keep that door even partly closed, he must have a regular occupation. Fortunately he was soon engaged in further literary enterprises, which, as usual, others suggested to him. His neighbor, the Reverend John Buchanan, advanced the idea for *The Four Ages of Man,* a poem that would deal in a philosophic fashion with childhood, youth, maturity, and old age. Cowper liked the subject and began writing, but he composed no more than thirty-eight lines.

A second proposal, made by his publisher, interested him still more. This was an invitation to edit the works of Milton. In preparing a new edition, he would translate the Latin and Italian poems, select the best text, and supply critical notes and commentaries. Cowper, who admired Milton above all other poets, saw in this work an opportunity to rescue his idol from the disparaging criticism of that "literary cossack" Dr. Johnson. Before accepting the assignment, however, he had to decide certain matters. He estimated that the task would require at least two years, leaving so much the less time for original composition. More important was the question of whether God wished him to undertake this project.

While Cowper believed in the mercies of Christ, mixed into his conception of the Deity was a strong fear of the Old Testament God of wrath. Believing that he had once offended God, he was concerned not to incur his further displeasure. But how was one to know God's intention? Under sentence himself, he felt incapable of interpreting the will of Providence. In this dilemma he turned to Samuel Teedon, the Olney schoolmaster whom he had known for several years. Two things recommended Teedon to the poet's regard. In the first place he was an Evangelical; secondly, although far from being a cultivated person, he had more book-learning than most of the Olney inhabitants. The schoolmaster, on his part, had the greatest respect for "Sir

Cowper." Earlier he had amused the poet by telling him that he had often prayed for the privilege of being on terms of intimacy with a man of genius. Providence had answered his prayers, he felt, by giving him the opportunity to know Cowper.

For several years the poet had regarded the schoolmaster with good-natured tolerance. Shortly after his recovery from the 1787 attack of insanity, he had written Lady Hesketh, "Poor Teedon, whom I dare say you remember, has never missed calling here once and generally twice a week since January last. The poor man has gratitude if he has not wit, and in the possession of that one good quality has a sufficient recommendation. I blame myself often for finding him tiresome, but cannot help it." [40] Eventually the schoolmaster came to play an important role in the lives of Cowper and Mrs. Unwin. During the period 1791–1794 some 277 letters passed between Teedon and his friends at the Lodge,[41] and the schoolmaster continued to be a frequent caller. The visits and letters were concerned chiefly with one topic, Cowper's state of mind, for Teedon had gradually advanced to being almost a spiritual adviser to the poet.

Cowper's reliance on the schoolmaster is not difficult to explain. Because of his obsession, the poet generally felt that he was barred from praying. Furthermore, although he frequently received what appeared to be monitions in the form of dreams or supernatural voices, he could not be certain whether the warnings came from God or the devil. Teedon, on the other hand, not only possessed assurance of his own salvation but also believed that a special form of grace permitted him to receive messages direct from the Deity. Of this ability Cowper had probably been sceptical at first, but at length he came to credit it to the extent that he allowed the schoolmaster to interpret his voices and dreams, to advise him when he had to make a decision, and to serve as his intercessor. Mrs. Unwin seems also to have credited Teedon's ability to communicate with the supernatural. At any rate she must have thought his influence good, and for a time perhaps it was. Although he was a foolish sycophant, he seems to have sincerely believed in his own powers, and he was pitifully eager to help. Whenever Cowper's voices appeared to be even slightly encouraging, he accorded them the most optimistic interpretation. Furthermore, he kept assuring the poet that all would come out right in the end.

When Cowper consulted him about undertaking the edition of Milton, Teedon prayed to know God's will and received a favorable answer. He passed this divination on to Cowper, who thereupon began translating Milton's Latin and Italian poems. Feeling great enthusiasm for the work, he now made Milton, rather than Homer, the chief topic of his letters. The autumn of 1791 passed pleasantly, but in December occurred an event that virtually put an end to his literary work.

Mrs. Unwin, now nearing seventy, had been in poor health for the past few years. In January 1789 she had slipped on an icy path at the Lodge, injuring her leg so badly that she had been unable to walk for several weeks. Although she suffered from headaches and general debility, she remained cheerful and had tried to keep Cowper from knowing when she was in pain. An illness of a more serious nature now developed. He described its appearance as follows: "On Saturday last, while I was at my desk near the window, and Mrs. Unwin at the fireside, opposite to it, I heard her suddenly exclaim, 'Oh! Mr. Cowper, don't let me fall!' I turned and saw her actually falling, together with her chair, and started to her side just in time to prevent her." [42] This first stroke, for that is what it proved to be, was only a slight one. It affected her speech for a few days; otherwise she showed no paralytic symptoms. The fortunate presence of Lady Hesketh helped to save Cowper from despair, but the illness of his elderly companion severely shook him. Because his devotion to her took priority over everything else, he virtually stopped his work on Milton in order to attend her. Meanwhile he sent urgent messages to Teedon, asking him to petition that Mrs. Unwin might be spared.

Another change that disturbed him was the loss of his neighbors. John Throckmorton, having succeeded to a title on the death of his grandfather, was taking his wife to live on their ancestral estate in Bucklands. Their departure filled Cowper with sadness. Yet, as he himself confessed, the situation at the Hall would not be much changed. Sir John's brother George, who had recently taken the surname of Courtenay, and whom the poet liked, was to become the new master. Furthermore, George was to bring to Weston as his bride the former Catharina Stapleton, a charming girl who had warmed Cowper's heart on her earlier visits. When the young couple took possession, they were as kind and hospitable to the poet as their predecessors had been, but because of his reluctance to leave Mrs. Unwin for even a few hours, he dined at the Hall less frequently than of old.

Since Mrs. Unwin was no longer able to bolster his faltering spirits, more than ever Cowper needed a strong-willed individual to give him strength and encouragement. Fortunately such a friend now appeared in the person of William Hayley. The circumstances of their acquaintance were somewhat unusual. Hayley, a rather well-known poet, had been commissioned by the publisher Boydell to write a life of Milton for an edition of the seventeenth-century poet. The newspapers, knowing that Cowper was preparing an edition of Milton for another publisher, tried to make the two men appear as rivals. Since neither of these mild-tempered poets shared Pope's zest for a pen-scratching squabble, they were both disturbed by the newspaper notices. To clear up the matter, Hayley sent his fellow poet a letter denying any intention of competing with him. Enclosed was a sonnet in which he called Cowper the true heir to Milton's genius. Touched by this friendly gesture, Cowper replied with a warm letter of acknowledgment. The correspondence continued, and before long Cowper was addressing Hayley as "My dear Friend and Brother" and telling him that he had never before felt so great an affection for one he had not seen. But, he protested, neither he nor Mrs. Unwin would be satisfied until they could greet their charming correspondent under their own roof. When could Hayley visit them?

Hayley arrived at Weston in May 1792. The man who had so quickly won Cowper's affection was a curious literary figure. As a boy he had been stricken by a paralysis which left him lame. Because of this impediment, he suffered from the cruel jests of his schoolmates at Eton. He had continued his education at Trinity Hall, Cambridge, but left without taking his degree. Like Cowper, he enrolled at the Temple, but a brief perusal of a few law books convinced him that a barrister's career was not for him. A few years later he married a Miss Eliza Ball and brought her to live at Eartham, an estate on the southern coast which he had inherited from his father. He spent much time developing this country home, which he made one of the show places of the region, enlarging the original small villa and introducing an elaborate system of landscape gardening. His wife bore him no children, but when he became the father of an illegitimate son, she generously took the child to live in the household. Her mind was not very strong, however, and she eventually developed a mild form of insanity. Although lucid much of the time, she came to hate Eartham. Finally in 1789 she left the place to pass the rest of her life at Derby and in London. Hayley, who seemed to value her more as a correspondent than he had as a wife, sent her long letters, couched in the sentimental language that characterized his literary works.[43]

A school of sentimental writers flourished in the last decades of the eighteenth century, but none of them, not even the author of *The Man of Feeling,* dipped his pen in treacle so often as Hayley. Although many professed admiration for his works, in literary circles he was a favorite subject for satire. One of the most amusing pieces was a burlesque poem published in 1789. The anonymous writer describes a scene in which various candidates for the poet laureateship present their credentials. Hayley, leading the procession, receives the following reply from the Lord Chamberlain:

> The polish'd period, the smooth flowing line,
> And faultless texture, all must own are thine;
> For this thy rank thou shalt unenvied keep,

While all must praise, but while they praise they sleep.
No fire of genius through thy verses burns,
Languour and sweetness take their place by turns,
No vig'rous lightning flashes through thy page,
To melt with pity, or inflame with rage:

. . . .

Correctly cold, your wishes here are vain,
To Eartham's pleasant shades return again.[44]

Several years later Byron put Hayley into *English Bards and Scotch Reviewers* among his dull writers. Hayley himself never wrote anything so sprightly as this satire, but as a man he must have had certain redeeming virtues. Southey later said of him, "Everything about the man is good except his poetry." [45] Certainly his friendship for Cowper was admirable and his first visit fortunately timed.

On May 22, 1792, a few days after Hayley's arrival, Mrs. Unwin had a second stroke. It contorted her face, paralyzed her limbs, and made her speech inarticulate. Hayley's presence and resourcefulness did much to help Cowper over this crisis. Having heard that an electric sparking machine was beneficial to paralytic patients, the visitor managed to borrow one of these new inventions and personally gave Mrs. Unwin treatments. He rendered his greatest service, however, in keeping Cowper from lonely meditation and giving him encouragement. According to Hayley, when Cowper first saw Mrs. Unwin's condition, he had talked wildly, saying, "There is a wall of separation between me and my God." His guest "looked fixedly in his face" and answered, "So there is, my friend, but I can inform you that I am the most resolute mortal on earth for pulling down old walls, and by the living God I will not leave a stone standing in that wall you speak of." Encouraged, Cowper became calmer and replied, "I believe you." [46]

Gradually Mrs. Unwin regained her powers of speech and some use of her limbs, though she was never to recover completely. At the end of a fortnight she was out of danger, and Hayley left, having won the lasting devotion of the elderly couple. After his departure Cowper wrote a sonnet to Hayley, in which he said he now knew that God could not be his enemy, because he had sent such a true friend to support him in his distress.

Johnny Johnson succeeded Hayley at Weston, but though Cowper loved this young cousin, he relied more on Teedon to give him comfort. Almost daily he advised the schoolmaster on Mrs. Unwin's condition and petitioned him to pray for her. In return Teedon transmitted messages of comfort, but Cowper was disappointed because none of them promised full recovery. Although Hayley had fortified him, the fear that Mrs. Unwin would be taken from him drove him to the verge of insanity. As always in this condition, he was harrowed by dreams. "My nocturnal experiences are all of the most terrible kind," he wrote Teedon. "Death, churchyards, and carcases, or else thunder-storms and lightenings, God angry, and myself wishing that I had never been born. Such are my dreams; and when I wake it is only to hear something terrible, of which she is generally the subject." [47]

At this juncture John Newton arrived in the region for a visit. Since Newton stayed with the Reverend Mr. Bean, Cowper apparently saw his old friend only a few times. After his departure he wrote Newton that the visit had awakened more spiritual feeling in him than he had experienced for years,[48] but the statement was probably more complimentary than sincere. He no longer treated the clergyman as his confidant. While Newton was at Weston, Cowper was already making plans to visit Hayley. Yet he said nothing on this subject, fearing perhaps that the old Calvinist would express disapproval. Instead the poet waited for the eve of his departure for Eartham and then wrote Newton that his address for the next month would be, care of William Hayley, near Chichester.

Cowper's decision to journey to Eartham was one of the bold-est he ever made. For twenty years neither he nor Mrs. Unwin had ventured more than a few miles from home. Now they were to make an arduous three-day trip to the southern coast. The visit had been discussed while Hayley was at Weston. Feeling a strong sense of gratitude to the man, Cowper had agreed to make the pilgrimage almost as a thank-offering, if Mrs. Unwin's health improved. During the next few months he frequently regretted his promise. Although somewhat better, Mrs. Unwin could walk only with assistance. Meanwhile Cowper's terrifying dreams kept his mind in a turmoil of anxiety and doubt. There was also the question of whether or not God willed that he should make the trip to Eartham. To help resolve this doubt, Teedon was asked to pray for directions. The message he received, as recorded in his Diary, was: *"Go & I will be with him* and afterwards *And he went to Bethel to enquire of the Lord who said I will go down with thee into Egypt & will bring thee up again."* [49]

This message seemed so favorable that Cowper gained a degree of confidence. Having decided to make the journey, he wrote Lady Hesketh: "Hayley interests himself so much in it, and I am persuaded it bids fair to do us both so much good that I am sincerely desirous of going. A thousand lions, monsters, and giants are in the way, but perhaps they will all vanish if I have but the courage to face them. Mrs. Unwin, whose weakness might justify her fears, has none. Her trust in the providence of God makes her calm on all occasions." [50]

The party set out on August 1, 1792. Besides the poet and Mrs. Unwin, it consisted of Johnny Johnson and the servants Sam and Nanny Roberts. Traveling in a coach drawn by four horses, they spent the first night at Barnet, where Samuel Rose was on hand to greet them. The second day the poet stopped at Kingston to dine with his relative General Cowper, and passed the night at Ripley. The third evening the party arrived at Eartham, both Cowper and Mrs. Unwin having made the trip without ill effects.

Shortly after their arrival young Johnson wrote his sister that the journey and the invigorating air of the south had greatly strengthened Mrs. Unwin. "As for our dearest cousin," he added, "he is ten times younger than ever I saw him — and laughs from morning till night." [51] No doubt Cowper did his best to appear cheerful, but Johnson's enthusiasm led him to exaggeration. Cowper himself wrote that he ate better and slept better at Eartham, but, as we shall see, he was far from happy.

Cowper remarked that the house at Eartham seemed to be brimful of guests. They included Mrs. Charlotte Smith, the novelist; Romney, the painter; and during the latter part of the sojourn, the Reverend James Hurdis, a correspondent of Cowper whom Hayley had invited to his home to meet his distinguished guest. Just before the departure from Weston, Cowper's picture had been painted by Abbot; now a second portrait was executed by the famous Romney. Fortunately Cowper did not have much leisure to brood. Part of the day he spent with Mrs. Unwin. Since she could not walk without help, he and Hayley's son drew her about the grounds in a little cart. The poet also devoted many hours to revising the translations of Milton's Italian and Latin poems, returning to this work after a lapse of several months. In this task he had the assistance of Hayley, who, according to Johnson, freely altered several of the translations and altered them for the worse. [52]

Hayley was clearly enraptured at having as his guest the most famous poet of the time. He wrote his wife in his customary vein of sentiment: "My dear brother bard of Buckinghamshire has accomplished his kind idea; and after being rooted in his own cell for twenty years, he has made a marvellous effort that has astonished all his acquaintances, and conducted his venerable muse to thank his physician under his own roof . . . She is still in such a state that we use electric fire to give energy to her weak limbs every day; and there is something at times so ghastly in her countenance that I should not be surprised if a third paralytic stroke put a sudden period to her life. Yet it is pleasing to see that she has some enjoyment of even the dregs of life." [53] In reply to Eliza's request for more details, Hayley supplied this general but nonetheless interesting thumbnail sketch of his visitor. "He is at the age of sixty-one, a florid, healthy figure . . . with an interesting countenance that expresses intelligence and energy of mind, with sweetness of manners and a certain tender and undescribable mixture of melancholy and cheerfulness, gravity and sportive humour, which give an admirable and delightful variety of attraction to his character." [54]

At Eartham Cowper found a country vastly different from the Olney region. Hayley's estate afforded a fine view of the sea, with the Isle of Wight in the distance. The grounds, moreover, were embellished in the eighteenth-century manner, with grottos, imitation Gothic towers, and symmetrical terraces and walks. But Cowper had little admiration for either the natural scenery or the artificial beauty of the landscaped grounds. For a genuinely appreciative description of the place, one must rely, not on the poet, but on his youthful cousin. Johnson wrote his sister:

"Mr. Hayley's grounds are nearly a mile round, and beautifully interspersed with rural grottos, ivy seats, and imitative Towers; from a lofty Terrace that terminates this elegant little Park is a noble view of the sea, beginning from Portsmouth and the Isle of Wight, and extending to the opposite point in the Horizon. On the other side are the beautiful South Downs, some of which are constantly covered with sheep, and others cloathed with hanging woods chiefly composed of Beech trees. They look superbly in prospect. The Isle of Wight is a grand object — having the appearance of a thick cloud in the Horizon — and such I took it to be for some time on account of its enormous height. The South Downs are also very steep, and it is no uncommon thing to see a cloud lodging upon the tops of the beautiful trees that grow upon them in great abundance." [55]

Cowper reacted very differently to the place. His descriptions of it are matter-of-fact and lacking in genuine enthusiasm. He wrote Samuel Greatheed that Hayley's grounds "occupy three sides of a hill, which in Buckinghamshire might well pass for a mountain, and from the summit of which is beheld a most magnificent landscape bounded by the sea." [56] He repeated this description, using almost the same words, when he wrote to Mrs. Courtenay and John Newton. Although he could recognize the distinguishing marks of beauty in the surroundings, he felt a psychological aversion to Eartham, as he indicates in a letter to Lady Hesketh: "This is, as I have already told you, a delightful place; more beautiful scenery I have never beheld or expect to behold; but the charms of it, uncommon as they are, have not in the least alienated my affections from Weston. The genius of that place suits me better, — it has an air of snug concealment, in which a disposition like mine finds itself peculiarly gratified; whereas from here I see from every window woods like forests, and hills like mountains — a wilderness in short, that rather increases my natural melancholy, and which, were it not for the agreeables I find within, would soon convince me that mere change of place can avail me little." [57]

Cowper here shows his temperamental sensitivity to his surroundings. As we shall see, his strong, almost pathological aversion to certain aspects of nature had a real bearing on his poetry. The longer he stayed at Eartham the more distasteful the place became, especially when the weather turned rainy and cold during the last days of the visit. Consequently he left without regret on September 17, the day previously set for the departure. From Kingston he addressed a note to Hayley, thanking him for his hospitality and expressing grief at the separation. His sentiments were quite sincere. The visit had increased his esteem for his fellow poet; nevertheless, he felt relieved when he was once more installed in his own household.

It soon became apparent that the change of scene had not altered his depressed state of mind. Mrs. Unwin's condition continued to worry him, and he felt incapable of work. He still had nightmarish dreams and heard voices which he interpreted as those of his evil and good monitors, but Satan seemed to speak to him more frequently than God. Only once did the cloud of despair lift. While he was walking in the garden, he wrote Teedon, "It pleased God to enable me once more to approach Him in prayer, and I prayed silently for everything that lay nearest my heart with a comfortable degree of liberty." [58] This sense of being restored to God's favor lasted for but a few days. His evil monitor again prevailed, and his experiences were more often of this kind: "Friday, November 16 — I have had a terrible night — such a one I believe I may say God knows no man ever had. Dreamed that in a state of the most insupportable misery I looked through the window of a strange room being all alone, and saw preparations making for my execution. That it was about four days distant, and then I was destined to suffer everlasting martyrdom in the fire, my body being prepared for the purpose and my dissolution made a thing impossible." [59]

Despite his mental agitation and his almost complete abandonment of hope, he still possessed enough control to be able to conduct his life with the appearance of normality. His letters, and he was writing frequently at this time, often sound quite cheerful. "It is even miraculous to my own eyes," he wrote Teedon, "that always occupied as I am in the contemplation of the most distressing subjects, I am not absolutely incapacitated for the common affairs of life." [60] Simulating cheerfulness became more difficult, however. When Samuel Rose and his wife visited him in December, he felt the need of laudanum to help him meet his obligations as a host. The drug soothed his nerves, enabling him to sleep more soundly and to feel more at ease during the day.

At Rose's suggestion he again began to revise his Homer in anticipation of a second edition. This work helped him through the dreaded month of January and the remainder of the winter. He spared only an hour or two a day to his revisions, performing his stint before breakfast so that he should not have to deprive Mrs. Unwin of his attention after she had awakened. He was never to complete the edition of Milton. After translating the Latin and Italian poems, he had intended to prepare a general commentary on the poet. With this purpose in mind, he had started to reread *Paradise Lost*, but in the plight of Satan, doomed for all eternity by an offended God, he seemed to find an analogy to his own situation, and he abandoned this uncongenial reading. Years later, after Cowper was dead, Hayley published an edition of Milton with the translations his friend had made.

After a summer with few guests, the autumn of 1793 brought several visitors to the Lodge. Samuel Rose came for a few days, accompanied by the painter Thomas Lawrence. Lawrence sketched a likeness of the poet and later supplied a verbal description, which Joseph Farington set down in his diary:

"He said Cowper's manner seemed to him to answer the description given of Addison, by Steele: — It was pleasant, with a tendency to delicate satire. His appearance was that of a gentleman, but rather of a former fashion, what is now called *The Old Court*. He avowed himself what the world would call a *Methodist*; — on the window seat of his sitting room Lawrence found a heap of 3 penny & sixpenny pamphlets, published by various Methodistical enthusiasts. Lord Thurlow, the old companion of Cowper when they were students in the Temple, proposed to have visited Cowper, but he declined receiving his Lordship from apprehension, it was believed, that their manners would not suit each other. He had heard that Lord Thurlow was accustomed to swear & to be very decisive. Mrs. Unwin, — Cowper's valuable female friend said little. Once she remarked, while the company was speaking of Dr. Johnson, 'that he seemed to have been born with *No Sir* coming out of his mouth.' " [61]

This rough sketch of the poet is extremely interesting. The circumstances of his refusal to see Thurlow may be incorrectly given, but the glimpses of Cowper as a gentleman of the old school, of his window seat piled with Evangelical tracts, of Mrs. Unwin, generally silent but still capable of a witticism — these details have the ring of truth.

When Hayley paid a second visit to Weston, in November of 1793, he was alarmed by Cowper's condition. He still possessed all his faculties, Hayley wrote, "but there was something indescribable in his appearance which led me to apprehend that without some signal event in his favour, to re-animate his spirits, they would gradually sink into hopeless dejection." [62] Mrs. Unwin, according to Hayley, seemed on the verge of second childhood. Yet she was petulantly determined to keep dominion over the household and her beloved consort.

Lady Hesketh arrived a few days after Hayley's departure. She had intended to stay a couple of months, but circumstances caused her to remain for a much longer period. In January 1794 Cowper sank into complete dejection. Although he attempted no violent measures, he almost never spoke unless someone addressed a question to him. His correspondence ceased, except for an occasional letter filled with gloomy reflections. At times he would turn to his revisions of Homer, and except for gross delusions about himself, he was often capable of rational thought. But for the rest of his life he remained shut up within himself, a prisoner chained to despair by the conviction that he was eternally damned.

Lady Hesketh now had two invalids to care for, besides the management of the household. She sent frantic calls for assistance to Johnny Johnson, but the young clergyman, who had been ordained the previous December, was detained by his appointment to a church in Hampnell, Norfolk. When he finally arrived at Weston, he found Cowper's condition worse even than he had expected. He reported to his sister: "He is extremely low and wretched, indeed — so much so as to make all our attempts to cheer him ineffectual. The dear soul hardly ever speaks, but sits by the hour together with his eyes on the ground in the deepest silence, which he never interrupts except when he breaks out into the most distressing speeches that can be conceived — all of which sufficiently convinces us that he feels more than tongue can express. Dear Soul! his firm opinion is that he shall be torn away by an armed force and executed in the face of all the Universe. This is the whole complaint." [63]

The formerly pleasant Lodge now became a household pervaded by gloom and undercurrents of discord. For the past few years Lady Hesketh and Johnny Johnson had been secretly planning what to do about Cowper when Mrs. Unwin died. Hayley had offered to provide a home for him at Eartham, but the poet had indicated that he never wished to return to that place. Lady Hesketh knew that he would be equally averse to living in her house in London. The best solution, it was agreed, would be for Johnny to take him to Norfolk when the old lady died. But she had lived on, in defiance of their expectations. To Lady Hesketh, who now referred to her as "the enchantress," Mrs. Unwin seemed to present the chief obstacle to Cowper's recovery. When the fourth attack of insanity occurred, Lady Hesketh had written to Dr. Francis Willis, describing her cousin's condition. Willis, who had the credit of restoring George III to sanity after his 1788 attack, was now the country's most eminent specialist in mental diseases. From the report he received, he judged Cowper's life to be in grave danger. Because of this opinion, Lady Hesketh felt that the poet's only chance of recovery was under the care of Willis. She approached Mrs. Unwin on the delicate subject, asking her to help persuade Cowper to spend a few weeks in the doctor's private asylum. But the old lady turned to stone at the suggestion of being separated from her consort. In no uncertain terms she told Lady Hesketh that "if the Angel Gabriel was to persuade her to let him leave her she would not comply." [64]

Sending him to an asylum would probably have been of no avail in any event. Later Dr. Willis called to see Cowper, but the prescriptions he left failed to help the patient. No physician was now capable of administering to his diseased mind. Yet in some respects he remained unchanged. Although Mrs. Unwin had become a fretful old woman, he never lost his chivalric devotion to her. The record of his indebtedness had been written in two poems composed a year or two earlier, the *Sonnet to Mrs. Unwin* and *To Mary*. No one at his advanced age had perhaps ever written such inspired love poems, for that is essentially what they are. Of the two the second is the more original, with its repetition of "My Mary" sounding like an invocation at vesper service. In this poem he blamed himself for her declining health when he said:

> Thy spirits have a fainter flow,
> I see thee daily weaker grow;
> 'Twas my distress that brought thee low,
> My Mary!

184

In May 1794 Mrs. Unwin suffered a third paralytic stroke. It distorted her face and made her speech incomprehensible, but she survived. A few days after she was stricken she insisted upon taking a walk in the garden, and Cowper roused sufficiently from his dejection to lend her his arm. Enraged by this incident, Lady Hesketh wrote, "She has made our wretched cousin drag her round the garden though Samuel can scarce support her." [65] But perhaps Mrs. Unwin understood Cowper better than his titled cousin. Having nursed him through two earlier periods of insanity, she probably realized, inarticulate though she was, that extreme measures were sometimes necessary to rouse him from his sedentary brooding.

Hayley, hoping to cheer his friend in this latest crisis, arrived for his third visit in April 1794. The stricken poet seemed scarcely conscious of his presence. Drained of all emotion except grief, he was incapable even of expressing gratitude to Hayley for a notable act of friendship. For the past two years Hayley had been working indefatigably to obtain a pension for him. After his first visit to Weston, he had stopped in London and broached the subject to Lord Thurlow. Thurlow was sympathetic to the idea of helping his old schoolmate, but before he could act, his enmity for Pitt led him to resign the lord chancellorship. Hayley next applied by letter to the Prime Minister, and when no answer was forthcoming, secured an interview. Pitt promised that he would try to get Cowper a pension, even though times were difficult, but further delays ensued. Finally, through the good offices of Lord Spencer, a favorable decision was reached. On April 23, 1794, during Hayley's visit, the announcement came that henceforth Cowper would receive an annuity of three hundred pounds. This grant, besides being a signal honor, would remove all financial worries. But much to the disappointment of Lady Hesketh and Hayley, Cowper failed to show even "a faint glimmering of joy" at the news. [66]

At the urging of Lady Hesketh, Johnson had resigned from his clerical appointment in order to help care for his cousin. A year passed in which these two spelled each other at Weston. They had hoped that Cowper would eventually recover, as he had recovered from the earlier attacks, but there was no change. He continued in a stupor of dejection, while his aged companion lived on, a helpless invalid. At last, worn out by her duties, Lady Hesketh felt no longer able to preside over the household, especially since there had been difficulties with the servants. Johnny, eager to return to his own region, decided that the best plan would be to take the two invalids with him. Mrs. Unwin greeted with childish delight the idea of making a journey to Norfolk. Cowper resigned himself to the proposal, though a diary he kept at this time shows that he felt there would be something fateful about the trip. Two days before he left he wrote, "Awoke this morning and lay awake 4 hours. Oh in what agonizing terrours! I have, I can have no faith in this Norfolk journey, but am sure that either I shall never begin it, or shall never reach the place. Could ye spare me, what mercy should I account it." [67]

The brief diary, kept for a few days before his departure, is a curious record of his frightful delusions. Although only partly coherent, it reveals that he was tormented with the old conviction that he had offended God by failing to destroy himself in 1773. Yet the diary contains no key to the fundamental nature of his disorder. It simply records the state of mental agony in which he lived, an agony often expressed in vivid imagery, as the following excerpts show. "It is I who have been the hunted hare and He who turn'd me out to be hunted . . . Oh miserable Being that I am! Can any sin committed in so terrible and tempestuous a moment deserve what I must suffer? . . . What sort of mercy is that which a poor, forlorn creature reduced to childish imbecility through infinite distress may forfeit for ever in a moment? . . . I have been a poor Fly entangled in a thousand webs from the beginning." [68]

On July 28, 1795, Cowper and Mrs. Unwin left Weston, never more to return. Realizing, perhaps, that the separation would be permanent, he wrote on the shutter of his bedchamber:

186

At Weston

Farewell, dear scenes, for ever closed to me;
Oh, for what sorrows must I now exchange ye!

His literary career now virtually at an end, he was to live on for five years more. Before considering this last dismal chapter in his life, however, let us turn to a general estimate of the man and the poet.

The Man and the Poet

There is a pleasure in poetic pains
Which only poets know.

TASK II. 285–286

Wʜᴇɴ Cowper began to write for publication at the age of fifty, his situation was unusual. "I reckon it among my principal advantages as a composer of verses that I have not read an English poet these thirteen years, and but one these twenty years," he wrote on November 24, 1781. "Imitation, even of the best models, is my aversion; it is servile and mechanical." [1] Besides objecting on principle to imitation, he was opposed to the practice of contemporary poets. Most of them, he felt, sacrificed thought and substance for the sake of producing verses that appealed chiefly to the ear:

Modern taste
Is so refined and delicate and chaste
That verse, whatever fire the fancy warms,
Without a creamy smoothness has no charms.

TABLE TALK 510–513

He believed that the poet should express himself with vigor and feeling, even at the cost of sacrificing rhythmical smoothness:

Give me the line that ploughs its stately course
Like a proud swan, conquering the stream by force:
That like some cottage beauty strikes the heart,
Quite unindebted to the tricks of art.

TABLE TALK 522–525

Like Wordsworth, Cowper felt that poetry should consist of simple language, such as the homely similes in the passage above. Although he did not go so far as to say that verse should resemble the discourse of rustics, he believed that it should be only slightly more formal than the spoken language of cultivated persons. What he aimed at was a good familiar style. The poet who had best mastered this style was Matthew Prior, he said. But Prior's simplicity of language had been most apparent in his lighter verse. Cowper was striving to produce a simple, colloquial style even in his more serious poems. He remarks: "Every man conversant with verse-writing knows, and knows by painful experience, that the familiar style is of all styles the most difficult to succeed in. To make verse speak the language of prose, without being prosaic — to marshall the words of it in such an order as they might naturally take in falling from the lips of an extemporary speaker, yet without meanness, harmoniously, elegantly, and without seeming to displace a syllable for the sake of rhyme, is one of the most arduous tasks a poet can undertake." [2]

Cowper achieved this simplicity and naturalness most often in shorter poems, like his verses *On the Loss of the Royal George*. These well-known stanzas, so artless and yet so effective, drew the following comment from Leslie Stephen: "Given an ordinary newspaper paragraph about wreck or battle, turn it into the simplest possible language, do not introduce a single metaphor or figure of speech, indulge in none but the most obvious of all reflections — as, for example, that when a man is once drowned he won't win any more battles, and produce as the result a copy of verses which nobody can ever read without instantly knowing them by heart." [3] Actually the poem does contain at least one metaphor. The ship can "plough" the wave no more, and in Cowper's metonymy the ship's cannon are "thunder." But the images are so natural that one does not think of them as poetic embellishments.

Needless to say, Cowper did not always succeed so well in capturing the familiar style. In his longer poems he sometimes sinks to the level of common prose; in numerous examples, like the following, he rises on the false wings of eighteenth-century poetic diction. Virgil is "the Mantuan swain," he refers to women as "the fair," barnyard fowls are "the feathered tribes domestic," a telescope is a "philosophic tube," snow, a "fleecy flood," and tea, "the fragrant lymph." Classical influences appear in his use of such terms from Greek and Latin as "arthritic," "tramontaine," "vitreous," "vermicular," "peccancy," and "vortiginous." Nevertheless, his Latinized vocabulary is smaller than that of Thomson and his followers.[4]

A certain formality of language also resulted from Cowper's indebtedness to Milton — his favorite poet since childhood. Like Wordsworth, Cowper constantly thought of Milton as the great and "inimitable" example for poets. "He intended neither to neglect nor follow this inimitable example, and he did neither," Professor R. D. Havens observes, "but he little realized how subtly, how variously, and how extensively his admiration for his 'idol' had affected his writings." Milton particularly influenced Cowper's blank verse, especially his translation of Homer, which he loaded with Miltonic inversions, appositives, and distortions, with the result that he lost much of the simplicity of the original. Frequent "reverberations from *Paradise Lost*" also appear in *The Task*, owing to Cowper's use of such typically Miltonic devices as inversion of the normal word order, parenthetical expressions, compound epithets, and poetical ellipses. But Cowper was no mere copyist. If Milton often served as his model, that was because he felt that "non-Miltonic blank verse was a contradiction in terms." Furthermore, he knew Milton so well that when he seems to echo him he does so with the naturalness of a man speaking his own tongue. Finally, although Milton's poetry was in his blood, he retained the gift of the easy, conversational style which he employs so effectively in *The Task* and in his shorter poems.[5]

The simplicity and naturalness of Cowper's diction owed much to his familiarity with the Bible, his one constant book during those long years when he read almost nothing else.

Like most Evangelicals, he knew the King James version by chapter and verse, and having a poet's sensitive ear, he could appreciate the effectiveness of its terse, simple diction. His knowledge of the Bible stood him in good stead when he wrote his hymns. Since these religious poems were intended to make one more familiar with Scripture, they include numerous phrases taken directly from the Bible, with the particular book and chapter designated by footnotes. Although Cowper did not elsewhere indicate his source in this manner, time and again he relied upon Holy Writ for a thought, a phrase, or an image. Indeed, the language of Scripture was so much in his mind that he probably came to use Biblical imagery almost as second nature. This practice was not uncommon with people who constantly read the Bible, but Cowper, having a poet's mind, often fused the images to form distinctive patterns. Some of these patterns express typical Evangelical sentiments; others seem to be symbolic utterances of his innermost reflections, particularly of his fear and despair.

A good example of his Biblical imagery exists in his frequent use of "worm" as a metaphor. To be sure, this term is frequently found in the Evangelical vocabulary, where it is generally used to describe the natural depravity of man. Possibly Cowper acquired the habit of employing the metaphor from associating with other Evangelicals, but more likely it developed from his familiarity with the frequent and often vivid use of this figure in Scripture. He introduces the term at least six times in his hymns. In number v he writes:

> Now Lord thy feeble *worm* prepare!
> For strife with earth and hell begins.*

In number xLi he refers to himself as "thy rebellious worm" and in number xLii he is "but a worm." He alludes to his conversion in Hymn Lii, when he says, "God has breathed upon a worm." In Hymn Lxii men in general are "sordid worms," and in Hymn Lxiv man is a "vain-glorious worm" who can never be saved by

* The italics here and throughout this chapter are mine.

works alone. The same image is later used in *Truth* to describe the vanity of man:

> So sings he, charmed with his own mind and form,
> The song magnificent — the theme a *worm*!
>
> LL. 411–412

In *Charity* God sheds his mercies "upon worms below," and in *Hope* Cowper writes:

> Now let the bright reverse be known abroad;
> Say man's a *worm*, and power belongs to God.
>
> LL. 710–711

Occasionally the image changes slightly, and instead of describing man as a worm, the term designates some evil that afflicts him. Thus in *Expostulation* (line 90) Cowper refers to "the worm of pride" that exists in man, and in *The Progress of Error* (line 7) the "insinuating worm" is an appositive for "the Serpent Error" that "twines round human hearts."

Another image, common to both speech and poetry, is that which employs the term "thorns." Cowper uses the metaphor in various ways. In Hymn XLIV he observes:

> Ah! were I buffeted all day,
>   Mocked, crowned with *thorns*, and spit upon,
> I yet would have no right to say,
>   My great distress is mine alone.

In two instances he rather closely paraphrases Isaiah 55:13: "Instead of the thorn shall come up the fir tree, and instead of the brier shall come up the myrtle tree; and it shall be to the Lord for a name, for an everlasting sign that shall not be cut off." With this passage in mind Cowper writes in Hymn LIV:

> I want the grace that springs from thee,
>   That quickens all things where it flows,
> And makes a wretched *thorn* like me
>   Bloom as the myrtle, or the rose.

A more specific paraphrase of the passage occurs in *Hope*:

> Well spake the prophet, "Let the desert sing:
> Where sprang the *thorn*, the spiry fir shall spring;

192

And where unsightly and rank thistles grew,
Shall grow the myrtle and luxuriant yew.

LL. 524–527

The "thorn" image is used most frequently, however, to describe the sufferings that beset the Christian on the road to eternity. In Hymn x Cowper refers to "thorns of heartfelt tribulation," and in Hymn LXII he writes:

No more I ask or hope to find
  Delight or happiness below;
Sorrow may well possess the mind
  That feeds where *thorns* and thistles grow.

Here he was probably thinking of the curse put upon Adam: "Thorns also and thistles shall it [the earth] bring forth to thee; and thou shalt eat of the herb of the field" (Genesis 3:18). Cowper uses this image again in his poem *To an Afflicted Protestant Lady*, where he remarks that the traveler seeking salvation has always found "thorns and briers in his road."

The adjective "thorny" also appears in a metaphorical sense. In *Truth* (line 454) Cowper speaks of "the Christian's thorny road," and in *The Winter Evening* (lines 333ff) he says it is the better part of wisdom for one to compare his lot with those less fortunate, for in this "world, so thorny" happiness does not exist without some "thistly sorrow at its side." Again in *Retirement* (lines 753–754) he remarks that not knowing God

we reap with bleeding hands
Flowers of rank odour upon *thorny* lands.

Although other poets have often used the "thorn" image, Cowper's special addiction to it indicates that it had a strong personal meaning for him. This view gains support from the remarkably subjective use of the metaphor in one of his letters to Newton. "My brier is a wintry one," he writes in despair, "the flowers are withered, but the *thorn* remains. My days are spent in vanity, and it is impossible for me to spend them otherwise. No man upon earth is more sensible of the unprofitableness of a life like mine than I am, or groans more heavily under the burthen; but this too is vanity, because it is vain; my groans will not bring the remedy, because there is no remedy for me." [6]

Several other Biblical metaphors appear in Cowper's poetry with varying frequency. Among them are such terms as "chains," "fetters," "rods," "arrows," and "deserts." His use of "wilderness" in a scriptural sense is also significant, as we shall see. The most notable image that he employs, however, is that of a mariner on a storm-tossed sea. To project this image, he usually introduces one or more of the following terms: "tempests," "storms," "mariner," "floods," "ship," "shipwreck," and, of course, "the sea." For the figurative use of "storms" and "tempests" he was probably indebted to the Bible, but some of the other terms may have become fixed in his mind from reading the works of such voyagers as Byron, Cook, and Forster. Obviously there is nothing original in this imagery, which has been used hundreds of times by other poets. What is remarkable is the frequency with which Cowper employs it and the strong personal meaning he attaches to it. It recurs not only in his verse but keeps cropping up in his letters and even appears in his short *Memoir*.

Generally "storms" and "tempests" represent the difficulties and anxieties that plagued the poet. In the *Memoir* the terms are used particularly to refer to his mental stress and the first period of insanity. He thus describes his fear of the near approach of the time when he was to take an examination before the House of Lords: "I looked forward to the approaching winter, and regretted the flight of every moment that brought it nearer; like a man borne away by a rapid *torrent*, into a strong *sea*." Temporarily he found relief by fixing his mind on other thoughts, but, he says, "the stress of the *tempest* was yet to come." Later in the *Memoir* he borrows an apostrophe from Psalm 42:7, to express the anguish he felt after attempting suicide: "O, Lord, thou didst vex me with all thy *storms*, all thy *billows* went over me." [7]

In his correspondence "storms" and "tempests" are often metaphors for a period of insanity, for his fear of damnation, or, as in the following example, for both. "It pleased the Almighty in great mercy to set all my misdeeds before me," he wrote after leaving Dr. Cotton's asylum. "At length the *storm* being passed, a quiet and peaceful serenity of soul succeeded." [8] In a letter to Joseph Hill he specifically referred to his first attack of insanity: "The *storm* of sixty-three made a *wreck* of the friendships I had contracted in the course of many years, yours excepted, which has survived the *tempest*." [9] In other letters these terms are used to describe various afflictions. He wrote Newton on October 2, 1787, "Never was the mind of man benighted to the degree that mine has been. The *storms* that have assailed me would have overset the faith of every man that ever had any." Still later (December 4, 1792) he confessed to Samuel Teedon that "my days are, many of them, *stormy* in the extreme, and the best of them are darkly clouded with melancholy."

In the hymns "storms" and "tempests" signify the tribulations of mankind and the poet, but in these earlier verses Cowper regards afflictions as heaven-sent, either to try the good Christian or to punish the wicked. He might have had in mind various passages of the Bible which employ the metaphor to express both views. For example, "So persecute them with thy tempest, and make them afraid with thy storm" (Psalm 83:15), and, "O, thou afflicted, tossed with tempest, and not comforted, behold I will lay thy stones with fair colors, and lay thy foundations with sapphires" (Isaiah 54:11). But whatever the source, Cowper made the image his own. In Hymn xix he writes:

> Fierce passions discompose the mind
> As *tempests* vex the sea,
> But calm content and peace we find
> When, Lord, we turn to thee.

And in Hymn lxii he says:

> But God shall fight with all his *storms*
> Against the idol of your trust.

So far mention has been made of "storms" and "tempests" as simple equivalents for periods of insanity or other trials. Cowper developed his imagery in other passages, however, to create a picture of a man or a ship traversing the stormy sea of life. The goal is a peaceful shore, representing salvation or a happy hereafter. The ship is "tempest-tossed," its sails are often tattered, and sometimes its rudder is lost. In *Truth*, for instance, he describes a soul redeemed after a period of anguish:

> 'Tis done — the raging *storm* is heard no more.
> Mercy receives him on her *peaceful shore.*
> LL. 275–276

In *The Winter Walk at Noon* (lines 738–739) "this tempestuous state of human things" is likened to "the working of a sea." What is human life? is asked in *Hope*, and the sage replies (line 3):

> A *painful passage* o'er a *restless flood.*

Cowper's vision of life as a voyage over a tempestuous sea is developed most fully in a hymn entitled *Temptation*. Here, as if anticipating another period of melancholia, he cries out to God, the "pilot" of his battered bark, to bring him safely to the peaceful shore.

> The billows swell, the winds are high,
> Clouds overcast my wintry sky;
> Out of the depths to thee I call, —
> My fears are great, my strength is small.
>
> O Lord the pilot's part perform,
> And guard and guide me through the storm,
> Defend me from each threatening ill,
> Control the waves, — say, "Peace! be still."
>
> Amidst the roaring of the sea
> My soul still hangs her hope on thee;
> Thy constant love, thy faithful care,
> Is all that saves me from despair.
>
> Dangers of every shape and name
> Attend the followers of the Lamb
> Who leave the world's deceitful shore,
> And leave it to return no more.

Though tempest-tost and half a wreck,
My Saviour through the floods I seek;
Let neither winds nor stormy main
Force back my shattered bark again.

In various other poems Cowper describes, not himself, but man in general as an unhappy "mariner" on a storm-tossed sea. For example, in *Certainty of Death*, he says:

Thus the wretched mariner may strive
Some desert shore to gain,
Secure of life, if he survive
The fury of the main.

Truth begins with the statement:

Man, on the dubious waves of error tossed,
His ship half foundered, and his compass lost,
Sees, far as human optics may command,
A sleeping fog, and fancies it dry land.

Stanzas five and six of *Human Frailty* develop the image even further:

Bound on a voyage of awful length
And dangers little known,
A stranger to superior strength,
Man vainly trusts his own.

But oars alone can ne'er prevail
To reach the distant coast,
The breath of heaven must swell the sail,
Or all the toil be lost.

Unlike Lord Byron, Cowper does not view the ocean romantically, nor does he generally consider it a superbly beautiful aspect of nature. Although the sea always fascinated him, it appealed more to his sense of wonder and awe than to his sense of beauty. "In all its various forms," he told William Unwin, "it is an object of all others the most suited to affect us with lasting impressions of the awful Power that created and controls it." He considers it "the most magnificent object under heaven," and he "cannot but feel an unpolite species of astonishment" at those "that view it without emotion, and even without reflection." [10] Yet he had found after a few experiences aboard ship that sea life was wearisome. "I seldom have sailed so far as from Hampton River to Portsmouth," he wrote John Newton, "without feeling the confinement irksome, and sometimes to a degree that was almost insupportable." [11]

Although Newton had probably told Cowper about his experiences at sea, when the poet wrote to the clergyman he was more inclined to speak of the ocean in metaphor than in literal terms. *To the Reverend Mr. John Newton on His Return from Ramsgate* begins with Cowper saying that he, too, had once seen the ocean at that resort, but as the poem continues the literal references develop into the familiar image, and the poem concludes with this stanza.

> Your sea of troubles you have past,
>   And found the peaceful shore;
> I, tempest-tossed, and wrecked at last,
>   Come home to port no more.

The image of the voyager on a stormy sea was so much in Cowper's mind that he seems to have used it as unconsciously as he did literal language. In a letter to Newton he describes Mrs. Unwin's state of health as follows: "Mrs. Unwin, whose poor bark is still held together, though shattered by being tossed and agitated so long at the side of mine, does not forget yours and Mrs. Newton's kindness." [12] A still more striking use of the metaphor occurs in a letter addressed to Newton just before the 1787 attack of insanity. Cowper here explains that he had undertaken the translation of Homer, chiefly as a means of diverting his mind from melancholy. He then describes the relief that the work has afforded him, writing a passage that teems with imagery: "A thousand times it has served at least to divert my attention, in some degree, from such terrible *tempests* as I believe have seldom been permitted to beat upon a human mind. Let my friends, therefore, who wish me some little measure of tranquility in the performance of the most *turbulent voyage* that ever Christian *mariner* made, be contented that, having Homer's mountains and forests to windward, I escape under their shelter, from the force of many a *gust,* that would almost overset me." [13]

Why did this image of a passage over a stormy sea become such a favorite with Cowper? Perhaps in the beginning "storms" and "tempests" were convenient euphemisms for words like "insanity" and "madness." Or possibly nightmares of shipwreck haunted his sleep, as did other horrible sights. One thing is certain. Cowper used the sea and storm imagery most often when he could speak freely of his afflictions, as in the letters to Newton, or when he was most deeply moved, as in the poem *On the Receipt of My Mother's Picture.* In this poem, employing the familiar image with remarkable effectiveness, he likens his mother's death and salvation to the coming into port of a ship:

> Then, as a gallant bark from Albion's coast
> (The storms all weathered and the ocean crossed)
> Shoots into port at some well-havened isle,
>
> . . . .
>
> So thou, with sails how swift! hast reached the shore,
> "Where tempests never beat nor billows roar."

But he felt that for one damned like himself there would be no furling of canvas in a pleasant harbor. In the same poem he speaks of his own situation as nearly hopeless:

> Me howling blasts drive devious, tempest tost,
> Sails ripped, seams opening wide, and compass lost,
> And day by day some current's threatening force
> Sets me more distant from a prosperous course.

At the end of his life Cowper would return to his sea imagery and would employ it with an interesting variation in his final poem, *The Castaway.* We must forego consideration of these valedictory stanzas, however, until the last chapter.

William Hazlitt's estimate of Cowper was, on the whole, a favorable one: "He is a genuine poet and deserves all his reputation." [14] However, the great critic of the romantic period detected in Cowper certain limitations, upon which he made this rather acidic comment: "With all his boasted simplicity and love of the country, he seldom launches out into general descriptions of nature: he looks at her over his clipped hedges, and from his well-swept garden walks: or if he makes a bolder experiment now and then, it is with an air of precaution, as if he were afraid of being caught in a shower of rain, or of not being able to make his retreat home." [15]

The limitations of Cowper are undeniable. His world lay literally at his feet, in the small compass of Olney and Weston. He writes charmingly of this little area, describing his garden, the Throckmorton park, and the trees and flowers of the region, but he seldom dwells with pleasure upon the more awe-inspiring aspects of nature. In his verse are no great expanses of heath or panoramic views. Although the sea provides him with many an image, he almost never regards it as a beautiful spectacle. Also missing are appreciative descriptions of mountains, torrential streams, and rugged stretches of coast line. These are real limitations, but Hazlitt too glibly accounts for Cowper's restricted range when he attributes it to "the finicalness of the private gentleman." [16] That was not the whole reason.

Cowper, first of all, had traveled relatively little. As a youth he had seen Norfolk and various points on the southern coast, but the only sections he knew well were the Berkhampstead area, where he grew up, and the Olney countryside. Secondly, and this is less obvious, he definitely ruled out certain subjects when he wrote verse. We have seen that he always regarded writing as a diversion which helped him to escape momentarily from his melancholy thoughts. This purpose would have been defeated had he dwelt on matters that increased his melancholy, and certain phenomena of nature had just such an effect upon him. In an oft-quoted line, he described himself as "a stricken deer that left the herd," trailing an arrow in its side. Moving to the country, he had found a measure of relief by living among peaceful, rural scenes. But only a cultivated landscape could provide that soothing effect; the stricken deer avoided the thorn-invested wilderness. In short, Cowper's limitations as a nature poet were owing, in no small measure, to the peculiarities of his temperament.

Myra Reynolds, one of the many critics who have observed his limitations, remarks that "mountains are merely mentioned. Night is nowhere described. Moonlight plays no part in his poetry." [17] This statement is slightly exaggerated. As we shall see, he does at least once describe a mountain, and he occasionally introduces night scenes. It is true, however, that there are no *appreciative* descriptions of mountains in his verse. An obvious explanation is that he had never seen a real mountain, not having visited Wales, Scotland, or the Lake Country. In a letter of November 16, 1791, he expresses regret that he has missed this opportunity, especially when he recalls that Dr. Johnson had once "pronounced that no man is qualified to be a poet who has never seen a mountain." Cowper adds that he will probably never have this experience, unless it be in a dream.[18]

Contrary to his expectations, however, he came upon at least some remarkable hills when he journeyed south the next year on his visit to Hayley. His reaction was extremely curious. Upon reaching Eartham, he wrote Samuel Teedon: "This journey, of which we all had some fears, and I a thousand, has by the mercy of God been happily and well performed, and we have met with no terrors by the way. I indeed myself was a little daunted by the tremendous height of the Sussex hills, in comparison of which all that I have seen elsewhere are dwarfs: but I alone was alarmed." [19] He alludes to this experience again in a letter to a second correspondent. At Ripley, he remarks, "We slept well, and rose perfectly refreshed; and except some terrors that I felt at passing over the Sussex hills by moonlight, met with little to complain of." [20] A normal man would hardly suffer "terrors" at crossing a range of hills.

Wild and rugged scenes brought his melancholy to the surface, as he admitted when he explained his failure to appreciate Eartham. "I see from every window," he wrote Lady Hesketh, "woods like forests, and hills like mountains — a wilderness in short, that rather increases my natural melancholy." [21] He used almost the same terms to describe Eartham to John Newton. "The prospects, though grand and magnificent," he wrote, were "rather of a melancholy cast, and consequently not very propitious to me. The cultivated appearance of Weston suits my frame of mind far better than wild hills that aspire to be mountains, covered with vast unfrequented woods, and here and there affording a peep between their summits at the distant ocean." [22] Later, when it was proposed that he repeat his visit to Hayley, Cowper refused. Johnny Johnson reported his reaction to the suggestion as follows: "He told me yesterday that the *melancholy wildness* of the scenes about Eartham is more than he can bear — the extensive prospects that present nothing to the view but uncultivated Hills, rising beyond Hills, and the vallies are so uninhabited that you see no signs of life, look where you will — nothing but one vast and desolate country." [23]

Such was the light in which Cowper regarded a landscape that appeared magnificent to others. Obviously mountains and other places of desolation led him to reflect upon his own unhappy state. Consequently he seldom included appreciative descriptions of wildly romantic scenes in his poetry. The only occasion on which he does describe a mountain at length is in *Heroism*, and here, significantly, he draws a picture of Mount Aetna erupting. There is no beauty in the picture; on the contrary, it is a scene of terrible desolation:

> Dark and voluminous the vapours rise,
> And hang their horrors in the neighbouring skies,
> While through the Stygian veil that blots the day
> In dazzling streaks the vivid lightnings play.
> But oh! what muse, and in what powers of song,
> Can trace the torrent as it burns along?
> Havoc and devastation in the van,
> It marches o'er the prostrate works of man,
> Vines, olives, herbage, forests disappear,
> And all the charms of a Sicilian year.
>
> LL. 15–24

In the remainder of the poem Cowper describes the volcanic fires as "emblematic" of the chaos and "mischiefs" produced by proud rulers of foreign nations, and he gives thanks that he is an Englishman, living in a "heaven-protected isle."

Several elements entered into Cowper's association of rougher scenes of nature with the personal evils that beset him. First, his Evangelical religious beliefs and his fundamentalist interpretation of the Bible led him to regard certain phenomena with superstitious awe. Second, because he dwelt much of the time on the borderline between sanity and insanity, his mental obsessions often served to refract his view. Finally, with his poet's mind, symbols were more important to him than to most.

Like many Evangelicals, he strongly believed in the interposition of God in human affairs. Often it is the angry God of the Old Testament, chastising man by casting thunderbolts and letting loose plagues and tempests. In *The Task* the "spruce philosopher" who attempts to explain such phenomena in terms of science is labeled "Thou Fool." Stoutly affirming that God still employs convulsions of nature to express his displeasure, just as he did in Biblical times, Cowper writes:

> God proclaims
> His hot displeasure against foolish men
> That live an atheist life: involves the heaven
> In tempests; quits his grasp upon the winds,
> And gives them all their fury; bids a plague
> Kindle a fiery boil upon the skin,
> And putrefy the breath of blooming health.
> He calls for famine and the meagre fiend
> Blows mildew from between his shrivelled lips,
> And taints the golden ear.
>
> II.178–187

Since Cowper thinks of floods, earthquakes, and tempests as manifestations of God's anger, he cannot view such phenomena with pleasure. Similarly he seems to regard mountains and deserts as symbols of an angry God, while smiling landscapes and cultivated scenes reflect a benevolent Deity. He asks,

> What is his creation less
> Than a capacious reservoir of means
> Formed for his use, and ready at his will?
>
> TASK II.200–202

Ready, one might add, to express either God's favor or displeasure toward man. Under these circumstances, Cowper chose to write about the pleasant rural countryside instead of the rougher aspects of nature. The latter, however, are frequently referred to symbolically to describe the evils that beset all men, but especially the poet himself.

We have already seen how he adopts "storms" and "tempests" as figures for his insanity or religious uncertainties. Certain other words are put to a similarly symbolic use. Especially notable is the recurrence of such nature images as "wilderness," "deserts," "gulfs," and "precipices." Several of these metaphors appear in a series of letters Cowper wrote to his aunt after his release from Dr. Cotton's asylum. He describes his mental illness, for instance, as "that *wilderness* from which He has just delivered me." In another allusion to his derangement he speaks of the "dangers and *precipices*, and the *bottomless pit* from whence He has plucked me." Referring to his unenlightened state of mind at the Temple, he says, "While it was thus with me the world, which till then had satisfied me, could satisfy me no longer; I found it was a mere *wilderness*, a dark, uncomfortable scene." A still more remarkable set of images appears in a letter of June 9, 1772. Here, though he still clings to the hope of salvation, he reveals that he is assailed by the doubts and fears that eventually led to his second attack of insanity. He writes, "That part of the *wilderness* I walk through is a *romantick* scene, there is but little level ground in it, but *mountains* hard to ascend, deep and *dark valleys, wild torrents, caves* and *dens* in abundance: but when I hear my Lord invite me from afar and say, Come to me, my spouse, come from the Lebanon, from the top of Amana, from the *lions' dens*, from the *mountains* and the *leopards*, then I can reply with cheerfulness: Behold I come unto Thee, for Thou art the Lord my God." [24]

While Cowper is here writing about his personal conflicts, much of the imagery is borrowed in actual paraphrase from the Bible. The last excerpt, indeed, is a very close rendition of the Song of Solomon 4:8, "Come with me from Lebanon, my spouse, with me from Lebanon: look from the top of Amana, from the top of Shenir and Hermon, from the lions' dens, from the mountains of the leopards." Cowper slightly misquotes the text, probably because he is relying upon his memory. Although scores of other Biblical texts were as well fixed in his memory, a psychologist might see special significance in the fact that Cowper was so intimately acquainted with this particular chapter of the Song of Solomon, in which the bridegroom speaks to the bride in imagery that is extremely sensual. The consistent references to periods of religious doubt or unenlightenment as a "wilderness" are also based on Scripture. There are several places in the Bible where a "wilderness" or "desert" represents a place of spiritual unenlightenment, but the most notable example occurs in Numbers 14:33, where the rebellious Israelites are doomed to wander in the wilderness for forty years. Cowper may have taken the symbol directly from the Bible, or, more likely, he may have borrowed it from other Evangelicals, who used it commonly to signify darkness of the soul or weakness of faith. John Wesley, besides using this term in his letters, preached a sermon on "The Wilderness State." According to Wesley, it is a condition into which many fall after they have once believed. The person in this situation, he says, suffers from loss of the inner light and a true love of God, loss of peace, accompanied by a "servile fear," and loss of power over sin. Causes of the wilderness state are sins of omission or commission, punishment for past sins, ignorance of Scripture or of the work of God in the soul.[25]

Although it was borrowed, the term was much more than a conventional metaphor or an abstract symbol to Cowper. His poetic imagination, combined with his aberrations, led him to think of the "wilderness" as a place of rough mountains and gaping valleys, peopled by ferocious animals lurking in dens and caves for their prey. Clearly this world is a projection by his imagination of the uncertainties, conflicts, and fears that filled his mind.

In his poetry, too, Cowper frequently employs "wilderness" as a synonym for something evil or abhorrent. The one notable exception occurs in the opening lines of the second book of *The Task*, where he exclaims:

> O for a lodge in some vast wilderness,
> Some boundless contiguity of shade,
> Where rumor of oppression and deceit,
> Of unsuccessful or successful war,
> Might never reach me more!

The romantic connotation which he here attaches to the term "wilderness" may be explained by the fact that this passage is an echo of Virgil's Georgic II (lines 488–489). Generally "wilderness" appears in his verse as a metaphor to express chaos. Such is the meaning given to it in *Heroism*, when he describes people fleeing before the lava of erupting Aetna:

> Earth seems a garden in its loveliest dress
> Before them, and behind a *wilderness*.
>
> LL. 57–58

In *Hope* he characterizes those who live only for pleasure as

> Born capable indeed of heavenly truth;
> But down to latest age, from earliest youth,
> Their minds a *wilderness* through want of care.
>
> LL. 231–233

Again he remarks:

> But not to understand a treasure's worth
> Till time has stolen away the slighted good
> Is cause of half the poverty we feel,
> And makes the world the *wilderness* it is.
>
> TASK VI.50–53

Here the whole misguided and unenlightened world is a wilderness, since it is peopled by those who either fail to pray or else pray for the wrong things. At the end of his life he would again speak of the world as a wilderness, but in this later instance, as we shall see, the world seemed a wilderness chiefly because it appeared to mirror the chaos of his own mind.

So far in this section we have tried to establish two related points. First, Cowper purposely refrained from writing detailed and appreciative descriptions of the wilder aspects of nature.

Second, he used such terms as "mountains," "wilderness," "gulfs," and "precipices" chiefly as synonyms for something evil. God made the country, man made the town, but the uninhabited wastelands, volcanic mountains, and yawning gulfs appeared to be the works of an angry God. As such they might more appropriately belong to Satan's kingdom. Better by far to write of the pleasant and soothing landscape of the Olney region, where one could daily perceive in nature evidence of God's love for mankind.

The idea that nature proves the existence of an all-wise, benevolent God occurs frequently in Cowper's poetry. To be sure, he never goes so far as the Deists of his age who placed natural evidence above Scripture. Always orthodox on this subject, Cowper writes:

> Instruct me, guide me to the heavenly day
> Thy words, more clearly than thy works, display.
> RETIREMENT 96–97

Nevertheless, it is interesting to observe that he was not unaffected by the apologists of the eighteenth century who argued the existence of a deity on the basis of natural evidence. Ever since Isaac Newton had made his discoveries, writers had been fond of demonstrating that the perfection and complexity of the universe prove that there must have been a creator. Instead of strengthening orthodox belief, however, this argument often led to the neglect or denial of traditional Christian teachings. To the deist virtually the only article of faith was that the God who created the universe must have been a superb engineer. Others, while not neglecting Christianity entirely, were so much enraptured with the new rationalistic evidence that they developed a special vocabulary when writing about the supernatural. In this lexicon Christ is seldom mentioned; the great Pattern-Maker of the universe is called "the Prime Mover," "the Great First Cause," or simply "the Deity"; and the universe itself is referred to as "the spheres," "the tremendous whole," or "the circling orbs."

Cowper shows the influence of the rationalistic thinkers chiefly in the use he makes of their special vocabulary. When he speaks of the God of the universe, for instance, his language is not so different from that of Pope's *Essay on Man*:

> Nature is but a name for an effect
> Whose cause is God. He feeds the secret fire
> By which the mighty process is maintained,
> Who sleeps not, is not weary; in whose sight
> Slow-circling ages are as transient days;
> Whose work is without labour; whose designs
> No flaw deforms, no difficulty thwarts.
>
> TASK VI.223–229

Another echo of Pope's school occurs in *Retirement*, when Cowper calls upon nature to be his second muse:

> O Nature! whose Elysian scenes disclose
> His bright perfections, at whose word they rose,
> Next to that Power, who formed thee and sustains,
> Be thou the great inspirer of my strains,
> Still, as I touch the lyre, do thou expand
> Thy genuine charms, and guide an artless hand,
> That I may catch a fire but rarely known,
> Give useful light, though I should miss renown,
> And, poring on thy page, whose every line
> Bears proof of an intelligence divine,
> May feel a heart enriched by what it pays.
> That builds its glory in its Maker's praise.
>
> LL. 199–210

There is much more here, however, than mere eighteenth-century adulation of the wonders of nature. Cowper humbly asks that his writing may bring "useful light" to others, even though he misses fame. What he wants is to arouse man's belief by helping him to see God reflected in nature, but, as we have observed, he was generally too stalwart an Evangelical to place natural evidence before the works of Scripture. And though he may slip into the deistical vocabulary of his age, we know beyond a shadow of doubt that the atonement of Christ was at the root of his faith. Finally, there can be no mistaking his meaning in the passage above, for he concludes by warning man against the danger of worshiping the gifts of nature instead of the Giver:

> Woe to the man whose wit disclaims its use,
> Glittering in vain, or only to seduce,
> Who studies nature with a wanton eye,
> Admires the work, but slips the lesson by.
>
> RETIREMENT 211–214

Another prevalent eighteenth-century idea to which Cowper alludes is the great chain of being. According to this philosophic concept, God had created a world in which all forms of being, from the simplest to the most complex, form an unbroken chain. All groups in the continuum serve higher groups, with man the penultimate and God the ultimate links in the chain. Cowper refers to this theory approvingly in *Tirocinium* and again in *Retirement* (lines 99–117).

More closely associated with his individual religious beliefs is the oft-repeated assertion that the spiritually enlightened can perceive a harmony and beauty in nature that elude the ordinary man. This idea, really the positive expression of his view that the world is a wilderness to the unenlightened, follows an interesting development. We encounter it first in a letter of 1780, in which he says that it would be better for a man never to be born than to be blind to the real meaning of the wonders of the world. "I delight in baubles and know them to be so," he wrote Newton; "for rested in, and viewed without a reference to their Author, what is the earth — what are the planets — what is the sun itself but a bauble? Better for a man never to have seen them, or to see them with the eyes of a brute, stupid and unconscious of what he beholds, than not to be able to say, 'The Maker of all these wonders is my friend.' " [26]

The core of the idea, as Cowper develops it, is that unregenerate or even careless men see a mere physical beauty which at best is but an ashen mockery of the visionary splendor that an intimate knowledge of God imparts to natural phenomena. In other words nature is a mere trinket unless one can read in it the lesson that God is all-powerful, ever present, and constantly providing for mankind. This theme is played upon in his poetry with interesting variations.

He introduces the idea in *Retirement* just after he describes the situation of an insane person. The world mistakenly thinks of a madman as suffering chiefly from wild dreams, he says, but actually the chief symptom is a deadening of his perceptions and the failure to appreciate the world about him:

> 'Tis not, as heads that never ache suppose,
> Forgery of fancy, and a dream of woes;
> Man is a harp whose chords elude the sight,
> Each yielding harmony, disposed aright;
> The screws reversed (a task which if He please
> God in a moment executes with ease)
> Ten thousand thousand strings at once go loose,
> Lost, till He tune them, all their power and use.
> Then neither heathy wilds, nor scenes as fair
> As ever recompensed the peasant's care,
> Nor soft declivities with tufted hills,
> Nor view of waters turning busy mills,
> Parks in which Art preceptress Nature weds,
> Nor gardens interspersed with flowery beds,
> Nor gales, that catch the scent of blooming groves,
> And waft it to the mourner as he roves,
> Can call up life into his faded eye
> That passes all he sees unheeded by.

LL. 323–340

From such a bereft feeling only God can rescue one, Cowper adds. Having his own experience so much in mind, however, he describes the restoration to sanity as accompanied by, if not contingent upon, a religious awakening. Once the light of reason and of grace has been attained by seeking God, the former madman can perceive, not just the ordinary beauties of nature, but a much more resplendent world than meets the eye of the spiritually blind:

> Nature, assuming a more lovely face,
> Borrowing a beauty from the works of grace,
> Shall be despised and overlooked no more,
> Shall fill thee with delights unfelt before.

RETIREMENT 357–360

Another variation of this theme occurs in *The Task*. In Book V, after dwelling upon the evils of slavery, Cowper observes that no tyranny can enslave the spirit of an enlightened man, for

He is the freeman whom the truth makes free.

Though he be in bondage, a man possessing the light of grace can appreciate beauties of nature that his captor fails to see. Thus the slave whom God loves is really the freeman, and his unenlightened owner, not enjoying the liberty to know God's works, is a bondsman to ignorance. Cowper concludes this discussion with an exhortation to all those who do not possess grace:

Acquaint thyself with God, if thou wouldst taste
His works. Admitted once to his embrace,
Thou shalt perceive that thou wast blind before;
Thine eye shalt be instructed, and thine heart,
Made pure, shall relish with divine delight,
Till then unfelt, what hands divine have wrought.

TASK V.779–784

The theme reaches its climax in the final book of *The Task*, when Cowper urges, not simply the unregenerate, but all men to awaken to the wonders of creation. Although he had always had a religious purpose in writing, heretofore he had been a preacher of gospel truths. In this final book of *The Task*, he momentarily turns aside from Scripture to exhort men to learn religious truths from nature. The knowledge gleaned from books, he says, is often a "rude unprofitable mass" that hoodwinks man. Nature, teaching humble wisdom, deceives no student. Unlike book-learning that yields only to "slow solicitation," the transcendental truths of nature "seize at once the roving thought." Here, and perhaps only here in all his verse, nature is regarded as a book of revelation wherein one may find indisputable evidence of God's existence and beneficence. Temporarily Cowper seems to be freed from his Calvinism, for the elect are no longer merely those predestined to salvation; they include all who can understand the miracles of God's creation. This ability, moreover, appears to be largely a matter of the will, since the wonders of nature are everywhere. If man fails to perceive them, the cause may simply be careless inattention. Consequently the poet endeavors to open men's eyes to the marvelous world in which they live:

> Should God again,
> As Once in Gibeon, interrupt the race
> Of the undeviating and punctual sun,
> How would the world admire! But speaks it less
> An agency divine, to make him know
> His moment when to sink and when to rise,
> Age after age, than to arrest his course?
> All we behold is miracle, but seen
> So duly, all is miracle in vain.

TASK VI.125–133

Cowper proceeds to show that God's handiwork is revealed in everything that lives and grows. It appears in the operation of the planetary bodies, in the changes of the seasons, in the abundance and variety of trees and flowers. Even the minutiae of nature — the delicate tracery of a leaf, the scent and coloring of a flower — attest that "there lives and works a soul in all things." That is the lesson that nature teaches, and the man who can read it aright will find more than the naked beauty that strikes the eye. For him all natural objects will be invested with a transcendental luster that far surpasses the material beauty that others enjoy:

> Happy who walks with him! whom what he finds
> Of flavour or of scent in fruit or flower,
> Of what he views of beautiful or grand
> In nature, from the broad majestic oak
> To the green blade that twinkles in the sun,
> Prompts with remembrance of a present God.
> His presence, who made all so fair, perceived,
> Makes all still fairer.

TASK VI.247–254

Cowper's vision of God in nature supplies a second reason for his preoccupation with smiling landscapes and cultivated scenes. He can admit descriptions of winter into his poetry, for he thinks of this season as a time of rest, when God works in a mysterious way his wonders to perform. But the hand of God was not so easy to discern in the wilder aspects of nature; these, as we have observed, seemed to be more the handiwork of an angry God. To what extent do these distinctive views impose limitations on his verse? For one thing, they generally prevent his using a broad expanse of canvas. He is a painter of vignettes. Even in his descriptions of winter, he provides a picture of limited dimensions. We see the poet's shadow, the cattle huddled together in the barnyard, the village steeple topped with snow, but we do not get expansive views of snow-clad hills or spreading heaths. In the second place, Cowper's association of nature with the Divinity causes him to lack a pagan sense of wonder, that sheer physical delight in natural phenomena that we find in most great nature poets. These are real artistic limitations, but they grew directly out of his temperamental peculiarities and his religious beliefs. Thus they were fundamental in the personality of the poet, and not, as Hazlitt believed, the mere whims of a finical private gentleman.

Turning to other aspects of Cowper's poetry, we find him stoutly maintaining the superiority of nature to art. A chief reason which he adduces is the diversity of nature's appeal. The painter's skill, though great, he says, can only please the eye. Nature addresses all our senses:

> The air salubrious of her lofty hills,
> The cheering fragrance of her dewy vales,
> And music of her woods — no works of man
> May rival these.

TASK I.428–431

Having confessed the inferiority of art, Cowper succeeds, better than any poet of his age, in showing the infinite variety of nature's appeal. He does this largely by providing a wealth of details, by dwelling on the particular phenomena that the more typical poets of the eighteenth century usually omitted. When he describes a tree, it is not simply an abstraction of arboreal beauty. Each tree has a name and distinguishing marks and colors. The poplar "with silver lines his leaf," the willow is "wannish gray," and the sycamore is "now green, now tawny," and in late summer dressed "in scarlet colors bright." An experienced gardener, he dwells with unself-conscious love upon the color, odor, and shape of flowers — the syringa, "ivory pure"; the lilac, "now white, now sanguine," or "set with purple spikes pyramidal"; the woodbine, with "never-cloying odours"; the broom, "yellow and bright as bullion unalloyed"; and the "laburnum rich in streaming gold."

Cowper was stimulated by the sounds and smells of his little world almost as much as by its visible splendor. His is not the lush, physical sensuousness of Keats; rather it is the delight of one who has come to know nature through long years of quiet intimacy. His sensitive ear catches the whisper of a fountain, the trill of a stream, the music of the wind sweeping through a forest, a rhythmical sound "not unlike the dash of ocean" on the shore. He rejoices in the songs of birds — melodies that "nice fingered art" can never imitate. Even the calls of the jay, the pie, and the "boding owl," though harsh and inharmonious, can be pleasing when heard "in scenes where peace for ever reigns." This last statement particularly attracted William Wordsworth. In a letter to John Wilson he remarked that Cowper's observation on the owl illustrated his own belief that the poet "ought to travel before men occasionally as well as at their sides," in order to make the feelings of humanity "more consonant with nature." [27]

Like Keats, Cowper knew that the sounds of nature are never completely stilled. Having observed a redbreast in winter flitting from spray to spray, he observes:

> Where'er he rests he shakes
> From many a twig the pendent drops of ice,
> That tinkle in the withered leaves below.
> Stillness, accompanied with sounds so soft,
> Charms more than silence.
>
> TASK VI.80–84

Besides these little noiseless noises, he liked to hear the clear chimes of Olney ringing on a frosty morn. The church bells, he remarks, touch a familiar chord and lead him to recall other days:

> Wherever I have heard
> A kindred melody, the scene recurs,
> And with it all its pleasures and its pains.
> Such comprehensive views the spirit takes,
> That in a few short moments I retrace
> (As in a map the voyager his course)
> The windings of my way through many years.
>
> TASK VI.12–18

In this passage Cowper shows a keen awareness of the process of association, in which one element of the past, such as the church bells, acts as a stimulus to restore the whole scene to mind.

To a remarkable degree Cowper anticipates the poets of the romantic period. Like them, he insists upon the importance of personal liberty, even though he feels that liberty can best be achieved under British constitutional monarchy. One of his favorite themes is the brotherhood of man; another is the broader brotherhood of all living creatures. He is especially Wordsworthian in his belief in the healing power of nature, in his assertion that the emotions are often a better guide than reason, and in the conviction that nature may teach more profound lessons than books. Wordsworth says:

> One impulse from a vernal wood
> Can teach us more of man,
> Of moral evil and of good
> Than all the sages can.

And Cowper, writing several years earlier, observes that

> the heart
> May give a useful lesson to the head,
> And learning wiser grow without his books.

Similarities of this kind may be partly explained by the younger poet's great admiration for the elder one. "With the exception of Burns and Cowper," Wordsworth wrote, "there is little of recent verse however much it may interest me, that sticks to my memory (I mean which I get by heart)." [28]

In several other respects, however, Cowper was far removed from the swelling romantic current of the late eighteenth century. Despite his admiration for the ballad form, he seems never to have read Percy's *Reliques*. He shows no interest in the Middle Ages, nor shares in the contemporary vogue for that era, as reflected in the poems of Ossian, the verse of Chatterton, or novels like *The Castle of Otranto*. In the second place, he has no sympathy for the cult of primitivism. Reflecting on the fate of Omai, a savage that Captain Cook had brought to England from the South Seas, Cowper pictures him restored to his native island, but sorrowing over its uncultivated state and longing to taste again the joys of civilization. Nor does he ever express the typical pre-romantic longing for solitude, but writes wittily:

> How sweet, how passing sweet, is solitude!
> But grant me still a friend in my retreat,
> Whom I may whisper, solitude is sweet.
> RETIREMENT 740–742

One would be ill-advised to classify Cowper as a member of any school of writers. Although he frequently expresses an idea of the romantics, he is the least self-conscious member of that group. When he broke with the older generation of writers, he wrote no declaration of emancipation. When he asserted that the heart can be a better guide than reason, he merely repeated a cardinal principle of the Evangelical revival. Although he influenced later romantic poets, he was never aware that he was blazing a new trail. Even Burns, despite his genuine simplicity, was more consciously a path-breaker.

Today Cowper is best considered as a transitional poet — typical of his age in his admiration for the classics, in choosing to write moral satires and didactic verse, in celebrating the reasonableness of a life of retirement, in his penchant for witty and aphoristic observations. At the same time he stands apart as the one great poet of the Evangelical movement and is further individualized by the reflection in his writing of his peculiar religious obsessions. Finally, he is distinctly a precursor of the romantic movement in his feeling of kinship with nature and

all living creatures, in his relatively simple diction and strong
lyrical qualities, and, above all, in restoring to verse passion and
an intimate personal note.

More than any other quality, his strong personal tone contributed to the change in poetical taste. For many decades a kind
of false modesty had caused poets to expunge the personal pro-
noun from their verses. This reluctance to unmask their emotions had led many writers to speak more like oracles than men.
Then came Cowper, a poet whose physical isolation kept him
from being a mere imitator, a man so harassed by emotional conflicts that writing became a form of sublimation. Thus, despite
his shy, retiring nature, his compelling need to express his feelings led him to speak out with candid and colloquial directness.
The subjective quality of his verse restored to English poetry a
personal note that had long been missing. The full significance
of this contribution has been excellently described by Stopford
Brooke, who writes:

"These personal passages and poems are the re-introduction into
English poetry — after a long interval — of the intimate revelation to the public of the personal cry, the lyric centre of the poet,
Shakespeare did this, but with a veil, in the Sonnets. Milton did
it now and then, but with his own dignity, so that none could
smile nor frown. And there was no misery, no torment, no weakness to reveal. Then after Milton all personal revelation, save in
light love-poems where it did not matter, ceased till Cowper
spoke. Since his time, this strange opening of the doors to show
the world the state of soul which it seems natural to hide is not
uncommon in poetry." [29]

While Cowper's distinctive personal note appears most often
in his shorter pieces, it frequently breaks out in his longer
poems, imparting to particular passages an intensity which,
though never mystical, has the inspired fervor of the mystics.
Such a passage, and one of the best he ever wrote, appears in
The Winter Morning Walk. Here the personal tone combines
with his religious ardor in a passionate invocation:

> Tell me, ye shining hosts
> That navigate a sea that knows no storms,

Beneath a vault unsullied with a cloud,
If from your elevation, whence ye view
Distinctly scenes invisible to man,
And systems of whose birth no tidings yet
Have reached this nether world, ye spy a race
Favoured as ours, transgressors from the womb
And hasting to a grave, yet doomed to rise,
And to possess a brighter heaven than yours?
As one who long detained on foreign shores
Pants to return, and when he sees afar
His country's weather-bleached and battered rocks
From the green wave emerging, darts an eye
Radiant with joy towards the happy land,
So I with animated hopes behold,
And many an aching wish, your beamy fires,
That show like beacons in the blue abyss
Ordained to guide the embodied spirit home
From toilsome life to never-ending rest.
Love kindles as I gaze. I feel desires
That give assurance of their own success,
And that, infused from Heaven, must thither tend.

TASK V.822–844

Most of his shorter poems, from the early verses addressed to Delia to the final lines of *The Castaway*, contain a strong personal note. Sometimes it is playful, as in the lighter pieces on his pets. Sometimes it occurs in the form of an analogy, as in *The Poplar Field*, where he reflects that his life may be nearly as short as that of the trees cut down in their prime. He also sees a symbol of himself in the long-lasting oak when he observes:

Thou, like myself, hast stage by stage attained
Life's wintry bourn; thou, after many years,
I after few; but few, or many prove
A span in retrospect.

YARDLEY OAK

Even in the lines on Alexander Selkirk, although it is the marooned sailor that speaks in the first person, his isolation from society is clearly a symbol of Cowper's spiritual isolation.

Besides introducing frequent references to himself, Cowper achieves a sense of intimacy in his verse by employing the direct query and the apostrophe. Alexander Selkirk, for instance, calls upon the winds in his loneliness to bring him reports from friends at home. The tree in *Yardley Oak* is consistently addressed in the second person and often by way of apostrophe. These devices, combined with personal references, are especially effective in expressing pathos and passion. *To the Nightingale,* a poem inspired by Cowper's hearing a lone bird singing on New Year's Day, 1792, is a good example:

> Whence is it that amazed I hear
>   From yonder withered spray,
> This foremost morn of all the year,
>   The melody of May?
>
> And why, since thousands would be proud
>   Of such a favour shown,
> Am I selected from the crowd
>   To witness it alone?
>
> Sing'st thou, sweet Philomel, to me,
>   For that I also long
> Have practised in the groves like thee,
>   Though not like thee in song?
>
> Or sing'st thou rather under force
>   Of some divine command,
> Commissioned to presage a course
>   Of happier days at hand?
>
> Thrice welcome then! for many a long
>   And joyless year have I,
> As thou to-day, put forth my song
>   Beneath a wintry sky.
>
> But thee no wintry skies can harm,
>   Who only need'st to sing
> To make ev'n January charm,
>   And every season Spring.

Cowper's subjectivity appears to special advantage in his warm tributes to those he loved. His poem to William Unwin and his sonnets to Hayley and Romney are good examples, but the best of all his tributes to his male friends is the gracious and manly *Epistle to Joseph Hill*. In expressing his gratitude to those who had helped make life bearable, Cowper frequently refers to the wretchedness caused by his religious conflicts and periods of insanity. Yet he has such a fine feeling for the appropriate word that he never becomes mawkish. No reader questions his sincerity, and no one can doubt that he speaks from the heart in his lines on his mother's picture or in the two poems to Mary Unwin. As Stopford Brooke has observed, "There is nothing more pathetic and yet more simple in English poetry" than these tributes to his real and to his adopted mother.[30]

"I am glad you have taken to Cowper," the youthful Edward Fitzgerald wrote Thackeray; "some of his little poems are affecting beyond anything in the English language: not heroic, but they make me cry." [31] Of how many eighteenth-century poets could one make the same affirmation? Most of them, indeed, would have been embarrassed by such a response on the part of their readers. One of the many ironies of literature is that a shy recluse, given to fits of insanity, was the first of his time to break through the convention of stubborn taciturnity. In this respect it was not the sensitive poet who was inhibited. The age itself had an emotional block. But the barrier was now broken, and henceforth poetry would be more truly the personal expression of human emotions.

❧ X ❧

The Castaway

The night contradicts the day and I go down the torrent of time into the gulf that I have expected to
plunge into so long.

LETTER TO LADY HESKETH, FEBRUARY 19, 1796

THE final years of Cowper's life form a brief and painful
chronicle. Uprooted from the region he loved, he passed the
remaining five years in Norfolk, almost completely detached
from the world about him. Hope having deserted him, he now
felt certain of his doom. Yet this certitude so numbed his mind
that, though he continued to suffer, his agony was perhaps less
keen than it had been during the long period when hope and
despair had kept him in conflict. At least once it seemed that
he might shake off his melancholy. On the trip from Weston to
Norfolk the party stayed the first night at the village of Eaton.
When the others were settled at the inn, he and Johnson walked
in the churchyard by moonlight. There, surrounded by the dead,
his spirits came momentarily to life, and he spoke with his old
conversational brilliance about the poet Thomson. But this was
the last glow of animation. "During all the years that he lived
after this," Johnson wrote, "I never heard him talk so much at
ease again." [1]

Upon arriving in Norfolk, Johnson installed his two invalids
in a parsonage at North Tuddenham for a fortnight. From there
they went to Mundesley on the coast and, in the fall, settled at
Dunham Lodge, a spacious dwelling near Swaffham. They stayed

there a year; then, after another sojourn at Mundesley, they moved to Johnson's house in East Dereham. Because this dwelling faced the market place, Johnson had feared that the noise would disturb Cowper, but the accommodations suited him so well that, except for trips to Mundesley, he remained at East Dereham until the end. Young Johnson managed the household and supervised the care of the invalids. This difficult task he performed with patience and fortitude, though he sometimes made serious mistakes of judgment. Cowper's servants, Sam and Nanny Roberts, returned to Weston after the first year, and other attendants took their place. The most helpful of these, a Miss Perowne, served as Cowper's nurse and won his affection by her kindness.

Cowper's days were passed in gloomy silence. Occasionally he could be persuaded to write to Lady Hesketh or Newton, but he could no longer force a smile or make a witty comment, and the letters contain little more than an account of his sufferings. Johnson found that the best way to keep his patients diverted was to read novels to them. The poet would listen in silence, but Mrs. Unwin would sometimes venture an appreciative comment. Her son-in-law and daughter visited them at Dunham Lodge, and during their stay they instituted the practice of reading her a chapter from Scripture each morning. When the Powleys left, Johnson continued this custom. Cowper always attended him to Mrs. Unwin's room, but appeared to take no notice of what was read.

So much were his thoughts turned inward that he seemed scarcely aware of the comings and goings in the household. Johnson reported that he took no notice of the Powleys. When the dowager Lady Spencer, to whom he had dedicated his *Odyssey*, called at Dereham, he answered her questions briefly but volunteered no remarks. Sir John Throckmorton, his old neighbor at Weston, also paid him a visit. Again the poet seemed hardly to notice his guest, though he later wrote Lady Hesketh that Sir John had called and looked much older.

Because of his numbed state of mind, he met with relative apathy an event that earlier would have profoundly moved him.

After a long period of invalidism Mrs. Unwin finally died on December 17, 1796. She had been failing for days, and Cowper realized that the end was near. The morning of her death he said to a maid that entered his room, "Sally, is there life above stairs?" Later in the day Johnson conducted him to the bedside of the dying woman. "Death was in her countenance and he could not but see it was," the clergyman wrote. "He bore the sight, however, better than I expected, and went down with me into the study to our customary employment." She died a half-hour later. Toward evening Johnson escorted him to see the remains. "After looking at her for a few seconds, with one hand holding back the bed-curtain, he bore himself away in an agony, and clasping his hands together, he lifted them up with great violence and exclaimed, looking towards the ceiling of the room — 'Oh God, was it for this?' " [2]

Mrs. Unwin was buried by torch light in St. Edmund's chapel, in the church of East Dereham. An interment at night had been decided upon so that Cowper might not be aware of the funeral until afterward. But he never inquired when or where she was to be buried, nor, according to Johnson, "did he seem ever to think of her more." [3] At one time the prospect of her death had helped to drive him mad; now the barrier that separated him from the outside world seemed to exclude from his thoughts even the woman who had been so long a part of his existence.

Neither Lady Hesketh nor Hayley visited Cowper in Norfolk, but Johnson kept these friends informed of his condition. Always the optimist, Hayley felt that a recovery would be likely after the death of Mrs. Unwin. Meanwhile he filled his letters to Johnson with nostrums and plans to help effect a cure. Having moved to a smaller house in the summer of 1797, he suggested that Johnson and Lady Hesketh take his mansion at Eartham and bring Cowper there to live. This proposal met with no enthusiasm. Johnson knew that Cowper disliked the place, and Lady Hesketh, now a semi-invalid, pleaded that poor health would prevent her from making a change.

Hayley's ingenuity is best seen in an elaborate plan which he

designed with the hope and expectation that it would restore
Cowper's peace of mind. The poet's closest associates knew that
before this last period of melancholy he had looked for a sign
that would assure him that God had restored him to grace. Upon
several occasions a pleasant dream or hallucination had raised a
fleeting hope, but the portents were never convincing enough
for a lasting effect, and after a few days despair had always returned. Hayley's scheme was to create a situation that would
compel him to believe that he was not excluded from salvation.
Since Cowper's own dreams failed to carry conviction, Hayley
proposed to tell him of a dream-vision of his own in which Cowper's salvation was promised. To give the dream the appearance
of a supernatural message, Hayley would include certain minor
prophecies. The fulfillment of these, he believed, would persuade
Cowper that the promise of his restoration to God's mercy was
genuine.[4]

Having won Johnson's enthusiastic approval of the plan,
Hayley dispatched a letter to Norfolk, in which he described his
dream as follows: "I beheld the throne of God whose splendour,
though in excess, did not strike me blind, but left me power to
discern, on the steps of it, two kneeling angelic forms." The two
angelic figures were Cowper's mother and Hayley's mother, both
of whom were petitioning for the poet's security of mind. Hayley,
interrupting their supplications, sprang forward and asked Cowper's mother what her son's destiny was to be. She turned to him
with "a look of seraphic dignity" and replied: "Warmest of
earthly friends! moderate the anxiety of thy zeal, lest it distract
thy declining faculties and know, as a reward for thy kindness,
that my son shall be restored to himself and to friendship. But
the All-merciful and Almighty ordains that his peace with
Heaven shall be preceded by the following extraordinary circumstances of signal honour on earth — He shall receive letters
from Members of Parliament, from Judges, and from Bishops to
thank him for the service he has rendered to the Christian world
by his devotional poetry. These shall be followed by a letter
from the Prime Minister to the same effect, and this by thanks

expressed to him on the same account in the hand of the King himself. Tell him when these events take place, he may confide in his celestial emancipation from despair." The angelic voice concluded by urging Hayley to impart his vision to Cowper.[5]

When Johnson read this letter to him, Cowper listened but made no comment. Several weeks now ensued while Hayley worked on the second step of his plan — the fulfillment of the prediction that Cowper would receive various testimonials. To this end, Hayley appealed to certain dignitaries in church and state to write complimentary letters to Cowper on his religious poetry. Hayley did not mention the predictive dream; he merely said that he hoped to raise the poet's spirits by supplying him with testimonials of his contribution to the cause of religion. For his member of parliament he selected William Wilberforce, who readily consented to help. Richard Watson, Bishop of Landaff, also agreed to write a letter, as did Beilby Porteus, Bishop of London. In order to obtain a comment from a judge, Hayley approached Thurlow and asked him to appeal to Chief Justice Lord Kenyon for a testimonial. Thurlow did his part, but apparently Kenyon failed to write the letter. Whether Hayley also tried to persuade the prime minister and the king to contribute letters in accordance with the prophecy does not appear.[6]

The testimonials that Hayley did succeed in securing eventually reached East Dereham. Wilberforce wrote Cowper, "Other authors have written poems of a religious nature, but it was reserved for you to add the charms of poetry to a distinct explanation of the leading principles of the Gospel." [7] Bishop Porteus, an Evangelical sympathizer, said that except for the Bible he knew of no work better "calculated to improve, exalt, and sanctify the soul" than Cowper's poems.[8] Bishop Watson, stressing the high moral tone of the verse, commented, "In an age when religion is rejected, morality outraged, and the concerns of futurity lost in dissipation and sensual indulgence, it must give every serious mind sincere satisfaction to see the impressive manner in which you support the cause of piety and virtue." [9]

When the letters arrived, Johnson and Cowper read them together. Then Johnson pretended suddenly to remember the predictive vision and started to look for Hayley's letter. Cowper restrained him, saying, "No, pray don't." Feeling that the whole point might be missed, Johnson pointed out that the testimonials showed "a kind of accomplishment of what is predicted." "Well," replied his cousin, "Be it so. I know there is, and I knew there would be; and I knew what it meant." [10] He never alluded to the subject again. What he thought no one knew. Hayley felt that the scheme had accomplished some good when he heard that Cowper had resumed work on his Homer, but the ruse seems to have been entirely ineffectual. When Cowper said, "I knew what it meant," perhaps he intended to convey that he was aware that the whole business was a fraud. He, too, had experienced visions, but in none of them did celestial beings speak in the mawkish prose of William Hayley.

Meanwhile Johnson was engaged in an experiment of his own. Knowing that Cowper was distracted by dreams and voices, the young clergyman had hit upon a scheme designed to counteract their ill effects. He had a workman cut a groove in the wall behind Cowper's bed and then inserted a tube through which he or someone else could speak in comforting terms to the poet.[11] During the course of this experiment Johnson quizzed Cowper each morning on his dreams and voices and set down his remarks in a diary. Although the voice that came through the wall had as little effect as Hayley's ruse, Johnson's record of Cowper's dreams and hallucinations supplies further evidence of his tortured state of mind.

The diary indicates that he had three predominant fears at this time. In the first place he was harassed by the thought that some dreadful, imminent change would cause him to be torn from the household and the protection of Johnson. When asked about his experiences during the night, he gave such answers as: "I was told I should not be here another day, and I shall not." "When Mr. Johnson is gone, they will pelt you with stones." "I was told last night that I would never sleep in that room again." "I saw myself driven from hence," and "I shall go to the torture on Monday." Once a voice announced that Johnson was going to send him to Bedlam, sometimes he dreamt that he would be completely impoverished, and he constantly received messages telling him that the next time would be the last occasion on which he would eat, dress, or sleep in his bed.[12]

His sense of insecurity was complicated by obsessions about his health. For years he had suffered from piles or a prolapsus. This condition led him to dream that his bowels would stop functioning, and once he heard a voice say, "You will never have another evacuation." Another time he reported, "I dream that what I eat forms a Monster within me." He also heard these words, "Every morsel of your food is poisoned." But apparently this voice did not cause him to become fearful about what he ate, as was the case during an earlier period of insanity.[13]

His most constant dream was that a group of bailiffs or soldiers were about to seize him and lead him off to a public execution. This apprehension appears to have arisen from an obsession that he would be made to suffer public shame. "If you were at the bottom of Mount Aetna or Vesuvius," a voice told him, "you would not escape ignominy." Once when Johnson asked him about his dreams of the previous night, he said he could not recall them but that he must have had at least six. "Some were dreams of contempt and horror — some of shame — and some were dreams of ignominy and torture." Apparently the sense of guilt that had helped to bring on the earlier attacks of insanity still troubled him. Once he heard the prediction, "The tyrant's head will be upon a pole within a week's time." When Johnson asked him what it meant, he replied, "I am the tyrant, because I despaired of mercy in the year seventy three." [14]

Johnson's diary records only a couple of the messages that came to Cowper through the tube, but they are sufficient to show the failure of this telephonic experiment. In December 1797 the voice spoken through the wall announced, "Here's a happy New Year coming for Mr. Cowper in this very house." Instead of being cheered by this message, however, Cowper reported that it was spoken "rapidly, to tell him that the time is come." Admitting defeat, Johnson adds, "I suppose he means the time of his torments." [15]

Using more direct methods, in the autumn of 1797 Johnson persuaded Cowper to return to the revision of his Homer. At first the poet felt that the work would be useless, since he would never be allowed to complete it. Once he had been coaxed into the task, however, it kept him occupied for two years, despite the fact that he now felt it was impossible to produce a good English translation of Homer. The only reason he continued with his corrections, he said, was that he felt a compulsion to proceed with the work. [16]

He still found some diversion in the novels that Johnson read to him. After they had exhausted a great many, the clergyman hit upon the idea of reading the poet's own compositions. To these Cowper listened with silent attention, but when his cousin came to *John Gilpin*, he protested that he could not bear to hear this comic poem which he had penned during happier times.

Cowper and Johnson made several trips to Mundesley in the summer and fall of 1798. Occasionally, as when they rowed out to inspect Happisburgh Lighthouse, Cowper showed a flicker of interest. Most of the time, however, he remained completely apathetic to the charms of the region. Even in his earlier days, when he was most deeply dejected, nature could afford neither solace nor escape. Now, although he was in a part of the country that had once delighted him, his perpetual melancholy kept him from responding to its scenic beauty. Nevertheless, he was still sufficiently analytical to be able to write a lucid description of his attitude. When Lady Hesketh wrote him an account of the region about Clifton, he replied: "You describe delightful scenes, but you describe them to one who, if he even saw them, could receive no delight from them — who has a faint recollection, and so faint as to be like an almost forgotten dream, that once he was susceptible of pleasure from such causes. The country you have had in prospect has been always famed for its beauties; but the wretch who can derive no gratification from a view of nature, even under the disadvantage of her most ordinary dress, will have no eyes to admire her in any. In one day, in one moment I should rather have said, she became an *universal blank* to me, and though from a different cause, yet with an effect as difficult to remove, as blindness itself." Cowper adds that from his window at Mundesley he can see hills, rivers, and the ocean itself — a view that once would have delighted him. But it no longer had that effect. "Why," he writes, "is scenery like this . . . now become . . . an insipid wilderness to me? . . . The reason is obvious. My state of mind is a medium through which the beauties of Paradise itself could not be communicated with any effect but a painful one." [17]

Although this is the letter of a man judged to be insane, it is a remarkably clear and consistent explanation of his attitude toward nature. To move him deeply, nature had always had to arouse, not pagan admiration, but a sense of wonder at the miracle of creation. Several times in his verse he had affirmed that the religiously enlightened man sees in nature not just simple beauty but "a ray of heavenly light gilding all forms terrestrial." Such, apparently, was his own experience when he had possessed hope of salvation, but now that despair had triumphed, the heavenly light had disappeared. Realizing his loss, moreover, he could no longer appreciate even the simple beauty enjoyed by the ordinary mortal. Hence Mundesley with all its charms seemed no more than "an insipid wilderness." This might at first appear like a strange term to use in describing a coastal scene, but the image is entirely consistent with the meaning he had earlier attached to it. In his lexicon a wilderness was a symbol of unredeemed chaos. But the chaos did not necessarily reside in the inherent characteristics of a scene. Any place that reminded him of the chaotic state of his own mind might be termed a wilderness. Earlier he had described Hayley's estate as a wilderness, chiefly because the rugged scenery of Eartham had brought his melancholy to the surface. Now not only Mundesley but the whole world loomed like an insipid wilderness, for the cloud of his despair had cast a permanent shadow on the face of the earth.

His ability to see a reflection of his grief in the world about him showed, however, that nature had not become a complete blank for him. He described his situation better when he said, "My mind is a medium through which the beauties of Paradise itself could not be communicated with any effect but a painful one." He could still observe details of his environment, but natural objects served merely as symbols of his plight. "My thoughts," he wrote, "are like loose and dry sand, which the closer it is grasped slips the sooner away." [18] Using a familiar image, he cried in despair, "The night contradicts the day, and I go down the torrent of time into the gulf that I have expected to plunge into so long." [19] The sea, as always, supplied him with stark symbols. "At two miles distance on the coast," he wrote Lady Hesketh, "is a solitary pillar of rock, that the crumbling cliff has left at the high water-mark. I have visited it twice, and have found it an emblem of myself. Torn from my natural connections, I stand alone and expect the storm that shall displace me." [20]

The sea was also the setting for the two amazing poems that Cowper wrote not long before his death. When he completed his revision of Homer, in March 1799, his friends sought to supply him with other projects. Johnson produced the text of *The Four Ages*, which Cowper had abandoned several years earlier. He revised a few lines and added one or two more, but laid it aside with the remark that it was too late in life to produce a long poem. After rejecting other proposals, he mentioned that he had some Latin verses in mind and within a few days he completed his *Montes Glaciales*. Later, at Miss Perowne's request, he translated it into English. The verses were based on a recent newspaper account of icebergs that had been seen floating in the German sea. Written in iambic pentameter couplets, the poem describes the huge blocks of ice rising to enormous heights in the Arctic. Then, breaking from the shelving beach with a roar, these "horrid wanderers of the deep" slip into the sea and float southward. The sun's rays make them shine "like burnished brass," but the poet predicts that Phoebus will destroy them unless they seek refuge in the place of their "hated birth." Although the icebergs are viewed as enemies of mankind, the poem seems to lack personal or subjective implications, unless one chooses to believe that Cowper regarded the icebergs as symbolic obstacles to man's endeavor to reach the peaceful shore of salvation.

About a week later Cowper produced *The Castaway*. This final poem, in which he returned to the image of a mariner on a storm-tossed sea, served as a fitting climax for a career of despondency. In these stanzas Cowper pictures the plight of a sailor washed overboard. His shipmates, unable to rescue him, toss casks and coops into the waves to keep him afloat, but the ship sails on, leaving the poor wretch to his certain fate.[21]

The analogy that Cowper makes between himself and the sailor is so pointed that no one acquainted with his life can read these verses without feeling sympathy for his suffering. Like the mariner's mates, his friends had tried to buoy him up, but their efforts had been in vain, and he now felt certain that his fate was sealed. It is for this reason, probably, that Cowper introduces an interesting variation in his familiar image of a storm-tossed mariner seeking the shore of salvation. In his earlier poems the ship is usually off its course, the sails are ripped, and the seams have opened, but it is always *shipwreck* that threatens to keep the voyager from his destination. In *The Castaway*, although the ship is buffeted by storms, it stays on its course. Thus the other members of the ship's company may happily reach port. Only the solitary sailor is destined to certain death, and he is lost, not by *shipwreck*, but by *drowning*. This variation of the image is significant. So long as Cowper possessed a slight hope of salvation, shipwreck was a proper symbol for his uncertain fate. But when he composed *The Castaway* he felt so sure of damnation that, in the last stanza, he not only compares his end to that of the drowned sailor, but even speaks of himself as one already dead:

> No voice divine the storm allayed,
> No light propitious shone,

> When, snatched from all effectual aid,
>   We perished, each alone:
> But I beneath a rougher sea,
> And whelmed in deeper gulfs than he.

The title of the poem is singularly fitting, especially if we think of its possible connotative meaning in addition to its specific application. Heretofore Cowper had seldom used the term, though one notable example appears in Hymn XXXVI, where he observes:

> Did I meet no trials here,
>   No chastisement by the way,
> Might I not with reason fear
> I should prove a *castaway?*

These lines, written when he had strong hope of salvation, were probably suggested by the text of St. Paul (I Corinthians 9:27), "But I keep under my body, and bring it into subjection: lest that by any means, when I have preached to others, I myself should be a castaway!" If this text was in Cowper's mind when he wrote his valedictory verses, he must have been stung by its bitter application to himself. For, like St. Paul, he had been a preacher of the gospel of salvation. Indeed, the chief purpose of his career as a poet had been to help spread Evangelical doctrines. But by a cruel irony the preacher who had often fired the faith of others had failed in hope himself, with the result that he could only think of himself as a castaway.

Cowper's life was now drawing to a close. Still seeking means to divert his mind, in the last months he made some English translations of the Latin epigrams and verses of his old schoolmaster, Vincent Bourne. He also translated into Latin several of the fables of John Gay. In December 1799 he moved with Johnson into a larger house in East Dereham. This change did not seem to disturb him, but in February his health became so poor that he was confined to his chamber. Because his legs were swollen, the doctor who was consulted diagnosed the case as dropsy, but Lady Hesketh may have been more nearly right when she attributed his illness to a general deterioration.

The elderly poet, who had never discarded his wig or the old-fashioned waistcoats of the dying century, lived to see the dawn of a new era. In western Europe the year 1800 was ushered in under red skies. Napoleon, having become dictator of France, had put an end to the revolution and was now waging a prolonged war with England and other nations. At home there had been threatened uprisings of democratic-minded citizens, but Pitt's government had sternly suppressed the English Jacobins. Other developments of great import were occurring, though no one could yet foresee their full significance. Evangelicalism, having spread through all the Protestant sects, had become the respectable and popular religion of the time. In the north crowded mill towns had sprung up and were manufacturing new machine-made products. In London new fads and fashions were taking the place of those of the previous century. Publishers were bringing out the works of Wordsworth, Coleridge, and Scott, and a revolution in literary taste was under way. Cowper himself had played an important part in developing the new trends in poetry, but the tired old man, now confined to his room in Johnson's house, had no interest in the new generation of writers or in the other innovations of the time.

When Samuel Rose visited him in March, the dying man took little notice of him, except to show signs of regret when Rose had to leave. Meanwhile Johnson kept other old friends informed of the condition of his patient. Lady Hesketh, who had shuddered when she read *The Castaway*, was torn between regret for the impending loss of her cousin and the consoling thought that he would soon be released from suffering. Hayley, his optimism temporarily dimmed by the fatal illness of his son, would find a new outlet for his sentimentalism as the official biographer of his fellow poet. John Newton, still active at seventy-five, would observe the death of his old companion by preaching a sermon in which the sturdy old Calvinist revealed that he was still puzzled that a man of such apparent merit could have doubts of his salvation.

The conviction that had made such a calamity of the poet's

life remained with him to the end. Toward the last his devoted but tactless cousin spoke to him about his approaching death, saying that he would soon be delivered from all bodily pain. Cowper, though able to understand him, made no reply. The clergyman then proceeded to speak of the merciful Redeemer who loved his children and would welcome him to a state of infinite happiness. These words, however, provoked an anguished cry from Cowper and he begged Johnson not to mention again the subject of an afterlife. He lingered for a few days; then on April 25, 1800, toward the latter end of a spring day, he breathed his last so quietly that those in the room did not at first realize that he was dead.

Notes

THE verse selections in this text are taken from *The Poems of William Cowper*, edited by J. C. Bailey, London, 1905. In quoting from Cowper's letters I have, wherever possible, used *The Correspondence of William Cowper*, edited by Thomas Wright, 4 volumes, New York and London, 1904. I have also, for the sake of easy reference, used the dates of composition which Wright assigned, even though he misdated certain letters. In quoting from letters not printed in Wright's collected edition, I have referred to the particular source in which they appear.

I. Youth

[1] *The Unpublished and Uncollected Letters of William Cowper*, ed. Thomas Wright (London, 1925), p. 18.

[2] *Memoir of the Most Remarkable and Interesting Parts of the Life of William Cowper, Esq.* (London, 1822), p. 14.

[3] John Sargeaunt, *Annals of Westminster School* (London, 1898).

[4] *Ibid.*, p. 170.

[5] *Ibid.*, p. 152.

[6] *Memoir*, pp. 16–17.

[7] To Mrs. King, March 3, 1788.

[8] *Memoir*, pp. 20–21.

[9] *Ibid.*, pp. 21–22.

[10] *Ibid.*, p. 22.

[11] Walter Bagehot, "William Cowper," *Estimations in Criticism* (London, 1908), Vol. I.

[12] *Connoisseur*, January 31, 1754.

[13] *Correspondence*, ed. Wright, I, 8 (undated letter).

[14] Eugene R. Page, *George Colman the Elder* (New York, 1935), pp. 39–40.

[15] To William Unwin, April 6, 1780.

[16] *Dictionary of National Biography*.

[17] *Cowper Memorials*, ed. H. P. Stokes (Olney, 1904), p. 19.

[18] To William Unwin, January 17, 1782.

[19] To "Dear Toby," February 21, 1754.

[20] "Preface," *Poems, the Early Productions of William Cowper*, ed. James Croft (London, 1825), p. vi.

[21] *Ibid.*

II. The Crisis

[1] *Diary of Mary Countess Cowper* (London, 1864), p. 42.

[2] Harry Graham, *Mother of Parliaments* (London, 1910), p. 242n.

[3] *Memoir*, p. 25.

[4] To Lady Hesketh, August 9, 1763.

[5] *Memoir*, p. 32.

[6] *Ibid.*, pp. 34 and 42.

[7] *Ibid.*, p. 36.

[8] *Ibid.*, p. 38.

[9] *Ibid.*, p. 40.

[10] *Ibid.*, p. 41.

[11] *Ibid.*, p. 46.

[12] *Ibid.*, p. 48.

[13] *Ibid.*, p. 49.

[14] *Ibid.*

[15] *Ibid.*, p. 50.

[16] *Ibid.*, p. 53.

[17] The discussion that follows in the text is based on my article "William Cowper and the Unpardonable Sin," *Journal of Religion*, XXIII (April, 1943), 110–116. For interpretations of the sin by early Church Fathers, see "Blasphème contre le Saint-Esprit," *Dictionnaire théologie catholique.* A summary of various views is found in Richard Baxter, "The Unpardonable Sin against the Holy Ghost," *Works* (London, 1830), Vol. XX.

[18] M. M. Knappen, *Tudor Puritanism* (Chicago, 1939), p. 396.

[19] Baxter, *op. cit.*, pp. 243ff.

[20] *Memoir*, p. 53.

[21] *Ibid.*, p. 50.

[22] *Ibid.*, p. 51.

[23] John Tillotson, *Works* (London, 1820), II, 176–177.

[24] *Ibid.*, p. 181.

[25] *Ibid.*, p. 188.

[26] *Memoir*, p. 59.

[27] *Ibid.*, p. 33.

[28] William Heberden, *Commentaries on the History and Cure of Diseases* (London, 1802), p. 226.

[29] James Hendrie Lloyd, "The Case of William Cowper," *Archives of Neurology and Psychology*, XXIV, 688–689.

[30] Gilbert Thomas, *William Cowper and the Eighteenth Century* (London, 1935), p. 126.

[31] David Cecil, *The Stricken Deer* (London, 1929), p. 165.

[32] *The Greville Memoirs*, ed. Henry Reeve (New York, 1875), II, 285.

[33] Frances M. Brookfield, *The Cambridge Apostles* (New York, 1906), p. 263.

[34] *The Greville Memoirs*, ed. Lytton Strachey and Roger Fulford (London, 1938), III, 85.

III. The Convert

[1] To John Newton, July 19, 1784.

[2] *Memoir*, p. 60.

[3] To Lady Hesketh, July 4, 1785.

[4] *Memoir*, p. 60.

[5] *Ibid.*, p. 63.

[6] *Ibid.*, p. 64.

[7] *Ibid.*, pp. 67–68.

[8] *Ibid.*, p. 66.

[9] July 3, 1765.

[10] To Lady Hesketh, September 14, 1765.

[11] *Unpublished Letters*, pp. 26–29 (To Mrs. Madan, June 11 and 18, 1768).

[12] To Lady Hesketh, April 3, 1786.

[13] To Joseph Hill, October 25, 1765.

[14] To Lady Hesketh, October 18, 1765.

[15] To Mrs. Cowper, October 20, 1766.

[16] *Unpublished Letters*, pp. 4–5 (To Mrs. Madan, July 10, 1767).

[17] *Ibid.*

[18] *Ibid.*, p. 11 (To Mrs. Madan, August 10, 1767).

[19] J. H. Lloyd, *op. cit.*, p. 685.

[20] Josiah Bull, "The Early Years of the Poet Cowper at Olney," *The Sunday at Home, A Family Magazine*, 1866, pp. 347–348. Letters of John Newton to Lord Dartmouth, *Manuscripts of the Earl of Dartmouth* (Historical Manuscripts Commission, 15th Report), Vol. III (London, 1896), Appendix, Part I, p. 183.

IV. A Disciple of Newton

[1] *Unpublished Letters*, p. 14 (To Mrs. Madan, September 26, 1767).

[2] Thomas Wright, *The Life of William Cowper* (London, 1892), p. 168.

[3] Letters of Newton to Lord Dartmouth (February 16, 1768), *op. cit.*, p. 186.

[4] John Newton, *Life* (New York: Am.

Tract Society, n.d.) For the most recent and the fullest life of Newton, see Bernard Martin, *John Newton*, London, 1950.

[5] John Newton, *Forty-one Letters on Religious Subjects* (London, 1807), p. 53.

[6] *Letters by the Reverend John Newton*, ed. Josiah Bull (London, 1869), p. 256.

[7] *John Newton*, ed. Josiah Bull (London, 1864), p. 212.

[8] Adelaide Thein, "The Religion of John Newton," *PQ*, XXI (April 1942), 164.

[9] John Newton, *Works* (London, 1816), IV, 246.

[10] *Letters . . . of Newton*, p. 159.

[11] *John Newton, op. cit.*, p. 189.

[12] *Life*, pp. 29ff.

[13] *Eclectic Notes*, ed. John H. Pratt (London, 1856), pp. 84–85.

[14] *Notes and Queries*, 10th Series, II, 42 (To Mrs. Madan, June 4, 1767).

[15] *Ibid.*, II, 84 (To Mrs. Madan, undated letter).

[16] *Ibid.* (To Mrs. Madan, December 10, 1767).

[17] To Mrs. Cowper, June 7, 1770.

[18] *John Newton, op. cit.*, p. 190.

[19] *Olney Hymns* (Edinburgh, 1821), p. vi.

[20] *Ibid.*, p. v.

[21] Louis F. Benson, *The English Hymn* (New York, 1915), p. 338.

v. The Olney Recluse

[1] "Early Years of the Poet William Cowper at Olney," *op. cit.*, p. 379.

[2] *Ibid.*

[3] *Notes and Queries*, 10th Series, II, 242 (June 9, 1772).

[4] John Newton, *op. cit.*, p. 181.

[5] *Ibid.*, p. 173.

[6] Robert Southey, *Life of William Cowper* (Boston, 1839), I, 185.

[7] Hoxie N. Fairchild, *Religious Trends in English Poetry* (New York, 1942), II, 176.

[8] Mary Whiting, "A Burning Bush," *Hibbert Journal*, XXIV, 305.

[9] To Lady Hesketh, April 3, 1786.

[10] Letters of Newton to Dartmouth, *op. cit.*, p. 201 (May 22, 1773).

[11] To Lady Hesketh, January 16, 1786.

[12] Mary Whiting, *op. cit.*, p. 306.

[13] Wright, *Life*, p. 206.

[14] Quoted by Southey, *Life*, I, 188.

[15] *Gospel Magazine and Theological Review*, V (November 1800), 437.

[16] To Newton.

[17] To Newton.

[18] October 27, 1782.

[19] Quoted by Southey, *Life*, I, 191. Bernard Martin, *John Newton*, p. 240, quotes a letter addressed to Newton by John Thornton, who expressed the opinion that it was scandalous to give shelter to the unmarried couple at the vicarage. Thornton urged Newton to get rid of them.

[20] To Newton, March 14, 1782.

[21] To Newton.

[22] To Newton.

[23] To Newton.

[24] *Gentleman's Magazine*, LIV (June 1784), 413.

[25] *Ibid.*, p. 414.

[26] To Newton, May 3, 1780.

[27] August 1, 1776.

[28] January 5, 1782.

[29] *Original Letters from the Rev. John Newton to the Rev. W. Barlass* (London, 1819), p. 52.

[30] To Mrs. Newton, March 4, 1780.

[31] *Letters by the Rev. John Newton*, ed. Bull, pp. 162–163.

[32] *Ibid.*

[33] Wright, *Life*, p. 235.

[34] To John Newton, October 16, 1785.

[35] W. P. Courtney, "Samuel Greatheed," *Notes and Queries*, 11th Series, V, 71.

VI. The Progress of Error

[1] November 27, 1781.

[2] To John Newton, January 26, 1783.

[3] *Poems of William Cowper*, ed. Bailey, p. lxxvii.

[4] John Wesley, "An Estimate of the Manners of the Present Time" [1782], *Works* (1856), XI, 152 and 154.

[5] *Letters . . . to . . . Barlass*, pp. 129ff.

[6] February 27, 1780.

[7] Martin Madan, *Thelypthora, or a Treatise on Female Ruin*, London, 1781.

[8] According to Louise Lanham, Sir Marmadan represents the Reverend Samuel Babcock, who satirized Madan's work in the *Monthly Review* (October and November 1780). See *The Poetry of William Cowper*, unpublished dissertation, Chapel Hill, N. C.

[9] To Newton, July 12, 1780.

[10] To William Unwin, February 6, 1781.

[11] To Newton, January 21, 1781.

[12] March 5, 1781.

[13] March 18, 1781.

[14] To Newton, August 25, 1781.

[15] February 18, 1781.

[16] October 19, 1781.

[17] April 1, 1782.

[18] *Critical Review*, LIII (April 1782), 287–290.

[19] *London Magazine*, LI (May 1782), 245.

[20] *Gentleman's Magazine*, LII (March 1782), 130.

[21] To William Unwin, June 12, 1782.

[22] *Monthly Review*, LXVII (October 1782), 262–265.

[23] *Gentleman's Magazine*, LV (December 1785), 986.

[24] See M. J. Quinlan, *Victorian Prelude* (New York, 1941), pp. 226ff.

[25] Wright, *Life*, letter of Franklin to Thornton quoted, p. 299.

[26] M. J. Quinlan, "An Intermediary between Cowper and Johnson," *RES*, XXIV (April 1948), 141–147.

VII. Second Spring

[1] William Hayley, *The Life and Posthumous Writings of William Cowper* (Chichester, 1806), II, 2.

[2] Kenneth Povey, "Cowper and Lady Austen," *RES*, X (October 1934), 424.

[3] July 7, 1781.

[4] *Ibid*.

[5] Povey, "Cowper and Lady Austen."

[6] *Ibid.*, p. 424.

[7] *Ibid.*, p. 422.

[8] To William Unwin, July 29, 1781.

[9] To Newton, August 16, 1781.

[10] August 21, 1781.

[11] To William Unwin, March 7, 1782.

[12] July 3 [1782].

[13] January 19, 1783.

[14] October 20, 1783.

[15] Povey, "Cowper and Lady Austen," p. 423.

[16] Kenneth Povey, "The Banishment of Lady Austen," *RES*, XV (October 1939), 395.

[17] *Ibid.*, pp. 393ff.

[18] *Ibid*.

[19] Dorothy L. Gilbert and Russell Pope, "The Cowper Translations of Mme. Guyon's Poems," *PMLA*, LIV (1939), 1097 and *passim*.

[20] Povey, "Cowper and Lady Austen," pp. 422–423.

[21] *Ibid*.

[22] Dwight Durling, *Georgic Tradition in English Poetry* (New York, 1935), pp. 84 and 152–157.

[23] *Gentleman's Magazine*, LV (December 1785), 985–988.

[24] *Monthly Review*, LXXIV (June 1786), 416–425.

[25] *Letters of the Reverend John Wesley* (London, 1931), VII, 342.

[26] *Letters of Robert Burns*, ed. J. DeLancey Ferguson (Oxford, 1931), I, 260; II, 225.

[27] To John Newton, December 15, 1783.

[28] To William Unwin, "about 24th of May, 1784."

[29] *Ibid.*

[30] October 12, 1785.

[31] To Lady Hesketh, December 7 [1785].

[32] *Thraliana, The Diary of Hester Lynch Thrale,* 1776–1809, ed. Katharine C. Balderston (Oxford, 1942), I, 478 (January 10, 1781).

[33] *Poems, The Early Productions of William Cowper,* ed. Croft, p. 58. (Extracts from Lady Hesketh's letters to Theodora are printed without dates.)

[34] *Ibid.,* p. 66.

[35] *New Review,* IX (March 1786), 164–165.

[36] To Newton, March 19, 1784.

[37] January 15, 1785.

[38] September 30, 1786.

VIII. At Weston

[1] December 9, 1786.

[2] December 4, 1786.

[3] January 14, 1787.

[4] Wright, *Life,* p. 452.

[5] *Private Papers of James Boswell from Malahide Castle,* ed. Geoffrey Scott and F. A. Pottle (1934), XVIII, 110.

[6] October 20, 1787.

[7] July 16, 1790.

[8] July 6, 1791.

[9] October 2, 1787.

[10] September 15, 1787.

[11] To Samuel Rose, July 24, 1787.

[12] April 12, 1788.

[13] To Lady Hesketh, February 26, 1790.

[14] To Mrs. King, March 12, 1790.

[15] To John Johnson, December 18, 1790.

[16] Rowland E. Prothers, "Horace Walpole and William Cowper," *Quarterly Review,* CCII (January 1905), 35.

[17] T. De Wyzewa, "A propos d'un recueil de lettres de William Cowper," *Revue des deux mondes,* July 15, 1912, p. 467.

[18] C. A. Sainte-Beuve, "William Cowper ou de la poésie domestique," *Causeries du lundi,* XI, 162–163.

[19] Lytton Strachey, *Characters and Commentaries* (New York, 1933), p. 48.

[20] Lodwick C. Hartley, *William Cowper, Humanitarian* (Chapel Hill, N. C., 1938).

[21] July 6, 1791.

[22] E. V. Lucas, "Evolution of Whimsicality," *Giving and Receiving* (London, 1922), pp. 48–63.

[23] February 5, 1791.

[24] November 27, 1787.

[25] May 28, 1790.

[26] May 25, 1788.

[27] To Mrs. King, June 14, 1790; Helperus R. V. Lier, *The Power of Grace Illustrated* (London, 1792).

[28] February 19, 1788.

[29] *Gentleman's Magazine,* LV (August 1785), 610–613.

[30] John Knowles, *The Life and Writings of Henry Fuseli* (London, 1831), I, 73.

[31] *Ibid.* and "Preface" to first edition of Cowper's Homer, *Works,* ed. Robert Southey (London, 1854), VII, xvi. (Cowper acknowledges in his Preface the assistance given him by Fuseli.)

[32] *The Farington Diary,* ed. James Grieg (London, 1923), II, 103.

[33] *Monthly Review,* VIII (August 1792), 431–443.

[34] *Ibid.,* XXIV (December 1797), 429.

[35] *Gentleman's Magazine,* LXI (September 1791), 845–846; (November 1791), 1034–1036; (December 1791), 1133–1134.

[36] *Ibid.,* LXII (July 1792), 616.

[37] Fuseli's review reprinted in Knowles, *op. cit.,* I, 81–109.

[38] February 17, 1793.

[39] *Henry Crabb Robinson on Books and Their Writers,* ed. Edith J. Morley (London [1938]), I, 72.

[40] October 5, 1787.

[41] Wright, *Correspondence*, IV, 121.

[42] To Samuel Rose, December 21, 1791.

[43] *Memoirs of the Life and Writings of William Hayley*, ed. John Johnson, 2 vols., London, 1823. The most recent and best biography is: Morchard Bishop, *Blake's Hayley*, London, 1951.

[44] *Analytical Review*, III (Appendix), 470.

[45] Wright, *Correspondence*, IV, 166n.

[46] Ernest Dowden, "Cowper and Hayley," *Atlantic Monthly*, C (July 1907), 83.

[47] June 5, 1792.

[48] July 30, 1792.

[49] *The Diary of Samuel Teedon*, ed. Thomas Wright (London, 1902), July 21, 1792.

[50] July 21, 1792.

[51] *Letters of Lady Hesketh to the Rev. John Johnson*, ed. Catherine B. Johnson (London, 1901), p. 20.

[52] *Ibid.*, p. 22.

[53] *Memoirs . . . of William Hayley*, I, 433.

[54] *Ibid.*, p. 434.

[55] *Letters of Lady Hesketh*, p. 19.

[56] August 6, 1792.

[57] September 9, 1792.

[58] October 16, 1792.

[59] November 17 [1792].

[60] November 21, 1792.

[61] *The Farington Diary*, II, 108.

[62] Hayley, *Life . . . of William Cowper*, IV, 115.

[63] *Letters of Lady Hesketh*, p. 33.

[64] *Ibid.*, p. 37.

[65] *Ibid.*

[66] Hayley, *Life . . . of William Cowper*, IV, 153; H. R. S. Caldicott, "How Cowper Got His Pension," *Cornhill Magazine*, XXXIV (April 1913), 493ff.

[67] "Cowper's Spiritual Diary," *London Mercury*, XV, 493–496.

[68] *Ibid.*

IX. The Man and the Poet

[1] To William Unwin, November 24, 1781.

[2] To William Unwin, January 17, 1782.

[3] Leslie Stephen, *Hours in a Library* (London, 1907), p. 45.

[4] Raymond D. Havens, *The Influence of Milton on English Poetry* (Cambridge, Mass., 1922), pp. 167–168.

[5] *Ibid.*, pp. 170ff.

[6] April 20, 1783.

[7] *Memoir*, pp. 31, 51.

[8] To Mrs. Cowper, April 4, 1766.

[9] September 25, 1770.

[10] September 26, 1781.

[11] September 24, 1785.

[12] October 2, 1787.

[13] January 13, 1787.

[14] William Hazlitt, *Lectures on the English Poets* (Philadelphia, 1818), pp. 181–182.

[15] *Ibid.*

[16] *Ibid.*

[17] Myra Reynolds, *The Treatment of Nature in English Poetry* (Chicago, 1909), p. 184.

[18] To John Newton.

[19] To Samuel Teedon, August 5, 1792.

[20] To Samuel Greatheed, August 6, 1792.

[21] September 9, 1792.

[22] October 18, 1792.

[23] *Letters of Lady Hesketh*, p. 22.

[24] The excerpts quoted in this paragraph are taken from a series of Cowper's letters published in *Notes and Queries*, 10th Series, II (July–December 1904), 84, 122, 243.

[25] John Wesley, "The Wilderness State," *Sermons on Several Occasions* (New York, 1828), I, 408ff.

[26] May 3, 1780.

[27] *Early Letters of William and Dorothy Wordsworth*, ed. Ernest De Selincourt (Oxford, 1935), pp. 295–296.

[28] *Letters of William and Dorothy Wordsworth*, ed. Ernest De Selincourt (Oxford, 1937), II, 615.

Notes

[29] Stopford Brooke, "Crabbe and Cowper," *Naturalism in English Poetry* (New York, 1920), pp. 111–112.

[30] Stopford Brooke, *Theology in English Poets* (New York, 1875), p. 61.

[31] Quoted from a letter of October 11, 1831, in Alfred M. Terhune, *The Life of Edward FitzGerald* (New Haven, 1947), p. 69.

x. The Castaway

[1] Robert F. Spiller, "A New Biographical Source for William Cowper," *PMLA*, XLII (December 1927), 951.

[2] *Ibid.*, p. 956.

[3] *Ibid.*

[4] Edward Dowden, "Cowper and Hayley," *op. cit.*, pp. 74–87.

[5] *Ibid.*, p. 75.

[6] *Ibid.*, p. 76.

[7] British Museum Add. MSS 38, 887, f. 187.

[8] *Ibid.*, ff. 189–190.

[9] Richard Watson, *Anecdotes* (London, 1817), p. 346.

[10] Dowden, *op. cit.*, p. 80.

[11] Spiller, *op. cit.*, p. 956.

[12] Transcript of a Diary kept by John Johnson, Cambridge University, Add. MSS 5993. (For a description of this Diary, see Hoxie N. Fairchild, "Additional Notes on John Johnson's Diary," *PMLA*, XLIII, 571–572.)

[13] *Ibid.*

[14] *Ibid.*

[15] *Ibid.*

[16] To Lady Hesketh, December 8, 1798.

[17] October 13, 1798.

[18] To Lady Hesketh, January 22, 1796.

[19] To Lady Hesketh, February 19, 1796.

[20] To Lady Hesketh, August 27, 1795.

[21] Hayley, *op. cit.*, IV, 181.

INDEX

Index

Index

JOY THE BAKER

Homemade Decadence

Irresistibly Sweet, Salty, Gooey, Sticky,
Fluffy, Creamy, Crunchy Treats

JOY WILSON

clarkson potter/publishers

new york

Published in the United States by Clarkson Potter/Publishers,
an imprint of the Crown Publishing Group, a division of Random House LLC,
a Penguin Random House Company, New York.
www.crownpublishing.com
www.clarksonpotter.com

CLARKSON POTTER is a trademark and POTTER with colophon
is a registered trademark of Random House LLC.

Library of Congress Cataloging-in-Publication Data
Wilson, Joy, 1981–
   Joy the baker homemade decadence / Joy Wilson. —First edition.
      pages cm
   Includes index.
   1. Desserts. 2. Baking. I. Title. II. Title: Homemade decadence.

TX773.W6977 2014
641.86—dc23

                              2013045976

ISBN: 978-0-385-34573-6
eBook ISBN: 978-0-385-34574-3

Printed in China

Cover and book design by Ashley Tucker
Cover and interior photography by Joy Wilson and Jon Melendez

10 9 8 7 6 5 4 3 2 1

First Edition

For Dede

Thank you for all of
the birthday cakes
and forehead kisses.

CONTENTS

INTRODUCTION

You should see my oven. You really should. It's a tiny apartment-size oven made to complement the tiny apartment-size refrigerator, inside the tiny apartment-size kitchen, housed in the very tiny bungalow in which I live and work, located in Venice, California.

By the looks of the oven and the mini baking sheets I've had to buy to accommodate it, you'd probably say that I have no business at all in the baking world. Thankfully, it's not the size of one's oven that makes a baker; it's the amount of butter in one's fridge and passion in one's heart.

My food blog, JoytheBaker.com, was born out of such passion (and butter, let's be real). I started the site in early 2008, during that weird time on the Internet when AOL chat rooms were uncool and Instagram didn't exist yet. I started it on a borrowed laptop, with a borrowed Internet connection, in a friend's kitchen. It was all very haphazard, but it was a place for me to scream into the void by way of sharing recipes, photos, and stories. Food blogs were just starting to emerge, authored by people utterly obsessed with food, and with Joy the Baker I found myself in humble but really enthusiastic company.

The Internet can teach us some pretty invaluable lessons (beyond how to tie a tie and poach an egg). It has taught me that people love to connect around food. We love to share recipes, gawk at pictures of chocolate chip cookies, and share our kitchen successes and occasional failures. In the past few years, Joy the Baker has grown from a solitary endeavor to a community of butter-loving bakers eager to share and learn together every day.

I'm a self-taught baker. Fueled by an unreasonable love of sweets and my parents' fondness for store-bought whole wheat fig bars, I taught myself how to bake as a survival skill. And yet I learned the heart of baking from my parents. My dad, who has a healthy appreciation for pies, taught me the art of a perfect pie crust; my mom, a cake enthusiast, imparted the importance of completely cooled cake layers in cake decorating. I may not put on a pastry chef coat every morning, but knowledge and confidence in the kitchen don't always come from a fancy uniform. Sometimes all you need is a great recipe and a trusty spatula.

In *Joy the Baker Homemade Decadence,* I'm diving deep into the edible wonders I explore every day in my kitchen and on Joy the Baker. I'm reaching beyond what we might need to get down to the nitty-gritty of what we really want. My wants generally include boozy brunches, chewy chocolate cookies, three-tiered cakes, and caramel in my ice cream. No shame! There's no such thing as out-of-bounds when it comes to dessert desires. My needs (as opposed to my wants) generally include shelter, sustenance, and a fork. Not as extravagant and severely lacking in caramel.

Let's talk about how to get more salty pretzels into our cakes, like in the Chocolate–Peanut Butter Pretzel Layer Cake (page 190). I've found a way to make ice cream taste like cheesecake! I call it Strawberry Cheesecake Ice Cream (page 245), and it's a revelation. We can totally have pizza for brunch, too, with Sausage and Blackberry Breakfast Pizza (page 59). And don't even get me started with the Apple Pie with Cheddar–Bacon Crust (page 135). It's beyond!

Decadent desserts shouldn't be reserved for fancy date nights at expensive restaurants. The recipes in this book are designed to make you look like a hero at the brunch table or neighborhood potluck. More than that, though, I want these sweet recipes to feel special. I know the biggest indulgence these days is having the time to make a pie crust from scratch and churn your own ice cream. Time is such a luxury, and for you to spend those precious moments making something truly wonderful for yourself and those you love is a big deal. I honor that.

I want you to feel confident in the kitchen. I want you to make scones for the first time, dust off that ice cream maker you got as a wedding present, and conquer your fear of meringue. I think you'll find that the time involved and love exuded will make a tasty, tasteful difference. I believe we can all use a little extra love and caramel in our treats these days. It can all be ours, no matter the size of our ovens.

BRUNCH

I BELIEVE THAT EVERY GREAT SATURDAY NIGHT IN THE HISTORY OF SATURDAY NIGHTS HAS BEEN PRECEDED BY OR FOLLOWED BY BRUNCH.

This meal is the beginning or end of every epic story.

Let's talk about the luxuries of brunch. Brunch is the lazy weekend meal that extends from the late morning into the mid-afternoon and is nothing short of entirely necessary and completely indulgent. It's a break in the weekend that invites you to linger. We so rarely linger these days. It almost feels . . . unnatural. I believe that as long as there is a warm cup of coffee in front of you on a Saturday or Sunday, you're allowed to linger.

Brunch is always what you need it to be. Maybe it's brunch for one on a quiet Sunday morning with buttered toast and cinnamon coffee. Maybe it's brunch for many set at a sprawling table where Bloody Marys flow, quiche is sliced generously, and new friends are extra chatty. Brunch can be serious business, a rowdy affair, or simply toast. It's wonderful every which way.

I've filled this brunch chapter with recipes and ingredients that I hope make you feel capable in the kitchen and praiseworthy at the breakfast table. I also want you to sleep in—and not worry about bed-head. These recipes are designed to feel comforting and indulgent, and a few can be made the evening before!

There's everything from Vanilla Sugar Doughnuts (page 31) to Braised Kale and Egg Breakfast Sandwiches (page 55). There are cocktails for a few or for many, and I also support spiking your carrot juice with champagne. It's the weekend. It's time to linger. It's time to live—and time to prepare for an epic night to follow.

FRESH RASPBERRY-HONEY butter

LEMON-POPPY SEED pancakes

yeasted OVERNIGHT PANCAKES

the ULTIMATE PANCAKE SYRUP

brown sugar & orange PANCAKE SYRUP

vanilla-blueberry QUICK JAM

PEAR, DARK CHOCOLATE & GINGER scones

SOUR CREAM scones

WHOLE WHEAT, PEACH & FRESH SAGE scones

vanilla sugar DOUGHNUTS

CINNAMON SUGAR & DARK CHOCOLATE croissants

HAWAIIAN SWEET PINEAPPLE breakfast rolls

cinnamon-sugar pull-apart cake WITH LEMON GLAZE

SOUR CREAM COFFEE CAKE with brown butter glaze

breakfast cobbler WITH OATMEAL DROP BISCUITS

blueberry pancake muffins WITH MAPLE GLAZE

ROASTED STRAWBERRY & BALSAMIC grits

roasted-potato BREAKFAST NACHOS

BRAISED KALE & EGG breakfast sandwiches

breakfast grilled cheese WITH HAM & CHERRY JAM

SAUSAGE & BLACKBERRY breakfast pizza

FRENCH ONION quiche

champagne-sorbet FLOATS

red snapper COCKTAIL

CARROT-ORANGE-GINGER mimosa punch

LAVENDER-LIME-CUCUMBER spritzers

MANGO-WATERMELON tequila sunrise

STRAWBERRY, BEET & chia seed SMOOTHIE

dirty CHAI LATTES

This is an exploration in making butter better. Futile? Unnecessary? Downright silly? Never. This sweetened butter is studded with fresh raspberries, and it's absolutely delicious slathered in hearty proportions on warm Sour Cream Scones (page 27) or Yeasted Overnight Pancakes (page 18). Breakfast divinity!

FRESH RASPBERRY–HONEY
butter

½ cup (1 stick) unsalted butter, at room temperature

8 fresh raspberries

2 tablespoons honey

¼ teaspoon salt

In a small bowl, use a fork to mash together the butter, raspberries, honey, and salt. Stir until the ingredients are combined but the raspberries are still somewhat chunky. It's okay if there are little pockets of honey and fruit. Scoop out the butter onto a piece of plastic wrap, form it into a disk shape, and wrap well. Chill until ready to use. The butter will keep, well wrapped in the refrigerator, for up to 3 days.

makes just over ½ cup

HAVE YOUR TOAST AND EAT IT, TOO:
simple and sublime

Toast is always worth mentioning. Toast is subtle, simple, and comforting. Toast is big, bold, and filling. Toast is for you, alone with a single cup of coffee. Toast is for many, topped with fancy cheese and dripping with honey. Toast is only and exactly toast, and it's perfect.

chocolate hazelnut spread with rainbow jimmies Toast a slice of bread. Spread it generously with chocolate hazelnut spread and sprinkle with rainbow jimmies. High-five yourself and then enjoy!

peanut butter, sliced banana, and honey Toast a slice of bread. Spread it with smooth all-natural peanut butter. Top with sliced banana and drizzle with honey. Sprinkle with raisins if you're feeling extra sweet.

cinnamon and sugar Toast a slice of bread. Spread it with room-temperature salted butter. Sprinkle generously with a mixture of cinnamon and sugar. Enjoy immediately.

melted cheese and pickled jalapeño Slice a bagel in half and scoop out some of the inside bread of each bagel half. Sprinkle with a bit of shredded Cheddar cheese. Add as many pickled jalapeños as you'd like. Top with more Cheddar cheese. Broil until melted and bubbly.

cream cheese, smoked salmon, sliced onion, and capers Slice a bagel in half. Spread it generously with cream cheese. Top with thinly sliced smoked salmon, thinly sliced onion, and capers.

ricotta, grape, honey, and herb Toast a baguette. Slather it with ricotta cheese. Top with sliced grapes, drizzle with honey, and sprinkle with fresh mint, thyme, or rosemary.

salted butter and radish Toast a baguette or thick slice of bread. Slather it with salted butter. Top with thinly sliced radishes and coarse sea salt.

smashed avocado and lemon Toast a baguette or a slice of bread. Spread it with smashed, ripe avocado. Drizzle with fresh lemon juice. Sprinkle with coarse sea salt and freshly cracked black pepper.

It was hard for me to justify pouring maple syrup over my favorite breakfast muffin, so I turned my beloved lemon-and-poppy-seed treat into a pancake. Totally reasonable. Now I can drench these flavors in maple syrup without getting any dirty looks. I'm nothing if not clever (and hungry).

LEMON-POPPY SEED
pancakes

- 2 tablespoons sugar
- 2 tablespoons grated lemon zest
- 2 cups all-purpose flour
- 2 teaspoons baking powder
- 1 teaspoon baking soda
- 1 teaspoon salt
- 2 cups buttermilk
- 2 large eggs
- 2 teaspoons pure vanilla extract
- 2 tablespoons fresh lemon juice
- ¼ cup (½ stick) unsalted butter, melted and cooled slightly, plus more for serving
- 2 tablespoons poppy seeds
- Butter, shortening, or vegetable oil, for the pan
- Maple syrup, warmed, for serving

1. In a small bowl, combine the sugar and lemon zest. Rub together with your fingers until the sugar is fragrant.

2. In a large bowl, whisk together the flour, baking powder, baking soda, and salt. Stir in the lemon sugar.

3. In a separate bowl (or a large liquid measuring cup), whisk together the buttermilk, eggs, vanilla, lemon juice, and melted butter. Pour the wet ingredients into the dry ingredients. Add the poppy seeds and stir well. If a few lumps remain, that's no problem. Let the batter rest for 10 minutes. The batter will thicken slightly as it rests.

4. Put a rack in the center of the oven, put a heat-proof plate on the rack, and preheat the oven to 150°F.

5. Heat a griddle or a nonstick sauté pan over medium heat. Melt a tablespoon of butter in the pan. Working in batches, spoon the batter onto the griddle. For small pancakes, I use about 2 tablespoons per pancake, and for larger pancakes, about ¼ cup. Cook until golden brown on the bottom and bubbling on top, about 4 minutes. Flip the pancakes and cook until golden brown on the second side, about 4 minutes. Repeat with the remaining batter. Transfer the cooked pancakes to the plate in the warm oven, cover with a clean kitchen towel, and keep warm until ready to serve.

6. Serve with butter and warm maple syrup.

makes 24 small pancakes

It takes some real kitchen tricks to feel like a superhero in the morning. There's something about bed-head and wrinkled pajama pants that doesn't instill a tremendous amount of confidence in your breakfast guests. Luckily you have tricks up your sleeve (and a giant mug of coffee in your hands). Yeast is your secret weapon.

This isn't one of those "sounds too good to be true" situations. This pancake batter comes together the night before cooking. While you're getting your beauty sleep, the yeast is working hard in the refrigerator to create a fluffy and flavorful dough. The pancakes bake up thick, but their texture is surprisingly light and fluffy. I love to serve them with The Ultimate Pancake Syrup (page 21). Oh! You should probably invite the neighbors over. They can smell what you're cooking up, and they promise not to judge your house slippers. It's cool.

Pancakes are perfect for add-ins. Some of my favorites include: 1 teaspoon grated orange zest and a handful of dark chocolate chips; ½ teaspoon ground cinnamon and a handful of fresh blueberries; 1 mashed banana and 1 heaping spoonful of peanut butter. Add these things after the batter has risen overnight, just before cooking.

yeasted
OVERNIGHT PANCAKES

1½ cups warm whole milk (about 105°F)

1 (.25-ounce) package active dry yeast (2¼ teaspoons)

2½ cups all-purpose flour

3 tablespoons sugar

¾ teaspoon salt

¼ teaspoon ground cinnamon

Pinch of freshly grated nutmeg

1. In a small bowl, whisk together the warm milk and yeast. Let stand for 5 minutes.

2. Meanwhile, in a large bowl, whisk together the flour, sugar, salt, cinnamon, and nutmeg.

3. Add the melted butter, eggs, and vanilla to the milk and yeast mixture. Pour the yeast mixture, all at once, into the dry ingredients. Stir until no lumps remain. Cover the bowl with plastic wrap and drape a clean kitchen towel over the covered bowl. Put the bowl on top of a plate in the refrigerator (in case the dough overflows) and let the pancake batter rest overnight.

4. When ready to make the pancakes, remove the batter from the fridge and let it sit at room temperature for 20 minutes.

5. Put a rack in the center of the oven, put a heat-proof plate on the rack, and preheat the oven to 150°F.

6. In a griddle or a nonstick sauté pan set over medium heat, melt 1 tablespoon of butter. Working in batches, spoon the batter onto the griddle. For small pancakes, I use about 2 tablespoons per pancake, and for larger pancakes, about ¼ cup. Cook until golden brown on the bottom, about 4 minutes. Carefully flip and cook the second side until golden brown, about 4 minutes. Repeat with the remaining batter. Transfer the cooked pancakes to the plate in the warm oven, cover with a clean kitchen towel, and keep warm until ready to serve.

makes 24 small pancakes

¼ cup (½ stick) unsalted butter, melted and cooled

2 large eggs, beaten

2 teaspoons pure vanilla extract

Butter or oil, for the pan

Are you one of those people who would rather ask for forgiveness than ask for permission? Are you one of those wild and crazy people who just live balls-to-the-wall with little regard for consequences? I admire you. You always seem like you're having the time of your life! You always hail cabs and order cocktails like you're majorly in charge. With this pancake syrup (inspired by NYC's Clinton Street Bakery), I'm channeling your bold nature. Let's combine crisp bacon, sweet maple syrup, and melted butter into one completely over-the-top pancake topping! We'll collect our praise and ask for forgiveness at a later date.

the
ULTIMATE PANCAKE SYRUP

1 (12-ounce) package bacon

1 cup pure Grade B maple syrup

1 cup (2 sticks) cold unsalted butter, cut into large cubes

2 teaspoons pure vanilla extract

¼ teaspoon salt

1. Put a rack in the center of the oven and preheat the oven to 375°F.

2. Arrange the bacon slices in a single layer across a rimmed baking sheet. Bake until the bacon is cooked through and crispy, 13 to 15 minutes. Transfer the bacon to paper towels to drain, and let cool. Roughly chop the bacon and set it aside.

3. Heat the maple syrup in a medium saucepan set over medium-low. Whisk in the butter, a few cubes at a time, until the mixture is thoroughly incorporated and emulsified.

4. Remove the pan from the heat and add the vanilla, salt, and bacon. Stir well. The syrup will keep in an airtight container in the refrigerator for up to 3 days.

makes 3 cups

There are some weekend mornings when the desire to make pancakes is trumped by the lack of maple syrup in your pantry. With a little brown sugar, your problem is solved. Reignite pancake cravings, and go!

brown sugar & orange
PANCAKE SYRUP

- 1½ **cups packed light brown sugar**
- ¼ **cup (½ stick) unsalted butter**
- ¼ **cup fresh orange juice**
- 1 **vanilla bean, split**
- ¼ **teaspoon salt**

In a 2-quart heavy saucepan set over medium heat, combine 1 cup water with the brown sugar, butter, orange juice, vanilla bean, and salt. Bring to a boil, stirring until the sugar is dissolved, and cook until the mixture is syrupy and has reduced to about 1½ cups, 12 to 15 minutes. Remove the pan from the heat and let cool until the syrup is just warm. Remove the vanilla bean just before serving. The syrup will keep in an airtight container in the refrigerator for up to 5 days.

makes about 1½ cups

The easier it is to make a jam, the more quickly we can slather it on our scones. This quick jam is a beautiful refrigerator pantry item. Because blueberries naturally have an ample amount of pectin, there's no need for commercial pectin. Also . . . I'm afraid of boiling jars, hence the quickness of this jam. Not to worry! This will last in the fridge for several days, through plenty of batches of scones.

vanilla-blueberry
QUICK JAM

About 3 cups (1 pound) fresh blueberries

1 cup sugar

½ cup light corn syrup

1 vanilla bean

⅓ cup fresh lemon juice

½ teaspoon grated lemon zest

1. In a medium saucepan set over medium heat, combine the blueberries, sugar, and corn syrup. Split the vanilla bean, scrape the seeds into the pan, and toss in the pod. Use a large spoon or potato masher to smash the blueberries and release their juice. Simmer until some of the berries begin to break down and the mixture thickens, about 12 to 16 minutes. Remove the pan from the heat and add the lemon juice and lemon zest, and stir well. Remove the vanilla bean pod and discard.

2. Ladle the warm jam into clean jars. Cover with a small piece of plastic wrap, pressing it to the surface of the jam to prevent a skin from forming. Let cool to room temperature.

3. Remove the plastic wrap. Secure the lids on the jars and refrigerate for at least 8 hours before serving. The jam will keep in the refrigerator for up to 4 days, or the cooled jam can be frozen for up to 2 months.

makes about 4 cups

"The strangest combinations make the most beautiful scones." That's an old proverb, right? Maybe I made it up, but it's no less true. Pear, chocolate, and ginger are my go-to autumn flavors. These scones are light and tender, thanks to a hearty dose of tangy buttermilk. I like to serve these scones warm from the oven because the chocolate will be wonderfully melty and make them all that much more indulgent. These are particularly over the top when served with Dirty Chai Lattes (page 71).

pear, dark chocolate & ginger
SCONES

3 cups all-purpose flour

¼ cup sugar

2½ teaspoons baking powder

½ teaspoon baking soda

½ teaspoon salt

¾ cup (1½ sticks) cold unsalted butter, cut into cubes

1 cup cold buttermilk

2 large eggs

1 cup peeled and chopped pear (I use Bosc or d'Anjou)

¾ cup dark chocolate chunks

½ cup coarsely chopped candied ginger

1. Put racks in the center and upper third of the oven and preheat the oven to 400°F. Line 2 baking sheets with parchment paper and set aside.

2. In a medium bowl, sift together the flour, sugar, baking powder, baking soda, and salt. Using your hands or a pastry cutter, cut in the butter until the mixture resembles a coarse meal.

3. In a separate bowl, using a fork, beat together the buttermilk and 1 egg. Pour it into the flour mixture and stir enough to make a soft and shaggy dough. Add the pear, chocolate, and candied ginger, dump the mixture onto a well-floured counter, and knead until the dough comes together, 10 to 15 turns. If your mixture is gooey and overly sticky, flour your hands to knead it and work on a well-floured counter. Roll or pat the dough out until it is 1 inch thick. Cut into rounds using a 2-inch biscuit cutter. Gather the dough scraps, press them until the dough is 1 inch thick, and cut into rounds with the biscuit cutter. Alternately, you can skip the round biscuit cutter and use a knife to cut the dough into 2 x 2-inch squares.

4. Put the scones on the prepared baking sheets. Lightly beat the remaining egg and brush the tops of the scones with it.

5. Bake until the tops are golden brown, 12 to 15 minutes. Serve warm. These scones are best eaten the day they're made but will keep for up to 2 days in an airtight container.

makes 12 to 14 scones

Some mornings require the warmth and simplicity of an earnest scone. This scone is simply the sum of its parts, baked. They're nothing more than they need to be, but they're generous in their flavor and tenderness. The sour cream perfectly moistens and flavors the scones, making them delightfully tender with just a hint of tang. These scones are certainly not overly sweet, so I like to serve them with something fancy like Fresh Raspberry–Honey Butter (page 13). Any left over should be enthusiastically consumed for dinner.

sour cream
SCONES

3 cups all-purpose flour

1 tablespoon sugar

2½ teaspoons baking powder

½ teaspoon baking soda

¾ teaspoon salt

¾ cup (1½ sticks) cold unsalted butter, cut into cubes

¾ cup cold sour cream

3 tablespoons cold water

2 large eggs

1. Put racks in the center and upper third of the oven and preheat the oven to 400°F. Line 2 baking sheets with parchment paper and set aside.

2. In a medium mixing bowl, sift together the flour, sugar, baking powder, baking soda, and salt. Using your fingers or a pastry cutter, cut in the butter until the mixture resembles a coarse meal.

3. In a separate bowl, combine the sour cream, water, and 1 egg. Beat lightly with a fork. Pour it into the flour mixture and stir enough to make a soft and shaggy dough. Dump the mixture onto a well-floured counter and knead until the dough comes together, 10 to 15 turns. Roll or pat the dough out until it is 1 inch thick. Cut into rounds using a 2-inch biscuit cutter. Gather the dough scraps, press them together until the dough is 1 inch thick, and cut into rounds with the biscuit cutter. Alternately, skip the round biscuit cutter and use a knife to cut the dough into 2 x 2-inch squares.

4. Put the scones on the prepared baking sheets. Lightly beat the remaining egg and brush the tops of the scones with it.

5. Bake until golden on top, 12 to 15 minutes. Serve warm. These scones are best eaten the day they're made, but will keep for up to 2 days.

makes 16 small scones

Herbs add a note of elegance to fruit-studded breakfast pastries. They lend an unexpected, though totally welcome, savory touch that I find irresistible. There's a play on sweet and savory here. The peach and sugar add the sweetness, while the sage and whole wheat flour play up the savory notes. These scones are hearty but still feel breakfast appropriate. I particularly love them with sweet, creamy coffee.

whole wheat, peach & fresh sage
SCONES

1½ cups all-purpose flour

1½ cups whole wheat flour

¼ cup plus 3 tablespoons sugar

2½ teaspoons baking powder

½ teaspoon baking soda

½ teaspoon salt

1 tablespoon finely chopped fresh sage

¾ cup (1½ sticks) cold unsalted butter, cut into cubes

¾ cup heavy cream, plus more for brushing

2 large eggs

1 large ripe peach, unpeeled, pitted, and thinly sliced

1. Put racks in the center and upper third of the oven and preheat the oven to 400°F. Line 2 baking sheets with parchment paper and set aside.

2. In a medium bowl, sift together the flours, the ¼ cup sugar, the baking powder, baking soda, and salt. Add the sage, and using your fingers or a pastry cutter, cut in the butter until the mixture resembles a coarse meal.

3. In a separate bowl, using a fork, beat together the heavy cream and 1 egg. Pour it into the flour mixture and stir enough to make a soft and shaggy dough. Dump the mixture onto a well-floured counter and knead until the dough comes together, 10 to 15 turns. Roll or pat the dough out until it is a little less than ½ inch thick. Brush half of the dough with a thin coating of cream. Arrange the peach slices in a single layer across the cream. Carefully fold the other side of the dough over the peaches. Press together gently. Add a bit of flour to your hands and press the edges of the dough in, creating more of a rectangle shape than a half-circle shape. Using a floured knife, slice the dough into 8 squares.

4. Transfer the scones to the prepared baking sheets, leaving about 1½ inches in between them. If the dough has warmed and feels mushy, chill it in the fridge for 20 minutes. Remove the pans from the fridge. Lightly beat the remaining egg and brush the tops of the scones with it. Sprinkle the scones with the 3 tablespoons sugar.

5. Bake until golden brown on top, 15 to 18 minutes. Serve warm. These scones are best eaten the day they're made but will keep for up to 2 days.

makes 8 scones

Do whatever you have to do to convince yourself to make these doughnuts. Maybe you have to convince yourself that you have the time. Maybe you have to talk yourself into working with yeast. Maybe you have to coach yourself through working with a pan of hot oil. Pep-talk yourself right into doughnut making, because the end result—the part where you get to eat a warm, sugar-coated doughnut fresh from the fryer—makes the doughnut-making journey worth it ten times over.

vanilla sugar
DOUGHNUTS

doughnuts

- 2 tablespoons warm water (about 105°)
- 1 (.25-ounce) package active dry yeast (2¼ teaspoons)
- 3¼ to 3¾ cups all-purpose flour, plus more for rolling
- 1 cup whole milk, at room temperature
- ¼ cup (½ stick) unsalted butter, at room temperature
- 3 large egg yolks
- 2 tablespoons sugar
- 1½ teaspoons salt
- ¼ teaspoon ground cinnamon

1. For the doughnuts, in a small bowl, stir together the warm water and yeast until the yeast is dissolved. Let stand until foamy, about 5 minutes. (If the yeast doesn't foam, discard and start over with new yeast.)

2. In the bowl of an electric stand mixer fitted with a dough hook, combine the yeast mixture, flour, milk, butter, egg yolks, sugar, salt, and cinnamon. Beat at low speed until a soft dough forms. Increase the speed to medium-high and beat 3 minutes more. The dough will be soft and sticky. If it's too sticky to handle, add up to ½ cup more flour.

3. Scrape the sides of the bowl and then lightly sprinkle the dough with flour (to keep a crust from forming). Cover the bowl with plastic wrap and a clean kitchen towel. Put the bowl in a warm place and let the dough rise until doubled in bulk, 1½ to 2 hours.

4. Dump the dough out onto a lightly floured counter. Using a lightly floured rolling pin, roll the dough out into a 12-inch round that's ½ inch thick. Cut out as many rounds as possible with a 3-inch cutter (or a doughnut cutter, if you prefer a hole in the middle) and transfer the doughnuts to a lightly floured baking sheet. Do not reroll scraps (they'll make for tough doughnuts). Cover the doughnuts with a clean kitchen towel and let rise in a warm place until slightly puffed, about 30 minutes.

recipe continues

vanilla sugar

1⅓ cups sugar

Two pinches of salt

1 vanilla bean

6 cups vegetable oil, for frying

5. While the cut doughnuts rise, make the vanilla sugar. In a medium bowl, combine the sugar and salt. Split the vanilla bean and scrape the seeds into the bowl. Using your fingers, blend the mixture, making sure the vanilla seeds are evenly distributed. Set aside.

6. Heat 2½ inches of oil in a deep 4-quart heavy pot until it registers 350°F on a thermometer. Fry the doughnuts, 2 at a time, turning occasionally, until puffed and golden brown, about 1 minute per side. Quickly submerge the doughnuts in the hot oil, and then immediately transfer them to the vanilla sugar. Toss well, transfer to a paper towel–lined baking sheet, and let cool.

7. Return the oil to 350°F between batches and continue until all of the doughnuts are fried. Doughnuts are best served the day they are made.

makes about 10 (3-inch) doughnuts

Croissants are considered "elite pastry" in my baking brain. I categorize them (along with baguettes) among the baked items that I have no business making at home. It's not that I can't make them at home; it's just that I shouldn't. I should, however, go across town to the French bakery for a proper croissant and a perfectly crunchy baguette. I know my limitations.

And yet, because I don't always want to trek across town, I've come up with an easy, but superdecadent, croissant recipe twist. I mix buttery puff pastry and dark chocolate with my very favorite toast toppings: cinnamon and sugar. The result is both classic and nostalgic. The fact that these croissants only take 30 minutes from start to finish makes them perfect for any morning, hurried or not.

cinnamon sugar & dark chocolate
CROISSANTS

⅓ cup granulated sugar

1 teaspoon ground cinnamon

1 (14-ounce) package frozen all-butter puff pastry, slightly thawed in the refrigerator for 2 to 3 hours

1 large egg, beaten

¼ cup 60% or 70% cacao dark chocolate pieces

A sprinkle of fine sea salt

1. Put a rack in the upper third of the oven and preheat the oven to 400°F. Line 2 baking sheets with parchment paper and set aside.

2. In a small bowl, whisk together the sugar and ground cinnamon.

3. On a lightly floured counter, gently unfold the slightly thawed puff pastry sheets. Lightly brush 1 sheet of pastry with the beaten egg. Sprinkle all but a few tablespoons of the cinnamon and sugar mixture on the egg wash. Put the second sheet of pastry on top of the cinnamon sugar and gently press with your fingers along the edges to seal. Using a lightly floured rolling pin, gently roll out the puff pastry, extending ½ inch on all sides. The dough will thaw as you work it. That's great. Add a bit of flour to the work surface if you find that the puff pastry is sticking.

4. If the pastry begins to thaw to the point that it becomes difficult to work with, return it to the refrigerator to chill for 20 minutes, or until solid enough to work with again.

recipe continues

5. Position the pastry sheet horizontally and make 3 vertical cuts, forming 4 strips of pastry. Cut each strip in half horizontally. You'll have 8 rectangles. Cut each rectangle in half diagonally, creating 16 triangles. Working with 1 piece at a time, position the triangle so that the wider part is toward you and the point is away from you. Put a few small pieces of chocolate about ½ inch above the bottom edge of the triangle. Carefully roll the pastry up toward the point, pinching in the chocolate chunks to ensure they don't ooze out during baking. Transfer the croissant to 1 of the prepared baking sheets and curl the ends toward the center slightly. Repeat with the remaining triangles.

6. Brush the croissants with the remaining egg and sprinkle each with the remaining cinnamon sugar mixture, as well as a sprinkling of sea salt

7. Bake the croissants until golden, puffed, and otherwise irresistible, 12 to 15 minutes. Croissants are best served the day they are made but will last 2 to 3 days well wrapped at room temperature.

makes 16 small croissants

I have a sweet spot for Hawaiian sweet rolls. I'm talking about the store-bought, yellow-hued rolls that are supersoft and slightly sweet. These cinnamon rolls are my homemade, breakfast version of those supermarket rolls. The roll dough is flavored with pineapple juice, and the inside is packed with crushed pineapple and toasted pecans. The combination is just beyond and I'm almost ready to set aside my obsession with the original roll.

To be honest, these rolls are a bit of a commitment to make. As with anything yeasty and divine, they require hours of your attention. But the moment you sit down with a warm, fragrant sweet roll on your plate is the moment that makes all the hours worthwhile. Also, the first rule of cinnamon-roll making is that the baker gets to eat all of the centers out of each and every roll, should he or she choose to do so. I don't make up the rules, I just enforce them.

hawaiian sweet pineapple
BREAKFAST ROLLS

dough

½ cup warm water (about 105°F)

2 (.25-ounce) packages active dry yeast (4½ teaspoons)

1 teaspoon honey

3 large eggs

1 cup pineapple juice

½ cup (1 stick) unsalted butter, melted, plus more for the pan

⅔ cup granulated sugar

6 to 6¾ cups all-purpose flour

1½ teaspoons salt

1. For the dough, put the warm water in a small bowl, sprinkle the yeast on top, and stir. The yeast may form lumps; that's okay. Add the honey and stir. Let sit for 5 minutes. The yeast should become foamy. If it does not, discard the yeast and water and start over.

2. In the bowl of an electric mixer fitted with the dough hook, whisk together ¼ cup cold water, the eggs, pineapple juice, butter, and sugar. Add 6 cups flour and the salt. Add the yeast mixture. Beat on medium speed until the dough begins to come together and becomes smooth, 6 to 8 minutes.

3. Dump the dough onto a lightly floured counter. Lightly flour your hands and knead the dough for about 4 minutes. The dough should be silky, smooth, and damp, but not sticky. If the dough is sticky, knead in up to ¾ cup more flour. Put the dough in a large, lightly greased bowl. Cover with plastic wrap and a clean kitchen towel. Put the bowl in a warm place in the house and let the dough rise until doubled in size, 1 to 1½ hours.

recipe continues

filling

½ cup packed dark brown sugar

¼ cup granulated sugar

½ cup coarsely chopped toasted pecans

1 tablespoon ground cinnamon

½ teaspoon freshly grated nutmeg

½ teaspoon salt

¼ cup (½ stick) unsalted butter, melted

1 cup canned crushed pineapple, well drained

icing

2 cups confectioners' sugar

¼ cup pineapple juice

4. Meanwhile, make the filling: Butter the bottom and sides of a 9 x 13-inch metal pan; set aside. In a large bowl, combine both sugars, the pecans, cinnamon, nutmeg, and salt. Stir well.

5. When the dough has doubled in size, dump it from the bowl onto a heavily floured counter. Gently knead the dough until it is no longer sticky, adding a bit more flour as needed, 1 to 2 minutes. Once it's no longer sticky, put a clean kitchen towel over the dough and let the dough rest for 5 minutes.

6. Using a floured rolling pin, roll the dough into a 10 x 10-inch square that's about ⅓ inch thick. Brush the top of the dough with the melted butter. Pour the filling onto the dough and spread it evenly, leaving a 1-inch border at the far edge of the dough so that the roll can be sealed. Put the crushed pineapple on the filling in an even layer. Lightly press the pecans and pineapple into the dough. Using your hands, lift up the bottom edge of the dough and roll it into a tight cylinder, pressing the edge to seal. Using a thin, sharp knife, trim off the uneven edges. Cut the cylinder into 8 equal slices. Nestle the slices, cut side up and evenly spaced, in the prepared pan. Cover the pan with plastic wrap, set in a warm place, and let rise for 1 hour. You may also refrigerate the rolls overnight instead of letting them rise at room temperature for 1 hour.

7. Preheat the oven to 375°F.

8. Uncover the rolls. If you refrigerated the rolls, let them sit at room temperature for 15 minutes before baking. Bake until golden brown and a wooden pick inserted in the center comes out clean, about 30 minutes.

9. Make the icing while the rolls are baking. Whisk together the confectioners' sugar and pineapple juice in a small bowl until smooth.

10. Let the rolls cool for 15 minutes. Dip the tines of a fork into the icing and drizzle it over the rolls. Serve immediately.

makes 8 large rolls

This yeasted pull-apart cake is, hands down, one of the most popular recipes on my website. I think it deserves a permanent place in print. There is something about this cake that speaks to your soul. I've tried for a long time to put my finger on that quality, and I think it's the simplicity of cinnamon sugar, which always smells like home. Warm pieces of yeast dough sandwich cinnamon sugar and easily peel apart for eating. If you're one of those people who goes in for just another "sliver" of cake and finds yourself eating 2 full slices in "slivers" alone, consider yourself a goner with this cake. It's all slivers! I tried to warn you!

CINNAMON-SUGAR PULL-APART CAKE
with lemon glaze

dough

- 3 to 3¼ cups all-purpose flour
- ¼ cup sugar
- 1 (.25-ounce) package active dry yeast (2¼ teaspoons)
- ½ teaspoon salt
- ⅓ cup whole milk
- ¼ cup (½ stick) unsalted butter
- 1 teaspoon pure vanilla extract
- 2 large eggs, at room temperature, beaten

1. For the dough, in a large bowl, whisk together 2 cups of the flour, sugar, yeast, and salt.

2. In a small saucepan set over medium-low heat, combine the milk and butter and heat until the butter has just melted, about 3 minutes. Remove the pan from the heat and add ¼ cup water and the vanilla. Let the mixture stand until it registers 115° to 125°F on a candy thermometer, 1 to 2 minutes. Pour the milk mixture into the flour mixture and stir with a spatula. Add the eggs and stir well. The eggs will feel soupy, and it'll seem like the dough will never come together. Keep stirring. Add the remaining 1 cup flour and stir with the spatula for about 2 minutes. The mixture will be sticky.

3. Transfer the dough to a large greased bowl. Cover the bowl with plastic wrap and a clean kitchen towel, put it in a warm space, and let rest until the dough has doubled in size, about 1 hour. If you'd like to bake off the bread the following morning, refrigerate the risen dough overnight. The next morning, let the dough rest on the counter for 30 minutes before continuing.

recipe continues

filling

- 1 cup sugar
- 2 teaspoons ground cinnamon
- ½ teaspoon freshly grated nutmeg
- ¼ cup (½ stick) unsalted butter

glaze

- 1½ cups confectioners' sugar
- 2 tablespoons fresh lemon juice
- 1 to 2 tablespoons whole milk

4. For the filling, in a small bowl, whisk together the sugar, cinnamon, and nutmeg.

5. In a small saucepan set over medium-low heat, melt the butter.

6. Put a rack in the center of the oven and preheat the oven to 350°F. Grease and flour a 9 x 5-inch loaf pan.

7. Turn the risen dough out onto a floured counter. Knead about 2 to 4 tablespoons of flour into the dough. Cover with a clean kitchen towel and let it rest for 5 minutes. On a lightly floured work surface, use a rolling pin to roll the dough out into a 12-inch-wide and 20-inch-long rectangle. Using a pastry brush, brush the melted butter on the dough. Sprinkle with all of the sugar and cinnamon mixture. It might seem like a lot of sugar. Seriously? Just go for it.

8. Slice the dough vertically into 6 equal strips. Stack the strips on top of one another and slice the stack crosswise into 6 equal slices. You'll have 6 stacks of 6 squares. Layer the dough squares in the loaf pan like a flip-book. Put a clean kitchen towel over the loaf pan and let it rest in a warm place until almost doubled in size, 30 to 45 minutes.

9. Bake until the top is very golden brown, 30 to 35 minutes. Let cool for 20 to 30 minutes.

10. While the cake cools, make the glaze. In a medium bowl, whisk together the confectioners' sugar, lemon juice, and 1 tablespoon milk. Add more milk as necessary to create a smooth and pourable consistency.

11. Run a butter knife around the edges of the pan to loosen the cake and invert it onto a clean board. Invert the cake again onto a cake stand or cake plate. Drizzle liberally with lemon glaze. Serve warm.

12. I think this cake is best served the day it's made, but it can also be wrapped and kept at room temperature for up to 2 days.

makes one 9 x 5-inch loaf

This coffee cake reminds me of my best friend, Tracy. The two of us live hundreds of miles apart, so when we do have the chance to be in the same place, there's always deep talks, good laughs, hot coffee, and cake! When we're not together, I find myself daydreaming about sitting at Tracy's kitchen table lingering over this fantastic sour cream coffee cake. The generous cinnamon and brown sugar swirl is studded with pecans, and on top, the brown butter glaze is rich and nutty—a decadent finish to an already triumphant cake.

SOUR CREAM COFFEE CAKE
with brown butter glaze

streusel

- ½ cup packed light brown sugar
- ½ cup cake flour
- 2 teaspoons ground cinnamon
- 1 teaspoon unsweetened cocoa powder
- ½ teaspoon salt
- ¼ cup (½ stick) cold unsalted butter, cut into small cubes
- ½ cup finely chopped pecans

cake

- 3 cups cake flour
- 2 teaspoons baking powder
- ½ teaspoon baking soda
- ½ teaspoon salt

1. Put a rack in the center of the oven and preheat the oven to 350°F. Grease a 10-inch Bundt pan with butter or vegetable shortening, dust with flour, and tap out any excess flour. Set aside.

2. For the streusel, in a medium bowl, whisk together the brown sugar, flour, cinnamon, cocoa, and salt. Add the cold butter, and using your hands, quickly break up the butter chunks in the dry ingredients. Some of the butter bits will be the size of small peas, others the size of oat flakes. Add the pecans and toss well. Set aside.

3. For the cake, in a medium bowl, whisk together the flour, baking powder, baking soda, and salt.

4. In the bowl of an electric mixer fitted with the paddle attachment, beat together the butter and sugar on medium speed until the mixture is light and fluffy, 4 to 5 minutes. Turn the mixer off, scrape down the sides of the bowl, and add 1 egg at a time, beating for 1 minute after each addition. Add the vanilla and beat well. Beat in the sour cream, stopping the mixer to scrape down the sides of the bowl to thoroughly mix.

5. Add the dry ingredients to the wet ingredients. Beat on low speed until the ingredients are almost entirely incorporated. Spoon half of the batter into the prepared pan. Sprinkle with two thirds of the streusel mixture.

recipe continues

- 1 cup (2 sticks) unsalted butter, at room temperature
- 1½ cups granulated sugar
- 3 large eggs
- 2 teaspoons pure vanilla extract
- 1¼ cups sour cream

glaze
- 3 tablespoons unsalted butter
- 1 cup confectioners' sugar
- 2 teaspoons pure vanilla extract
- 1 tablespoon water or milk, if needed
- Pinch of salt

Spoon in the remaining batter and smooth the top. Sprinkle the remaining streusel on the top. Use a butter knife to loosely swirl the streusel into the batter. Don't overswirl; just about 10 swirls will do.

6. Bake until a wooden pick inserted in the cake comes out moist but clean, 45 to 55 minutes.

7. Meanwhile, for the glaze, in a small saucepan set over medium heat, melt the butter. Cook until the butter cracks and sizzles, about 2 minutes. Continue cooking until the butter begins to smell nutty and there are little brown speckles on the bottom of the pan, about 2 more minutes. Remove the pan from the heat and immediately pour the browned butter into a small bowl. Add the confectioners' sugar and vanilla extract, and whisk until the glaze is thick enough to drizzle. Add a few drops of water or milk if you need to thin it out. Stir in a pinch of salt and set aside.

8. Remove the cake from the oven and let it cool for 10 minutes. Invert it onto a wire rack and let cool completely.

9. Spread the glaze onto the cooled cake and serve. The cake will keep in an airtight container for up to 4 days.

makes one 10-inch Bundt cake

In my family, cobbler is a big deal. It's a big deal when my dad starts to root through the kitchen cabinets looking for the large cobbler pan. This dessert is usually reserved for the big family Easter party, the all-family cookout, or Christmas. You know there's going to be a lot of happy gathering when that special pan emerges.

Leave it to me to find a way to turn cobbler into breakfast.

Breakfast is totally a special occasion, right? In this cobbler incarnation, we're combining juicy berries and drop biscuit batter. The result is somewhere between a berry pie and a berry scone. It's sweet and juicy, hearty and special.

BREAKFAST COBBLER
with oatmeal drop biscuits

filling

- 4 cups fresh mixed berries, or frozen, thawed and drained (strawberries aren't great in this recipe)
- 2 tablespoons cornstarch
- ¼ cup fresh orange juice
- ½ cup packed light brown sugar
- ¼ teaspoon salt

1. Put racks in the center of the oven and preheat the oven to 375°F. Grease an 8 x 8-inch square or 8-inch round pan with butter. Set aside. Line a baking sheet with foil and put it on the lower rack in the preheating oven.

2. In a medium bowl, combine the berries and cornstarch until the cornstarch dissolves. In a separate small bowl, combine the orange juice, brown sugar, and salt, and then pour it over the berries. Gently combine the mixture and pour it into the prepared baking pan.

3. Bake on the center rack until the berries soften and begin to burst, about 15 minutes.

recipe continues

4. For the biscuit topping, in a medium bowl, whisk together the flour, oats, the ¼ cup sugar, the baking powder, baking soda, cardamom, salt, and orange zest. Add the butter and, using your fingers, quickly break up the butter in the dry mixture until the butter is the size of small peas. Make a well in the center of the mixture. Pour in the buttermilk and gently stir until all of the flour mixture is moistened.

5. Remove the berry mixture from the oven. Dollop six ½ cup scoops of the biscuit topping onto the berry mixture. Sprinkle with the 2 tablespoons granulated sugar.

6. Return the pan to the center rack directly above the foil-lined baking sheet, which will catch any drippings. Bake until the biscuits are golden brown and the berries are bubbling and thick, 20 to 25 minutes. Let cool for 20 minutes before serving. This dish is best served the day it is made.

serves 6

biscuit topping

- 1½ cups all-purpose flour
- ½ cup old-fashioned oats
- ¼ cup plus 2 tablespoons granulated sugar
- 2 teaspoons baking powder
- ½ teaspoon baking soda
- ½ teaspoon ground cardamom
- ¼ teaspoon salt
- 1 teaspoon grated orange zest
- ½ cup (1 stick) cold unsalted butter, cut into small pieces
- 1 cup cold buttermilk

You can get away with so much when it comes to brunch. If you want to turn your blueberry muffins into pancakes, brunch is your safe space to do that. These muffins are blueberry-studded and maple syrup–dipped, and even in their simplicity, they've made an impression on my brunch brain. It's uncanny how much these muffins taste just like blueberry pancakes. The combination of bursting blueberries, maple syrup, and cake just cues the brain to recall pancakes. You get all the flavor credit without standing in front of the griddle and flipping.

BLUEBERRY PANCAKE MUFFINS
with maple glaze

muffins

⅓ cup whole milk

1 large egg

1 large egg yolk

1 tablespoon pure maple syrup

1 teaspoon pure vanilla extract

7 tablespoons unsalted butter, melted and cooled slightly

1½ cups all-purpose flour

¾ cup granulated sugar

1½ teaspoons baking powder

¾ teaspoon salt

¾ cup fresh blueberries

maple glaze

¾ cup pure maple syrup

1 tablespoon fresh lemon juice

1. Put a rack in the upper third of the oven and preheat the oven to 375°F. Line a 12-cup standard muffin pan with paper or foil liners.

2. For the muffins, in a medium bowl, whisk together the milk, egg, egg yolk, maple syrup, and vanilla. Add the butter and stir well.

3. In a separate bowl, whisk together the flour, sugar, baking powder, and salt. Add the milk mixture and stir gently. Fold in the blueberries. Divide the batter among the prepared muffin cups.

4. Bake until golden and a wooden pick inserted in the center of a muffin comes out clean, 18 to 20 minutes.

5. Meanwhile, for the maple glaze, in a small saucepan set over low heat, combine the maple syrup and lemon juice. Bring to a simmer and cook, stirring occasionally, until reduced to a thick (thicker than maple syrup) syrup, about 12 minutes. Remove the pan from the heat.

6. When the muffins are out of the oven and cool enough to handle, poke a few holes in each muffin top with a toothpick and drizzle a spoonful or two of glaze over each muffin. The muffins will keep for up to 2 days.

makes 12 muffins

There is a huge difference between boiling cornmeal and cooking grits. Boiling cornmeal involves water and meal. Making a pot of grits requires creamy whole milk, rich butter, salt and pepper, heart and soul. When I step into the kitchen to make these grits, I think about my grandmother standing in the kitchen making me breakfast. Okay . . . so she actually made me canned pears and cottage cheese, but I could tell even that was sprinkled with love. In this recipe, I've topped warm and buttery grits with roasted berries. Roasting strawberries gives them a tender bite and wonderfully intense flavor. These strawberries were inspired by a recipe on the "101 Cookbooks" blog.

roasted strawberry & balsamic
GRITS

strawberries

1½ pounds fresh strawberries, hulled and halved

⅓ cup pure maple syrup

2 tablespoons olive oil

¼ teaspoon salt

2 tablespoons balsamic vinegar, plus more for topping

grits

1 teaspoon salt

1 cup coarsely ground yellow or white cornmeal

2 cups whole milk

¼ cup (½ stick) unsalted butter

¼ to ½ teaspoon coarsely ground black pepper

1. Put a rack in the center of the oven and preheat the oven to 375°F.

2. Line a rimmed baking sheet with parchment paper. Spread the strawberries on the baking sheet in a single layer. Drizzle with the maple syrup and olive oil, and toss well. Sprinkle with the salt.

3. Roast, stirring once or twice, until the strawberries are soft and the juices have thickened, 30 to 40 minutes. Keep an eye on the strawberries to ensure that the juices don't burn. Transfer the warm berries and juices to a medium bowl and toss with the balsamic vinegar. Set aside.

4. For the grits, bring 3 cups of water to a boil in a medium pot. Add the salt, and while stirring constantly, slowly add the cornmeal. Reduce the heat to low and simmer until the grits are thickened to the consistency of a thick pudding, 5 to 8 minutes. Add the milk, butter, and black pepper and continue to cook, stirring constantly, until the grits are thick and creamy, 15 to 20 minutes.

5. Divide the grits among 4 bowls. Top with the roasted strawberries and a small drizzle of balsamic vinegar, if desired. Serve hot.

serves 4

Any dish consisting of roasted potatoes and fried eggs is automatically breakfast, even if we call it "nachos." This is a modified rendition of the traditional fried egg and hash brown breakfast. By adding fresh tomato, avocados, jalapeños, and cheese sauce, we're transforming hash browns into an all-out breakfast-nacho situation. Heck, yes, it's as good as it sounds.

roasted-potato
BREAKFAST NACHOS

nachos

1½ teaspoons salt

1 teaspoon freshly cracked black pepper

½ teaspoon garlic powder

½ teaspoon cayenne pepper

2½ pounds (about 5 small to medium) russet potatoes

3 tablespoons olive oil

3 Italian sausages (about 1 pound), casings removed

1 small onion, chopped

2 garlic cloves, minced

¼ teaspoon crushed red pepper flakes (optional)

2 tablespoons unsalted butter

1 tablespoon all-purpose flour

2 cups whole milk, warmed

1. Put a rack in the center of the oven and preheat the oven to 425°F. Line 2 baking sheets with aluminum foil.

2. In a small bowl, combine the salt, black pepper, garlic powder, and cayenne pepper.

3. Using a mandolin or a knife, thinly slice the potatoes into ½-inch-thick rounds. Put them on the prepared baking sheets in a single layer. Drizzle with the olive oil and sprinkle with half of the seasoning blend. Bake the potatoes, turning halfway through, until golden brown and crispy, 25 to 30 minutes.

4. Meanwhile, heat a 9- or 10-inch cast-iron skillet over medium heat. Put the sausages in the skillet and cook, using a wooden spoon to break up any lumps, until browned, about 5 minutes. Add the onion and garlic and cook until the onion is translucent, about 3 minutes. Add the red pepper flakes, if using. Reduce the heat to low and cook for 2 more minutes. Transfer to a bowl or plate.

5. In the same skillet, set over medium heat, melt 1 tablespoon of the butter. Sprinkle in the flour and whisk for a few seconds. While whisking constantly, slowly pour in the warmed milk. Season with the remaining seasoning blend and cook, whisking constantly, until the sauce has thickened slightly, about 6 minutes. Turn off the heat and whisk in the cheese until completely melted and smooth.

6. In a clean small nonstick skillet set over medium heat, melt the remaining 1 tablespoon butter. Crack in as many eggs as people you're serving and fry for 3 minutes, cover the pan with a lid, and cook until whites are cooked through and yolks are still soft, about 4 minutes.

7. Transfer the potatoes to a platter or individual bowls. Top with the cheese sauce and then the sausage mixture. Sprinkle with the toppings as you desire. Top with the fried eggs and serve immediately.

serves 4 to 6

2 cups shredded Irish Cheddar cheese (or white Cheddar cheese)

4 to 6 large eggs

toppings

1 tomato, chopped

2 scallions, sliced

⅓ to ½ cup sliced pickled jalapeños

2 avocados, peeled, pitted, and smashed with a squeeze of fresh lime juice

Sour cream

Fresh cilantro

In Southern California, we eat kale for brunch. I find this fact equal parts awesome and obnoxious. It's like we can't enjoy the indulgence of brunch without getting in our dose of health. It might be a compulsion.

I've infused my Southern California roots into this breakfast sandwich. The strong green is softened with the comforting flavors of garlic and chicken stock. Plump raisins add an unexpected sweet contrast. Serving these soft greens with rich brioche, soft eggs, and mustard makes it perfectly California cool.

braised kale & egg
BREAKFAST SANDWICHES

- 2 tablespoons olive oil
- 2 garlic cloves, minced
- ¾ cup low-sodium chicken stock
- 1 pound lacinato kale, stems and ribs removed, coarsely chopped
- ⅓ cup golden raisins
- 2 tablespoons unsalted butter
- 4 brioche buns
- 4 large eggs
  Salt and coarsely ground black pepper
- 2 to 4 tablespoons whole grain mustard

1. Heat the olive oil in a large pot over medium heat. Add the garlic and cook, stirring often, for about 1 minute. Add the stock. Add the kale a handful at a time, waiting for some of it to wilt before adding more. Add the raisins and toss well. Cover, reduce the heat to medium-low, and cook until kale is wilted and raisins are plumped, about 10 minutes. Remove the lid and toss the mixture.

2. Meanwhile, in a large nonstick skillet, melt the butter over medium heat. Cut the brioche buns in half and toast, cut side down, in the melted butter, about 4 minutes. Set aside.

3. Wipe out the skillet and set it back over medium heat. Crack the eggs into the skillet, and sprinkle with salt and pepper. Reduce the heat to low, cover, and cook until the yolks reach your desired doneness, about 4 minutes for my taste.

4. To assemble the sandwiches, divide the braised kale among the bottoms of the toasted buns. Top each with a fried egg. Spread the mustard on the bun tops, top the sandwiches, and serve immediately.

serves 4

Grilled cheese sandwiches are an any day, any time sandwich. They taste particularly good between the hours of midnight and 2 a.m., and 9 a.m. and noon. This sandwich is a play on sweet and salty, as it involves mixing cherry jam with thinly sliced ham. I think of Brie as butter's cheesy cousin. Butter makes everything better, so Brie can't be that far from awesome! This cheese adds a richness that helps this breakfast sandwich feel utterly inspired.

BREAKFAST GRILLED CHEESE
with ham & cherry jam

8 thick slices brioche bread

2 to 4 tablespoons whole grain mustard

12 thin slices Black Forest ham

¼ cup cherry jam

4 to 8 ounces Brie, cut into 4 wedges

Butter, for the pan

1. Put the slices of bread on a work surface. Smear 1 side of 4 of the pieces with the mustard and top with 3 slices of the ham each. Spread the remaining 4 slices of bread liberally with the cherry jam and top each with a wedge of Brie (rind and all). Sandwich the bread slices together.

2. Melt about 1 tablespoon of butter in a medium skillet over medium-low heat. Put 2 sandwiches in the heated skillet and cook, flipping once, until both sides of the sandwiches are golden brown and the Brie is melted, about 6 minutes total. Repeat with the remaining 2 sandwiches. Cut in half and serve promptly.

serves 4

While cold, leftover pizza is an understandable indulgence, I would argue that fresh pizza in the morning is the ultimate. I always love a sweet and salty combination at brunch, and the blackberries and sausage are playful and delicious atop this pizza. Fresh arugula adds a fresh, spicy green element.

sausage & blackberry
BREAKFAST PIZZA

pizza dough

- ¼ cup olive oil, plus more for the bowl
- ¾ cup warm water (about 105°F)
- 1 (.25 ounce) package active dry yeast (2¼ teaspoons)
- 1 tablespoon plus a pinch of granulated sugar
- 1 cup all-purpose flour, plus more for kneading
- 1 cup whole wheat flour
- ¾ teaspoon salt

pizza

- 1 cup pizza sauce
- 1½ to 2 cups shredded mozzarella cheese
- 2 cups cooked crumbled mild Italian sausage
- 1 cup blackberries, halved
- 1 big handful fresh arugula or spinach

1. Brush a large bowl with olive oil and set aside.

2. Put the warm water in a medium bowl. Sprinkle the yeast over the top and add a pinch of sugar. Let stand for 5 minutes until the mixture is foamy. If the yeast does not foam, discard and start over with another package of yeast.

3. Whisk 2 tablespoons of the olive oil and the 1 tablespoon sugar into the yeast mixture. Add the flours and salt, and use a wooden spoon to stir well. The dough should be thick, shaggy, and somewhat sticky. Transfer the dough to the oiled bowl, cover with plastic wrap and a clean kitchen towel, and set in a warm place. Let rise until doubled in size, about 1 hour.

4. Turn the dough out onto a well-floured counter. Flour your hands and knead until the dough is smooth and silky, about 15 turns. Loosely cover the dough with plastic wrap and let it rest for 15 minutes.

5. Put a rack in the upper third of the oven and preheat the oven to 450°F. Grease a 12-inch round pizza pan, or a rimmed baking sheet, with the remaining 2 tablespoons olive oil, or sprinkle a pizza stone with cornmeal. Set aside.

6. Using a floured rolling pin, roll the dough into a 12-inch round. Transfer the pizza dough to the prepared pan. Top with the pizza sauce, shredded cheese, cooked sausage, and blackberries.

7. Bake until the pizza crust is thick and golden and the cheese is bubbling, 18 to 20 minutes. Remove from the oven and let cool for 10 minutes. Top with the arugula, slice, and serve.

makes one 12-inch pizza

I think that caramelized onions are one of life's simple luxuries. It's amazing that something as aggressive as raw onions can become earthy and delicate with some coaxing from a hot pan, melted butter, and a bit of time.

No one should have to make pie crust before noon, so this quiche calls upon the wonders of puff pastry to do the heavy lifting of the crust. And because no French onion situation is complete without a hearty amount of Gruyère cheese, I happily oblige.

I think of this quiche as a midday brunch indulgence. It's lovely served with a fresh green salad and Lavender-Lime-Cucumber Spritzers (page 67).

french onion
QUICHE

onion mixture

- ¼ cup (½ stick) unsalted butter
- 2 tablespoons olive oil
- 3 medium yellow onions, cut in half and sliced ¼ inch thick
- 1½ teaspoons coarse sea salt
- 1 tablespoon fresh thyme leaves
- 1 teaspoon freshly cracked black pepper
- 1 teaspoon sugar
- ¼ cup plus 2 tablespoons vegetable broth, beer, or white wine

1. To caramelize the onions, put a medium, heavy-bottomed saucepan over medium heat. Add the butter and olive oil and stir until the butter is melted. Add the onions, stir well, and cook, undisturbed, for about 4 minutes. Add the salt, thyme, pepper, and sugar and stir. Cover the pan and cook, stirring occasionally, until the onions are brown and a soft, jam-like consistency, about 12 minutes. Lower the heat if the onions are browning too quickly. Add the broth to the pan and cook, scraping any browned bits off the bottom of the pan with a wooden spoon, about 30 seconds. The onions will be soft and tender, and most of the liquid will have cooked down. Remove the pan from the heat and set aside.

2. Put a baking sheet on the center rack and preheat the oven to 375°F.

3. For the quiche, on a lightly floured counter, roll the puff pastry out into a 13-inch square. Transfer the pastry to a 9-inch pie dish, letting the corners hang over the sides. Spread the onion mixture on the bottom of the pie crust and sprinkle with ½ cup of the cheese. Chill in the refrigerator while you assemble the filling.

recipe continues

quiche

  1 sheet frozen puff
    pastry (from a
    17¼-ounce package),
    thawed (I love Dufour
    puff pastry)

  1 cup shredded Gruyère
    cheese (about 4
    ounces)

  6 large eggs

1½ cups whole milk

  1 cup heavy cream

½ teaspoon salt

⅛ teaspoon freshly
    grated nutmeg

4. Whisk the eggs in a medium bowl until well combined and then whisk in the milk, cream, salt, and nutmeg. Pour the egg mixture through a fine-mesh strainer into the chilled pastry shell. Sprinkle with the remaining ½ cup cheese.

5. Set the pie dish on the baking sheet and bake until the center of the quiche is set, 45 minutes to 1 hour. The quiche will puff up in the oven and sink a bit once it's out and cooled. Transfer the pie dish to a wire rack to cool. Serve warm or at room temperature.

serves 8

There are two major perks of adulthood: drinking champagne in the morning and eating ice cream (or in this case, sorbet) any time we'd like. Champagne cocktails are a celebration of our adult independence. This cocktail gets more fruity as it melts. Enjoy it immediately with a few sips and a spoon, or let the sorbet melt into the champagne, creating an ice-cold, sweet drink. This float is reminiscent of a Bellini, made just slightly tart with the addition of lemon sorbet.

CHAMPAGNE-SORBET
floats

1 **pint lemon sorbet**

1 **pint raspberry sorbet**

1 **(750-milliliter) bottle champagne, chilled**

Put a small scoop of the lemon sorbet into each of 8 glasses. Top with a small scoop of the raspberry sorbet. Slowly fill the glasses with the champagne. Serve immediately.

serves 8

My favorite brunch cocktail is a Bloody Mary. A Red Snapper is a Bloody Mary made with gin instead of vodka. There are few things better than having a salty and spicy tomato cocktail right next to my cup of hot coffee. This version is inspired by a very ginny experience I had in London not long ago (humble brag). Since vodka is such a benign spirit, the gin adds an additional layer of flavor to the drink.

This recipe can be served either as a punch for many or as cocktails for individuals.

RED SNAPPER
cocktail

drink mix

- 3 cups low-sodium tomato juice
- 1½ ounces (scant 3 tablespoons) fresh lemon juice
- 1½ ounces (scant 3 tablespoons) fresh lime juice
- 2 tablespoons Worcestershire sauce
- 2 teaspoons prepared horseradish
- 1 teaspoon hot sauce (such as Tabasco)
- ½ teaspoon celery salt
- 1 teaspoon salt
- 1 teaspoon coarsely ground black pepper
- 1½ cups cold gin

garnish

- 6 celery stalks
- 6 pickled green beans
- 6 green olives

1. For the drink mix, in a large glass pitcher, stir together the tomato juice, lemon juice, lime juice, Worcestershire sauce, horseradish, hot sauce, celery salt, salt, and pepper. Refrigerate until ready to use or for up to 5 days, or freeze for up to 30 days.

2. When ready to serve, fill 6 tall glasses with ice. Pour 2 ounces of gin into each glass. Fill the remainder of the glass with the mix. Stir and garnish with the celery stalks, pickled green beans, and green olives.

serves 6

It's entirely possible to combine champagne and health food. I know. . . . You're welcome. Think of this as an elevated, California-living, Sunday Mimosa. The sweetness of carrot and orange juice is balanced by the spicy ginger and dry champagne. The vibrant orange color is also majorly inviting.

CARROT-ORANGE-GINGER
mimosa punch

1 cup fresh carrot juice

2 cups fresh orange juice

2 tablespoons freshly grated ginger

1 (750-milliliter) bottle champagne, chilled

1. In a large punch bowl, stir together the carrot juice, orange juice, and ginger. Gently stir in the champagne.

2. Serve in punch glasses or champagne flutes. Ice is optional.

serves 6

I love the dreamy fragrance that lavender adds to drinks. It feels fresh, floral, and feminine. This fragrant homemade soda is so refreshing alongside French Onion Quiche (page 60)!

LAVENDER-LIME-CUCUMBER
spritzers

decorative ice
Filtered water

12 thin slices cucumber

Juice of half a lime

lavender syrup
2 cups granulated sugar

⅓ cup dried lavender blossoms

spritzers
1 liter sparkling water

8 lime wedges

8 cucumber slices

1. For the ice, fill an ice tray with filtered water. Put a cucumber slice and a few drops of lime juice into each cup. Freeze until solid.

2. For the syrup, in a medium saucepan, combine 2 cups water, the sugar, and lavender blossoms. Bring to a boil, remove the pan from the heat, cover, and let steep for 15 minutes.

3. Strain the syrup through a fine-mesh strainer and discard the lavender blossoms. Pour the syrup into a glass jar, and let it cool completely before covering with a tight-fitting lid. The lavender syrup will keep in an airtight container in the refrigerator for up to 2 weeks.

4. For the spritzers, fill 8 tall glasses with the cucumber ice cubes. Pour 3 to 4 tablespoons of lavender syrup into each glass. Top with sparkling water. Squeeze a generous lime wedge into each drink. Add the cucumber slices to garnish. Serve immediately.

serves 8

There are very few instances when tequila is an acceptable breakfast item. Welcome to the one and only reason we need. This beautiful peachy pink–colored cocktail is perfect for late spring or summertime brunching.

This pretty pink cocktail calls for grenadine. I find that it's actually easier to make grenadine than it is to find it in stores. Try my homemade grenadine.

mango-watermelon
TEQUILA SUNRISE

2 cups mango nectar

1⅓ cups tequila (gold or silver)

6 tablespoons grenadine

2 cups watermelon juice

1. In a large liquid measuring cup, combine the mango nectar and tequila. Set aside.

2. Pour 1 tablespoon of the grenadine into each glass. Fill each glass with ice. Gently pour in the watermelon juice until each glass is half full. Top each glass with the mango and tequila mixture. Serve immediately.

serves 6

HOMEMADE GRENADINE

¼ cup sugar

1 cup unsweetened pomegranate juice

Juice of half a lemon

In a medium saucepan set over medium heat, combine the sugar and pomegranate juice. Bring to a boil and simmer until slightly thickened, about 10 minutes. Remove the pan from the heat. Stir in the lemon juice and let cool to room temperature. Store in an airtight container in the refrigerator for up to 2 months.

makes 1 cup

It's not just butter and sugar that make for a decadent brunch. Sometimes bright color and unexpected combinations can make brunch feel over the top. Here, I've transformed an earthy, sweet roasted beet into the most vibrant (and superhealthful) smoothie. I added chia seeds because they're packed with wonderful omega nutrients, they add a touch of crunch to the smoothie, and they're filling, too!

STRAWBERRY, BEET & CHIA SEED
smoothie

1 large beet, roasted and cut into chunks (about ⅔ cup)

2 bananas, sliced into chunks and frozen

2 heaping cups frozen sliced strawberries

2 heaping tablespoons chia seeds

2 cups almond, soy, coconut, or cow's milk

1. Put a rack in the upper third of the oven and preheat the oven to 375°F.

2. Rinse and scrub any dirt from the beet. Loosely wrap it in aluminum foil, place it on a small baking sheet, and put it in the oven. Roast until a knife inserted into the beet meets no resistance, about 20 to 30 minutes, depending on the size of the beet. Let cool completely. Rub the skin from the beet and discard the skin. Cut the beet into large chunks.

3. In a blender, combine the bananas, strawberries, beet, chia seeds, and milk. Blend until smooth. Add more milk if the smoothie is too thick for your taste. The chia seeds will begin to absorb the liquid of the smoothie as it sits. Enjoy immediately for a thinner smoothie, or let sit for 5 minutes for a slightly thicker smoothie.

serves 4

The flavors of chai and coffee are such unlikely partners, but the spice of chai joined with the heartiness of coffee is absolutely divine. This warm, milky coffee drink is lovely paired with Vanilla Sugar Doughnuts (page 31).

dirty
CHAI LATTES

4 cups low-fat milk

½ cup sugar

4 chai tea bags

1½ cups hot strong brewed coffee

1. In a medium saucepan set over medium heat, heat the milk until it is steaming and little bubbles form on the top, about 6 minutes. Add the sugar and stir until it is dissolved. Remove the pan from the heat and add the tea bags. Cover and let steep for 15 minutes.

2. Remove and discard the tea bags. Stir in the coffee, return the pan to low heat, and reheat the latte before serving.

3. Divide the latte among 4 mugs and serve immediately.

serves 4

COOKIES, BROWNIES & BARS

LET'S IMAGINE WHAT'S INSIDE OUR FANTASY COOKIE JARS. WHAT'S IN YOURS?

In mine, I have a fresh batch of brown butter–chocolate chip cookies. They're the fancy kind, with sea salt and pistachios (see page 80). You know what else is in my fantasy cookie jar? A tube of Dr Pepper lip balm, a small bag of cheese puffs, and my yellow sport Walkman with a Counting Crows cassette tape. Apparently my fantasy cookie jar is also my time capsule from 1993.

For this chapter, I dug deep into my cookie fantasies. These are my cookie dreams come to life, with every bit of dark chocolate, peanut butter filling, malt powder, lemon curd, and cornflakes cereal imaginable. These cookies are meant to celebrate our sweet tooth and reinforce our ability to put cereal in our cookies and to eat too many for breakfast . . . because now we're grown . . . and we can have cookies for breakfast, listen to Counting Crows, and wear our junior high Dr. Martens if we want to.

OATMEAL SANDWICH COOKIES
with creamy peanut butter filling

CHOCOLATE-MALTED
OATMEAL COOKIES with salted peanuts

DARK CHOCOLATE, PISTACHIO &
SMOKED SEA SALT cookies

black-and-white dipped PRETZELS

BLACK SESAME BROWN SUGAR shortbread

melt-y chocolate-truffle COOKIES

vanilla bean-confetti COOKIES

BLACKBERRY PIE cookies

chocolate-dipped BANANA BREAD BISCOTTI

pumpkin, cranberry & white chocolate CAKE COOKIES

strawberry shortcake COOKIES

CHOCOLATE-DIPPED cookie-dough balls

chocolate-coconut-ALMOND BITES

HONEY-ROASTED-PEANUT & STRAWBERRY thumbprint cookies

set it & (don't) forget it COOKIES

LEMON MERINGUE cookies

PEACH, BRIE & DARK CHOCOLATE s'mores

CLASSIC lemon bars

BOURBON-CHOCOLATE pecan pie bars (aka derby pie bars)

buttered popcorn CRISPY TREATS

RASPBERRY cream cheese brownies

toasted marshmallow SQUARES

LAVENDER palmiers

COOKIE EXPRESS

Two of the best things about making a big batch of cookies are licking the excess dough from the spatula and, less selfishly, sharing cookies with people you love. Many times, those folks aren't in easy cookie-sharing distance. It's important to know the best way to pack up our creations so that they can make a safe trip through the mail and into the hands of your loved one.

Taking the time to bake cookies is *all* love. Wrapping cookies, labeling them, adding a bow, and carefully packaging them for shipment—that's *extraspecial* care.

Here are some tips to successfully pull it off.

choose your cookie wisely Select a hearty and simple cookie for shipment. Delicate ones may have a tendency to crumble in shipment, chocolate-dipped ones might melt along the way, and cakey cookies have too much moisture and might mold.

Some of my favorite cookies to ship are the Dark Chocolate, Pistachio, and Smoked Sea Salt Cookies (page 80), Buttered Popcorn Crispy Treats (page 115), Black Sesame Brown Sugar Shortbread (page 84), Vanilla Bean–Confetti Cookies (page 88), and Lavender Palmiers (page 122). These cookies are as durable as they are delicious. Perfect for shipment!

wrap and double wrap We want our cookies to arrive as fresh as possible. Wrap each cookie individually in plastic wrap. Then bundle a few cookies together, put them in a small plastic bag, and tie the bag closed with a small bow. Double-wrapped cookies will stay fresh and look extraspecial when they come out of the box. Double win!

Once the cookies are in their baggies, it's best to put them in a small box inside of the larger shipping box. Small craft boxes lined with tissue paper are a perfect fit.

proper padding is essential We have our cookies double wrapped and safely packed away inside a tissue-paper-cushioned box. Now it's time to make sure all of our deliberate packaging work gets there safely.

You'll want about 2 to 3 inches of bubble wrap, or eco-friendly foam popcorn, to surround the sides of your cookie box. Yeah, that's a lot of cushion. You're going to need a big box. Generously line box with cushion, put the box in the center, and surround it with more cushioning.

Tape it up. Add an address. Ship it off as quickly as possible. Don't think about the fact that the mail people might throw the box around. If they knew it had cookies inside, they'd probably be much nicer.

Let me tell you a little something about myself: I can sell you a box of Girl Scout cookies like you wouldn't believe. You might think you can ignore me. You might think that you don't have the time or money. You might think that, for some weird reason, you're not in the mood for cookies. Well . . . you are. I have 12 years (which is almost awkward) of Girl Scout cookie–selling experience on my side. I have the bow-and-arrow badge, I can still recite the pledge, and I am one fine seller of cookies.

Lucky for you, I'm not here to sell you cookies. This recipe is inspired by my favorite Girl Scout cookies. My version is thick and chewy, loaded with oats, brown sugar, and butter. With a sweet nutty filling, these cookies make for the perfect sandwich situation. I like to wrap these cookies individually and keep them in my freezer for occasional snacking. Come to think of it, I bet I could sell these cookies outside my local grocery store. Hmm . . . I've just got to find that Girl Scout sash. This won't be awkward at all. . . .

OATMEAL SANDWICH COOKIES
with creamy peanut butter filling

cookies

- ½ cup (1 stick) unsalted butter, at room temperature
- 1 cup packed light brown sugar
- 1 large egg
- 1 teaspoon pure vanilla extract
- 1¼ cups old-fashioned oats
- 1 cup all-purpose flour
- ½ teaspoon baking powder
- ½ teaspoon baking soda

1. Put racks in the center and upper third of the oven and preheat the oven to 350°F. Line 2 baking sheets with parchment paper.

2. For the cookies, in the bowl of an electric mixer fitted with the paddle attachment, beat the butter and sugar until creamy, 3 to 4 minutes. Add the egg and beat on medium speed for about 1 minute. Add the vanilla and beat until incorporated.

3. In a medium bowl, whisk together the oats, flour, baking powder, baking soda, cinnamon, nutmeg, and salt. Add this mixture to the butter mixture and beat on low speed until just incorporated. Stir in the pecans.

4. Scoop up 1 heaping teaspoon of cookie dough, roll it into a ball in your hands, and put it on 1 of the prepared baking sheets. Repeat with the remaining dough, leaving about 1½ inches in between cookies. If the dough begins to stick to your hands, rinse your hands and work with just slightly damp hands.

5. Bake until the cookies are a little underdone, about 10 minutes, or up to 13 minutes, if you prefer them more done. Let cool on the baking sheets for 5 minutes before transferring to wire racks to cool completely.

6. For the filling, in the bowl of a stand mixer fitted with the paddle attachment, beat the butter, peanut butter, and confectioners' sugar on medium speed until smooth and creamy, 3 to 5 minutes. With the mixer running, drizzle in the vanilla. Scrape down the bowl as necessary. Add the milk, 1 tablespoon at a time, until the filling is smooth and will spread easily.

7. When the cookies are completely cool, flip them over and spread half of the cookie bottoms with the filling. Top with a similar-size cookie. Wrap individually and store in the refrigerator. The cookies are best served slightly chilled. They will last, well wrapped, in the fridge, for about 5 days.

makes about 24 sandwich cookies

1 teaspoon ground cinnamon

¼ teaspoon freshly ground nutmeg

½ teaspoon salt

½ cup coarsely chopped pecans

filling

3 tablespoons unsalted butter, at room temperature

½ cup smooth all-natural peanut butter

1 cup confectioners' sugar

1 teaspoon pure vanilla extract

3 to 4 tablespoons milk

You know that lady at the office who can pack on the eye makeup and lipstick and super gloss and look absolutely amazing? If I were to wear the same amount of makeup, I'd look like I had dipped my face in scary clown makeup. Oatmeal is that lady. It just has the ability to hold its own against chocolate chunks, salted peanuts, and anything else you might throw in its direction. How about some malt powder? Sure! Oatmeal can take it. Feel free to throw in dried fruit, white chocolate, spicy pecans, or any other tasty morsels you may find in your kitchen.

CHOCOLATE-MALTED OATMEAL
cookies with salted peanuts

2½ cups old-fashioned oats

2 cups all-purpose flour

¾ cup malted milk powder

1 teaspoon baking powder

1 teaspoon baking soda

¾ teaspoon salt

1 cup (2 sticks) unsalted butter, at room temperature

1 cup packed light brown sugar

½ cup granulated sugar

2 large eggs

¼ cup whole milk

1 tablespoon pure vanilla extract

1½ cups milk chocolate chips

1½ cups chopped salted peanuts

1. Put racks in the center and upper third of the oven and preheat the oven to 350°F. Line 2 baking sheets with parchment paper.

2. In a large bowl, whisk together the oats, flour, malted milk powder, baking powder, baking soda, and salt.

3. In an electric mixer fitted with the paddle attachment, beat together the butter and sugars on medium speed until light and fluffy, 3 to 4 minutes. Add the eggs one at a time, beating well and scraping the bowl after each addition. Reduce the speed to medium-low and slowly add the milk and then the vanilla. Mix until well combined. Reduce the mixer speed to low and gradually add the oat mixture, mixing until barely combined. Using a rubber spatula, stir in the chocolate chips and peanuts.

4. Scoop the cookie dough, about 2 tablespoons per cookie, onto the prepared baking sheets, leaving about 2 inches in between each cookie. Bake until they are just set and golden around the edges, about 12 minutes. Let cool on the baking sheets for 5 minutes and then transfer to wire racks to cool completely. The cookies will keep in an airtight container at room temperature for up to 4 days.

makes about 36 cookies

There's just something about chocolate chip cookies that always feels like a treat. They make you feel thought of, cared for, and special—even if you're just making a big batch for yourself. They're the chicken soup of cookies.

This version of the classic chocolate chip cookie is elevated to dream-status. It's packed with dark chocolate chunks and salty roasted pistachios, and topped with smoked sea salt. The smoky salt enhances the flavor of the dark chocolate and balances the sweetness of the cookie—it's seriously good, so don't skip it. The pistachios add a soft crunch and pretty green flecks throughout the cookie.

This is a treat-yo'self cookie. You're worth it. Every bit.

dark chocolate, pistachio &
SMOKED SEA SALT COOKIES

½ cup (1 stick) unsalted butter, at room temperature

½ cup granulated sugar

½ cup packed light brown sugar

1 large egg

1 teaspoon pure vanilla extract

1¼ cups all-purpose flour

½ teaspoon baking soda

¼ teaspoon salt

1½ cups dark chocolate chips

1 cup shelled pistachios, coarsely chopped

Smoked sea salt, for sprinkling

1. Put racks in the center and upper third of the oven and preheat the oven to 350°F. Line 2 baking sheets with parchment paper.

2. In the bowl of an electric mixer fitted with the paddle attachment, beat the butter and sugars until pale and fluffy, about 4 minutes. Add the egg and beat for about 1 minute. Add the vanilla and beat until incorporated.

3. In a medium bowl, whisk together the flour, baking soda, and salt. Add this mixture all at once to the butter mixture. Beat on low speed until just incorporated. Beat in the chocolate chips and nuts.

4. Scoop the cookie dough, about 2 tablespoons per cookie, onto the prepared baking sheets, leaving about 2 inches in between each cookie. Sprinkle generously with smoked sea salt.

5. Bake until just golden brown, 10 to 12 minutes. Let the cookies cool on the pans for 5 minutes before transferring them to wire racks to cool completely. The cookies will last, well wrapped, at room temperature for up to 4 days . . . as if they'll last that long.

makes about 24 cookies

One of my favorite guilty pleasures is chocolate-covered pretzels. I like the sweet and salty combination so much that I've been known to eat them for dinner. As long as we're being honest, I should also mention that I have a tendency to eat these chocolate-dipped pretzels as a meal, in excess, on the couch, with wine.

BLACK-AND-WHITE
dipped pretzels

1 heaping cup white nonpareil sprinkles

12 ounces white chocolate

12 ounces dark chocolate

About 36 small hard pretzels (I use about half of a 16-ounce bag)

1. Line a baking sheet with parchment paper and set aside. Put the sprinkles in a medium bowl and set aside.

2. Put the white chocolate and dark chocolate in separate heat-proof bowls. Simmer 2 inches of water in a medium saucepan over medium heat. Put the bowl of white chocolate over the simmering water, making sure that the bottom of the bowl does not touch the water. Gently stir until the white chocolate is melted and perfectly smooth, about 4 minutes. Remove from the heat.

3. Dip half of a pretzel into the warm melted white chocolate. Shake off a bit of the excess chocolate and use a knife or fork to wipe some of the chocolate off the back side of the pretzel. You'll want the pretzels to have their holes free of chocolate. Put the coated pretzel in the sprinkle bowl and coat well. Put the dipped and sprinkled pretzel on a piece of parchment paper and let the chocolate harden while you dip and coat the remaining pretzels. Put the coated pretzels in the freezer and freeze until hard, about 15 minutes.

4. While the pretzels set, melt the dark chocolate over the simmering water as you did for the white chocolate.

5. Remove the pretzels from the freezer, and using tongs, gently dip the other half of the pretzels in the warm melted dark chocolate. Add more sprinkles if you'd like. Return to the freezer and freeze until hard, about 15 minutes.

6. The pretzels will keep in an airtight container at a cool room temperature for up to 3 days.

makes about 36 pretzels

Shortbread doesn't like to brag. It doesn't mind that some cookies are packed with chocolate chunks and colorful confetti. It doesn't need to prove its worth with cream filling or extra glaze. Shortbread can just sit back content in the knowledge that it's the most buttery, melt-in-your-mouth, make-you-weak-in-the-knees cookie on the block. Shortbread has nothing to prove. It doesn't necessarily need a lift from brown sugar and black sesame seeds, but it doesn't mind the classy company.

black sesame brown sugar
SHORTBREAD

1 cup (2 sticks) unsalted butter, at room temperature

½ cup packed light brown sugar

2¼ cups all-purpose flour

2 tablespoons cornstarch

½ teaspoon salt

2 tablespoons plus 2 teaspoons black sesame seeds

1. Put racks in the center and upper third of the oven and preheat the oven to 325°F. Line 2 baking sheets with parchment paper.

2. In the bowl of an electric mixer fitted with the paddle attachment, beat together the butter and sugar until light and fluffy, 3 to 4 minutes.

3. In a small bowl, whisk together the flour, cornstarch, salt, and sesame seeds. Add the flour mixture to the butter mixture, 1 cup at a time, beating after each addition, until it is all incorporated. The mixture will be thick and crumbly. Transfer it to a counter and knead it into a smooth dough. Wrap the dough in plastic wrap and refrigerate for 20 minutes.

4. Transfer the chilled dough to a lightly floured counter and roll it into a ½-inch-thick rectangle. Cut it into 2-inch squares, and cut each square into triangles. Transfer to the prepared baking sheets.

5. Bake until just lightly golden brown around the edges, 20 to 22 minutes. Remove from the oven and let cool. The cookies will keep in an airtight container at room temperature for up to 7 days.

makes about 50 cookies

Let's be the kind of people who throw dinner parties with matching china. Let's be the kind of people who don't knock over their wine glasses during a very animated reenactment of their favorite scenes from *Anchorman* (because, yeah, we're still talking about that movie). Let's be the kind of people who have coffee brewed and little dessert cookies ready for serving. These are them. Good luck with the wine spill.

melt-y
CHOCOLATE-TRUFFLE COOKIES

½ cup all-purpose flour

½ cup sugar

¼ cup unsweetened Dutch-processed cocoa powder

½ teaspoon baking powder

¼ teaspoon salt

1 teaspoon espresso powder (optional)

2 tablespoons unsalted butter, cut into chunks, at room temperature

⅓ cup (about 3 ounces) chopped dark chocolate (I used a 70% cacao chocolate)

1 large egg

1 tablespoon pure vanilla extract

1 cup confectioners' sugar

1. Put racks in the center and upper third of the oven and preheat the oven to 375°F. Line 2 baking sheets with parchment paper.

2. In a medium bowl, whisk together the flour, sugar, cocoa powder, baking powder, salt, and espresso powder, if using. Add the butter and rub the butter into the dry ingredients until thoroughly combined. The mixture will be relatively dry and resemble breadcrumbs. Add the chopped chocolate and toss well.

3. In a small bowl, whisk together the egg and vanilla. Add the egg mixture to the chocolate mixture and stir with a fork until the mixture is slightly moistened. Use your hands to press the dough into a ball. Wrap the dough in plastic wrap and refrigerate for about 30 minutes.

4. Put the confectioners' sugar in a medium bowl. Remove the dough from the refrigerator and shape it into tablespoon-size balls. Generously coat the balls, one at a time, in the confectioners' sugar and place on the prepared baking sheets. Leave about 2 inches of space between each cookie. Bake until the cookies are just set, but still slightly undercooked on the inside, about 10 minutes. Let cool on the pans for 5 minutes before transferring to wire racks to cool completely. Serve warm (preferably right after dinner). The cookies will keep in an airtight container for up to 4 days.

makes about 18 cookies

I like to think that, on good days, each of us is filled to the brim with happiness, color, and confetti. Now, thanks to this cookie, we can eat exactly how we feel.

vanilla bean
CONFETTI COOKIES

1½ cups all-purpose flour

1 teaspoon baking powder

1 teaspoon cream of tartar

½ teaspoon baking soda

½ teaspoon salt

½ cup (1 stick) unsalted butter, at room temperature

¾ cup sugar

1 vanilla bean

1 large egg

1 teaspoon pure vanilla extract

½ cup sprinkles (I prefer jimmies over nonpareils)

1. In a medium bowl, whisk together the flour, baking powder, cream of tartar, baking soda, and salt.

2. In the bowl of an electric mixer fitted with the paddle attachment, beat the butter and sugar at medium speed until light and fluffy, 3 to 4 minutes. Split the vanilla bean and scrape the seeds into the bowl. Add the egg and vanilla extract, and beat until thoroughly combined.

3. Reduce the mixer speed to low, and slowly add the dry ingredients to the wet ingredients. The dough will be thick (you may have to finish incorporating the mixture with a spatula). Fold in ¼ cup of the sprinkles.

4. Put the remaining ¼ cup sprinkles in a bowl. Scoop up 2 tablespoons of dough and roll it into a ball. Dip the ball into the bowl of sprinkles to cover lightly. Put the ball on a plate. Repeat with the remaining sprinkles and dough, and chill for at least 2 hours.

5. Put racks in the center and upper third of the oven and preheat the oven to 350°F. Line 2 large baking sheets with parchment paper.

6. Transfer the chilled dough balls to the prepared baking sheets, leaving about 2 inches of space in between each ball.

7. Bake until the cookies have spread and are just beginning to brown around the edges, but are mostly pale and soft, 8 to 10 minutes. Let cool on the cookie sheets for 5 minutes before transferring to wire racks to cool completely. The cookies will keep in an airtight container for up to 4 days.

makes about 18 cookies

Think of these cookies as picnic pie. Think of these cookies as purse pie. Think of these cookies as pie you can eat in the car while stuck in traffic. Think of these cookies as pie on the go, with a deep purple fruity filling, forever and always.

BLACKBERRY PIE
cookies

3 cups fresh blackberries

½ cup plus 3 tablespoons sugar

3 tablespoons cornstarch

1 teaspoon ground cinnamon

1 teaspoon grated lemon zest

Pinch of salt

Buttermilk Pie Crust (page 128)

1 large egg

1 tablespoon whole milk

1. Line 2 baking sheets with parchment paper and set aside.

2. Cut the berries into small (½-inch) pieces and put them in a medium bowl. (This could stain your fingers purple, just FYI.) Add ½ cup of sugar, the cornstarch, ½ teaspoon cinnamon, the lemon zest, and the salt, and toss well.

3. Roll each disk of crust out until it is ¼ inch thick. Use a 2½-inch round cookie or biscuit cutter to cut circles out of the dough, rerolling once. Transfer the rounds to the prepared baking sheets. Freeze the dough rounds for 20 to 30 minutes.

4. Put racks in the center and upper third of the oven and preheat the oven to 375°F.

5. In a small bowl, whisk together the eggs and milk. In a separate small bowl, stir together the remaining 3 tablespoons of sugar and ½ teaspoon cinnamon.

6. To assemble the pie cookies, lightly brush 1 dough circle with the egg wash. Spoon about 2 teaspoons of the filling into the center. Put a second dough circle over the fruit filling. Using a fork, crimp the edges. Using a sharp knife, cut a small X into the top crust. Put the pie cookie on 1 of the prepared baking sheets and repeat with the remaining ingredients. Lightly brush the tops of the cookies with the egg wash and sprinkle with the cinnamon sugar.

7. Bake until golden brown and puffed, 20 to 25 minutes. Let cool on the baking sheets for 10 minutes before transferring to wire racks to cool completely.

makes about 24 cookies

I'm convinced that most regular biscotti cookies are on a mission to send me straight to the dentist with a broken tooth. Why are they so hard!?

This biscotti recipe is softer than its traditional counterpart. You can choose to bake them once for a soft cookie feel, or twice for a bit more bite. Either way, these biscotti have both sweet banana flavor and spice, essentially making them dunkable banana bread. Let's just be real.

chocolate-dipped
BANANA BREAD BISCOTTI

2	cups all-purpose flour
1½	teaspoons ground cinnamon
1	teaspoon baking powder
¼	teaspoon salt
¼	cup (½ stick) unsalted butter, at room temperature
¾	cup plus 2 tablespoons sugar
1	medium overripe banana, peeled and mashed well (about ½ cup)
2	large eggs
1	teaspoon pure vanilla extract
8	ounces dark chocolate

1. Put racks in the center and upper third of the oven and preheat the oven to 325°F. Line 2 baking sheets with parchment paper.

2. In a medium bowl, whisk together the flour, 1 teaspoon of the cinnamon, the baking powder, and salt.

3. In the bowl of an electric mixer fitted with the paddle attachment, beat the butter and the ¾ cup sugar until light and fluffy, 3 to 4 minutes. Beat in the banana and 1 of the eggs. Beat in the vanilla extract. Add the flour mixture to the butter mixture and, using the mixer or a spatula, stir until a somewhat stiff dough is formed.

4. Divide the dough between the 2 prepared baking sheets. Shape each half of dough into a log that is 9 inches long and 1½ inches wide. In a small bowl, beat the remaining 1 egg with 1 tablespoon water, and brush the egg wash over both logs. In another small bowl, whisk together the remaining ½ teaspoon cinnamon with the 2 tablespoons sugar. Sprinkle over the biscotti logs.

5. Bake on 2 different racks for 20 minutes. Rotate the cookie sheets and bake until golden and firm to the touch, 20 to 25 more minutes.

6. Remove the pans from the oven, but keep the oven on if you're going to crisp the biscotti. Let the biscotti cool until you're able to handle them. Using a serrated knife, cut the logs into ½-inch-wide diagonal slices. Put the biscotti, cut side down, on a baking sheet. For a soft biscotti, you're done! No need for a second bake. For a bit of firmness, bake for 5 more minutes. For a crisp biscotti, bake for 10 to 12 more minutes. Let cool until the biscotti are cool enough to handle.

7. Put a medium pot filled with 2 inches of water over medium heat. Bring the water to a simmer. Put the chocolate in a heat-proof bowl and put the bowl over the simmering water. Stir the chocolate as it melts. Once the chocolate has melted, remove the pan from the heat, but keep the bowl over the hot water. Dip about 2 inches of the biscotti into the dark chocolate. Shake off the excess chocolate, put the biscotti on a piece of parchment paper, and let cool completely.

8. Store in an airtight container in the refrigerator (if it's warm in your kitchen) for up to 1 week.

makes about 24 cookies

These cookies represent what it might be like to celebrate Thanksgiving and Christmas on the same day. Get in all your holiday spirit in one day, and in one cookie! They're just perfect for sitting around the fire and singing carols about what we're thankful for.

pumpkin, cranberry &
WHITE CHOCOLATE CAKE COOKIES

1 cup pumpkin puree

½ cup (1 stick) unsalted butter

1 teaspoon ground cinnamon

½ teaspoon ground ginger

¼ teaspoon freshly grated nutmeg

¼ teaspoon ground cloves

¼ teaspoon ground cardamom

½ teaspoon grated orange zest

2 cups all-purpose flour

1 teaspoon baking powder

1 teaspoon baking soda

½ teaspoon salt

2 large eggs

1 cup packed light brown sugar

1 teaspoon pure vanilla extract

1 cup fresh cranberries, coarsely chopped

1 cup white chocolate chips

Confectioners' sugar, for dusting

1. Put racks in the upper third and center of the oven and preheat the oven to 325°F. Line 2 baking sheets with parchment paper.

2. In a medium saucepan set over medium heat, combine the pumpkin, butter, cinnamon, ginger, nutmeg, cloves, cardamom, and orange zest. Heat until the butter is melted and the mixture is warm and fragrant, about 5 minutes. Remove the pan from the heat and let cool slightly.

3. In a large bowl, whisk together the flour, baking powder, baking soda, and salt.

4. Once the pumpkin mixture is about room temperature, whisk in the eggs, brown sugar, and vanilla. Add the pumpkin mixture to the flour mixture. Stir well and then stir in the cranberries and white chocolate.

5. Spoon the cookie dough, about 2 heaping tablespoons per cookie, onto the prepared baking sheets, leaving about 2 inches in between each cookie. Bake until the tops feel firm and cooked through, about 16 minutes. Let cool on the baking sheets for 5 minutes before using a wide metal spatula to transfer the cookies to wire racks to cool completely.

6. Dust the cooled cookies lightly with confectioners' sugar. The cookies will keep in an airtight container, with parchment paper between the stacked layers, for up to 4 days.

makes 24 cookies

This is a biscuit/scone/cookie hybrid that couldn't be more perfect for summertime picnics and parties. They were inspired by the ladies of the Spoon Fork Bacon blog.

STRAWBERRY SHORTCAKE
cookies

strawberries

- 1 cup chopped fresh strawberries
- 1 teaspoon fresh lemon juice
- 2 tablespoons sugar
- 1 tablespoon cornstarch

cookies

- 2 cups all-purpose flour
- ¾ cup sugar
- 1½ teaspoons baking powder
- ¼ teaspoon baking soda
- ½ teaspoon salt
- ¼ teaspoon freshly grated nutmeg
- ½ cup (1 stick) cold unsalted butter, cut into cubes
- 1 large egg yolk
- 2 teaspoons pure vanilla extract
- ½ cup plus 2 tablespoons cold buttermilk

glaze

- 1 cup confectioners' sugar
- 2 tablespoons milk or water
- 1 teaspoon pure vanilla extract

1. Put racks in the center and upper third of the oven and preheat the oven to 375°F. Line 2 baking sheets with parchment paper and set aside.

2. In a small bowl, toss together the strawberries, lemon juice, sugar, and cornstarch. Set aside.

3. In a medium bowl, whisk together the flour, sugar, baking powder, baking soda, salt, and nutmeg. Using your fingers or a pastry cutter, cut in the butter until some of the butter pieces are the size of peas and some are the size of oat flakes.

4. In a small bowl, whisk together the egg yolk, vanilla, and buttermilk. Pour this mixture into the flour mixture. Stir with a fork until all of the flour bits are moistened. Fold in the strawberries and any strawberry juice.

5. Scoop the batter, about 2 tablespoons per cookie, onto the prepared baking sheets, leaving 2 inches in between each cookie. Bake until the cookies are baked through and just beginning to brown on top, 18 to 20 minutes. Remove from the oven and let cool completely before glazing.

6. For the glaze, in a small bowl, whisk together the confectioners' sugar, milk, and vanilla. Add a dash more milk if your glaze is too thick. Use the tines of a fork to drizzle the glaze over the cooled cookies. The cookies will keep in an airtight container at room temperature for up to 3 days.

makes about 20 cookies

Guilty! It was me who ate half of the raw cookie dough before baking off a single cookie. I'm sorry/I'm not sorry.

I've found a solution to my dough-eating dilemma: cookie dough that is meant to stay cookie dough! This recipe for dough balls includes all of the cookie-dough miracle flavors we know and love: butter, brown sugar, and heady vanilla. It also keeps the baking soda in the cookie dough even though the dough is not actually baked, because it will add that familiar sour tang. What these cookie-dough balls lack is raw eggs. My replacement is applesauce, which helps the dough bind together without contributing much flavor. I love these on a stick, dipped in chocolate, and stored in the freezer. Totally snackable. You're welcome/I'm sorry. Seriously.

chocolate-dipped
COOKIE-DOUGH BALLS

½ cup (1 stick) unsalted butter, at room temperature

½ cup packed light brown sugar

⅓ cup granulated sugar

¼ cup applesauce

1 teaspoon pure vanilla extract

1¼ cups all-purpose flour

½ teaspoon baking soda

¾ teaspoon salt

2½ cups semisweet chocolate chips

½ cup chopped walnuts (optional)

1. Line 2 baking sheets with parchment paper.

2. In the bowl of an electric mixer fitted with the paddle attachment, beat together the butter and sugars on medium speed until light and fluffy, about 3 minutes. Beat in the applesauce and vanilla.

3. In a medium bowl, whisk together the flour, baking soda, and salt. Add the flour mixture to the butter mixture and stir until incorporated. Fold in 1 cup of the chocolate chips and the walnuts, if using.

4. Use a small cookie scoop to portion out the dough onto the prepared baking sheets. Spear each dough ball with a Popsicle stick. Freeze overnight, or until frozen, at least 3 hours.

5. When ready to dip the balls, melt the remaining 1½ cups chocolate chips in a double boiler or in the microwave. Remove the balls from the freezer, dip them into the warm chocolate, and return them to the baking sheets. Freeze until hard, at least 30 minutes. Serve cold from the freezer.

makes 24 balls

Welcome to the very sweet union of the macaroon and the candy bar. These coconut bites are essentially no-bake cookies (save for roasting the almonds). The coconut is sweet and crunchy, and the melted chocolate is the little bit of glue needed to hold the almond in place. Such good bites! It's impossible to eat just one.

chocolate-coconut-
ALMOND BITES

30 almonds

½ cup sweetened condensed milk

¾ cup confectioners' sugar

1 tablespoon pure vanilla extract

Pinch of salt

1½ cups unsweetened flaked coconut

8 ounces good-quality semisweet chocolate chips

1. Put a rack in the upper third of the oven and preheat the oven to 350°F. Spread the almonds on a baking sheet and toast them until fragrant, about 10 minutes. Remove from the oven and let cool.

2. In a medium bowl, whisk together the sweetened condensed milk, confectioners' sugar, vanilla, and salt. Stir in the coconut. The mixture will be thick. Put the mixture in the freezer for 30 minutes.

3. Line a baking sheet with parchment paper. Remove the coconut mixture from the freezer. Scoop up 1 heaping teaspoon of the mixture, roll it into a ball in your hands, and put it on the prepared baking sheet. Repeat with the remaining mixture. Rinse your hands if they get too sticky. Press your pinkie finger into each ball, creating a small indentation. Don't worry if the bites crack; just press them back together. Chill in the refrigerator for 15 minutes.

4. Put a medium pot filled with 2 inches of water over medium heat. Bring the water to a simmer. Put the chocolate in a heat-proof bowl and put the bowl over the simmering water. Stir the chocolate until melted. Remove the pan from the heat, but keep the bowl over the hot water.

5. Remove the bites from the fridge. Dollop about ½ teaspoon of melted chocolate into the center of each bite. Top with a roasted almond. You can also drizzle them with a bit of chocolate. Let cool for about 1 hour. (Refrigerate to speed the hardening process along.) Store in an airtight container, with parchment or wax paper between the layers, at room temperature or in the refrigerator for up to 7 days.

makes about 30 bites

This is what a peanut butter and jelly sandwich would look like all grown up and transformed into a cookie. I grind up honey-roasted peanuts and stir them into a shortbread cookie dough. The result is a delicately flavored, crisp cookie. Strawberry jam feels perfectly classic in the cookie indentation. Definitely splurge on the good jam. We're grown-ups and so are our cookies.

honey-roasted-peanut & strawberry
THUMBPRINT COOKIES

1¾ cups finely ground honey-roasted peanuts

1¾ cups all-purpose flour

1 cup (2 sticks) unsalted butter, at room temperature

¾ cup granulated sugar

1 large egg yolk

2 teaspoons pure vanilla extract

Confectioners' sugar, for dusting

1 cup good-quality strawberry jam

1. Put racks in the center and upper third of the oven and preheat the oven to 350°F. Line 2 baking sheets with parchment paper.

2. In a food processor, finely grind the peanuts. Transfer to a medium bowl, add the flour, and whisk together.

3. In the bowl of an electric mixer fitted with the paddle attachment, beat the butter and sugar together on medium speed until light and fluffy, 3 to 4 minutes. Add the egg yolk and vanilla and beat well. Reduce the speed to low and gradually add the flour mixture, mixing only until just incorporated. Use a spatula to finish hand mixing.

4. Scoop up 1 tablespoon of cookie dough, roll it into a ball in your hands, and put it on 1 of the prepared baking sheets. Repeat with the remaining dough, leaving about 2 inches in between cookies. Steadying each cookie with the thumb and finger of 1 hand, use the pinkie of your other hand to make an indention in the center of each cookie. Be careful; you don't want to press all the way down to the cookie sheet.

5. Bake until the cookies are slightly browned, 12 to 15 minutes. Let the cookies cool on the baking sheets for 5 minutes before transferring them to cooling racks to cool completely.

6. Using a fine-mesh strainer, generously sift confectioners' sugar onto the cookies. Spoon the strawberry jam into each indentation. The cookies will keep in an airtight container, with the layers separated by parchment or wax paper, in the refrigerator for up to 4 days.

makes about 30 cookies

These cookies are full of secrets. For the record, I'm terrible at keeping secrets, so here I go, spilling the beans. First secret: They are chock-full of cornflake cereal, which makes them crispy and crunchy. Second secret: They're baked superslow overnight! That means that you can bake at midnight and be a hero at work . . . the well-rested, totally-wearing-mascara-and-matching-socks hero! If all you can find is sweetened shredded coconut, decrease the sugar by ¼ cup.

SET IT & (DON'T) FORGET IT
cookies

1 cup unsweetened flaked coconut

2 large egg whites

⅛ teaspoon cream of tartar

Pinch of salt

1 cup sugar

½ cup dark chocolate chunks

1½ cups cornflake cereal

1. Put racks in the center and upper third of the oven and preheat the oven to 350°F.

2. Line 2 baking sheets with parchment paper. Sprinkle the coconut flakes on 1 of the prepared baking sheets. Toast the coconut until it is golden brown, 5 to 8 minutes. Keep an eye on it! Let cool completely. Leave the oven on.

3. Put the egg whites in the bowl of an electric mixer fitted with the whisk attachment. Make sure your bowl is completely dry and free of any residual grease. Beat on medium speed until frothy, about 2 minutes. Add the cream of tartar and salt. Slowly add the sugar, increase the speed to medium-high, and continue to add the sugar slowly. The egg whites will begin to thicken. Beat until all of the sugar is added and the eggs whites hold stiff peaks, about 6 minutes. They'll be glossy and resemble melted marshmallow.

4. Fold in the cooled coconut, the chocolate chunks, and cereal. Use a gentle hand while folding the ingredients together. Egg whites have a temper. Dollop the batter, 2 tablespoons per cookie, onto the prepared baking sheets, and put the baking sheets in the hot oven.

5. Turn the oven off and let the cookies cook overnight (or for at least 6 hours). Don't open the oven to peek! The cookies will be crisp and chewy. They will keep in an airtight container at room temperature for up to 3 days.

makes about 20 cookies

I sometimes hit a roadblock in the kitchen. I want all the flavor of a certain kind of pie, but I don't want to spend all of the time and wash all of the dishes necessary to actually make the pie. The crust, the filling, the foofy topping . . . it seems like a lot. Never mind the fact that I don't have a proper windowsill to cool my pies on. (Kidding . . . mostly.) These cookies are an excellent compromise. Pie bites in a cookie, they involve crisp meringue studded with graham cracker bits and filled with sweet-and-sour lemon curd. Roadblock cleared.

LEMON MERINGUE
cookies

meringues
- 2 **large egg whites**
- **Pinch of salt**
- ⅔ **cup sugar**
- 1 **teaspoon lemon zest**
- 1 **teaspoon pure vanilla extract**
- ½ **cup graham cracker crumbs**

lemon curd
- ½ **cup sugar**
- ½ **cup fresh lemon juice**
- 2 **large eggs**
- 2 **large egg yolks**
- **Pinch of salt**
- 6 **tablespoons (¾ stick) unsalted butter**

1. Put racks in the center and upper third of the oven and preheat the oven to 200°F. Line 2 baking sheets with parchment paper.

2. For the meringues, put the egg whites in the bowl of an electric mixer fitted with the whisk attachment. Beat on medium speed until foamy, about 2 minutes. Add the salt and increase the speed to medium-high. Slowly begin to sprinkle in the sugar. Beat until all of the sugar is added and the egg whites become thick and glossy and hold stiff peaks, about 6 minutes. They'll resemble melted marshmallow.

3. Remove the bowl from the mixer and fold in the lemon zest, vanilla extract, and graham cracker crumbs. Spoon the meringue, about 2 tablespoons per cookie, onto the prepared baking sheets. The cookies can be fairly close together, as the meringue won't spread. Use the back of a spoon to spread the meringue out into 2-inch circles. Create a ½-inch well in the center of each cookie for the lemon curd.

4. Bake the cookies until they are no longer sticky, but are firm and hardened, about 2 hours. Remove the pans from the oven and let the cookies cool completely on the baking sheets before filling.

5. For the lemon curd, put a fine-mesh strainer over a medium bowl and set aside.

recipe continues

6. In a medium saucepan, whisk together the sugar, lemon juice, eggs, egg yolks, and salt. Put the pan over medium-low heat and add the butter. Beat with a whisk as the mixture heats. Occasionally scrape the pan with a spatula to get into the corners of the pan and prevent any curd from overcooking. Cook the curd until the butter is melted, the mixture is the thickness of warm hot fudge, and the whisk leaves a trail of whisk marks, about 8 minutes.

7. Remove the pan from the heat and immediately pour the curd into the fine-mesh strainer set over the medium bowl. Press through the strainer, discarding any solids. Pour the curd into a jar, press a piece of plastic wrap directly onto the surface of the curd, and refrigerate until completely cold.

8. When ready to serve the cookies, spoon about 2 teaspoons of cooled lemon curd into the well of each meringue cookie. The curd and the cookies are kept separate until ready to serve. Serve within a few hours of assembling. The curd will keep in an airtight container in the refrigerator for about 1 week (you'll have extra). The meringues will keep in an airtight container, in a dry area, at room temperature, for about 3 days (humidity will make them sticky balls).

makes about 24 cookies

In this installment of "Never Leave Well Enough Alone," let's transform the already delicious s'more. What would happen if we substituted melty, buttery Brie cheese for the marshmallows? What if we added roasted peaches to the mix? We're taking decadence to a whole new level! These treats are gooey, show-stopping, and yummy-unique.

peach, brie & dark chocolate
S'MORES

4 graham crackers, halved

About 2 ounces 70% cacao chocolate, divided into 4 pieces

4 ounces Brie, cut into 4 wedges

1 ripe peach, unpeeled, pitted, and sliced

1. Preheat the broiler.

2. Arrange the graham crackers on a baking sheet. Top 4 of the graham cracker halves with a piece of dark chocolate. Top each piece of dark chocolate with a wedge of Brie. Put 2 peach slices on each of the remaining 4 graham crackers.

3. Broil for just a few seconds. Thirty seconds should be the maximum amount of time needed to melt the chocolate and soften the cheese. Don't walk away from the oven while the s'mores broil, as they'll burn quickly. Remove the pan from the oven. Top each melted-cheese graham cracker with a peach graham cracker and serve the sandwiches immediately.

serves 4

There's a page in one of my oldest cookbooks that is tattered, butter-stained, and dusted with flour. It's the page for a recipe for classic lemon bars, which was one of my favorite treats to make as a kid. The press-in crust makes me feel like I'm playing with my food, and the simple lemon filling comes together with a whisk. The bars are buttery, tart, and sweet, and so easy a child could make them. I'm proof.

classic
LEMON BARS

crust

- ½ cup (1 stick) unsalted butter, room temperature, plus more for pan
- ½ cup sugar
- 1 cup all-purpose flour
- Pinch of salt

topping

- 2 large eggs
- ¾ cup sugar
- 3 tablespoons all-purpose flour
- 1 teaspoon grated lemon zest
- ¼ cup fresh lemon juice

1. Put a rack in the upper third of the oven and preheat oven to 350°F. Grease an 8 × 8-inch baking pan with butter, line with parchment paper so that it overhangs the pan slightly, and grease the parchment paper. Set aside.

2. For the crust, in the bowl of a stand mixer fitted with the paddle attachment, beat together the butter and sugar until light and fluffy, 3 to 5 minutes. Scrape down the sides of the bowl. Add flour and salt, and beat on low speed until incorporated. The dough may come together, but if it remains shaggy, that's fine, too. Dump the crust into the prepared pan and, using your fingertips, press it into the bottom of the pan.

3. Bake until it is just browned around the edges, 15 to 18 minutes. Let cool slightly.

4. Meanwhile, for the filling, in a medium bowl, whisk together the eggs and sugar until well combined and slightly thick. Add the flour, lemon juice, and zest and whisk well.

5. Pour the filling over the warm baked crust. Return the pan to the oven and bake until lightly browned on top and no longer jiggling in the center, 18 to 20 minutes. Let cool completely in the pan. Run a knife around the edges of the pan and slice the lemon bars into nine squares. Use the overhanging parchment paper to lift the squares out. The lemon bars will keep in an airtight container, the layers separated by wax paper, for up to 1 week.

makes 9 squares

I know a lovely girl from Kentucky. When you know a lovely girl from Kentucky, two things are certain: You develop a taste for Kentucky bourbon, and you celebrate Derby Day every May. On Derby Day, one is required to wear an unreasonably large hat, drink generous amounts of mint juleps, and relentlessly cheer for running horses for a solid 90 seconds. It's glorious, and Derby Pie Bars are just the icing on this bourbon-y cake.

bourbon-chocolate
PECAN PIE BARS
(aka derby pie bars)

shortbread crust

- 2 cups all-purpose flour
- ¾ cup confectioners' sugar
- 1 cup (2 sticks) unsalted butter, at room temperature
- ½ teaspoon salt

filling

- ¼ cup (½ stick) unsalted butter, melted
- ¾ cup packed light brown sugar
- ½ cup light corn syrup
- 3 large eggs
- 2 tablespoons bourbon
- ½ teaspoon salt
- 2 cups toasted pecan halves, coarsely chopped
- 1 cup dark chocolate chunks

1. Put a rack in the upper third of the oven and preheat the oven to 350°F. Grease a 9 x 13-inch baking dish with butter, line it with parchment paper, and grease the parchment paper. The parchment paper will ensure that the bars are easy to remove from the pan, but it's not entirely necessary.

2. For the crust, in an electric mixer fitted with the paddle attachment, combine the flour, confectioners' sugar, butter, and salt. Beat until the mixture is combined, but crumbly, about 4 minutes. Dump the mixture into the prepared baking dish and use your fingers to press the crust evenly across the bottom.

3. Bake until lightly browned, 12 to 15 minutes. Remove from the oven, but leave the oven on.

4. For the filling, in a medium bowl, whisk together the butter, brown sugar, corn syrup, eggs, bourbon, and salt until thoroughly combined and glossy. Stir in the pecan pieces and chocolate chunks. Pour the mixture over the baked crust, distributing the pecans and chocolate pieces evenly.

5. Bake until set, 25 to 30 minutes. Let cool completely in the baking dish before slicing into bars. The bars will keep in an airtight container in the refrigerator for up to 4 days.

makes about 36 bars

Only one thing could make sticky, sweet marshmallow treats better than they already are. For once the answer is not bourbon—it's buttered popcorn!

buttered popcorn
CRISPY TREATS

- 3 tablespoons vegetable oil
- ¼ cup yellow corn kernels
- ¼ teaspoon salt
- 4 cups crisp rice cereal, such as Rice Krispies
- ¼ cup (½ stick) salted butter
- 1 (10-ounce) bag large marshmallows (about 40)

  Coarse sea salt, for sprinkling

1. Generously butter a 9 x 13-inch baking dish.

2. In a medium saucepan set over medium heat, heat the oil. Add the corn kernels and put a lid over the pan, keeping the lid slightly askew. Listen as the popcorn begins to pop. Once the popping slows, turn off the heat. Remove the lid and add the salt to the popcorn.

3. Measure 3 heaping cups of popcorn into a large bowl. Add the crisp rice cereal. (You may have a bit of extra popcorn. That's for you to munch on.)

4. In the same pan that you popped the popcorn in, melt the butter over medium heat. Stir in the marshmallows until they are melted and glossy. Quickly pour the warm marshmallow mixture over the popcorn and cereal mixture. Stir with a wooden spoon until all of the popcorn and cereal are coated in marshmallow and evenly distributed. Spoon the mixture into the prepared baking dish and use the back of a wooden spoon to press the mixture into the baking dish. It may help to butter the back of the spoon several times. That will help the marshmallow not stick to the spoon. Sprinkle the top lightly with sea salt. Let cool for at least 1 hour.

5. Cut the treats into 32 squares and wrap individually. The treats will last, individually wrapped and at room temperature, for up to 1 week.

makes 32 squares

Brownies were the first thing I learned how to bake. I distinctly remember the experience. The unsweetened chocolate products were all kept on the lower baking shelf, well within reach of my grubby eight-year-old hands. The sweetened chocolate chips and candy pieces were kept on a higher shelf, way out of reach. It was common knowledge in our house that if I could reach the chocolate, I'd demolish it with no remorse. With the unsweetened chocolate, sugar, and flour within reach, I taught myself how to make brownies. There really was no stopping this sweet tooth.

In this version of brownie-madness, I'm combining my favorite classic brownie with equally decadent raspberry-infused cream cheese. It's where brownies and cheesecake collide. Now that I'm grown, and I can reach everything in the kitchen, it's time to get down to business!

raspberry cream cheese
BROWNIES

brownies

- 4 ounces bittersweet chocolate, coarsely chopped
- ¼ cup (½ stick) unsalted butter
- 2 large eggs
- ¾ cup sugar
- ½ cup all-purpose flour
- ½ teaspoon baking powder
- ½ teaspoon salt
- 1 teaspoon pure vanilla extract

1. Put a rack in the upper third of the oven and preheat the oven to 350°F. Grease an 8-inch square pan with butter, line it with parchment paper, and grease and flour the parchment paper. The parchment paper will ensure that the brownies are easy to remove from the pan, but if you don't have any on hand, simply greasing and flouring the pan will suffice.

2. For the brownies, bring 2 inches of water to a simmer in a medium saucepan. Put the chocolate and butter in a heat-proof bowl and put the bowl over the simmering water. Melt the chocolate and butter together, stirring occasionally, about 5 minutes. Remove the bowl from the pan and let the mixture cool slightly.

3. In a small bowl, beat the eggs. Whisk the eggs into the slightly cooled chocolate mixture. Add the sugar and beat until combined. Add the flour, baking powder, and salt. Stir well. Stir in the vanilla. Spread the brownie batter in the prepared pan.

recipe continues

cream cheese layer

- 4 ounces cream cheese, at room temperature
- 2 tablespoons unsalted butter, at room temperature
- 2 tablespoons sugar
- 2 tablespoons raspberry jam
- 1 large egg
- 1 tablespoon all-purpose flour
- ½ teaspoon pure vanilla extract
- ½ cup fresh raspberries

4. For the cream cheese layer, in a medium bowl, stir together the cream cheese and butter until smooth and thoroughly combined. Add the sugar, jam, and egg and mix well. Stir in the flour and vanilla. Dollop the mixture onto the brownie batter in the pan. Use a butter knife to swirl the cream cheese mixture into the brownies. Press a few fresh raspberries into the top.

5. Bake until a wooden pick inserted in the center comes out with only a few moist crumbs, 35 to 40 minutes (check after 30 minutes). Let cool completely before slicing and serving. The brownies will keep, wrapped individually and stored in the refrigerator, for up to 4 days.

makes 9 brownies

A toasted marshmallow is never just a toasted marshmallow. A toasted marshmallow is my first time at sleep-away camp. A toasted marshmallow is the first time I could remember all the words to John Denver's "Leaving on a Jet Plane" and join my friends in singing around the campfire. A toasted marshmallow is smoke in my eyes, a crackling fire, and red-hot clothes-hanger skewers. A toasted marshmallow is a season, a childhood friend, a sky full of stars, a friend playing the guitar. A toasted marshmallow is somehow so much, and somehow just melted, toasty sugar.

These squares are the buttery shortbread, at-home version of summertime s'mores. The chocolate-hazelnut spread feels both elevated and familiar, and being able to pull toasted marshmallow memories from the broiler is just the best thing ever.

TOASTED MARSHMALLOW
squares

½ cup (1 stick) unsalted butter, at room temperature

½ cup sugar

1 vanilla bean, split lengthwise, or 1 teaspoon pure vanilla extract

1 large egg yolk

1 cup plus 2 tablespoons all-purpose flour

¼ teaspoon salt

⅓ cup chocolate-hazelnut spread

15 large marshmallows, cut in half

1. Put a rack in the center of the oven and preheat the oven to 350°F. Line an 8-inch square baking pan with parchment paper and grease it with butter.

2. In the bowl of an electric mixer fitted with the paddle attachment, beat the butter and sugar on medium speed until light and fluffy, 3 to 4 minutes. Stop the mixer, scrape down the sides of the bowl, and then scrape the vanilla seeds into the bowl. Add the egg yolk and beat well. Stop the mixer and add the flour and salt. Beat on low speed until completely incorporated.

3. Spoon the batter into the prepared pan. Sprinkle the top with a little flour. Using your fingers, press the dough into the bottom of the pan. Try to make the shortbread crust as even as possible.

4. Bake until the crust is golden brown around the edges, but still slightly soft in the center, 20 to 24 minutes. Remove the pan from the oven (leave the oven on) and let the crust cool for 20 minutes.

recipe continues

5. Run a thin butter knife around the edges of the pan. Use the parchment paper to carefully remove the crust. Run a butter knife between the crust and the paper and carefully slide the crust from the paper and onto a baking sheet.

6. Top the crust with a thin layer of the chocolate-hazelnut spread. Arrange the marshmallow pieces on top. Return the pan to the oven and bake until the marshmallows are warm and soft, about 4 minutes. Remove the pan from the oven and turn on the broiler. Use the back of a spoon to gently press and smash the top of each marshmallow.

7. Broil the marshmallows. Keep a very, very, very, very close eye on them, because they'll toast in seconds. They'll burn in seconds. Don't even close the broiler door. They just need a kiss of broiler action. Remove the pan from the oven and let the s'more rest for 10 minutes before slicing. The squares can be served slightly warm or at room temperature. They'll keep, well-wrapped and at room temperature, for up to 4 days.

makes 9 squares

I imagine that these are the days I'll look back on with fondness when I'm old and fit perfectly into a rocking chair. The days when I stood in the kitchen and made ridiculous amounts of cookies, took pictures of everything I ate, and shared it on a new thing called the Internet. I'll look back and feel like . . . yeah . . . I totally did my thing. Then I'll call for my grandchildren and make them go to the kitchen to fetch me a plate of these Lavender Palmiers and a glass of lemonade. I'll eat them greedily and rock back and forth until someone tells me they've made dinner for me, at which point I'll slowly hoist myself from rocking and mosey inside for chicken potpie with an extra side of mashed potatoes. My old-age fantasies are very specific.

lavender
PALMIERS

1⅓ cups sugar

2 sheets frozen all-butter puff pastry, thawed but still cold

2 tablespoons dried lavender

A few pinches of salt

1. Dust a clean counter with ⅓ cup sugar. Put 1 of the puff pastry sheets on the sugar, and dust it with another ⅓ cup sugar. Sprinkle evenly with 1 tablespoon of the lavender. Sprinkle with salt. Use a rolling pin to press the sugar and lavender into the puff pastry, and then roll out the pastry, extending the ends about ½ inch on all sides. The sugar on the counter should keep the puff pastry from sticking, but lift the pastry occasionally to ensure that it's not sticking. If the pastry rips at the seams a bit, don't worry. Just press it back together with your fingers.

2. Beginning at the left vertical side of the pastry, evenly and tightly roll it toward the center of the sheet. Roll the right vertical side into the center in the same manner to meet the other side. Gently press the pastry together. Wrap in plastic wrap and refrigerate for 30 minutes. Repeat this same process with the remaining sheet of puff pastry. Leave the sugar counter as is; we're going to use it in a bit.

3. Put racks in the center and upper third of the oven and preheat the oven to 400°F. Line 2 baking sheets with parchment paper.

4. Transfer the chilled pastry to the sugared work surface. Use a sharp knife to slice the pastry logs into ½-inch-thick slices. Put the cookies on the prepared baking sheets.

5. Bake until the cookies are a deep golden brown, 12 to 15 minutes. Keep a close eye on the cookies after 12 minutes, as the sugar can burn quickly. Let cool on the pans before serving. The cookies will keep in an airtight container at room temperature for up to 3 days.

makes about 36 cookies

PIES, CRUMBLES & COBBLERS

THE PIE CHAPTER IN MY LIFE DOES NOT BEGIN HERE.

It began in 1989, when an eight-year-old Joy began helping her father make pies in their tiny, pea-green wallpapered family kitchen.

Let's take it back. In that kitchen my dad taught me the importance of cold butter and chilled buttermilk. It was there that my dad taught me how to gather dough rather than knead it, about fast-finger and quick rolling, while he perfected his sweet potato pie recipe and worked on his meringues. It was by no means a pie bakery—just a family kitchen with a heck of a lot of pies. Dad guided me through the ins and outs of making a good pie crust, peeling apples, and barely boiling peaches to loosen their furry skins. I watched it all, sneaking scraps of pie dough along the way. What was a hobby for him became a childhood meditation for me.

There is deep satisfaction in pie baking. Each moment is important, and the sum of those moments is stunning. The way the butter is incorporated into the flour influences the way the crust is marbled after rolling it out on the counter. The way the custard is whisked and cooked speaks to how smoothly the pie slices 4 hours later. The way the top crust is brushed with egg affects its ability to turn a rich golden brown, eliciting oohs and aahs when it's presented at the table. Making a pie is all about taking the time to layer delicious moments. A baking meditation.

Pie is both humble and luxurious. Pie can be a simple mishmash of leftover buttermilk, sugar, and a few eggs. Pie can also be as decadent as butterscotch pudding and marshmallow meringue. It can be as simple or fussy as you need it to be. Pie is a luxury because it often requires time. A good buttermilk pie crust asks that you pay it some mind for at least an hour. A good apple pie filling requires your attention, knife skills, and patience. It's time well spent. It's time you can taste. But it's time nonetheless, and it feels like we have so little of it lately.

Pie is our precious time, made edible.

This chapter starts with buttermilk pie crust tips and tricks. The crust is usually the part of pie baking that psyches people out. Half of the battle when it comes to making pie crust is confidence. I totally get it. Hopefully my tutorial will give you a better understanding of crust and you can approach your ingredients with poise. Believe it or not, the ingredients can smell your fear. The other half of the battle is temperature, and I have some good techniques for keeping that under control.

After the crust recipes, you'll find all of the complete pie recipes. I kept the crusts separate from the fillings so that you can mix and match as you see fit. Pies can be flexible, so feel free to try Salty Pretzel Crust (page 130) with every filling ever. You can't go wrong.

Enjoy pie baking. Enjoy showing off the sum of your moments. Enjoy the meditation. Enjoy the first piece, because though it's always the ugliest, it's often the most satisfying.

buttermilk PIE CRUST

salty pretzel CRUST

GRAHAM CRACKER crust

cold-butter CRUST

APPLE PIE with cheddar-bacon crust

double-crusted LEMON-BLUEBERRY PIE

LEMON-BUTTERMILK PIE
with maple-cranberry sauce

PINEAPPLE-COCONUT ambrosia pie

pumpkin pie WITH PECAN PRALINE TOPPING

HAPPY BIRTHDAY brownie pie

peanut butter-BANANA CREAM PUDDING PIE

CHOCOLATE PUDDING pie

peanut butter CREAM PIE

BUTTERSCOTCH CREAM PIE with thyme-marshmallow meringue

RHUBARB cornmeal crostata

APPLE-AND-FENNEL brown betty

strawberry-ginger CRUMB COBBLER

pear-cranberry-pecan CRUMBLE

ROASTED-PLUM TARTE TATIN with citrus-honey yogurt

CHURCH PARTY PEACH COBBLER with orange & cinnamon dumplings

BROWN SUGAR-ROSEMARY CHEESECAKE with bourbon-burnt caramel sauce

MANGO-ROSE WATER cheesecake

HOW TO MAKE PERFECT BUTTERMILK PIE CRUST

(aka you can totally do this!)

INGREDIENTS:

cold unsalted butter • salt and granulated sugar • all-purpose flour • cold buttermilk

I cannot let you step away from this book without instilling in you a deep love for homemade buttermilk pie crust. This pie crust is generous, forgiving, and, best of all, it's rooting for you. It's the kind of pie crust that wants to do a good job for you. It wants to be your soldier.

If you keep your butter chilled and your buttermilk cold, this crust will be the new love of your life. It bakes up supremely buttery and wildly flaky. I adore this crust with Lemon-Buttermilk Pie (see page 140) and Lemon-Blueberry Pie (see page 139).

cold unsalted butter Why are bakers so specific about the flavor and temperature of their butter? Butter is *everything*. When we step into the kitchen to make a pie crust, we're essentially deciding what to do with our butter.

You want to use unsalted butter because you want to be able to control the amount of salt that goes into the crust. Different companies use different amounts of salt for their salted butters, so if we start with unsalted butter, we know exactly what we're getting ourselves into when we add 1 teaspoon of salt.

Cold butter is absolutely essential to a successful pie crust. When broken down into the dry ingredients, it creates flaky pockets of flavor. You just won't get the same effect with mushy, room-temperature butter (save that for the cake chapter). The science: The water in the butter will quickly evaporate when the chilled crust (with all its butter pockets) hits the oven. The water evaporation will cause the crust to rise and create a flaky and layered crust.

If our butter is cold and stays cold, I promise we're halfway to success!

salt and sugar Let's flavor this crust! We're relying on butter to do a major amount of the heavy lifting when it comes to the crust. Pie crust should be a simple base to accompany the flavors of the pie. The pie crust should be simple, but not entirely tasteless. That's where salt and sugar come in! The salt and sugar will add a balancing flavor, enhancing both the butter and the flavors of the pie.

all-purpose flour As with most recipes in this book, my pie crust recipes call for all-purpose flour. My favorite brand is King Arthur Flour. I keep my flour stored in a large jar, tightly sealed, and at room temperature. When measuring, I fluff the flour with a large spoon, lightly spoon it into a measuring cup, and, using a butter knife, level the flour flush with the measuring cup.

cold buttermilk I've already lectured you about the importance of cold butter, and the same thing goes for buttermilk. We want cold on cold buttermilk.

I also love using buttermilk because it adds yet another layer of flavor. Buttermilk adds a creamy tang to our pie crusts. The hint of acid in the buttermilk will also help the texture. If you're fresh out of buttermilk, you can also use ice-cold water. The results will be delicious. I promise.

2½ cups all-purpose flour

2 tablespoons sugar

1 teaspoon salt

1 cup (2 sticks) cold unsalted butter, cut into cubes

½ cup plus 1 tablespoon cold buttermilk

1. In a medium bowl, whisk together the flour, sugar, and salt. Add the butter and, using your fingers or a pastry cutter, quickly work the butter into the flour mixture until some butter pieces are the size of oat flakes and some are the size of peas. Make a well in the mixture, pour in the buttermilk, and using a fork, stir until a dough forms. Turn the dough out onto a lightly floured counter. It will be moist and shaggy. Divide the dough in 2 and gently knead each half into a disk. Wrap each disk in plastic wrap and refrigerate for 1 hour.

2. To roll out the pie crust, on a well-floured counter, roll the bottom crust until it is ⅛ inch thick and about 12 inches in diameter. Occasionally move the crust around the floured counter during rolling to ensure that it's not sticking to the counter. Transfer it to a pie dish and trim the edges. For a single pie crust, fold the edges under and crimp with your fingers or a fork. Cover with plastic wrap and refrigerate for at least 30 minutes and up to 3 hours.

3. For a double-crusted pie, roll out the top crust in the same manner. Fill the pie and top with the second crust. Fold both layers of pie dough under and crimp with a fork or your fingers. Cover loosely with plastic wrap and chill in the refrigerator for 30 minutes before baking.

makes one 9-inch double pie crust

I believe Ben and Jerry of Ben & Jerry's ice cream were the first people to put salted pretzels into a dessert with their Chubby Hubby ice cream. I believe that was the beginning of the Pretzel Revolution. You've never heard of the Pretzel Revolution? It's real. It's strong.

This pie crust combines the traditional elements of an all-butter pie crust with the salt and crunch of pretzels. It pairs really well with the Butterscotch Cream Pie with Thyme-Marshmallow Meringue (page 155). Long live the revolution!

SALTY PRETZEL
crust

2½ cups all-purpose flour

¼ cup sugar

1 teaspoon salt

1 cup (2 sticks) cold unsalted butter, cut into cubes

½ cup plus 1 tablespoon cold buttermilk

16 to 20 small twisted pretzels

1. In a medium bowl, whisk together the flour, sugar, and salt. Add the butter and, using your fingers or a pastry cutter, work the butter into the flour mixture. Quickly break down the butter until some of the pieces are the size of oat flakes and some are the size of peas. Make a well in the mixture and pour in the buttermilk. Using a fork, stir the buttermilk into the flour until a dough forms. Turn the dough out onto a lightly floured counter. It will be moist and shaggy. That's perfect. Divide the dough in 2 and gently knead each half into a disk. Wrap each disk in plastic wrap and refrigerate for 1 hour.

2. To roll out the pie crust, on a well-floured counter, roll the bottom crust until it is ⅛ inch thick and about 12 inches in diameter. Occasionally move the crust around the floured counter during rolling to ensure that it's not sticking to the counter. Transfer it to a pie pan. Trim the edges almost even with the edges of the pan. Fold the edges under and use your fingers or the tines of a fork to shape the crust edges into a design. Gently press the pretzels into the bottom of the pie crust and onto the sides of the pan, so the rounded edges peek up slightly. Cover with plastic wrap and refrigerate the crust for at least 30 minutes and up to 3 hours.

3. To prebake the pie crust, put a rack in the center of the oven and preheat the oven to 350°F. Spray a piece of foil with nonstick cooking spray and press it, sprayed side down, into the chilled pie crust. Add pie weights or dried beans and bake for 10 minutes. Remove the pie crust from the oven and remove the foil and beans. Return the pie crust to the oven and bake until the crust is slightly golden and cooked through, 5 minutes more. Remove the dish from the oven and let cool completely before filling.

makes one 9-inch pie crust

This traditional graham cracker crust lends that bit of delicious familiarity to cheesecakes (like the Mango–Rose Water Cheesecake on page 175) and fruit cream pies. Crisp and slightly sweet, it's an ever-reliable vehicle for pie filling.

I use a food processor fitted with a blade attachment to grind the graham crackers into fine crumbs. If you don't have a food processor, you can put the crackers in a heavy-duty sealable plastic bag (maybe 2 plastic bags) and smash them with a rolling pin. The plastic bag method takes some more elbow grease to get really fine crumbs.

GRAHAM CRACKER
crust

- 1 cup graham cracker crumbs
- 1 tablespoon sugar
  Pinch of salt
- 5 tablespoons unsalted butter, melted and cooled slightly

1. Put a rack in the upper third of the oven and preheat the oven to 350°F.

2. In a medium bowl, combine the graham cracker crumbs, sugar, and salt. Add the butter and stir with a fork until the mixture is thoroughly moistened. The mixture will not form a dough ball, but will stay a crumby texture.

3. Dump the crumb mixture into a 9-inch pie dish and, using your fingers, evenly press the mixture along the bottom and sides of the dish.

4. Bake until the crust is slightly golden brown, 12 to 15 minutes. Remove the pie dish from the oven and let cool completely before filling.

makes one 9-inch pie crust

VARIATIONS

gingersnap cookie crust Replace the graham cracker crumbs with 2 cups gingersnap cookie crumbs, and the granulated sugar with packed light brown sugar.

chocolate cookie crust Replace the graham cracker crumbs with 2 cups chocolate wafer cookie crumbs.

Not everything in the world revolves around buttermilk . . . which is strange, because it should. This pie crust is mighty fine without it, as it uses cold water instead of buttermilk. The result is an equally flaky, buttery crust, with no need to run to the store because you're fresh out of buttermilk.

COLD-BUTTER
crust

- 2½ cups all-purpose flour
- 2 tablespoons sugar
- 1 teaspoon salt
- 1 cup (2 sticks) cold unsalted butter, cut into cubes
- 5 tablespoons plus 2 teaspoons cold water
- 1 teaspoon apple cider vinegar

1. In a medium bowl, whisk together the flour, sugar, and salt. Add the butter and, using your fingers or a pastry cutter, work the butter into the flour mixture. Quickly break down the butter until some of the pieces are the size of oat flakes and some are the size of peas. Make a well in the mixture and pour in the cold water and vinegar. Using a fork, stir the liquid into the flour until a dough forms. Turn the dough out onto a lightly floured counter. It will be moist and shaggy. That's perfect. Divide the dough in 2 and gently knead each half into a disk. Wrap each disk in plastic wrap and refrigerate for 1 hour.

2. To roll out the pie crust, on a well-floured counter, roll the bottom crust until it is ⅛ inch thick and about 12 inches in diameter. Occasionally move the crust around the floured counter during rolling to ensure that it's not sticking to the counter. Transfer it to a pie pan. Trim the edges almost even with the edges of the pan. If you're making a single pie crust, fold the edges under and crimp with your fingers or a fork. Cover with plastic wrap and refrigerate for at least 30 minutes and up to 3 hours.

3. For a double-crusted pie, roll out the top crust in the same manner. Fill the pie and top with the second crust. Fold both layers of pie dough under and crimp with a fork or your fingers. Cover loosely with plastic wrap and chill in the refrigerator for 30 minutes before baking.

makes one 9-inch double pie crust

Here I've taken a traditional apple pie and put not only Cheddar cheese, but also bacon in the crust. Yes, I've crossed the line into good-grief-what-have-you-done territory. Think about all the times you've bitten into an apple right after biting directly into the 5-pound block of Cheddar in your refrigerator. Think about all the times you've tried to work bacon into every course of a meal. I know you, because I'm just like you. Welcome to Cheddar-Bacon Crust Town, population: us.

APPLE PIE
with cheddar-bacon crust

crust
6 slices bacon

2½ cups all-purpose flour

1 tablespoon sugar

1 teaspoon salt

1 cup (2 sticks) cold unsalted butter, cut into cubes

1 cup coarsely grated sharp Cheddar cheese

½ cup plus 1 tablespoon buttermilk

filling
2½ pounds baking apples, peeled, cored, and sliced ¼ inch thick (I used a combination of Granny Smith, Fuji, and Pink Lady)

1 tablespoon fresh lemon juice

1. For the crust, put a rack in the upper third of the oven and preheat the oven to 375°F. Put the bacon on a foil-lined baking sheet and bake until it is crisp, 15 to 18 minutes. Remove the pan from the oven, transfer the bacon to a paper towel to drain, and let cool. Finely chop the bacon and set aside.

2. In a medium bowl, whisk together the flour, sugar, and salt. Add the butter and, using your fingers or a pastry cutter, work the butter into the flour mixture. Quickly break down the butter until some of the pieces are the size of oat flakes and some are the size of peas. Add the cheese and chopped bacon and toss well. Make a well in the mixture and pour in the buttermilk. Using a fork, stir the buttermilk into the flour mixture until a dough forms. Turn the dough out onto a lightly floured counter. It will be moist and shaggy. That's perfect. Divide the dough in 2 and gently knead each half into a disk. Wrap each disk in plastic wrap and refrigerate for 1 hour.

3. For the filling, in a large bowl, combine the apples, lemon juice, brown sugar, ¼ cup of granulated sugar, cinnamon, nutmeg, and salt. Cover and let sit at room temperature for 30 minutes.

4. Transfer the apples and their juices to a colander set over a bowl. Let drain until you have at least ½ cup of liquid. Bring the liquid to a boil in a small saucepan (preferably nonstick) set over medium-high heat. Add the butter, and cook until it is syrupy and lightly caramelized and reduced to about ⅓ cup, about 5 minutes. Swirl the liquid; there's no real need to stir.

recipe continues

¼ cup packed light brown sugar

¼ cup plus 2 tablespoons granulated sugar

½ to 1½ teaspoons ground cinnamon

¼ teaspoon freshly grated nutmeg

¼ teaspoon salt

2 tablespoons unsalted butter

1 tablespoon plus 1 teaspoon cornstarch

1 large egg, beaten

French Vanilla Bean Ice Cream (page 226), for serving

5. Meanwhile, transfer the apples to a bowl and toss them with the cornstarch. Pour the syrup over the apples and toss gently. (Do not be concerned if the liquid hardens on contact with the apples; it will dissolve during baking.)

6. Roll out the bottom pie crust on a well-floured surface until it is ⅛ inch thick or less and 12 inches in diameter. Occasionally move the crust around the floured counter during rolling to ensure that it's not sticking to the counter. Transfer it to a pie dish. Trim the edges almost even with the edges of the pie dish. Cover with plastic wrap and refrigerate for at least 30 minutes and up to 3 hours. Roll out the top crust large enough to cut a 12-inch circle.

7. Transfer the apple mixture to the pie shell. Lightly brush the border of the bottom crust with water and put the top crust over the fruit. Trim the overhang so that the crust overhangs by only ½ inch. Tuck the overhang under the bottom crust and press to seal. Crimp the border using the tines of a fork or your fingers, and cut about 5 evenly spaced 2-inch vents in the top. Cover the pie loosely with plastic wrap and refrigerate for 1 hour before baking.

8. Put a rack in the center of the oven and preheat the oven to 400°F. Put a foil-lined baking sheet on the center rack of the oven.

9. Brush the top of the pie with the egg and sprinkle generously with remaining 2 tablespoons granulated sugar. Put the pie on the foil-lined baking sheet and bake for 20 minutes. Reduce the oven temperature to 350°F, and bake until the juices bubble and the apples feel tender, but not mushy, when a small sharp knife is inserted through a vent, 35 to 40 minutes. If the pie seems to be browning too quickly, make a loose foil tent to put over the pie while it bakes.

10. Transfer the pie to a rack and let cool for at least 4 hours before cutting. Serve warm or at room temperature with vanilla ice cream.

makes one 9-inch double crust pie

Sharing a slice of this pie is just like giving someone a big bundle of bright yellow roses. The filling comes together effortlessly, since there's no peeling or slicing to contend with, and the lemon helps highlight the fresh berry flavor. I find that this pie is best served the day after it has been baked. I let it cool to room temperature and then refrigerate it overnight so that the flavors meld and the juices thicken.

double-crusted
LEMON-BLUEBERRY PIE

3 pints fresh blueberries

1 cup sugar, plus more for sprinkling

½ cup all-purpose flour

1 tablespoon grated lemon zest

3 tablespoons fresh lemon juice

Generous pinch of salt

Buttermilk Pie Crust (page 128)

1 large egg

1. In a large bowl, gently combine the blueberries, sugar, flour, lemon zest and juice, and salt. Let sit for 5 minutes.

2. Remove the chilled pie crust from the fridge and roll it out on a well-floured counter. Transfer 1 piece to a pie dish and trim the excess, leaving about ½ inch of overhang. Scoop the fruit mixture into the pie.

3. In a small bowl, beat the egg with a splash of water. Moisten the edges of the pie dough with the egg wash. Drape the second pie dough piece over the pie and trim the excess, leaving a ½-inch overhang. Tuck the 2 pie crusts under a bit so that the dough is flush with the edge of the pie dish. Crimp with the tines of a fork or your fingers to seal. Cut 4 vents into the top of the pie crust. Refrigerate the pie for 30 minutes.

4. Put a rack in the center of the oven and preheat the oven to 400°F. Line a baking sheet with aluminum foil and put it on the lowest rack.

5. Brush the top and sides of the pie with the egg wash. Sprinkle generously with sugar. Place the pie on the prepared baking sheet. Bake for 30 minutes and then reduce the oven temperature to 375°F. Bake until the crust is a beautiful golden brown and the filling is bubbling, about 30 minutes. If the pie browns too quickly, make a loose foil tent to put over the pie.

6. Transfer the pie to a rack and let cool for at least 1 hour. You can serve it warm, though it's best if you refrigerate the pie overnight before serving.

makes one 9-inch pie

This classic Southern pie is a beautifully fragrant baked custard. It's mostly sweet and slightly tart, and humility is its grace. Together the flavors taste wintery.

LEMON-BUTTERMILK PIE
with maple-cranberry sauce

filling

- 1 cup granulated sugar
- 1 tablespoon grated lemon zest
- ¼ cup all-purpose flour
- ½ teaspoon salt
- ¼ teaspoon freshly grated nutmeg
- 2 cups buttermilk
- 4 large eggs
- 3 tablespoons fresh lemon juice
- 1 teaspoon pure vanilla extract

  Single Buttermilk Pie Crust (see page 128)

sauce

- ½ cup fresh orange juice
- ⅓ cup pure maple syrup
- ¼ cup packed light brown sugar
- Pinch of salt
- 1 (12-ounce) bag fresh cranberries
- 1 tablespoon pure vanilla extract

1. Put a rack in the center of the oven and preheat the oven to 350° F.

2. For the filling, in a medium bowl, combine the sugar and lemon zest. Using your fingers, rub the mixture together. The sugar will become slightly moist and fragrant. Whisk in the flour, salt, and nutmeg.

3. In a large liquid measuring cup, whisk together the buttermilk and eggs. Whisk in the lemon juice and vanilla extract. Add the wet ingredients to the dry ingredients and whisk to combine. Pour the filling into the prepared unbaked pie shell. Bake until the pie no longer jiggles in the center, 45 to 55 minutes.

4. Meanwhile, for the sauce, in a medium saucepan set over medium heat, combine ½ cup of water with the orange juice, maple syrup, brown sugar, and salt. Cook, stirring, until the sugar is dissolved, about 4 minutes. Add the cranberries and cook, stirring, until the cranberries begin to pop, about 6 minutes. Continue to cook the cranberries, stirring occasionally, for about 10 minutes. The sauce will thicken as the cranberries cook down. Once thick, remove from the heat and add the vanilla extract. Stir to incorporate and set aside to cool to room temperature.

5. Let the pie cool completely. Top with the cranberry sauce just before serving.

6. The sauce can be made up to 3 days in advance.

7. The pie will last, well wrapped in the refrigerator, for up to 4 days.

makes one 9-inch pie

My aunt Judy makes the most delicious ambrosia. I'm pretty sure all she does is mix coconut, canned fruit, marshmallows, and whipped cream together in a bowl, and yet I can't resist it. I find myself sneaking to the kitchen during family gatherings to shove ambrosia into my mouth with the serving spoon. No shame in my game. This pie is my cheeky homage to ambrosia. I really only added some cream cheese to a basic ambrosia and put it all in a graham cracker crust. It's light and creamy and totally easy to make. I'm nothing if not classy.

pineapple-coconut
AMBROSIA PIE

1½ cups unsweetened flaked coconut

1 cup heavy cream

1 (8-ounce) package cream cheese, at room temperature

1½ cups sweetened condensed milk

Pinch of salt

2 teaspoons pure vanilla extract

1 cup drained crushed pineapple

3 cups mini marshmallows

Graham Cracker Crust (page 132)

1. Put a rack in the upper third of the oven and preheat the oven to 350°F.

2. Spread the coconut in a single layer on a baking sheet. Toast until golden brown, 4 to 6 minutes. Keep a close eye on the coconut, as it can burn quickly.

3. In the bowl of an electric mixer fitted with the whisk attachment, beat the cream until it holds soft peaks, about 5 minutes. Transfer to a small bowl.

4. In the same mixing bowl, beat the cream cheese until completely smooth. Add the sweetened condensed milk, salt, and vanilla, and beat until creamy, about 4 minutes. Remove the bowl from the mixer and stir in the crushed pineapple and 1 cup toasted coconut. Fold in the whipped cream. Fold in 1½ cups of the marshmallows.

5. Spoon the filling into the prepared pie crust. Top with the remaining 1½ cups marshmallows and remaining ½ cup toasted coconut. Refrigerate for at least 4 hours before serving.

6. The pie will last, well wrapped in the refrigerator, for up to 4 days.

makes one 9-inch pie

No one *really* wants turkey on Thanksgiving. We all just skip past the turkey and green beans to load our plates up with mashed potatoes, mac and cheese, and gravy, right!? The turkey is just a formality. After a quick nap on the couch, we wake up refreshed and ready for pumpkin pie and a hot cup of coffee. This is my Thanksgiving pie. The traditional pumpkin base is covered with an über-decadent pecan praline sauce. Totally over the top! Welcome to my world. It's sweet.

PUMPKIN PIE
with pecan praline topping

Half recipe Buttermilk Pie Crust (page 128)

filling

 2 cups pumpkin puree
 ½ cup packed light brown sugar
 ¼ cup granulated sugar
 2 teaspoons ground cinnamon
 1 teaspoon ground ginger
 ½ teaspoon freshly grated nutmeg
 ½ teaspoon allspice
 ¼ teaspoon ground cloves
 ¼ teaspoon ground cardamom
 ¼ teaspoon salt
 1½ cups cold heavy cream
 2 large eggs, lightly beaten
 1 teaspoon pure vanilla extract

1. Put a rack in the center of the oven and preheat the oven to 400°F.

2. Roll out the pie crust, put it in a pie dish, and refrigerate until ready to fill.

3. For the filling, combine the pumpkin puree, brown and granulated sugars, cinnamon, ginger, nutmeg, allspice, cloves, cardamom, and salt in a medium saucepan set over medium heat. Cook, stirring, until the mixture begins to bubble and become fragrant, 5 to 7 minutes. Transfer the mixture to a medium bowl. Stir in the heavy cream. Whisk in the eggs and vanilla.

4. Transfer the filling to the prepared pie crust. Bake for 15 minutes. Reduce the oven temperature to 350°F and bake until the pie no longer jiggles in the center, 40 to 50 minutes.

5. Meanwhile, for the topping, in a medium saucepan set over medium-low heat, combine the brown sugar, butter, cream, and salt. Bring to a simmer and cook until thick and bubbly, 3 to 5 minutes. Remove the pan from the heat and stir in the vanilla and pecans.

6. Let the pie cool for 30 minutes before topping. The pie will settle and deflate slightly. That's great.

7. Check to see that the praline topping is still pourable. If it has hardened too much, heat it over low heat until just pourable, or microwave for 30 seconds. Pour the topping evenly over the pie. The topping may seem loose, but will thicken and harden as it cools. Let cool completely before

serving. I like my pumpkin pie served cold, so I store my pie in the refrigerator until serving time.

8. The pie will last, well wrapped in the refrigerator, for up to 4 days.

makes one 9-inch pie

topping

- ½ cup packed light brown sugar
- 6 tablespoons (¾ stick) unsalted butter
- 3 tablespoons heavy cream
- ¼ teaspoon salt
- 1 teaspoon pure vanilla extract
- ¾ cup very coarsely chopped pecans (some halved pecan pieces are fine)

I know what everyone wants for their birthdays: diamonds, cashmere, kittens, sprinkles, and a pony. I tried and tried, but I just couldn't combine all of those things into one delicious cake. I hope this pie will satisfy your greatest birthday desires regardless. I made this with mint chocolate chip ice cream, because it was my party. You can make it with whatever flavor you like best!

happy birthday
BROWNIE PIE

½ cup all-purpose flour

½ cup Dutch-processed cocoa powder

½ teaspoon baking powder

½ teaspoon salt

1 cup granulated sugar

½ cup (1 stick) unsalted butter, melted and cooled

2 large eggs

3 teaspoons pure vanilla extract

½ cup milk chocolate chips

½ cup coarsely chopped walnuts (optional)

1 cup heavy cream

2 tablespoons confectioners' sugar

1 quart mint chocolate chip ice cream

Rainbow sprinkles

Birthday candles

1. Put a rack in the upper third of the oven and preheat the oven to 350°F. Grease and flour a 9-inch round pie dish.

2. In a small bowl, whisk together the flour, cocoa powder, baking powder, and salt.

3. In a separate medium bowl, whisk together the sugar, melted butter, eggs, and 2 teaspoons vanilla. Add the dry ingredients and fold together with a spoon. Fold in the chocolate chips and walnuts, if using. Pour the batter into the prepared pie dish.

4. Bake until the top looks dry and a wooden pick inserted in the center comes out with only a few moist crumbs, 20 to 22 minutes. Let cool.

5. Meanwhile, for the whipped cream, in the bowl of an electric mixer fitted with the whisk attachment, beat the cream with the confectioners' sugar and remaining 1 teaspoon vanilla until it holds soft peaks, about 4 minutes. Refrigerate until ready to serve.

6. Scoop the ice cream into the center of the brownie. Freeze for at least 30 minutes, or until ready to serve.

7. To serve, spread the whipped cream over the brownie ice cream pie, sprinkle generously with rainbow sprinkles, and insert birthday candles. Light the candles and sing loudly.

8. The brownies can be made up to two days in advance.

makes one 9-inch pie

My first question when I approach a recipe is this: Can I put peanut butter in it? The answer is usually yes. This pudding pie has all of the delicious familiarity of banana cream pudding with a rousing dose of salty peanut butter. This is not a traditional pie. It's more of a layered pudding disguised as a pie.

peanut butter
BANANA CREAM PUDDING PIE

vanilla pudding

- ½ cup granulated sugar
- ¼ cup cornstarch
- ¼ teaspoon salt
- 2½ cups whole milk
- 3 large egg yolks
- 1 tablespoon pure vanilla extract
- 2 tablespoons unsalted butter

peanut butter whipped cream

- ¼ cup smooth all-natural peanut butter
- 2 cups heavy cream
- ⅓ cup confectioners' sugar
- Pinch of salt
- 1 tablespoon pure vanilla extract
- 1 (12-ounce) box vanilla wafers
- 3 ripe bananas, sliced

1. For the pudding, in a medium saucepan, whisk together the sugar, cornstarch, and salt. Whisk in the milk and egg yolks. Turn the heat on medium-low, bring the mixture to a boil while whisking constantly, and cook, whisking, until the mixture is thick enough to hold the lines of the whisk, 2 to 3 minutes. Remove the pan from the heat and whisk in the vanilla and butter until the butter is melted. Transfer the mixture to a bowl, cover with plastic wrap so that the plastic touches the top of the custard, and refrigerate until chilled through, about 2 hours.

2. Meanwhile, for the whipped cream, microwave the peanut butter for 15 to 25 seconds, until warm and pourable.

3. In the bowl of an electric mixer fitted with the whisk attachment, beat the heavy cream, confectioners' sugar, and salt on medium speed. Beat until soft peaks form, about 4 minutes. Drizzle in the warm peanut butter and the vanilla and increase the speed to high. Beat until the whipped cream is pillow-y and holds its shape, but is still smooth, about 2 minutes.

4. To assemble the pie, line the bottom of a 9-inch pie dish with the vanilla wafers in a single layer, to create a crust. Dollop half the vanilla pudding over the wafers and spread it in an even layer. Arrange half of the banana slices over the pudding. Add a thin layer of the whipped cream. Add another layer of the vanilla wafers and top with the remaining vanilla pudding. Add the remaining bananas, the remaining vanilla wafers, and top with the remaining whipped cream. Refrigerate for at least 4 hours before serving.

5. The pudding will last, well wrapped in the refrigerator, for up to 3 days.

makes one 9-inch pie

I like to work the depth of chocolate flavor by adding both cocoa powder and good-quality dark chocolate . . . you know, the kind of chocolate you're bummed to find has been mindlessly scarfed down by your roommate. That's the chocolate we want to flavor our pie with. Classic meets quality.

CHOCOLATE PUDDING
pie

chocolate pudding

- 1 cup packed light brown sugar
- ½ cup unsweetened cocoa powder
- ⅓ cup cornstarch
- ¼ teaspoon salt
- 3 cups whole milk
- 4 ounces 65% cacao dark chocolate, finely chopped
- 1 tablespoon unsalted butter
- 2 teaspoons pure vanilla extract

whipped cream

- 1½ cups heavy cream
- 1 teaspoon pure vanilla extract
- 3 tablespoons confectioners' sugar
- Pinch of salt

Chocolate Cookie Crust (page 132)

Finely chopped dark chocolate

1. For the pudding, in a medium saucepan, whisk together the brown sugar, cocoa powder, cornstarch, and salt. Slowly whisk in 1 cup of the milk. Whisk until the mixture is smooth. Whisk in the remaining 2 cups milk. Set the pan over medium-low heat and cook, whisking frequently, until the mixture has thickened, about 10 minutes. Bring the mixture to a simmer, reduce the heat to low, and cook, whisking constantly, for 2 minutes.

2. Remove the pan from the heat and add the chocolate, butter, and vanilla. Stir until the chocolate and butter are completely melted. Pour the pudding through a fine-mesh sieve into a medium bowl. Cover the bowl with plastic wrap so that the plastic touches the surface of the pudding. Refrigerate until chilled, about 2 hours.

3. Meanwhile, for the whipped cream, in the bowl of an electric mixer fitted with the whisk attachment, beat the cream, vanilla extract, confectioners' sugar, and salt. Beat until soft but firm peaks form, 4 to 5 minutes. The whipped cream will still be smooth, but will hold its shape on a spoon.

4. To assemble the pie, spoon the chilled pudding into the prepared pie crust. Top with the whipped cream and sprinkle generously with the chopped chocolate. Chill until ready to serve.

makes one 9-inch pie

Let's do backflips in the park, pull some stunts on the jungle gym, sit on a blanket in the backyard, sprinkle heaps of salted pretzels on top of our peanut butter pie, and make the world the most perfect place it can be.

peanut butter
CREAM PIE

filling

1½ cups heavy cream

1 (8-ounce) package cream cheese, at room temperature

¼ cup packed light brown sugar

¼ teaspoon salt

1 teaspoon pure vanilla extract

1 cup smooth all-natural peanut butter

Graham Cracker Crust (page 132) or Chocolate Cookie Crust (page 132)

whipped cream topping

1½ cups heavy cream

¼ cup confectioners' sugar

optional garnish

½ cup coarsely chopped peanut butter cups

½ cup coarsely chopped salted pretzels

2 ounces dark chocolate, melted

1. For the filling, in the bowl of an electric mixer fitted with the whisk attachment, beat the cream until it holds soft peaks, 4 to 5 minutes. Transfer to a medium bowl.

2. In the same bowl of the electric mixer (you don't have to rinse it out) fitted with the paddle attachment, beat the cream cheese on medium speed until smooth and pliable, about 3 minutes. Add the brown sugar, salt, and vanilla extract and beat well. Beat in the peanut butter until smooth. Remove the bowl from the mixer and gently fold in a quarter of the whipped cream. Gently fold in another quarter of the whipped cream. Repeat twice with the remaining whipped cream until the mixture is well incorporated but still fluffy. Spoon the filling into the prepared crust.

3. For the whipped cream topping, in the clean bowl of an electric mixer fitted with the whisk attachment, beat the cream and confectioners' sugar until it holds soft peaks, 4 to 5 minutes. Top the pie with the whipped cream mixture. Cover lightly with plastic wrap and refrigerate for at least 4 hours before serving.

4. Just before serving, generously sprinkle with the chopped peanut butter cups or salted pretzels, or drizzle with melted chocolate.

5. The pie will last, well wrapped in the refrigerator, for up to 4 days.

makes one 9-inch pie

How to bridge the gap between delicious and plain crazy? Put it all in a pie crust and own it. This pie combines the sweetness of butterscotch cream with an herby meringue. It's like skipping out in a plaid shirt and striped pants, and making everyone jealous with your amazing style and audacious nature.

BUTTERSCOTCH CREAM PIE
with thyme-marshmallow meringue

Salty Pretzel Crust (page 130) or Graham Cracker Crust (page 132) or Gingersnap Cookie Crust (page 132)

filling

- 3 tablespoons unsalted butter
- 4 large egg yolks (whites reserved for the meringue)
- 1 teaspoon molasses
- 1 cup packed light brown sugar
- ¼ cup plus 1 tablespoon cornstarch
- ½ teaspoon salt
- 2 cups whole milk
- 2 teaspoons pure vanilla extract

1. For the filling, let's brown some butter. In a small saucepan, melt the butter over medium-low heat. The butter will begin to crackle and pop; that's the water cooking out of it. Once the crackling subsides, keep an eye on the butter. The fat solids will begin to brown and the melted butter will smell nutty. It will take about 4 minutes, and then immediately transfer the butter to a small bowl to stop the cooking. Let cool while you prepare the rest of the filling.

2. In a clean medium saucepan set over medium-low heat, whisk together the egg yolks, molasses, brown sugar, cornstarch, and salt. Whisk in the milk and bring to a simmer. Reduce the heat to low and cook, whisking constantly, until the mixture is the consistency of warm pudding and will hold whisk marks when whisked, 1 to 2 minutes.

3. Remove the pan from the heat and stir in the browned butter and the vanilla. Transfer the custard to a bowl and cover with plastic wrap so that the plastic touches the custard. Refrigerate for at least 2 hours.

4. Meanwhile, for the meringue topping, in a small bowl, combine the granulated sugar and thyme. Using your fingers, rub the herb into the sugar. The sugar will become deliciously fragrant.

5. In a medium bowl, whisk the marshmallow creme to fluff it a bit.

recipe continues

meringue

¼ cup granulated sugar

2 teaspoons chopped fresh thyme

1 (7-ounce) jar marshmallow cream

4 large egg whites (reserved from the filling)

Pinch of salt

1 teaspoon pure vanilla extract

6. Make sure that your metal mixing bowl and whisk are clean, dry, and free of any residual fats. In the bowl of an electric mixer fitted with the whisk attachment, beat the egg whites on medium speed. When the eggs begin to froth, add a pinch of salt. Slowly add the thyme sugar 1 tablespoon at a time, while slowly increasing the mixer speed to medium-high. Beat until stiff peaks form and the egg whites are fluffy and glossy, about 5 minutes. Beat in the vanilla extract.

7. Gently fold about ½ cup of the egg whites into the marshmallow cream. The marshmallow cream will feel very thick and dense in contrast to the light egg whites, but don't worry, because it will loosen up. Fold in a third of the remaining egg whites. Fold in the remaining egg whites in 2 batches.

8. Put a rack in the upper third of the oven and preheat the oven to 400°F. Spoon the pie filling into the prepared crust. Top with the marshmallow meringue. Toast the pie in the oven just until the edges and tips of the meringue are lightly browned, 4 to 5 minutes, but keep a close eye on it, because the marshmallow topping may brown faster.

makes one 9-inch pie

In the sisterhood of produce, rhubarb would be considered the lanky middle child who reads horror novels and actually likes wearing the rubber bands on her braces. In the family talent show, she is the sister that does a spot-on impression of her favorite weatherman. It's awkward and endearing and entirely confusing, especially considering her older and younger sisters have choreographed a routine from *West Side Story*.

No one expects rhubarb to be the star of the show. Strawberries usually steal the spotlight. But with this crostata, rhubarb shines on its own. This rustic tart bakes up buttery, tender, and lightly sweet. It's surprisingly juicy, and that's what I love about it. It's not nearly as awkward as the lanky middle child, but every bit as endearing.

rhubarb
CORNMEAL CROSTATA

crust

- 1 large egg yolk
- ¼ cup cold buttermilk
- 1½ cups all-purpose flour
- ½ cup coarsely ground cornmeal
- 2 tablespoons granulated sugar
- ½ teaspoon salt
- ½ cup (1 stick) cold unsalted butter, cut into cubes

filling

- 5 cups chopped rhubarb (½- to ¾-inch chunks; about 1½ pounds)
- 3 tablespoons fresh orange juice
- 1 cup packed light brown sugar

1. For the crust, in a small bowl, whisk together the egg yolk and buttermilk. In a medium bowl, whisk together the flour, cornmeal, granulated sugar, and the salt. Add the butter and, using your fingers or a pastry cutter, work the butter into the flour mixture. Quickly break down the butter until some of the pieces are the size of oat flakes and some are the size of peas. Make a well in the flour mixture and pour in the buttermilk mixture. Using a fork, stir the buttermilk mixture into the flour until a dough forms. Turn the dough out onto a lightly floured counter. It will be moist and shaggy. That's perfect. Form the dough into a disk and wrap in plastic wrap. Refrigerate for 1 hour.

2. For the filling, in a medium bowl, toss together the rhubarb, orange juice, brown sugar, cornstarch, cardamom, nutmeg, cloves, and salt.

3. Put a rack in the upper third of the oven and preheat the oven to 375°F. Line a rimmed baking sheet with parchment paper.

4. Put the chilled dough on a well-floured counter and roll it into a circle that is ⅓ inch thick. Be sure to seal any cracks. Carefully transfer the crust to the prepared baking sheet. Pile the fruit filling into the center of the dough, leaving a 2-inch border. Fold the crust up around the fruit filling. Press the edges together to seal the crust a bit.

recipe continues

3 tablespoons cornstarch

½ teaspoon ground cardamom

½ teaspoon freshly grated nutmeg

⅛ teaspoon ground cloves

Pinch of salt

1 large egg white

1 tablespoon whole milk

Turbinado or granulated sugar, for sprinkling

French Vanilla Bean Ice Cream (page 226), for serving

5. Whisk together the egg white and milk in a small bowl. Lightly brush the crust with the egg wash. Sprinkle generously with granulated sugar.

6. Bake until the crust is a deep golden brown, the fruit is tender, and the juices are bubbling, 35 to 45 minutes. Remove the pan from the oven and let cool for 2 hours before serving. Serve slightly warm with vanilla ice cream.

makes one 9-inch free-form pie

I think of a brown betty as an alternative to apple pie and apple crisp. It lives in the middle-ground where apples are combined with bread and made into a unique dessert. Serve warm with Brown Sugar–Cream Cheese Ice Cream (page 237).

apple-and-fennel
BROWN BETTY

1 tablespoon unsalted butter, for the baking dish

6 cups cubed challah bread (about ½ loaf)

3 pounds (6 to 8) Granny Smith and Fuji apples, peeled, cored, and sliced thin

1 cup thinly sliced fennel bulb

1 cup packed light brown sugar

½ cup granulated sugar

1 tablespoon cornstarch

1 teaspoon grated lemon zest

1 teaspoon ground cinnamon

½ teaspoon freshly grated nutmeg

½ teaspoon ground ginger

¼ teaspoon salt

2 tablespoons fresh lemon juice

1½ cups unfiltered apple cider

¼ cup (½ stick) cold unsalted butter

1. Put a rack in the center of the oven and preheat the oven to 350°F. Generously grease a 9 x 13-inch baking dish with the butter.

2. Put the bread cubes on a baking sheet and toast until dried, 6 to 8 minutes. Use your fingers to break the cubes down into smaller chunks. Set aside.

3. In a large bowl, combine the apples, fennel, brown and granulated sugars, cornstarch, lemon zest, cinnamon, nutmeg, ginger, and salt. Add about ½ cup of the breadcrumbs and toss well. Spoon half of the apple mixture into the prepared baking dish. Top with half of the remaining breadcrumbs.

4. In a small bowl, stir together the lemon juice and apple cider. Drizzle the mixture over the apples and crumbs. Top with the remaining apple mixture and then the remaining breadcrumbs. Slice the cold butter into 8 to 10 slices and scatter them over the top.

5. Bake until the apples are nearly baked through and bubbling, 40 minutes. Gently stir the apples and continue baking until the apples are cooked through, 12 to 15 minutes. If your breadcrumbs are getting too brown, put a piece of foil over the baking dish for the last 15 minutes of baking.

6. Let rest for 20 minutes before serving warm.

serves 8 to 10

Let's talk for a moment about stress-free pie baking. It's totally possible. Our cheat—which totally isn't a cheat at all—is this crumb cobbler. We can set aside the cold butter and the pressures of the rolling pin. This crumble is all about warm fruit and hearty crumble topping. I love an almost dangerous amount of oat topping on my cobbler, and this recipe reflects those oat-overboard sentiments.

strawberry-ginger
CRUMB COBBLER

topping

- 1 cup all-purpose flour
- ⅔ cup packed light brown sugar
- ¼ teaspoon salt
- ½ cup (1 stick) cold unsalted butter, cut into cubes
- ½ cup old-fashioned oats
- ½ cup chopped pecans

filling

- 1½ pounds (about 4 cups) fresh strawberries, hulled and quartered
- 1 tablespoon grated peeled fresh ginger
- ⅓ cup granulated sugar
- ½ teaspoon ground ginger
- 2 teaspoons cornstarch

1. Put a rack in the upper third of the oven and preheat the oven to 350°F. Lightly butter a 9-inch baking dish.

2. For the topping, in a medium bowl, combine the flour, sugar, and salt. Add the butter and, using your fingers, work the butter into the flour mixture. Quickly break down the butter until some of the pieces are the size of oat flakes and some are the size of peas. Add the oats and pecans and toss together.

3. For the filling, in the prepared baking dish, toss together the strawberries, fresh ginger, sugar, ground ginger, and cornstarch. Toss well. Add a handful of the topping mixture to the fruit mixture and toss lightly. Sprinkle the remaining topping mixture over the top.

4. Bake until the fruit juices are bubbling and the top is golden brown, 40 to 45 minutes. Remove the baking dish from the oven and let cool for about 30 minutes before serving.

makes one 9-inch pan

I've never met one person who couldn't get down with a big bowl of warm fruit crumble. That would be like seeing a person who doesn't like cookies ride by on a unicorn. If you prefer to leave the nuts out, add an additional ½ cup of old-fashioned oats.

PEAR-CRANBERRY-PECAN
crumble

filling

- 4 ripe but still firm pears, preferably d'Anjou
- 1 heaping cup fresh cranberries
- 3 tablespoons granulated sugar
- ½ teaspoon ground cinnamon
- Squeeze of fresh lemon juice

topping

- ¾ cup all-purpose flour
- ¾ cup packed light brown sugar
- ⅓ cup old-fashioned oats
- 1 teaspoon ground cinnamon
- ¼ teaspoon freshly grated nutmeg
- ¼ teaspoon salt
- ½ cup (1 stick) unsalted butter, cut into cubes and at room temperature, plus more for the baking dish
- ½ cup chopped pecans

1. Put a rack in the center of the oven and preheat the oven to 350°F. Butter the bottom and sides of an 8 x 8-inch baking dish.

2. For the filling, cut the top stem and bottom butt off of each pear. The bottom will give you a stable base to peel the pears. Using a small paring knife, peel the pears. Slice each pear in half. Using a small teaspoon, gently run down the length of the inside of the pear, removing the fibrous inside spine and then scooping out the seeds. Chop the pears into hearty bite-size chunks and put them in the prepared dish. Pour the cranberries over the pears. Top with the sugar, cinnamon, and lemon juice. Toss lightly.

3. For the topping, whisk together the flour, brown sugar, oats, cinnamon, nutmeg, and salt. Add the butter and, using your fingers or a pastry cutter, work the butter into the flour mixture. Quickly break down the butter until some of the pieces are the size of oat flakes and some are the size of peas. Toss in the pecans.

4. Add about a third of the topping mixture to the pear and cranberry mixture and toss. Sprinkle the remaining topping mixture on top.

5. Bake until bubbly and browned on top, 40 to 45 minutes. Remove the baking dish from the oven and let cool for about 20 minutes before serving. Serve warm.

6. The crumble will keep, covered, in the fridge for up to 3 days.

serves 6

Plums should get more attention than they do. I think maybe they get a bad rap for turning into prunes in their old age. This tarte tatin lets plums simmer and soften, becoming richly flavored with the help of butter and puff pastry. The tangy yogurt cream is a really special alternative to whipped cream and might even inspire you to have a second helping. After all, it's just fruit and yogurt! If you'd like to be a little more indulgent, try the tart with Brown Sugar–Cream Cheese Ice Cream (page 237).

ROASTED-PLUM TARTE TATIN
with citrus-honey yogurt

tart

½ cup sugar

¼ teaspoon salt

¼ teaspoon freshly grated nutmeg

Pinch of freshly cracked black pepper

6 tablespoons (¾ stick) unsalted butter

8 to 10 ripe but still firm plums (about 2½ pounds), halved and pitted

1 sheet frozen puff pastry, thawed

yogurt

1 cup Greek yogurt

2 tablespoons honey

½ teaspoon grated lemon zest

Pinch of ground cloves

1. Put a rack in the upper third of the oven and preheat the oven to 400°F.

2. For the tart, in a small bowl, whisk together the sugar, salt, nutmeg, and pepper.

3. Put a 9-inch ovenproof skillet over medium-low heat. I use my cast-iron skillet. Melt the butter in the skillet. Evenly sprinkle the sugar mixture over the melted butter. Immediately add the plums, cut side up, to the skillet. The plums might seem bulky, but they'll cook down. Cook the plums, shaking the pan occasionally to make sure they don't stick, until the butter is a deep brown and purple color and the plums are soft, about 10 minutes.

4. Remove the pan from the heat and carefully put the puff pastry over the warm plums, tucking the edges into the sides of the pan. Carefully slice two 2-inch-long vents in the center of the puff pastry.

5. Bake the tart until puffed and golden brown, 20 to 25 minutes.

6. Meanwhile, for the yogurt, in a small bowl, stir together the yogurt, honey, lemon zest, and cloves. Refrigerate until ready to serve.

7. Remove the tart from the oven and let cool for 20 minutes. Run a knife around the edges of the skillet to loosen the puff pastry. Carefully invert the tart onto a serving plate. This will probably require 18 pot holders and a prayer. Serve warm with a dollop of the yogurt.

makes one 9-inch tart

Some pies have a day ascribed to them. This dumpling cobbler is a lazy afternoon of sunshine and fellowship with sweet tea and peach-scented air. This pie *is* Sunday afternoon.

I chose to forgo the traditional pie crust in favor of topping the sweet peaches with dumplings. I love to add flavor to every part of the recipe, so these dumplings are flavored with orange juice and cinnamon that mirror the flavors of the filling. This pie is scoopable and just begging for Brown Sugar–Cream Cheese Ice Cream (page 237).

CHURCH PARTY PEACH COBBLER
with orange & cinnamon dumplings

filling

- 6 to 8 fresh peaches, unpeeled and thinly sliced
- 1 cup sugar
- ¼ cup cornstarch
- 1½ teaspoons ground cinnamon
- 1 teaspoon freshly grated nutmeg
- ½ teaspoon ground cardamom
- ⅛ teaspoon ground cloves
- Pinch of salt
- ½ cup fresh orange juice

1. Put a rack in the upper third of the oven and preheat the oven to 400°F. Lightly grease the bottom and sides of a 9 x 13-inch pan.

2. For the filling, in a large bowl, toss together the peaches, sugar, cornstarch, cinnamon, nutmeg, cardamom, cloves, salt, and orange juice. Toss well. Spoon the peaches into the prepared pan.

3. For the dumplings, in a medium bowl, combine the ¼ cup sugar and the orange zest. Using your fingers, work the zest into the sugar. Whisk in the flour, baking powder, and salt. Add the butter and, using your fingers or a pastry cutter, work the butter into the flour mixture. Quickly break down the butter until some of the pieces are the size of oat flakes and some are the size of peas. Create a well in the mixture

4. In a small bowl (or liquid measuring cup), whisk together the egg and milk. Pour the milk mixture into the well in the flour mixture. Using a fork, stir the mixture until a dough forms. The dumpling mixture will be on the wet side. That's perfect. Dollop the dumpling dough by the heaping spoonful (about ¼ cup each) on top of the peaches. You should have 8 dumplings.

recipe continues

dumplings

- ¼ cup plus 3 tablespoons sugar
- 1 teaspoon grated orange zest
- 2 cups all-purpose flour
- 2 teaspoons baking powder
- ½ teaspoon salt
- ½ cup (1 stick) cold unsalted butter, cut into cubes
- 1 large egg
- 1 cup cold whole milk
- ½ teaspoon ground cinnamon

5. In a small bowl, combine the remaining 3 tablespoons sugar with the cinnamon. Sprinkle the cinnamon sugar on top of the dumplings.

6. Bake until the fruit is bubbling and the dumplings are golden brown, 30 to 35 minutes. If the dumplings begin to brown too quickly, put a loose piece of foil over the pan. Remove the pan from the oven and let cool for at least 20 minutes before serving. Serve warm.

7. The cobbler will last, well wrapped in the refrigerator, for up to 3 days.

serves 8 to 10

I love to blend traditionally savory elements like rosemary with delicious desserts like cheesecake. This feels like a winter cheesecake to me, with the woodsy rosemary, the depth of brown sugar, and a caramel sauce that teeters on the edge of burnt.

If you're thinking you might want to serve this cake on gold-rimmed plates next to the Christmas tree, I think you've totally got the right idea.

BROWN SUGAR–ROSEMARY CHEESECAKE
with bourbon–burnt caramel sauce

filling

- 1 cup packed light brown sugar
- 1 tablespoon plus 2 teaspoons chopped fresh rosemary leaves
- 2 (8-ounce) packages cream cheese, at room temperature
- ½ teaspoon salt
- 2 teaspoons pure vanilla extract
- 2 large eggs
- ½ cup heavy cream
- 1 teaspoon grated lemon zest

Graham Cracker Crust (page 132) or Gingersnap Cookie Crust (page 132)

1. Put a rack in the center of the oven and preheat the oven to 325°F.

2. For the filling, in a small bowl, combine the brown sugar and rosemary leaves. Using your fingers, rub the mixture together until fragrant.

3. In the bowl of an electric mixer fitted with the paddle attachment, beat together the cream cheese and brown sugar–rosemary mixture until light and fluffy, 3 to 5 minutes. Beat in the salt and vanilla. Add the eggs, one at a time, beating after each addition. Gradually add the cream, beating on medium-high until the mixture is creamy, about 4 minutes. Beat in the lemon zest. Pour the filling into the prepared crust.

4. Put a roasting pan in the center of the hot oven. Put the cheesecake dish into the roasting pan and carefully pour in boiling water until it reaches about a quarter of the way up the sides of the cheesecake dish.

5. Bake until the cheesecake is browned and puffed and doesn't jiggle in the center, 50 to 60 minutes. Turn the oven off and use a wooden spoon to prop the oven open slightly. Let the cheesecake rest for 45 minutes in the cooling oven. Remove the cheesecake from the oven and refrigerate for at least 4 hours, though overnight is best.

recipe continues

bourbon–burnt caramel sauce

½ cup granulated sugar

2 tablespoons corn syrup

⅓ cup heavy cream

2 tablespoons unsalted butter, at room temperature

½ teaspoon sea salt, plus more for topping

2 teaspoons bourbon

6. For the caramel, in a medium saucepan set over medium heat, combine 2 tablespoons water with the sugar and corn syrup. Bring to a boil, stirring once or twice, and cook until the sugar mixture begins to brown, about 6 minutes. Continue cooking until the mixture has become a medium amber color, 6 minutes. Immediately remove the pan from the heat and add the cream and butter. Be careful, because the mixture will bubble and foam. Stir well. Add the ½ teaspoon sea salt and bourbon and stir well. The caramel may seem thin, and that's okay. Transfer to a bowl, cover with plastic wrap, and refrigerate for at least 4 hours, though overnight is best.

7. Warm the caramel slightly by microwaving for 20 to 25 seconds. Pour the caramel over the cooled cheesecake, and refrigerate until ready to serve.

8. Sprinkle with a little sea salt, and serve. The cheesecake will keep, well wrapped in the refrigerator, for up to 4 days.

makes one 9-inch cheesecake

Am I the only one who walks out of an Indian restaurant with a mango lassi in hand thinking about cheesecake? That's pretty much how this recipe came about. When it comes to the nitty-gritty of making cheesecakes, I'm not the kind of baker who wants to fuss around with springform pans and foil lining. I make my cheesecakes in a standard pie plate. They aren't quite as tall as a traditional cheesecake, but the flavor and texture is just as divine.

MANGO–ROSE WATER
cheesecake

cheesecake

- 2 (8-ounce) packages cream cheese, at room temperature
- 1 cup sugar
- ½ teaspoon salt
- 2 teaspoons pure vanilla extract
- 2 large eggs
- ½ cup sour cream
- ¾ cup mango puree
- 3 tablespoons rose water

  Graham Cracker Crust (page 132)

sour cream topping

- 1 cup sour cream
- ⅓ cup confectioners' sugar
- 2 tablespoons rose water
- 2 tablespoons mashed fresh mango (optional)

1. Put a rack in the center of the oven and preheat the oven to 325°F.

2. In the bowl of an electric mixer fitted with the paddle attachment, beat together the cream cheese and sugar until light and fluffy, 3 to 5 minutes. Beat in the salt and vanilla extract. Add the eggs, one at a time, beating well after each addition. Slowly beat in the sour cream and mango puree, beating on medium-high until creamy, about 4 minutes. Beat in the rose water. Pour the mixture into the prepared crust.

3. Put a roasting pan in the center of the hot oven. Put the cheesecake in the roasting pan and carefully pour in boiling water until it reaches about a quarter of the way up the sides of the cheesecake dish.

4. Bake until browned and puffed and doesn't jiggle in the middle, 50 to 60 minutes. Turn the oven off and use a wooden spoon to prop the oven open slightly. Let the cheesecake sit for 45 minutes in the cooling oven.

5. Remove the cheesecake from the oven and let cool completely, at least 4 hours, though overnight in the refrigerator is best.

6. For the sour cream topping, in a medium bowl, whisk together the sour cream, confectioners' sugar, rose water, and mashed mango (if using).

7. When cool, spread the sour cream topping over top. Serve chilled. The cheesecake will keep, well wrapped in the refrigerator, for up to 4 days.

makes one 9-inch cheesecake

LAYER CAKES, CUPCAKES & SKILLET CAKES

WALKING INTO A PARTY WITH A CAKE IS LIKE WALKING INTO A PARTY WITH A TROPHY—A GIANT, GLOSSY TROPHY THAT EVERYONE WANTS TO EAT.

There are few things that match walking into a room with a cake, namely: walking into a party with a full piñata, or walking into a party in a dress made entirely out of edible candy. The latter is not advised.

Cakes, more than any other dessert, are all about the gathering, the occasion, the celebration. They require a bit of pomp and circumstance, both in their creation and in their presentation. They need confetti, shaved chocolate, and colored sprinkles. Even the most humble of chocolate loaf cakes deserves to be placed on the fancy silver cake platter. Why not?

Cake is a big deal.

There can be some pressure involved in baking up a celebration cake. Not to worry. I'm here with tools for you. This chapter opens with some cake-baking tips. Everything from how to get your cake out of the pan to how to frost a layer cake. I'm looking out for you.

I separated my cake recipes from my frosting recipes because they're all interchangeable—you can mix and match to suit your whim. I also included some composed recipes that combine the cake bases and frostings so that you can see how I like to play with flavors. And this chapter has more than just layer cakes, because I equally love cupcakes, cakey loaves, and skillet cakes. Everything is designed to make you look like a cake genius.

basic THREE-LAYER YELLOW CAKE

LEMON-HONEY yellow cake

MAPLE ORANGE & GINGER
CREAM CHEESE cake

BASIC three-layer chocolate cake

mint chocolate chip CAKE

double the chocolate CAKE

CHOCOLATE–PEANUT BUTTER
PRETZEL layer cake

s'more CAKE

CHOCOLATE POUND CAKE
with chips & chocolate glaze

vegan CHOCOLATE CAKE

BLACK-AND-WHITE-COOKIE cake

white chocolate, summer peach & STRAWBERRY CAKE

ALMOND ANGEL FOOD CAKE with vanilla-scented citrus

dark chocolate brownie CUPCAKES

BROWN SUGAR cupcakes

LEMON HONEY-brown butter cupcakes

carrot cake CUPCAKES

OLIVE OIL CORNMEAL cake

MAPLE-APPLE UPSIDE-DOWN cake

under-baked CHOCOLATE CHIP SKILLET CAKE

This is it! This is that basic yellow cake recipe that we should all just agree to commit to memory. It's light and tender, but has enough girth and body to be stable and stackable. It's a wonderful base for stellar fillings and toppings.

basic
THREE-LAYER YELLOW CAKE

4 cups cake flour

2 teaspoons baking powder

1½ teaspoons baking soda

1 teaspoon salt

1 cup (2 sticks) unsalted butter, at room temperature

2 cups sugar

1 tablespoon pure vanilla extract

4 large eggs, at room temperature

2 cups buttermilk

1. Put oven racks in the center and upper third of the oven and preheat the oven to 350°F. Grease and flour three 9-inch round baking pans.

2. In a medium bowl, whisk together the flour, baking powder, baking soda, and salt.

3. In the bowl of an electric mixer fitted with the paddle attachment, beat the butter and sugar on medium speed until light and fluffy, 3 to 4 minutes. Add the eggs, one at a time, beating for 1 minute between each addition. Beat in the vanilla extract. Reduce the mixer speed to low, add half of the flour mixture, and beat well. Add the buttermilk in a slow stream and beat well. Add the remaining flour mixture and beat until just combined. Finish stirring with a spatula. Divide the batter among the 3 prepared cake pans.

4. Bake until golden brown on top and a wooden pick inserted in the center comes out clean, 20 to 25 minutes. Let cool in the pans for 20 minutes before inverting onto wire racks to cool completely before frosting.

5. If you're not using right away, double-wrap the cake layers in plastic wrap, and freeze for up to 7 days. When ready to frost, remove from the freezer, unwrap, and frost frozen!

makes one 3-layer 9-inch cake

THE CLASSIC

I'm not sure if this cake is more about the tender cake, the vanilla-flavored buttercream frosting, or the major amount of sprinkles. I'm betting it's the sprinkles. Yeah . . . sprinkles always win.

Frost Basic Three-Layer Yellow Cake (page 179) with Classic Buttercream Frosting (recipe follows), adding a generous dose of rainbow jimmies between each layer. Finish with a thorough sprinkling of jimmies all over the cake.

classic buttercream frosting

- 2 cups (4 sticks) unsalted butter, at room temperature
- 5 to 6 cups confectioners' sugar, sifted
- ¼ teaspoon salt
- 3 teaspoons pure vanilla extract
- About ¼ cup heavy cream

In the bowl of an electric mixer fitted with the paddle attachment, beat the butter on medium speed until soft, about 1 minute. Add 2 cups of the confectioners' sugar, the salt, and vanilla. Beat on low speed until the sugar is well incorporated. Add another 2 cups sugar and the cream. Add remaining 2 cups of sugar as needed to thicken the frosting. Beat on medium speed until the frosting is smooth and fluffy, about 4 minutes.

makes about 4 cups

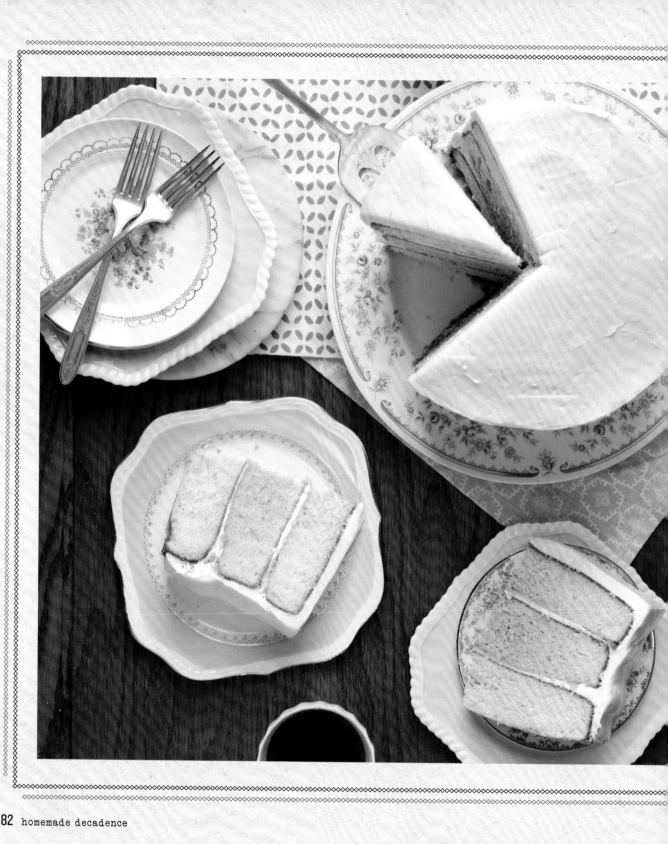

LEMON-HONEY YELLOW CAKE

This cake reminds me of springtime. It's bright and sweet, and for some reason it makes me think of sundresses and hummingbirds.

Frost Basic Three-Layer Yellow Cake (page 179) with Lemon-Honey Cream Cheese Frosting (recipe follows).

lemon-honey cream cheese frosting

2 (8-ounce) packages cream cheese, at room temperature

1½ cups (3 sticks) unsalted butter, at room temperature

⅓ cup honey

3 teaspoons pure vanilla extract

⅛ teaspoon salt

1½ teaspoons grated lemon zest

3 tablespoons fresh lemon juice

6 to 7 cups sifted confectioners' sugar

3 to 4 tablespoons whole milk

In the bowl of an electric mixer fitted with the paddle attachment, beat the cream cheese on medium speed for 1 minute. Add the butter and beat until incorporated, about 1 minute. Add the honey, vanilla, and salt and beat well. Add the lemon zest and juice and beat well. Turn off the mixer and add 2 cups of confectioners' sugar. Turn the mixer on low speed so that the sugar doesn't fly out of the bowl. Gradually add more sugar, alternately with the milk, until you reach your desired consistency. Beat on medium speed until the frosting is smooth and fluffy, about 4 minutes.

makes about 4 cups

MAPLE ORANGE & GINGER CREAM CHEESE CAKE

Citrus and ginger are an unusual but supercool combination. The citrus is round and bright, while the ginger is bold and spicy. When paired with good yellow cake and cream cheese frosting, this cake is unique and delicious!

Frost Basic Three-Layer Yellow Cake (page 179) with Maple-Orange Cream Cheese Frosting (recipe follows), sprinkling coarsely chopped candied ginger between the layers.

maple-orange cream cheese frosting

- 2 (8-ounce) packages cream cheese, at room temperature
- 1½ cups (3 sticks) unsalted butter, at room temperature
- ⅓ cup pure maple syrup
- 3 teaspoons pure vanilla extract
- ½ teaspoon orange extract
- ⅛ teaspoon salt
- 1½ teaspoons grated orange zest
- 6 to 7 cups sifted confectioners' sugar
- 3 to 4 tablespoons whole milk

In the bowl of an electric mixer fitted with the paddle attachment, beat the cream cheese on medium speed for 1 minute. Add the butter and beat until incorporated, about 1 minute. Add the maple syrup, vanilla, orange extract, salt, and orange zest and beat well. Turn off the mixer and add 2 cups of the confectioners' sugar. Turn the mixer on low speed so that the sugar doesn't fly out of the bowl. Gradually add more sugar, alternately with the milk, until you reach your desired consistency. Beat on medium speed until the frosting is smooth and fluffy, about 4 minutes.

makes about 4 cups

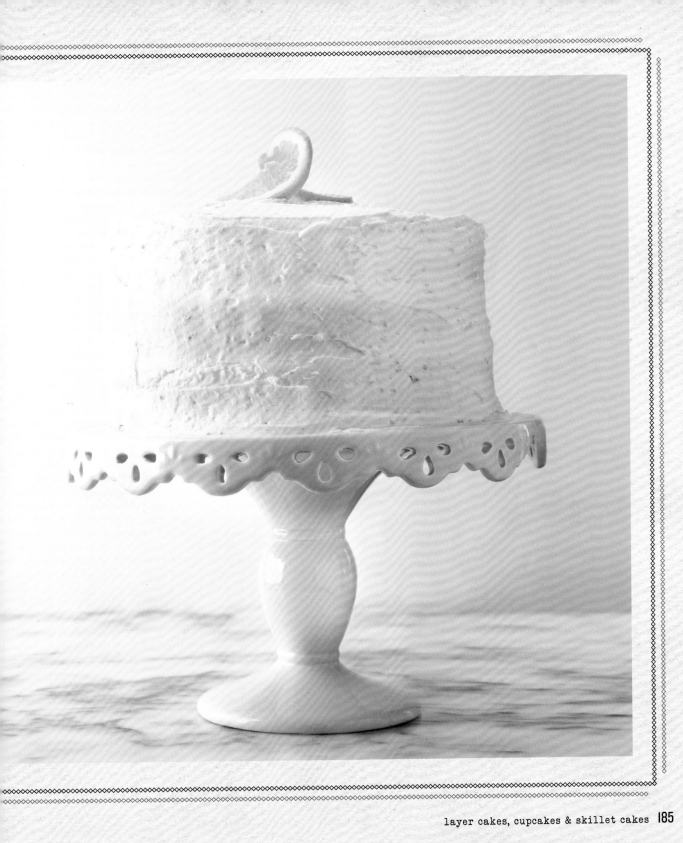

I'm always and forever a chocolate cake lover. With a tender crumb from the addition of buttermilk and a boost from espresso powder, this chocolate cake really is the perfect base.

basic
THREE-LAYER CHOCOLATE CAKE

3 cups cake flour

¾ cup unsweetened natural cocoa powder

2 teaspoons baking powder

1½ teaspoons baking soda

1 teaspoon salt

1 teaspoon instant espresso powder (optional)

1 cup (2 sticks) unsalted butter, at room temperature

1½ cups packed light brown sugar

1½ cups granulated sugar

4 large eggs, at room temperature

1 tablespoon pure vanilla extract

2 cups buttermilk

1. Put oven racks in the center and upper third of the oven and preheat the oven to 350°F. Grease and flour three 9-inch round baking pans.

2. In a medium bowl, whisk together the flour, cocoa powder, baking powder, baking soda, salt, and instant espresso powder, if using.

3. In the bowl of an electric mixer fitted with the paddle attachment, beat the butter and sugars together on medium speed until light and fluffy, 3 to 4 minutes. Add the eggs, one at a time, beating for 1 minute after each addition. Beat in the vanilla extract. Reduce the mixer speed to low, add half of the flour mixture, and beat until the flour mixture is incorporated. Add the buttermilk in a slow stream and beat until thoroughly combined. Add the remaining flour mixture and beat until just combined. Remove the bowl from the mixer and finish stirring with a spatula. Divide the batter among the 3 prepared cake pans.

4. Bake until golden brown on top and a wooden pick inserted in the center comes out clean, 20 to 25 minutes. Let cool in the pans for 20 minutes before inverting onto wire racks to cool completely before frosting.

5. If you're not frosting the cake right away, double-wrap in plastic wrap and store in the freezer. Cake layers will stay freshest for up to 7 days in the freezer. When ready to frost, remove from the freezer, unwrap, and frost frozen!

makes one 3-layer 9-inch cake

MINT CHOCOLATE CHIP CAKE

Mint chocolate chip is my very favorite ice cream flavor, reborn as a super-light and fluffy cake. The chocolate cake combined with the minty whipped-cream frosting feels like you're eating cake and ice cream combined! It's festive and familiar. This cake is made even more special with a good dose of sprinkles and birthday candles.

Frost Basic Three-Layer Chocolate Cake (opposite) with Mint Chocolate Chip Whipped Frosting (recipe follows). Decorate the cake with ½ cup finely chopped 60% cacao dark chocolate, chocolate jimmies, or colored sprinkles.

mint chocolate chip whipped frosting

- ¼ cup confectioners' sugar
- 3 cups heavy cream
- 2 teaspoons pure vanilla extract
- ½ to ¾ teaspoon mint extract
- ½ cup finely chopped 60% cacao dark chocolate, plus more for decorating

In the bowl of an electric mixer fitted with the whisk attachment, beat together the confectioners' sugar, cream, vanilla, and mint extract on medium speed until soft peaks form, about 4 minutes. Add the chopped chocolate and beat until combined, about 1 more minute.

makes about 3½ cups

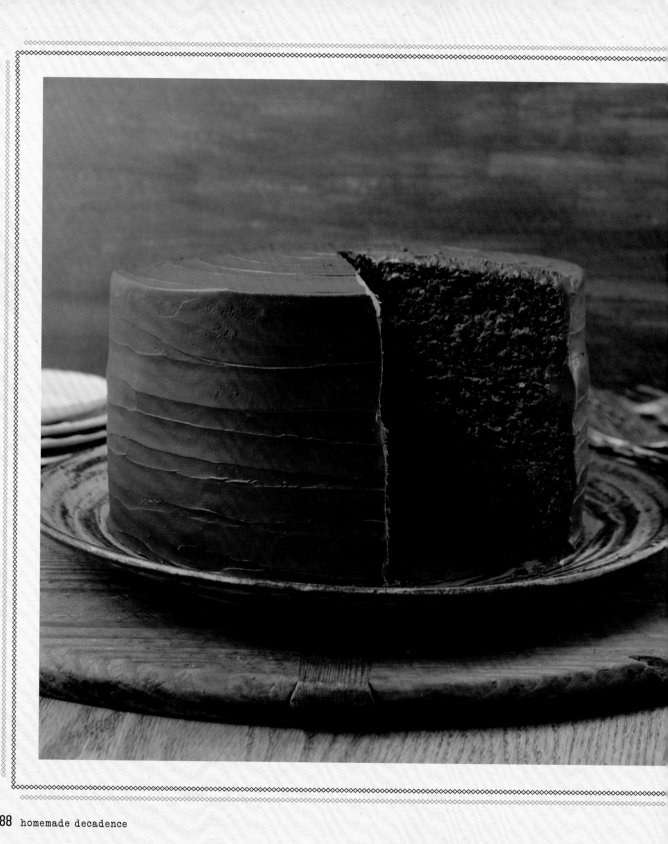

DOUBLE THE CHOCOLATE CAKE

Frost Basic Three-Layer Chocolate Cake (page 186) with Glossy Chocolate Sour Cream Frosting (recipe follows), which is a quirky recipe. Instead of creaming butter with cocoa powder, you combine melted chocolate with sour cream. The result is a beautifully glossy, wonderfully creamy, and super-spreadable frosting. Though the frosting is very loose when you first mix it together, it thickens as it cools.

glossy chocolate sour cream frosting

- 1 pound semisweet or dark chocolate, coarsely chopped (I like 60% cacao dark chocolate)
- 1 teaspoon instant espresso powder
- 2 cups sour cream
- ¼ cup light corn syrup
- 2 teaspoons pure vanilla extract
- Pinch of salt

Put the chopped chocolate in a heat-proof bowl and put the bowl over a saucepan of simmering water, making sure that the bottom of the bowl does not touch the simmering water. Stir the chocolate until it melts. Remove the bowl from the pan and stir the espresso powder into the chocolate. Let cool slightly.

In a small bowl, whisk together the sour cream, corn syrup, vanilla, and salt. Add the mixture to the melted chocolate and stir until thoroughly combined. Let cool to room temperature. The frosting will thicken as it cools. If you're in a hurry, chill it in the refrigerator. When it reaches your desired consistency, frost the cake or use on cupcakes.

makes about 4½ cups

CHOCOLATE-PEANUT BUTTER PRETZEL LAYER CAKE

My very favorite desserts are a combination of sweet and salty. Throwing chocolate in the mix? That's just perfection. This cake is a combination of tender chocolate cake, creamy peanut butter frosting, and crunchy pretzel bits. Big bites of chocolate meet little flecks of salt. There's really nothing more I need from life.

Start with Basic Three-Layer Chocolate Cake (page 186), 1 cup coarsely crushed pretzels, 4 ounces 60% cacao dark chocolate, coarsely chopped, and a few handfuls of whole mini pretzel twists. Frost the cake with Salted Peanut Butter Buttercream Frosting (recipe follows), adding a handful of the crushed pretzels and the chocolate pieces between each layer. Scatter roasted salted peanuts and the remaining chocolate pieces on top, and decorate the sides with the whole pretzel twists.

salted peanut butter buttercream frosting

- 2 cups (4 sticks) unsalted butter, at room temperature
- 1½ cups smooth all-natural peanut butter
- ½ teaspoon salt
- 1 tablespoon pure vanilla extract
- 6 to 7 cups confectioners' sugar
- 3 to 4 tablespoons heavy cream

In the bowl of an electric mixer fitted with the paddle attachment, beat the butter on medium speed until softened, about 1 minute. Add the peanut butter, salt, and vanilla extract and beat well. Add 2 cups of the confectioners' sugar and beat until well combined. Add another 2 cups of sugar along with 3 tablespoons of heavy cream. Add the remaining 2 to 3 cups of sugar and remaining cream and beat until it is your desired thickness. Beat on medium speed until the frosting is smooth and fluffy, about 4 minutes.

makes about 4½ cups

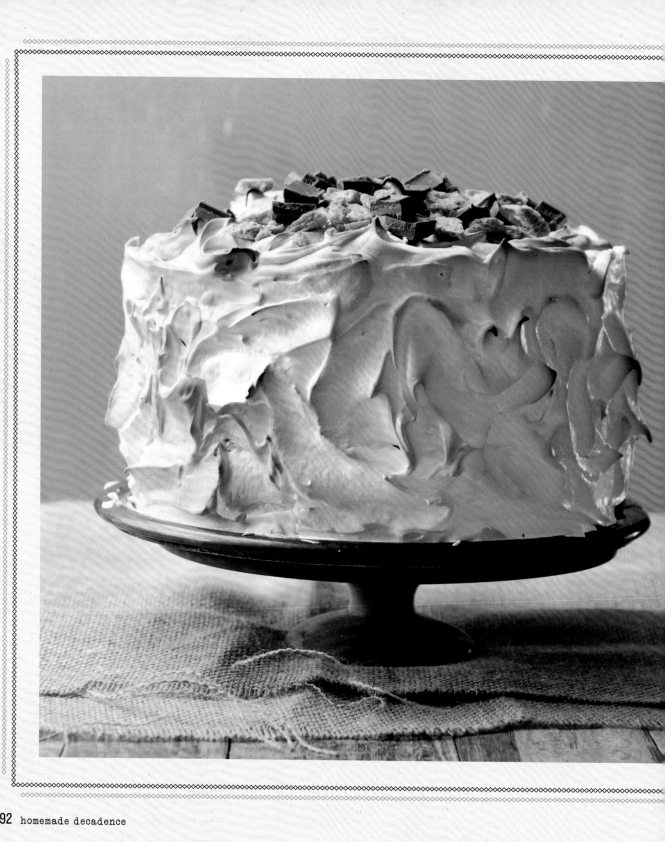

S'MORE CAKE

Toasted marshmallow makes my heart race. It's the ultimate indulgence to have an entire cake coated in toasted marshmallow frosting. Chocolate cake and crushed graham crackers just complete the s'more trifecta.

Frost Basic Three-Layer Chocolate Cake (page 186) with Marshmallow Meringue Frosting (recipe follows), sprinkling crushed graham crackers between each frosted layer. To serve, sprinkle the cake with big chunks of graham cracker. Toast the meringue by grazing the topping with the flame of a kitchen torch until it is golden brown. Alternately, you can toast the cake in a 375°F oven for about 4 minutes. Keep an eye on the cake. It toasts quickly.

marshmallow meringue frosting

- 5 large egg whites
- ½ cup plus 2 tablespoons light corn syrup
- 1¾ cups sugar
-    Large pinch of salt
- 2 teaspoons pure vanilla extract

In a large, heat-proof bowl, whisk together the egg whites, corn syrup, sugar, and salt. Put the bowl over a saucepan of simmering water, making sure that the bottom of the bowl does not touch the simmering water. Whisk the mixture as it heats and cook until the sugar dissolves, about 5 minutes.

Transfer the mixture to the bowl of an electric mixer fitted with the whisk attachment. Beat the egg whites on high speed until stiff peaks form, about 5 minutes. The mixture will be fluffy and glossy and look like melted marshmallows. It'll be sticky, too. Beat in the vanilla. Frost cake just after frosting is made.

makes about 5 cups

Can we just call this our everyday chocolate cake? It's loaf size and approachable. We can have a small slice with our breakfast coffee, or maybe a little after dinner.

CHOCOLATE POUND CAKE
with chips & chocolate glaze

cake

- ⅓ cup unsweetened Dutch-processed cocoa powder
- ⅓ cup hot coffee
- 1¾ cups cake flour
- 1 teaspoon baking powder
- ½ teaspoon salt
- 1 cup (2 sticks) unsalted butter, at room temperature
- 1 cup granulated sugar
- 2 large eggs
- 2 teaspoons pure vanilla extract
- ¼ cup buttermilk
- ¾ cup dark chocolate chips

glaze

- 1½ cups confectioners' sugar, sifted
- 3 tablespoons unsweetened Dutch-processed cocoa powder
- Pinch of salt
- 3 to 4 tablespoons milk or water
- 2 teaspoons pure vanilla extract

1. Put a rack in the center of the oven and preheat the oven to 350°F. Grease and flour a 9 x 5-inch loaf pan and set aside.

2. For the cake, in a small bowl, whisk together the cocoa powder and hot coffee.

3. In a medium bowl, whisk together the flour, baking powder, and salt.

4. In the bowl of an electric mixer fitted with the paddle attachment, beat the butter and sugar on medium speed until light and fluffy, about 3 minutes. Reduce the speed to low and add the eggs, one at a time, beating for 1 minute after each addition. Beat in the vanilla. With the mixer on low speed, gradually add the flour mixture and beat until just combined. Add the cocoa-coffee mixture and beat well. Beat in the buttermilk. Fold in the chocolate chips. Spoon the batter into the prepared pan and smooth the top.

5. Bake until a wooden pick inserted in the center of the cake comes out clean, with just a few crumbs, 50 to 60 minutes. Let cool for 20 minutes before inverting the cake onto a wire rack to cool completely.

6. Meanwhile, for the glaze, in a small bowl, whisk together the confectioners' sugar, cocoa powder, salt, milk, and vanilla.

7. Once the cake has completely cooled, drizzle the chocolate glaze on top. Let set for 30 minutes before serving.

8. The cake will keep, well wrapped and at room temperature, for up to 4 days.

makes one 9 x 5-inch loaf

When it comes to vegan cakes, I think chocolate are best. They maintain their flavor and moisture beautifully. I like to boost my vegan cakes with a bit of avocado, which mimics the fat of butter and is virtually tasteless in the chocolate cake. Vegan secrets!

This cake pairs beautifully with Vegan Chocolate Frosting (opposite). I'd pile on some toasted coconut to finish. Divine!

vegan
CHOCOLATE CAKE

- 3 cups all-purpose flour
- 2 cups sugar
- ½ cup unsweetened natural cocoa powder
- 2 teaspoons baking powder
- 1½ teaspoons baking soda
- 1 teaspoon salt
- ⅓ cup vegetable oil
- ½ cup mashed ripe avocado (about 1 medium avocado)
- 2 tablespoons apple cider vinegar
- 2 teaspoons pure vanilla extract

1. Put oven racks in the center and upper third of the oven and preheat the oven to 350°F. Grease and flour two 9-inch round pans.

2. In a large bowl, whisk together the flour, sugar, cocoa powder, baking powder, baking soda, and salt.

3. In a medium bowl, whisk together the oil and mashed avocado until very few lumps remain. Add 2 cups of water, the vinegar, and vanilla and whisk well. Pour the avocado mixture into the flour mixture and whisk together. Divide the batter between the prepared pans.

4. Bake until a wooden pick inserted in the center of the cake comes out clean or with just a few crumbs, 25 to 30 minutes. Let cool in the pans for 20 minutes before inverting onto wire racks to cool completely before frosting.

makes one 2-layer 9-inch cake

VEGAN CHOCOLATE FROSTING

Skip the cow's milk butter and substitute a vegan alternative for this super-chocolaty frosting. It's packed with so much chocolate flavor, you won't even miss the butter.

- 2 **cups vegan margarine**
- ⅓ **cup unsweetened natural cocoa powder**
- ¼ **teaspoon salt**
- 24 **ounces 60% cacao dark chocolate, coarsely chopped and melted**
- 6 **to 7 cups confectioners' sugar**
- 2 **teaspoons pure vanilla extract**
- 4 **to 5 tablespoons almond milk**

In the bowl of an electric mixer fitted with the paddle attachment, beat the margarine on medium-low speed until soft, about 1 minute. Add the cocoa powder and salt and beat well. Add the melted chocolate and 2 cups of the confectioners' sugar and beat well. Add another 2 cups confectioners' sugar and the vanilla, and add the almond milk 1 tablespoon at a time, beating well until the mixture is well combined. Add the remaining sugar, if necessary, until your desired consistency is reached.

makes about 4 cups

I love that the classic black-and-white cookie is essentially a small, frosted cake in disguise. Let's take this cookie to its logical cake conclusion. Here, I've made a single-layer cake that is tender and spongy and dripping with simple chocolate and vanilla glazes. I dare you to pick it up and eat it like a cookie. That's what I would do.

BLACK-AND-WHITE-COOKIE
cake

cake

2½ cups all-purpose flour

2 teaspoons baking powder

½ teaspoon baking soda

½ teaspoon salt

¼ teaspoon ground cardamom

½ cup sugar

1½ cups buttermilk

2 large eggs

1. Put a rack in the center of the oven and preheat the oven to 375°F. Butter and flour a 10-inch cake pan.

2. For the cake, in a medium bowl, whisk together the flour, baking powder, baking soda, salt, cardamom, and sugar.

3. In a small bowl, whisk together the buttermilk, eggs, and butter. Whisk in the vanilla and almond extracts. Add the buttermilk mixture to the flour mixture and stir until just combined. Spoon the batter into the prepared pan and smooth the top.

4. Bake until a wooden skewer inserted in the center of the cake comes out clean, 20 to 25 minutes. Let cool in the pan for 20 minutes and then turn the cake out onto a wire rack to cool completely.

5. For the chocolate glaze, put the butter and chocolate in a heat-proof bowl and put the bowl over a saucepan of simmering water, making sure that the bottom of the bowl does not touch the simmering water. Stir until the butter and chocolate are melted. Remove the bowl from the pan and stir in the corn syrup and salt. Set aside until ready to glaze the cake. The glaze should be smooth and glossy. If the frosting thickens too much, loosen it by putting it back over the simmering water once again, or microwave for a few seconds.

6. For the vanilla glaze, in a medium bowl, whisk together the confectioners' sugar, vanilla, corn syrup, and milk until smooth. Set aside until ready to glaze the cake.

7. To glaze the cake, put the cake on a serving platter. Using a butter knife, gently spread the chocolate glaze over half of the cake, allowing the glaze to drip over the sides. Carefully pour the vanilla glaze over the other half of the cake, allowing the glaze to drip over the sides. Refrigerate the cake for 30 minutes before serving.

8. The cake will keep, well wrapped in the refrigerator, for up to 3 days.

makes one 9-inch cake

¼ cup (½ stick) unsalted butter, melted and slightly cooled

1 teaspoon pure vanilla extract

½ teaspoon pure almond extract

chocolate glaze

3 tablespoons unsalted butter

4 ounces semisweet chocolate, coarsely chopped

1 tablespoon light corn syrup

Pinch of salt

vanilla glaze

2 cups confectioners' sugar

1 teaspoon pure vanilla extract

1 teaspoon light corn syrup

2 tablespoons whole milk

With flecks of white chocolate and bites of fresh summer fruit, this cake feels like a super-fancy shortcake recipe, all layered and pretty.

I love the combination of peach and strawberry, but raspberries and blueberries would be lovely if you're going for a midsummer Fourth of July theme.

WHITE CHOCOLATE, SUMMER PEACH & STRAWBERRY
cake

cake

- 4 cups cake flour
- 2 teaspoons baking powder
- 1½ teaspoons baking soda
- 1 teaspoon salt
- 1 cup (2 sticks) unsalted butter, at room temperature
- 2 cups sugar
- 1 tablespoon pure vanilla extract
- 4 large eggs, at room temperature
- 2 cups buttermilk
- 1 cup finely chopped white chocolate

1. Put racks in the center and upper third of the oven and preheat the oven to 350°F. Butter and flour three 9-inch round cake pans.

2. For the cake, in a large bowl, whisk together the flour, baking powder, baking soda, and salt.

3. In the bowl of an electric mixer fitted with the paddle attachment, beat the butter and sugar at medium speed until pale and fluffy, 3 to 4 minutes. Add the eggs, one at a time, beating for 1 minute after each addition. Beat in the vanilla. Reduce the mixer speed to low, add half of the flour mixture, and beat until incorporated. Add 1 cup of the buttermilk and beat until just combined. Add the remaining flour mixture, followed by the remaining 1 cup buttermilk, and beat until just combined. Remove the bowl from the mixer and finish stirring with a spatula. Fold in ½ cup of white chocolate. Divide the batter among the prepared cake pans. Spread the batter evenly in each pan and then rap each pan on the counter to release any air bubbles.

4. Bake until golden brown and a wooden pick inserted in the center of the cake comes out clean, about 20 minutes. Let the cakes cool in the pans for 10 minutes before inverting them onto wire racks to cool completely.

recipe continues

frosting and filling

- 3 cups heavy cream
- 2 teaspoons pure vanilla extract
- ¼ cup confectioners' sugar
- 2 cups sliced strawberries
- 2 ripe peaches, pitted and thinly sliced

5. For the frosting, in the bowl of a stand mixer fitted with the whisk attachment, beat the cream, vanilla, and confectioners' sugar on medium speed until soft peaks form, about 4 minutes. Watching closely, continue beating just past the soft-peak stage, about 2 more minutes. The frosting should hold its shape, but still be smooth and spreadable.

6. To assemble the cake, put a cake layer on a serving plate. Put a dollop of the whipped-cream frosting on the layer. Arrange 1 cup each of the sliced strawberries and peaches on the frosting and sprinkle with half of the remaining white chocolate. Press the fruit and chocolate into the frosting a bit. Top with another cake layer and another dollop of the whipped-cream frosting.

7. Arrange the remaining 1 cup sliced strawberries and 1 cup sliced peaches on top, and sprinkle with the remaining white chocolate. Put the last cake layer on top and frost the cake all over with the remaining whipped-cream frosting.

8. Refrigerate the cake until ready to serve.

makes one 3-layer 9-inch cake

The lightest of all cakes is also my favorite. This is the one thing that's worth the work of separating 12 eggs. If you've never made an angel food cake, you may find the idea intimidating, and I can understand that. It requires a special pan. You have to employ a technique called "folding," and after baking, the cake is supposed to rest safely *upside down*! It all sounds like madness. I totally understand.

Try this recipe. I believe in you. You can gently fold ingredients and you can confidently cool a cake upside down. With those two skills, you're practically home free. This cake is flavored with almond extract and paired with juicy winter citrus. If you find yourself making this cake in the summer, replace the citrus with fresh strawberries, and you will be the happiest person ever.

ALMOND ANGEL FOOD CAKE
with vanilla-scented citrus

1¾ cups sugar

1 cup cake flour

¼ teaspoon salt

12 large egg whites, at room temperature

⅓ cup warm water

1 teaspoon pure vanilla extract

1½ teaspoons cream of tartar

½ teaspoon pure almond extract

vanilla-scented citrus

3 navel oranges

3 blood oranges

2 Ruby Red grapefruit

1 vanilla bean

3 tablespoons sugar

1. Put a rack in the center of the oven and preheat the oven to 350°F.

2. For the cake, in the bowl of a food processor fitted with the blade attachment, process the sugar until it is finely ground, about 2 minutes. A superfine sugar will be more easily absorbed into the egg whites. Reserve half of the sugar in a small bowl.

3. In a large bowl, sift together the remaining sugar, the cake flour, and salt.

4. In the bowl of an electric mixer fitted with the whisk attachment, beat the egg whites, water, vanilla, and cream of tartar on medium speed until combined. Gradually add the reserved sugar and continue beating until medium (not stiff) peaks form, 4 to 6 minutes. Beat in the almond extract. The meringue will hold a trail of the beaters through it, be glossy, and won't be overly foamy.

5. Remove the bowl from the mixer and sift in one-quarter of the flour and sugar mixture. Fold with a spatula. Try to avoid stirring the mixture too much. Instead, sweep the egg whites from the bottom of the bowl to

recipe continues

the top, incorporating the flour mixture. Repeat with the remaining flour mixture, adding it in 3 more batches. Fold until thoroughly combined, but don't overmix or deflate the egg whites. Spoon the batter into an ungreased tube pan. *Ungreased* is important, as it will help the cake rise. The tube pan will be full.

6. Bake until a wooden pick inserted in the center of the cake comes out clean, 45 to 50 minutes. Remove the cake from the oven and carefully invert it, propping it upside down on a bottle. Let cool for at least 1 hour before trying to remove it from the pan.

7. As the cake cools, it will begin to pull away from the sides of the pan. To remove it from the pan, tap the pan with a butter knife, or carefully run a butter knife around the edges between the cake and the pan. Turn it out onto a serving plate.

8. For the vanilla-scented citrus, cut the fruit into segments into a medium bowl: First slice off about ½ inch of the bottom and top of 1 of the oranges. Slice down the sides of the orange, cutting through all of the peel and pith to reveal the orange flesh. It's just like peeling an orange with a knife. Cut into the fruit at an angle, slicing in between the natural orange segments. A clean orange slice should pop out. Repeat until all the fruit has been cut into segments.

9. Split the vanilla bean lengthwise and scrape the seeds into a small bowl. Add the sugar and rub together with your fingers until the vanilla seeds are evenly distributed. Add the vanilla sugar to the citrus segments and toss. Refrigerate for 30 minutes, or until ready to serve. The citrus will keep in the refrigerator for up to 3 days.

10. To serve, cut generous slices of cake, put them on serving plates, and top with the citrus segments and juice.

11. The cake will keep, well wrapped and at room temperature, for up to 3 days.

makes 1 tube cake

cake magic
HOW TO GET YOUR CAKE OUT OF THE PAN

Preparing a cake pan for baking is one way to ensure a successful cake-making experience. Here's how to do it:

Start with solid vegetable shortening and a pastry brush. If you don't have a pastry brush, a paper towel will also work. Spread a thin layer of shortening in the bottom and up the sides of the cake pan. Don't miss the corners! That's where cake can't wait to stick.

After greasing, some bakers put a precisely cut piece of parchment paper in the bottom of the cake pan and then grease the paper. I generally find this step to be a bit redundant, but it certainly ensures that cakes will fall out of the pan in one piece.

Next, sprinkle in a few tablespoons of all-purpose flour. Tip and tap the pan over and around to thoroughly dust the pan with flour. Tap out and discard any remaining flour.

Add the cake batter and bake away!

Wait! Your job is not done!

When the cake comes out of the oven, let the cake cool in the pan for 10 to 20 minutes before inverting onto a wire rack to cool completely. The cake should be just warm (not screaming hot) when you invert it onto a wire rack. Is a wire rack really that important? Well, yes. The wire rack helps every surface of the cake to cool, and no surface is subject to sogginess from steam.

HOW TO FROST A CAKE

1. Always start with completely cool cake layers. If your cake is slightly warm, you're late to a party, and you're trying to slap the cake together and run out the door, I'm telling you now: disaster. Your cake must be completely room temperature, chilled from the refrigerator, or even straight out of the freezer.

2. Arrange 3 small pieces of parchment or waxed paper in a triangle shape on the cake plate, cake stand, or board that you're presenting your cake on. This will keep any messy frosting bits off the pretty presentation area. Put the first cake layer, top side up, on the paper pieces.

3. Dollop about ½ to ¾ cup frosting onto the first cake layer. Using a butter knife, spread evenly to the edges.

4. Put the second cake layer on the cake. If this is a 2-layer cake, put it bottom side up. If this is a 3-layer cake, put it top side up.

5. Dollop about ½ to ¾ cup frosting on the layer and spread evenly.

6. Clean the knife in a glass of warm water. It's important to frost the outside of the cake with a clean knife. When frosting is loaded up on the knife, it's hard to get a smooth finish. Spread a thick layer of frosting on the top of the cake and push the excess frosting to the edges of the cake, smoothing the frosting down the sides of the cake.

7. Clean the knife frequently and spread the frosting around the sides of the cake to your desired thickness.

8. Gently pull the paper pieces out from under the cake. Smooth the frosting at the base and refrigerate the cake before serving.

These brownie cups are deep, dark, and melt-y in their chocolate flavor. They're rich. Totally unapologetic.

I love these cupcakes with Salted Peanut Butter Buttercream Frosting (page 190) or Salted Caramel Frosting (page 210). Now that's decadent.

dark chocolate
BROWNIE CUPCAKES

1 cup (2 sticks) unsalted butter

8 ounces 60% cacao dark chocolate, coarsely chopped

1 cup packed light brown sugar

1 teaspoon instant espresso powder (optional)

2 teaspoons pure vanilla extract

4 large eggs

1 cup all-purpose flour

½ teaspoon salt

¼ teaspoon baking powder

½ cup bittersweet chocolate chips

1. Put a rack in the upper third of the oven and preheat the oven to 350°F. Line 1 cupcake pan with paper or foil liners.

2. Put the butter and chocolate in a heat-proof bowl and put the bowl over a saucepan of simmering water, making sure that the bottom of the bowl does not touch the simmering water. Stir until the butter and chocolate melt. Whisk in the brown sugar, espresso powder, if using, and vanilla. Let cool slightly.

3. Once the chocolate mixture has cooled a bit, whisk in the eggs, one at a time, until thoroughly combined. Whisk in the flour, salt, and baking powder. Fold in the chocolate chips. Divide the batter among the prepared cupcake cups.

4. Bake until a wooden pick inserted in the center of a cupcake comes out clean, or with just a few moist crumbs, 20 to 25 minutes. Let cool in the pan for 20 minutes before transferring to a wire rack to cool completely.

makes 12 rich cupcakes

recipe continues

SALTED CARAMEL FROSTING

This sweet caramel frosting is rich. It'll raise your eyebrows; it's that good. This makes enough for a 2-layer cake or a double batch of cupcakes.

½ cup (1 stick) unsalted butter

½ cup heavy cream

2 teaspoons pure vanilla extract

1 cup packed light brown sugar

½ teaspoon salt

3 to 4 cups confectioners' sugar, sifted

In a medium saucepan set over medium heat, combine the butter, cream, vanilla, brown sugar, and salt. Cook, stirring occasionally, until the sugar melts and the mixture begins to simmer, about 4 minutes.

Transfer the mixture to the bowl of an electric mixer fitted with the whisk attachment. Add 2 cups of the confectioners' sugar and beat on medium-low speed until thoroughly combined. Add another 1 to 2 cups confectioners' sugar and beat until thick and fluffy, 4 to 6 minutes.

makes about 3 cups

These are simple cupcakes with a half-twist. The brown sugar simply deepens the flavor and makes these cupcakes the perfect match for Salted Caramel Frosting (opposite).

BROWN SUGAR
cupcakes

3 cups all-purpose flour

1½ teaspoons baking powder

½ teaspoon baking soda

1 teaspoon salt

¼ teaspoon ground cinnamon

1 cup (2 sticks) unsalted butter, melted and cooled

2 large eggs

1 large egg yolk

2 teaspoons pure vanilla extract

2 cups packed light brown sugar

1½ cups buttermilk

1. Put racks in the center and upper third of the oven and preheat the oven to 350°F. Line 2 cupcake pans with paper or foil liners.

2. In a large bowl, whisk together the flour, baking powder, baking soda, salt, and cinnamon.

3. In a medium bowl, whisk together the melted butter, eggs and egg yolk, vanilla, and brown sugar. Add the brown sugar mixture all at once to the flour mixture and stir well. Add the buttermilk and stir well. Divide the batter among the prepared cupcake cups. Bake until lightly golden on top and a wooden skewer inserted in the center of a cupcake comes out clean, or with just a few moist crumbs, 20 to 23 minutes. Let cool in the pans for 20 minutes before transferring to wire racks to cool completely.

4. The cupcakes will keep, unfrosted and well wrapped, at room temperature for up to 3 days. Cupcakes can also be wrapped and frozen for up to 7 days. Once frosted, they should be stored in the refrigerator.

makes 24 cupcakes

Matching these tender cupcakes with Lemon-Honey Cream Cheese Frosting (page 183) isn't overkill . . . it's *juuuust* right.

lemon honey
BROWN BUTTER CUPCAKES

3 cups all-purpose flour

1½ teaspoons baking powder

1 teaspoon baking soda

1 teaspoon salt

1 cup (2 sticks) plus 2 tablespoons unsalted butter

1½ cups sugar

1 tablespoon grated lemon zest

¼ cup honey

4 large eggs

⅔ cup buttermilk

2 tablespoons fresh lemon juice

2 teaspoons pure vanilla extract

1. Put racks in the center and upper third of the oven and preheat the oven to 350°F. Line 2 cupcake pans with paper or foil liners.

2. In a medium bowl, whisk together the flour, baking powder, baking soda, and salt.

3. In a medium stainless steel skillet set over medium heat, melt the butter and cook until it begins to crackle and pop as the water cooks out of it, about 3 minutes. Reduce the heat to medium-low and continue to cook the butter until the solids brown and it becomes fragrant, about 3 minutes more. Immediately transfer the butter to a small bowl. Let cool slightly.

4. In the bowl of an electric mixer fitted with the paddle attachment, beat the brown butter, sugar, lemon zest, and honey. Add the eggs, one at a time, beating for 1 minute after each addition. Add half of the flour mixture and beat on low speed until incorporated. Add the buttermilk, lemon juice, and vanilla and beat well. Add the remaining flour mixture and beat on low speed until just combined. Finish stirring with a spatula. Divide the batter between the prepared cupcake pans.

5. Bake until a wooden pick inserted in the center of a cupcake comes out clean, or with just a few moist crumbs, 18 to 20 minutes. Let cool in the pans for 20 minutes before transferring to wire racks to cool completely.

6. The cupcakes will keep, unfrosted and well wrapped, at room temperature for up to 3 days. Cupcakes can also be wrapped and frozen for up to 7 days. Once frosted, they should be stored in the refrigerator.

makes 24 cupcakes

We generally try to keep our vegetables out of our cupcakes. Here, though, the combination is magic. These cupcakes are familiar and spiced, studded with dried cranberries, and ready to go for every season. I especially love to frost these cupcakes with Maple-Orange Cream Cheese Frosting (page 184). It's a classic, with an extra kick from maple and orange.

CARROT CAKE
cupcakes

- 3 cups all-purpose flour
- 1½ teaspoons baking powder
- 1 teaspoon baking soda
- 1 teaspoon salt
- 1 teaspoon ground cinnamon
- 1 teaspoon ground ginger
- ½ teaspoon freshly grated nutmeg
- ¼ teaspoon ground cloves
- 1 cup granulated sugar
- 1 cup packed light brown sugar
- 1 cup canola oil
- 2 large eggs
- 2 tablespoons pure vanilla extract
- 4 cups finely grated carrots
- ½ cup dried cranberries
- ½ cup coarsely chopped walnuts

1. Put racks in the center and upper third of the oven and preheat the oven to 350°F. Line 2 cupcake pans with paper or foil liners.

2. In a large bowl, whisk together the flour, baking powder, baking soda, salt, cinnamon, ginger, nutmeg, and cloves.

3. In a medium bowl, whisk together the sugars, oil, eggs, and vanilla. Fold in the carrots, cranberries, and walnuts. Add the carrot mixture to the flour mixture and fold together until thoroughly incorporated. Divide the batter between the prepared cupcake pans.

4. Bake until a wooden pick inserted in the center of a cupcake comes out clean, or with just a few moist crumbs, 20 to 25 minutes. Let cool in the pans for 20 minutes. Transfer the cupcakes to wire racks and let cool completely. The cupcakes will keep, unfrosted and well wrapped, at room temperature for up to 3 days. Once frosted, they should be stored in the refrigerator.

makes 24 cupcakes

Some of the greatest cakes are those made with a bowl, a wooden spoon, and a cast-iron skillet. This is one of those! Pour the batter into the skillet and top with any combination of sweet raspberries, dried cranberries, sliced apples, or toasted sliced almonds. The cake is lightly flavored with olive oil and owes a bit of its texture to cornmeal. If you don't have a cast-iron skillet, you can bake the cake in a regular 9-inch round baking pan. I love this with a scoop of Brown Sugar–Cream Cheese Ice Cream (page 237).

OLIVE OIL
cornmeal cake

1¼ cups all-purpose flour

½ cup yellow cornmeal

1 teaspoon baking powder

½ teaspoon baking soda

½ teaspoon salt

½ cup buttermilk

½ cup olive oil

2 large eggs

¾ cup packed light brown sugar

½ teaspoon freshly grated nutmeg

topping options

1 cup fresh raspberries or ½ cup toasted sliced almonds or ⅓ cup dried cranberries or 1 thinly sliced Bosc pear or 1 thinly sliced apple

Turbinado or granulated sugar, for sprinkling

1. Put a rack in the upper third of the oven and preheat the oven to 350°F. Grease and flour a 9-inch cast-iron skillet.

2. In a medium bowl, whisk together the flour, cornmeal, baking powder, baking soda, and salt.

3. In a separate bowl, whisk together the buttermilk, olive oil, eggs, brown sugar, and nutmeg. Add the olive oil mixture to the flour mixture and gently stir until just combined. Pour the batter into the prepared skillet. Lightly press whatever toppings you've chosen into the top of the battter. Sprinkle generously with turbinado sugar.

4. Bake until a wooden pick inserted in the center comes out clean, 30 to 35 minutes. Let cool for at least 1 hour before slicing and serving.

5. The cake will keep, well wrapped and at room temperature, for up to 3 days.

makes one 9-inch cake

I'm a girl that loves summer sun, summer fruit, and huge summer ice-cream cones. No matter how much I love everything involving that season, I always find myself craving this decidedly fall-flavored cake come mid-August. Packed with sweet apples, spices, and pure maple syrup, it is so endearing that by late September, I've probably pulled it out of my oven at least twice. This recipe is inspired by a cake I enjoyed at The King Arthur Flour Bakery in Vermont.

maple-apple
UPSIDE-DOWN CAKE

apples

- 2 medium Fuji or Granny Smith apples, peeled, cored, and sliced into ½-inch-thick wedges
- ½ cup pure maple syrup
- 4 tablespoons (½ stick) unsalted butter
- ½ cup firmly packed light brown sugar
- ¼ teaspoon ground cinnamon
- ¼ teaspoon freshly grated nutmeg

cake

- 1½ cups all-purpose flour
- 1 teaspoon baking soda
- 1 teaspoon ground cinnamon
- ½ teaspoon freshly grated nutmeg
- ½ teaspoon ground ginger

1. Put a rack in the upper third of the oven and preheat the oven to 350°F. Grease a 9 x 2-inch round baking dish with butter.

2. For the apples, arrange the apple wedges in the bottom of the prepared baking dish, fanning the apples out in a circle.

3. In a medium saucepan set over medium-low heat, combine the maple syrup, the 4 tablespoons butter, the brown sugar, cinnamon, and nutmeg. Heat until the butter melts and the mixture begins to simmer, about 4 minutes. Remove the pan from the heat. Pour half of the syrup over the apples in the baking dish. Reserve the remaining half for after the cake is baked.

4. For the cake, in a large bowl, whisk together the flour, baking soda, cinnamon, nutmeg, ginger, and salt.

5. In a separate bowl, combine the melted butter, eggs, maple syrup, brown sugar, and grated apple. Add the apple mixture to the flour mixture and stir well. Dollop the batter onto the apples in the baking dish and gently smooth the top.

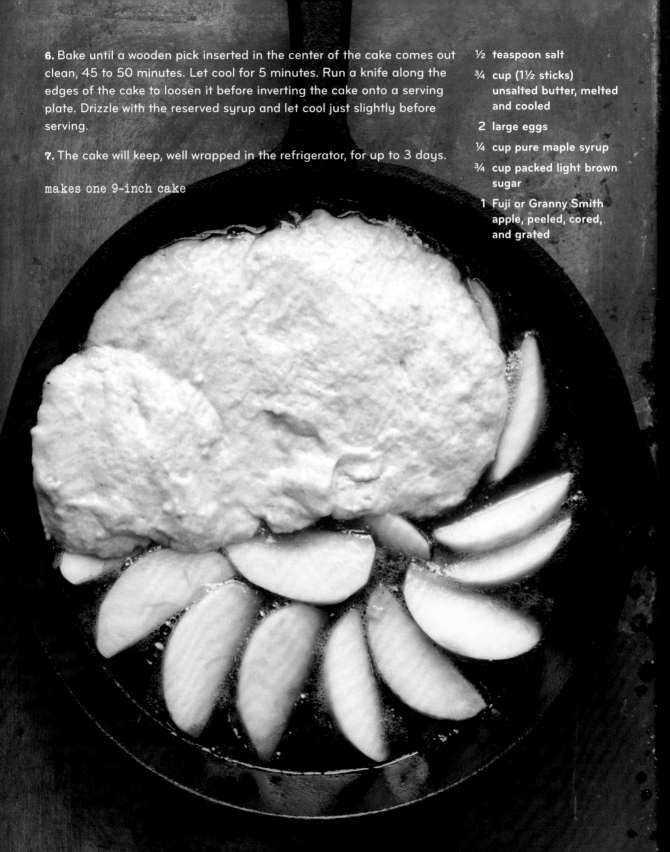

6. Bake until a wooden pick inserted in the center of the cake comes out clean, 45 to 50 minutes. Let cool for 5 minutes. Run a knife along the edges of the cake to loosen it before inverting the cake onto a serving plate. Drizzle with the reserved syrup and let cool just slightly before serving.

7. The cake will keep, well wrapped in the refrigerator, for up to 3 days.

makes one 9-inch cake

½ teaspoon salt

¾ cup (1½ sticks) unsalted butter, melted and cooled

2 large eggs

¼ cup pure maple syrup

¾ cup packed light brown sugar

1 Fuji or Granny Smith apple, peeled, cored, and grated

We all have a preference when it comes to our chocolate chip cookies. There are the flat and crispy fans. There are the thick and doughy enthusiasts. Then there are people who just eat the cookie dough unbaked—and who could blame them?

I love my cookies under-baked: crisp on the outside and just underdone in the center. This cake is that cookie, giant-size, because we can.

under-baked
CHOCOLATE CHIP SKILLET CAKE

- 2 cups all-purpose flour
- 1 teaspoon baking soda
- ½ teaspoon salt
- ¾ cup (1½ sticks) unsalted butter, at room temperature
- ½ cup granulated sugar
- ½ cup packed light brown sugar
- 1 large egg
- 1 large egg yolk
- 2 teaspoons pure vanilla extract
- 1 cup semisweet chocolate chips
- French Vanilla Bean Ice Cream (page 226), for serving

1. Put a rack in the upper third of the oven and preheat the oven to 350°F. Grease and flour a 9-inch ovenproof skillet.

2. In a medium bowl, whisk together the flour, baking soda, and salt.

3. In the bowl of an electric mixer fitted with the paddle attachment, beat the butter, granulated sugar, and brown sugar on medium speed until light and fluffy, about 3 minutes. Reduce the speed to low and beat in the egg. Add the egg yolk, followed by the vanilla, and beat well. Add the flour mixture and beat on low speed until just combined. Remove the bowl from the mixer, and using a spatula, fold in the chocolate chips. Smooth the batter in the prepared pan.

4. Bake until the cookie is baked on the outside, but still slightly under-cooked in the center, 18 to 20 minutes. Let cool for 10 minutes before serving. Serve with big scoops of ice cream in the center.

5. This cookie is best served warm the day it is made but will last, well wrapped and at room temperature, for up to 2 days.

makes one 9-inch cookie cake

ICE CREAM
SOCIAL

I USE ICE CREAM TO MARK MILESTONES IN MY LIFE.

This is totally normal, right? You do this too, don't you? It turns out, it's a great timeline.

I think back to the first time I was tall enough (standing on tippy toes) to peer inside the ice cream case. That was the first time I laid eyes on electric blue Bubble Gum ice cream. It was love at first sight.

The first time I was old enough to pick my own ice cream flavors at my fifth birthday party was a big day. I picked plain vanilla ice cream when I knew in my heart I wanted mint chocolate chip. Don't hesitate to go big, young Joy. Take this ice cream lesson as an analogy for how you should live your life! Ironically, now I adore plain vanilla ice cream.

The first time my sister dropped her ice cream cone in a grocery store parking lot, she burst into tears and I burst into uncontrollable laughter. That might have been the first time I realized that siblings are allowed to suspend compassion when ice cream humor is involved.

The first time I babysat, I snuck into the freezer and ate every last bite of their Rocky Road ice cream. That taught me the very dangerous lesson of asking for forgiveness over asking for permission.

The first time I snuck in past curfew, I found my mom standing in front of the open freezer eating ice cream straight from the container. I told her a story about how I had lost my glasses in the movie theater. She told me a story about how she woke up with a sweet tooth. I'd made up the story about losing my glasses. My mama was telling the truth about her sweet tooth.

I remember the first time I consciously chose to eat a pint of ice cream for dinner. It was Ben & Jerry's Chubby Hubby ice cream; I was a broke college student, writing a term paper about *Macbeth*.

I also recall the day I got my own ice cream maker. I felt a mixture of pride and fear of adulthood. Sort of like the first time you file your own taxes, but more delicious than IRS-y.

This chapter extends my ice cream timeline, as I hope it does yours. I understand that the idea of making ice cream can be a bit overwhelming. It requires special kitchen equipment and often calls for multiple bowls and spatulas. It's a lot. I totally understand. If you can get past a few roadblocks, you'll find that making ice cream is a simple pleasure, and eating freshly churned ice cream directly from the machine is an absolute luxury.

Some recipes in this chapter call for cream, milk, and egg yolks, with which you make a custard ice cream base. By cooking the cream with the egg yolks, the proteins in the yolks will help thicken the cream. Custard bases require a bit of standing, stirring, faith, and practice, but the result is a supremely deluxe ice cream. Other recipes in this chapter are a simple mixture of cream and milk. These recipes generally require less time and attention, and the result is a mighty fine, mega-creamy ice cream.

You'll also find ice cream–based treats like milkshakes and ice cream sandwiches, along with a handful of edible (and, some might argue, essential) ice cream accessories. My great hope is that you find yourself picking fresh strawberry chunks out of and swirling caramel into your very own homemade ice cream in no time. Let's add some quality notches to our ice cream–life timeline.

french vanilla bean ICE CREAM

ROSE WATER ICE CREAM with pistachios & white chocolate

salted dark chocolate & orange ICE CREAM

DOUBLE PEANUT BUTTER ice cream

dark-chocolate-dipped SUGAR CONES

CRUMBLED CHOCOLATE-COVERED potato chips

chocolate-dipped MARSHMALLOWS

CANDIED BACON bits

chocolate-drizzled SALTY PEANUTS

WHITE CHOCOLATE sprinkle clusters

chocolate-dipped SUGAR CONES

mocha FUDGE SAUCE

SALTED CARAMEL sauce

blueberry–goat cheese ICE CREAM

BROWN SUGAR–CREAM CHEESE ice cream

lavender–earl grey ICE CREAM

CARAMEL-SWIRLED sweet corn ice cream

avocado ice cream WITH TOASTED COCONUT

STRAWBERRY CHEESECAKE ice cream

cookie no-dough ICE CREAM

RUM-APRICOT ice cream

bread & brown butter ICE CREAM

HORCHATA ice cream

pumpkin spice ICE CREAM

EGGNOG ice cream

honey-and-pistachio FROZEN YOGURT

MINT-LEMONADE sorbet

strawberry–rosé SANGRIA GRANITA

STRAWBERRY-BALSAMIC pops

sweet coffee & fresh fig POPS

CREAMY MILK CHOCOLATE pops

peach & buttermilk MILKSHAKE

I'm the first person to add chocolate chunks and/or orange zest to basically anything and everything. Some things, however, should remain as pure as they're intended. This ice cream focuses on the simple and divine flavors created by a marriage of vanilla bean, egg yolks, and gloriously heavy cream. It's rich, luscious, and perfectly vanilla.

FRENCH VANILLA BEAN
ice cream

1 vanilla bean

¾ cup sugar

5 large egg yolks

2 cups heavy cream

1 cup whole milk

Pinch of salt

1 teaspoon bourbon (optional)

1. Split the vanilla bean lengthwise. Using the back of a knife, scrape the seeds into a small bowl. Add the sugar and rub the mixture together with your fingers until the sugar is fragrant.

2. In a medium bowl, whisk together the egg yolks and half of the vanilla sugar until the mixture is pale and thick, about 3 minutes.

3. In a medium saucepan set over medium-low heat, heat the remaining vanilla sugar, the cream, milk, and salt until steaming and just boiling, about 5 minutes. Gradually pour the hot cream mixture into the egg yolk and sugar mixture, whisking constantly to ensure that the hot cream does not cook the eggs. Return the mixture to the saucepan and cook, stirring constantly, over medium-low heat until it thickens and begins to coat the back of a spoon, about 10 minutes. Pour the custard through a fine-mesh strainer into a medium bowl. Add the bourbon, if using. Cover with plastic wrap so that the plastic wrap touches the top of the custard, and refrigerate for 4 hours, or until chilled through.

4. Churn the custard in an ice cream maker according to the manufacturer's instructions. Transfer to a freezer-safe container and freeze for 2 hours before serving.

5. Ice cream is best served within 3 days of churning.

makes about 4 cups

This ice cream is the manifestation of the expression "stopping to smell the roses." It's deliciously perfumed. By adding pistachios and white chocolate to the rose-scented base, you're adding salty and sweet elements that will really make this gathering of flavors sing. One more splash of rose water just before serving will really tickle your senses. Stopping to smell the ice cream. You'll see what I mean.

ROSE WATER ICE CREAM
with pistachios & white chocolate

¾ cup sugar

5 large egg yolks

2 cups heavy cream

1½ cups whole milk

Pinch of salt

2 tablespoons rose water, plus more for serving

1 teaspoon vodka (optional)

1 cup shelled and coarsely chopped pistachios, plus more for serving

4 ounces coarsely chopped white chocolate

1. In a medium bowl, whisk together about half of the sugar and all the egg yolks until pale yellow and thick, about 3 minutes.

2. In a medium saucepan set over medium-low heat, heat the remaining sugar, the cream, milk, and salt until steaming and just boiling, about 5 minutes. Gradually pour the hot cream mixture into the egg yolk mixture, whisking constantly. Return the mixture to the saucepan and cook over medium-low heat, stirring constantly, until it thickens and begins to coat the back of a spoon, about 10 minutes. Pour the mixture through a fine-mesh strainer and into a medium bowl. Stir in the 2 tablespoons rose water and the vodka, if using. Cover with plastic wrap so the plastic wrap touches the top of the cream mixture and refrigerate for 4 hours, or until chilled through.

3. Churn the custard in an ice cream maker according to the manufacturer's instructions. During the last minute of churning, add the 1 cup pistachios and the white chocolate. Transfer to a freezer-safe container and freeze for 2 hours before serving.

4. To serve, scoop the ice cream into bowls, drizzle with about 1 teaspoon of rose water, and sprinkle with chopped pistachios.

5. Ice cream is best served within 3 days of churning.

makes about 4 cups

This slightly bonkers ice cream combination can be blamed solely on my very logical dessert brain. My well-seasoned, acutely tuned dessert brain tells me that salt makes chocolate better, orange makes chocolate better, and a clever combination of salt and orange brings chocolate to its highest ice cream potential: brain-freezingly good!

I add just a splash of vodka to this ice cream base to help it maintain a scoopable texture in the freezer. The alcohol (which doesn't freeze) helps the ice cream stay just slightly soft.

SALTED DARK CHOCOLATE & ORANGE
ice cream

- 1 cup sugar
- 2 tablespoons grated orange zest
- 2 tablespoons unsweetened natural cocoa powder
- 5 large egg yolks
- 1½ cups heavy cream
- 2 cups whole milk
- 7 ounces 70% cacao dark chocolate, finely chopped
- ¼ teaspoon coarse sea salt, plus more for sprinkling
- 1 teaspoon vodka (optional)

1. In a small bowl, combine the sugar and orange zest. Rub together with your fingers until the sugar is fragrant. Whisk in the cocoa powder.

2. In a medium bowl, whisk together the egg yolks and half of the orange-and-cocoa sugar mixture until the mixture is thick, about 3 minutes.

3. In a medium saucepan set over medium-low heat, heat the cream and milk until steaming and just boiling, about 5 minutes. Gradually pour the hot cream mixture into the egg yolk mixture, whisking constantly to ensure that the hot cream does not cook the eggs. Return the mixture to the saucepan, add the remaining orange-and-cocoa sugar mixture, and cook, stirring constantly, over low heat until it thickens enough to coat the back of a spoon, about 10 minutes. Remove the pan from the heat and add the chocolate, salt, and vodka, if using. Stir until the chocolate is melted. Pour the custard through a fine-mesh strainer into a medium bowl. Cover with plastic wrap so that the plastic wrap touches the top of the custard, and refrigerate for 4 hours, or until chilled through.

4. Churn the custard in an ice cream maker according to the manufacturer's instructions. Transfer to a freezer-safe container and freeze for 2 hours before serving.

5. Ice cream is best served within 3 days of churning.

makes about 4 cups

This ice cream has a 0% chance of not being totally delicious. Ice cream double negative. This ice cream guarantees that you will win over the world with grace and favor. It's that unstoppable. Consider serving this ice cream with the Basic Three-Layer Yellow Cake (page 179), or with the Black-and-White-Cookie Cake (page 198), or on a giant serving spoon taken straight to the face. To seriously outdo yourself, serve the ice cream topped with chopped chocolate-covered malted milk candies. Yeah, I know.

DOUBLE PEANUT BUTTER
ice cream

1½ cups smooth all-natural peanut butter

⅔ cup packed light brown sugar

1 tablespoon pure vanilla extract

⅛ teaspoon salt

1 cup whole milk

2 cups heavy cream

1. In the bowl of a food processor, combine 1 cup of the peanut butter, the brown sugar, vanilla, and salt. Pulse until blended. With the processor running, slowly stream in the milk. Transfer to a medium bowl and slowly stir in the cream.

2. Churn the custard in an ice cream maker according to the manufacturer's instructions.

3. Put the remaining ½ cup peanut butter in a small bowl and microwave until pourable, 10 to 15 seconds. Pour the peanut butter into the ice cream, and using a spatula, quickly stir by hand to swirl it in. Transfer to a freezer-safe container and freeze for 4 hours before serving.

4. Ice cream is best served within 3 days of churning.

makes about 4 cups

If we've gone through all the trouble of making our very own ice cream, that ice cream must be properly accessorized. This is simple enough: Dip store-bought cones into glossy dark chocolate and then sprinkle them with fancies. I adore these cones speckled with salty chopped pistachios and topped with French Vanilla Bean Ice Cream (page 226).

These cones are extra delicious if the insides are coated in chocolate, too. Once the outside chocolate has frozen, drizzle a bit of chocolate inside each cone and swirl it around to coat. Set the cones on their sides and freeze once again to harden the chocolate inside.

dark-chocolate-dipped
SUGAR CONES

1 cup coarsely chopped pistachios

½ cup sprinkles

½ cup cocoa nibs

2 cups dark chocolate chunks

12 store-bought ice cream cones

1. Line a baking sheet with parchment paper.

2. Put the pistachios, sprinkles, and cocoa nibs into 3 separate small bowls.

3. Put the chocolate chunks in a heat-proof bowl. Fill a medium saucepan with 1 inch of water and set it over medium heat. Bring the water to a boil. Put the bowl of chocolate over the simmering water, making sure that the bottom of the bowl does not touch the water. Gently stir the chocolate until it's melted and smooth, about 6 minutes.

4. Holding the tip of each cone, dip about 2 inches of the top into the melted chocolate. Allow the excess chocolate to drip off. Put the cones, tip side up, onto the prepared baking sheet. Let the chocolate set for about 30 seconds before sprinkling with nuts, sprinkles, or cocoa nibs. Dip and dress each cone as you desire.

5. Put the dipped and dressed cones in the freezer to harden for about 30 minutes.

6. Put the frozen cones in a sealable plastic bag and store in the freezer until ready to top with ice cream and serve. The cones will last for up to 1 month in the freezer.

makes 12 cones

TREATS & TOPPINGS!

The best part of making beautiful food is designing entire gatherings around that food. An ice cream social is the perfect excuse to bust out the homemade quarts, fill small bowls with toppings, and scatter colorful sprinkles across the table. Make sure you have enough spoons, cones, and ice water (with all this sugar, you'll need it!) for the crowd, and then sit back and watch the ice cream fly!

TOPPINGS

crumbled chocolate-covered potato chips

Melt semisweet chocolate in a heat-proof bowl set over a saucepan of simmering water. Remove the pan from the heat, but keep the bowl of melted chocolate over the steaming water. Dip whole potato chips (I like to use Ruffles) halfway into the chocolate, shake off any excess, and put the chips a parchment paper–lined baking sheet. Place the baking sheet in the freezer until the chocolate is set, about 8 minutes. Remove from the freezer and coarsely crumble the chips. The chips will keep in a plastic zip-top bag in the freezer for up to 1 week.

BEST MATCHES:
French Vanilla Bean Ice Cream (page 226) or Double Peanut Butter Ice Cream (page 230)

chocolate-dipped marshmallows

Melt semisweet chocolate in a heat-proof bowl set over a saucepan of simmering water. Remove the pan from the heat, but keep the bowl of melted chocolate over the steaming water. Dip marshmallows halfway into the melted chocolate, shake off any excess, and put the marshmallows on a parchment paper–lined baking sheet. Place the baking sheet in the refrigerator until the chocolate is set, about 10 minutes. The marshmallows will keep in a plastic zip-top bag at room temperature or in the refrigerator for up to 5 days.

BEST MATCHES:
Salted Dark Chocolate & Orange Ice Cream (page 228) or Cookie No-Dough Ice Cream (page 246)

candied bacon bits

Put an oven rack in the upper third of the oven and preheat the oven to 375°F. Line a baking sheet with aluminum foil. Lay 6 strips of bacon in a single layer on the baking sheet. Sprinkle with 2 to 3 tablespoons light brown sugar. Bake until crisp, 15 to 17 minutes. Remove from the oven and let cool. Once cool enough to handle, finely chop the bacon. The bacon will keep in an airtight container in the refrigerator for up to 3 days.

BEST MATCHES:
Double Peanut Butter Ice Cream (page 230) or Eggnog Ice Cream (page 256)

chocolate-drizzled salty peanuts

Spread salted peanuts over a parchment paper–lined baking sheet. Drizzle with melted dark chocolate. Put the baking sheet in the freezer until the chocolate is set, about 8 minutes. Scrape chocolate and nuts off of the parchment paper. The nuts will keep in a plastic zip-top bag in the freezer for up to 1 week.

BEST MATCHES:
Double Peanut Butter Ice Cream (page 230) or Brown Sugar–Cream Cheese Ice Cream (page 237)

white chocolate sprinkle clusters

Line a baking sheet with parchment paper. Melt white chocolate in a heat-proof bowl set over a saucepan of simmering water. Spoon the white chocolate by the teaspoonful onto the prepared pan. Generously sprinkle each white chocolate mound with color sprinkles before the chocolate sets. Put the baking sheet in the freezer until the chocolate is set, about 8 minutes. The clusters will keep in a plastic zip-top bag for up to 1 week.

BEST MATCHES:
Strawberry Cheesecake Ice Cream (page 245) or Cookie No-Dough Ice Cream (page 246)

chocolate-dipped sugar cones

Melt semisweet chocolate in a heat-proof bowl set over a saucepan of simmering water.

Remove the pan from the heat, but keep the bowl of melted chocolate over the steaming water. Line a baking sheet with parchment paper. Dip the open end of the cones about 1 inch into the melted chocolate, shake off any excess, and put the cones on the prepared baking sheet. Before the chocolate hardens, you can sprinkle the cones with rainbow sprinkles, coarsely chopped pistachios, crumbled chocolate sandwich cookies, or crumbled potato chips, if you like. Let cool at room temperature until the chocolate is set, 10 minutes, or place the cones in the freezer to harden the chocolate more quickly. To store the cones, stack them inside one another, put them in a plastic zip-top bag, and store in the freezer for up to 1 week.

SAUCES

mocha fudge sauce

This deep, dark chocolate sauce is irresistible on absolutely everything it touches. It's a classic pair with the French Vanilla Bean Ice Cream (page 226) and makes for a thoroughly chocolate situation atop the Salted Dark Chocolate & Orange Ice Cream (page 228). I've also been known to enjoy this sauce with a spoon straight from the pot. It's that good.

1 teaspoon instant espresso powder

1½ teaspoons hot water

⅔ cup heavy cream

½ cup light corn syrup

¼ cup unsweetened Dutch-processed cocoa powder

⅓ cup packed light brown sugar

6 ounces good bittersweet chocolate, finely chopped

¼ teaspoon salt

2 tablespoon unsalted butter, cut into ½ tablespoons

1 teaspoon pure vanilla extract

1. In a small bowl, combine the espresso powder and hot water and stir until dissolved. In a 2-quart heavy saucepan set over medium heat, combine the cream, corn syrup, cocoa powder, brown sugar, half of the chocolate, and salt. Cook, stirring constantly, until chocolate is melted, about 4 minutes. Bring the mixture to a low boil and cook, stirring occasionally, until thoroughly combined and glossy, about 5 minutes.

2. Remove the pan from the heat, add the remaining chocolate, the butter, vanilla extract, and espresso mixture. Stir until smooth. Let cool slightly before serving. The sauce will keep in an airtight container in the refrigerator for up to 1 week. Reheat over low heat.

Makes about 2 cups

salted caramel sauce Caramelized sugar mixed with cream and butter makes a dream topping for ultracreamy desserts like ice cream. I love adding a generous hint of salt to cut the sweetness. This sauce is especially over-the-top when paired with Cookie No-Dough Ice Cream (page 246) and Rum-Apricot Ice Cream (page 249).

1 cup sugar

¼ cup light corn syrup

⅔ cup heavy cream

4 tablespoons (½ stick) unsalted butter

1 teaspoon sea salt

1. In a medium saucepan set over medium heat, combine ¼ cup water with the sugar and corn syrup. Bring to a boil and cook, stirring once or twice, until the sugar has melted and turned a medium amber color, 6 to 8 minutes. Remove the pan from the heat and immediately add heavy cream and butter. Be careful; the mixture will boil and foam. Stir well, add the salt, and stir well again. The caramel may seem thin; that's ok. Transfer to a bowl, cover with plastic wrap, and put in the refrigerator to cool for at least 4 hours (overnight is best).

2. The caramel will keep in an airtight container in the refrigerator for up to 1 week.

Makes about 2 cups

Dorie Greenspan—one of my favorite bakers of all time—introduced me to the wonders of blueberry ice cream in her stellar book *Baking*. In this homage to her creation, I've added goat cheese, which imparts a mild but distinct tang. It's a fancy cheese plate with fresh blueberries and goat cheese brought to life in an ice cream. It would be my instinct to scoop this beautifully purple ice cream and drizzle each serving with a touch of honey.

BLUEBERRY-GOAT CHEESE
ice cream

1 cup blueberries, fresh or frozen (if frozen, thaw and drain the berries)

½ cup packed light brown sugar

Pinch of salt

2 cups heavy cream

1 cup whole milk

1 teaspoon vodka (optional)

4 ounces goat cheese, coarsely crumbled

1. In a medium saucepan set over medium heat, combine ¼ cup water with the blueberries, brown sugar, and salt. Cook until the berries are softened and begin to burst, about 5 minutes. Transfer to a blender and puree until smooth. (Actually, it's okay if a few chunks remain.) Add the cream, milk, and vodka, if using, and blend well. Add the goat cheese and pulse until mostly incorporated. Pour the mixture into a bowl, cover with plastic wrap, and refrigerate until chilled through, about 1 hour.

2. Churn the custard in an ice cream maker according to the manufacturer's instructions. Transfer to a freezer-safe container and freeze for 2 hours before serving.

3. Ice cream is best served within 5 days of churning.

makes about 4 cups

Maybe you have your mother-in-law coming over with her famous apple pie—the pie that you dare not tell her is a touch too dry. Lucky for you, there's a container of this ice cream in your freezer, and it is the perfect addition. Familiar and comforting, it also boasts a hint of molasses and an irresistibly tangy cream cheese flavor. Best of all, it's not nearly as aggressive as making another pie to compete with your mother-in-law's. Good for you!

BROWN SUGAR–CREAM CHEESE
ice cream

1 (8-ounce) package cream cheese, at room temperature

2½ cups cold half-and-half

1 cup packed light brown sugar

¼ teaspoon salt

1 tablespoon bourbon (optional)

1. Combine the cream cheese, half-and-half, brown sugar, salt, and bourbon, if using, in the bowl of a food processor fitted with the blade attachment. Blend on high speed until smooth. Transfer the mixture to an ice cream maker and churn according to the manufacturer's instructions. Transfer to a freezer-safe bowl and freeze for at least 4 hours before serving.

2. The ice cream can be stored in an airtight container in the freezer for up to 1 week.

makes about 4 cups

We're sophisticated. We're as classy as warm scones and clotted cream. The combination of delicate lavender and fragrant Earl Grey tea feels like a natural fit. This ice cream makes you sit up straight and lift your head a little higher, and even if you do have an ice cream cone dripping down your hands, pinkie up, always!

LAVENDER-EARL GREY
ice cream

2 cups heavy cream

1½ cups whole milk

½ cup sugar

1 tablespoon dried lavender

4 Earl Grey tea bags

5 large egg yolks

1 teaspoon pure vanilla extract

1 teaspoon vodka (optional)

1. In a medium saucepan set over medium-low heat, combine the cream, milk, and ¼ cup of the sugar. Cook, stirring, until the sugar is dissolved and the milk is steaming and just boiling, about 5 minutes. Add the lavender and tea bags, remove the pan from the heat, cover, and let steep for 7 minutes. Remove the tea bags, cover the pan, and let the lavender continue to steep for 15 more minutes.

2. Pour the cream mixture though a fine-mesh strainer and discard the lavender.

3. In a medium bowl, whisk together the egg yolks and the remaining ¼ cup sugar. Slowly pour the warm cream mixture into the egg mixture, whisking constantly. Return the mixture to the saucepan and cook over medium-low heat, stirring constantly, until it thickens and begins to coat the back of a spoon, about 10 minutes. Pour the custard through a fine-mesh strainer and into a medium bowl. Stir in the vanilla and vodka, if using. Cover with plastic wrap so that the plastic wrap touches the top of the cream mixture and refrigerate for 4 hours, or until chilled through.

4. Churn the custard in an ice cream maker according to the manufacturer's instructions. Transfer to a freezer-safe container and freeze for 2 hours before serving.

5. Ice cream is best served within 3 days of churning.

makes about 4 cups

In order to have the best ice-cream-shop experience possible, always just ask. The fifteen-year-old behind the counter knows what's what at any given moment. He knows that the Cookies 'n' Cream ice cream is chock-full of more cookies than usual, that the Rocky Road is particularly marshmallow-y at the moment, and that the waffle cones are superfresh. He knows these things because he's covered in ice cream from elbow to fingertip.

My favorite ice cream shop in Los Angeles is Sweet Rose Creamery. During the summer months, the guys behind the counter always recommend the Sweet Corn ice cream. This recipe is my homage to that creation. I added a swirl of caramel because caramel is always the right move. With a pinch of sea salt on top, this ice cream is beyond!

caramel-swirled
SWEET CORN ICE CREAM

caramel
- ½ cup sugar
- ⅓ cup light corn syrup
- ¼ teaspoon salt
- ½ cup heavy cream
- 1 teaspoon pure vanilla extract

ice cream
- 3 ears of corn, kernels cut and scraped, cobs reserved
- 1½ cups whole milk
- 2 cups heavy cream
- ½ teaspoon salt
- ½ cup sugar
- 5 large egg yolks

1. For the caramel, in a medium saucepan set over medium heat, combine ¼ cup water with the sugar, corn syrup, and salt. Bring to a boil, swirling the pan occasionally, and cook until the mixture is a deep amber color, about 8 minutes. Remove the pan from the heat and carefully stir in the cream. The mixture will bubble and froth and the sugar might seize, but that's normal. If the sugar seizes, return the pan to low heat and cook until the sugar dissolves, about 2 minutes. Remove the pan from the heat. Stir in the vanilla, transfer the caramel to a small bowl, and let cool in the refrigerator for 30 minutes. The caramel can be made up to 5 days in advance. Bring to room temperature or heat just slightly in a microwave or on the stovetop if the caramel is too thick for drizzling.

2. For the ice cream, in a large saucepan set over medium-low heat, combine the corn kernels and cobs, milk, cream, and salt. Heat until steaming and nearly boiling, about 5 minutes. Remove the pan from the heat and cover. Let the mixture steep for 30 minutes.

recipe continues

1 teaspoon pure vanilla
extract

2 teaspoons vodka or
bourbon (optional)

3. Remove the corn cobs and discard. Blend the mixture until smooth with either an immersion blender or a regular blender in 2 batches. Always be careful when blending hot liquids! Strain the mixture and return it to the saucepan.

4. In a small bowl, whisk together the sugar and egg yolks until thick and pale yellow, about 3 minutes. Whisk the egg yolk mixture into the corn mixture. Cook over medium-low heat, stirring constantly, until the mixture thickens and coats the back of a spoon, about 10 minutes. Remove the pan from the heat and stir in the vanilla and vodka, if using. Transfer to a bowl and cover with plastic wrap so that the plastic wrap touches the surface of the ice cream base. Refrigerate for 4 hours, or until chilled through.

5. Churn the custard in an ice cream maker according to the manufacturer's instructions. During the last 10 seconds of churning, drizzle in most of the caramel sauce. Transfer to a freezer-safe container and swirl in the remaining caramel. Freeze for 2 hours before serving.

6. Ice cream is best served within 3 days of churning.

makes about 4 cups

This ice cream was *not* the cool kid in high school. It was just too weird to be cool. But these days, it is the awesome dude who plays banjo in the band that is just too weird *not* to like. It's funny how that works!

It may surprise you to know that avocados lend themselves very easily to sweet interpretations. This ice cream is pale green, sweet, and deliciously strange. The coconut adds a toothsome texture and an almost tropical feel. I love this ice cream served alongside the Double the Chocolate Cake (page 189).

AVOCADO ICE CREAM
with toasted coconut

1 cup sweetened shredded coconut

1½ cups mashed ripe avocados (from 3 medium avocados)

1½ cups whole milk

2 tablespoons fresh lime juice

½ cup sugar

Pinch of salt

1 cup heavy cream

1 teaspoon pure vanilla extract

1 teaspoon vodka (optional)

1. Put a rack in the upper third of the oven and preheat the oven to 350°F.

2. Spread the coconut out on a baking sheet and toast until golden brown and fragrant, 4 to 6 minutes. Let cool completely.

3. In a blender, combine the avocados, milk, lime juice, sugar, and salt. Blend until smooth. Add the cream, vanilla, and vodka, if using. Blend well.

4. Churn the mixture in an ice cream maker according to the manufacturer's instructions. During the last minute of churning, add the toasted coconut. Transfer to a freezer-safe container and freeze for 2 hours before serving.

5. Ice cream is best served within 5 days of churning.

makes about 4 cups

By combining sweet strawberries with a cream cheese base and a touch of crumbled graham crackers, we have an ice cream that tastes just like strawberry cheesecake in the most delicious, frozen way possible.

STRAWBERRY CHEESECAKE
ice cream

2½ cups cold half-and-half

1 tablespoon fresh lemon juice

1 teaspoon pure vanilla extract

1 tablespoon vodka (optional)

1 (8-ounce) package cream cheese, at room temperature

½ cup sugar

¼ teaspoon salt

1 pint fresh strawberries, hulled and coarsely chopped

1 cup coarsely crumbled graham crackers (optional)

1. In a blender, combine the half-and-half, lemon juice, vanilla, vodka, if using, cream cheese, sugar, and salt. Blend on high until smooth. Add ½ cup of strawberries to the blender. Blend until smooth.

2. Churn the mixture in an ice cream maker according to the manufacturer's instructions. During the last minute of churning, add the remaining strawberries and the graham cracker crumbs, if using. Transfer to a freezer-safe container and freeze for at least 4 hours before serving.

3. Ice cream is best served within 5 days of churning.

makes about 4 cups

I have to be honest. You should never ask me to house-sit for you. I can't be trusted alone with your freezer full of ice cream. I'll eat it all—and if I don't eat it all, I'll at least eat all of the yummy chunks out of your Chocolate Chip Cookie Dough ice cream. The only solution to this special sort of rudeness is this recipe. It's got all the flavor of cookie dough without all the digging for chunks.

COOKIE NO-DOUGH
ice cream

¼ cup (½ stick) unsalted butter

5 large egg yolks

⅔ cup packed light brown sugar

¼ teaspoon salt

2 cups heavy cream

1½ cups whole milk

2 teaspoons pure vanilla extract

¼ teaspoon baking soda

4 ounces 65% cacao dark chocolate, coarsely chopped

1. In a small saucepan set over medium-low heat, melt the butter. Cook until it starts to crackle and sizzle, about 3 minutes. Continue cooking until the butter begins to smell nutty and there are little brown speckles on the bottom of the pan, about 2 more minutes. Remove the pan from the heat and immediately pour the brown butter into a small bowl.

2. In a medium bowl, whisk together the egg yolks, brown sugar, and salt until the mixture is slightly paler and thick, about 3 minutes.

3. In a medium saucepan combine the cream, milk, and brown butter. Cook until steaming and almost boiling, about 5 minutes. Slowly pour the cream mixture into the egg yolk mixture, whisking constantly. Return the mixture to the saucepan and cook over low heat, stirring constantly, until the mixture is thickened. Continue to stir constantly until it thickens and coats the back of a spoon, about 10 minutes. Remove the pan from the heat and stir in the vanilla and baking soda. Transfer to a bowl and cover with plastic wrap so that the plastic wrap touches the ice cream mixture. Refrigerate for 4 hours or until chilled through.

4. Churn the custard in an ice cream maker according to the manufacturer's instructions. During the last minute of churning, add the chocolate chunks. Transfer to a freezer-safe container and freeze for 2 hours before serving.

5. Ice cream is best served within 3 days of churning.

makes about 4 cups

Let's just be honest with ourselves: No one likes raisins. (Totally not true. I'm just making big statements.) I'm probably not a fan of raisins because my parents too often tried to pass them off as candy when I was growing up. No way.

I don't want raisins to keep me from my rum ice cream, so let's switch it up! Apricots! We won't scoop around apricots. We can't scoop around the rum! Perfect. Now we're all in!

RUM-APRICOT
ice cream

apricots
- ¾ cup coarsely chopped dried apricots
- ¾ cup spiced rum

ice cream
- 2 cups heavy cream
- 1½ cups whole milk
- ⅔ cup packed light brown sugar
- 1 tablespoon pure vanilla extract

1. In a medium saucepan set over medium-low heat, combine the apricots and rum. Cook until hot and steaming, about 5 minutes. Remove the pan from the heat, cover, and let steep until the apricots are extra plump, about 30 minutes. Reserve 3 tablespoons of rum from the steeped apricots.

2. For the ice cream base, in a medium saucepan set over medium-low heat, whisk together the cream, milk, brown sugar, vanilla, and reserved rum until the sugar is dissolved, about 4 minutes. Transfer to a bowl, cover with plastic wrap, and refrigerate until chilled, about 1 hour.

3. Churn the mixture in an ice cream maker according to the manufacturer's instructions. During the last minute of churning, add the steeped apricots. Transfer to a freezer-safe container and freeze for 4 hours before serving.

4. Ice cream is best served within 4 or 5 days of churning.

makes about 4 cups

To think that a recipe can combine melted butter with stale bread and somehow turn it into ice cream is ludicrous. However, it's totally possible. It's also totally delicious. I really want you to trust me, here. You and I should totally share a giant bowl with 2 spoons. The end.

BREAD & BROWN BUTTER
ice cream

bread crumbs

- 4 slices pumpernickel bread, cut into cubes
- ¼ cup (½ stick) salted butter
- ⅓ cup granulated sugar
- ¼ teaspoon freshly grated nutmeg

ice cream

- ¼ cup (½ stick) salted butter
- ⅔ cup packed light brown sugar
- 5 large egg yolks
- 2 teaspoons molasses
- 1½ cups whole milk
- 2 cups heavy cream
- 1 teaspoon pure vanilla extract
- 1 teaspoon bourbon (optional)

1. Put a rack in the upper third of the oven and preheat the oven to 375°F. Line a baking sheet with parchment paper.

2. Put the bread cubes on the baking sheet in a single layer. Toast in the oven until dried on the outside, about 6 minutes. Transfer the bread cubes to the bowl of a food processor fitted with the blade attachment. Pulse until the bread is crumbled.

3. In a small saucepan set over medium-low heat, melt the butter. Pour the butter into a medium bowl and add the bread crumbs, sugar, and nutmeg. Toss well and spread the buttered crumbs again on the prepared baking sheet. Bake until toasted and even more browned, 15 to 20 minutes. Let cool completely.

4. For the ice cream, in a small saucepan set over medium heat, melt the butter. Cook until the butter cracks and sizzles, about 3 minutes. Continue cooking until the butter begins to smell nutty and there are little brown speckles on the bottom of the pan, about 2 more minutes. Remove the pan from the heat and immediately pour the brown butter into a small bowl. You'll have just over 2 tablespoons of brown butter.

5. In a medium bowl, whisk together ⅓ cup of the brown sugar, the egg yolks, and molasses.

6. In a medium saucepan, heat the remaining ⅓ cup brown sugar, the milk, and cream. Cook, stirring, until the sugar is dissolved and the mixture begins to steam, about 5 minutes. Slowly pour the hot cream mixture over the egg mixture, whisking constantly. Return the mixture to the saucepan

and heat over medium-low heat, stirring constantly, until it thickens and begins to coat the back of a spoon, about 10 minutes. Pour the custard through a fine-mesh strainer and into a medium bowl. Stir in the brown butter, vanilla, and bourbon, if using. Cover with plastic wrap so that the plastic wrap touches the top of the cream mixture and refrigerate for 4 hours, or until chilled through.

7. Churn the custard in an ice cream maker according to the manufacturer's instructions. During the last minute of churning, add the toasted bread crumbs. Transfer to a freezer-safe container and freeze for 2 hours before serving.

8. Ice cream is best served within 3 days of churning.

makes about 4 cups

Horchata is traditionally a creamy beverage that's made with soaked ground rice, cinnamon, and sugar. It's an incredibly comforting and soothing iced drink. If you've ever lived in Los Angeles, you've probably crouched over a plate of spicy taco-truck tacos and desperately sipped your horchata from a Styrofoam cup, hoping it'll tame the heat of the spicy fare. Once horchata, the drink, is turned into ice cream, it's soothing comfort is magnified!

HORCHATA
ice cream

⋄⋄⋄

- ⅓ cup long-grain rice
- 2 cups whole milk
- 3 cinnamon sticks
- 2 cups heavy cream
- 5 large egg yolks
- ½ cup sugar
- ½ teaspoon ground cinnamon
- ¼ teaspoon salt
- 2 teaspoons pure vanilla extract
- 1 teaspoon bourbon (optional)

1. In a medium saucepan set over medium heat, toast the rice until fragrant and golden, about 2 minutes. Add the milk and cinnamon sticks. Heat until the milk is steaming and nearly boiling, about 3 minutes. Remove the pan from the heat, cover, and let steep for 30 minutes. Remove the cinnamon sticks and pour the milk mixture into a blender. Blend until the mixture is almost smooth. Pour the mixture through a fine-mesh strainer and into a medium bowl. Press the rice solids to release as much milk as possible, and discard. Stir in the cream.

2. In a medium bowl, whisk together the egg yolks, sugar, cinnamon, and salt until pale yellow and thick, about 3 minutes. Slowly pour the milk mixture into the egg mixture, whisking constantly. Return it to the saucepan and cook over low heat, stirring constantly, until it thickens enough to coat the back of a spoon, about 10 minutes. Remove the pan from the heat and add the vanilla and bourbon, if using. Transfer to a bowl and cover with plastic wrap so that the plastic wrap touches the top of the milk mixture. Refrigerate for 4 hours, or until chilled through.

3. Churn the custard in an ice cream maker according to the manufacturer's instructions. Transfer to a freezer-safe container and freeze for 2 hours before serving.

4. Ice cream is best served within 3 days of churning.

makes about 4 cups

A few times a year, we have an obligation to "pumpkin" things. We pumpkin our pies. We pumpkin our cakes. We pumpkin our fancy coffee drinks. Why not also pumpkin our ice cream? This ice cream has all of the pomp and circumstance of a flavorful pie, and the mascarpone adds a creamy sweetness that melds well with big pumpkin spices.

Warning: This will totally have you thinking of all of the other things you'll want to "pumpkin" this fall.

PUMPKIN SPICE
ice cream

1 cup canned pumpkin puree

1 teaspoon ground cinnamon

½ teaspoon ground ginger

½ teaspoon freshly grated nutmeg

¼ teaspoon ground allspice

¼ teaspoon salt

Pinch of ground cloves

2 cups heavy cream

1 cup whole milk

5 large egg yolks

½ cup packed light brown sugar

2 teaspoons pure vanilla extract

1 teaspoon bourbon (optional)

1 cup coarsely crumbled gingersnap cookies, for serving

1. In a medium saucepan set over medium heat, combine the pumpkin puree, cinnamon, ginger, nutmeg, allspice, salt, and cloves. Heat until bubbling and fragrant, 3 to 5 minutes. Remove the pan from the heat.

2. In a medium saucepan set over medium-low heat, heat the cream and milk until steaming and almost bubbling, about 5 minutes.

3. In a medium bowl, whisk together the egg yolks and brown sugar. Slowly pour the hot cream mixture into the egg yolk mixture, whisking constantly. Return the mixture to the saucepan and cook over medium-low heat, stirring constantly, until it thickens and begins to coat the back of a spoon, about 10 minutes. Pour it through a fine-mesh strainer and into a medium bowl. Stir in the vanilla and bourbon, if using. Whisk in the spiced pumpkin mixture. Cover with plastic wrap so that the plastic wrap touches the top of the cream mixture and refrigerate for 4 hours, or until chilled through.

4. Churn the custard in an ice cream maker according to the manufacturer's instructions. Transfer to a freezer-safe container and freeze for 2 hours before serving.

5. Ice cream is best served within 3 days.

makes about 5 cups

You know it's about to be a great holiday party when someone shows up with the eggnog! Freeze it. Add extra rum. Now it's an ice cream party!

EGGNOG
ice cream

2 cups heavy cream

1½ cups whole milk

½ cup packed light brown sugar

5 large egg yolks

½ teaspoon freshly grated nutmeg

3 tablespoons dark rum

1 teaspoon pure vanilla extract

1. In a medium saucepan set over medium-low heat, combine the cream, milk, and ¼ cup of the brown sugar. Heat until the sugar is dissolved and the mixture is steaming hot and just boiling, about 5 minutes.

2. In a medium bowl, whisk together the remaining ¼ cup brown sugar, the egg yolks, and nutmeg. Slowly pour the hot cream mixture over the yolk mixture, whisking constantly. Return the mixture to the saucepan and cook over medium-low heat, stirring constantly, until it thickens and begins to coat the back of a spoon, about 10 minutes. Pour it through a fine-mesh strainer and into a medium bowl. Stir in the rum and the vanilla extract. Cover with plastic wrap so that the plastic wrap touches the top of the cream mixture and refrigerate for 4 hours, or until chilled through.

3. Churn the custard in an ice cream maker according to the manufacturer's instructions. Transfer to a freezer-safe container and freeze for 2 hours before serving.

4. Ice cream is best served within 3 days.

makes about 4 cups

This frozen yogurt is full of integrity. This recipe is exactly what its ingredients suggest. Tart yogurt combines with sweet honey and salty pistachios. It's wonderfully balanced and (gasp!) healthy, too! I love to serve this frozen yogurt with an extra drizzle of honey on top. The honey freezes slightly and becomes the consistency of taffy.

honey-and-pistachio
FROZEN YOGURT

- 1 cup shelled salted pistachios, coarsely chopped
- 3 cups Greek yogurt (whole milk or low fat is best)
- ½ cup honey, plus more for topping
- 1 tablespoon vodka (optional)

1. Put half of the pistachios in a spice grinder and grind to a powder. If a few chunks remain, that's just fine.

2. In a medium bowl, stir together the ground pistachios, yogurt, the ½ cup honey, and the vodka, if using.

3. Churn the mixture in an ice cream maker according to the manufacturer's instructions. During the last minute of churning, add the remaining chopped pistachios. Transfer to a freezer-safe container and freeze for at least 4 hours before serving. Drizzle each scoop with a bit of honey just before serving.

4. Yogurt is best served within 5 days.

makes about 4 cups

Can dessert also be refreshing? That sounds kind of odd, but this sorbet is so bright and herby that no other description so perfectly sums it up. It's the sort of dessert that makes your face pucker and a smile break out at the same time.

MINT-LEMONADE
sorbet

1 cup sugar

1 large handful (about ½ cup) fresh mint leaves

1 cup fresh lemon juice

2 teaspoons vodka

1 teaspoon grated lemon zest

1. In a medium saucepan set over medium heat, combine 1 cup of water with the sugar. Cook, stirring, until the sugar is completely dissolved, about 2 minutes. Remove the pan from the heat. Add the mint leaves, stir, cover, and let steep for 15 minutes. Strain the syrup, discarding the mint leaves. Stir in the lemon juice, vodka, and zest. Pour the mixture into a pitcher. Cover and refrigerate until completely chilled, about 1 hour.

2. Churn the mixture in an ice cream maker according to the manufacturer's instructions. The sorbet will be about the consistency of thick (though icy) pudding. Transfer to a freezer-safe container and freeze for at least 2 hours before serving.

makes 2 cups

I look forward to the months between April and September, because during those summer months I have every reason to indulge in pretty pink wine, also known as rosé. When combined with strawberries, vanilla, and fresh citrus, rosé transforms into a refreshing and icy sweet summer treat. It's part snow cone, part happy hour, part dessert.

strawberry–rosé
SANGRIA GRANITA

½ cup sugar

½ vanilla bean (optional)

1 pint strawberries, hulled

2 cups rosé wine

Juice of 1 orange

Juice of 1 lemon

Juice of 1 lime

1. In a medium saucepan set over medium heat, combine ½ cup water with the sugar, and scrape the seeds of the vanilla bean into the pan, if using. Cook, stirring, until the sugar is dissolved, about 2 minutes.

2. Puree the strawberries in a blender or food processor. Pour the puree into the pan and add the wine, orange juice, lemon juice, and lime juice.

3. Pour the mixture into an 8 x 8-inch baking dish. Put the dish in the freezer and chill for 45 minutes. Run a fork through the mixture, stirring up any ice crystals. Return the baking dish to the freezer and freeze for another hour. Run a fork through the mixture again. Repeat this process until all of the mixture is crystallized and frozen, about 5 more times.

4. To serve, scrape and stir the granita again and spoon heaping mounds of the granita into serving dishes.

serves 4 to 6

The simple flavor of strawberries can also be pleasingly complex when a splash of balsamic vinegar and a sprinkling of black pepper are added to the mix. These ice pops are perfect in the middle of summer when strawberries are supersweet and juicy.

STRAWBERRY-BALSAMIC
pops

2 pounds fresh strawberries, hulled and sliced

¼ cup sugar

2 tablespoons balsamic vinegar

Pinch of salt

⅛ teaspoon coarsely ground black pepper

1. In a medium bowl, toss together the strawberries and sugar. Let sit and macerate for 30 minutes.

2. Transfer the strawberries and their juices to a blender and add the vinegar, salt, and pepper. Blend until relatively smooth. Pour the mixture into ice pop molds, insert sticks, and freeze until frozen through, about 6 hours.

3. To remove the ice pops, put each mold in warm water for 30 seconds. Gently but firmly tug at the stick of each ice pop to remove the pop. Wrap the pops individually in sealable plastic bags and store in the freezer. The ice pops will keep well wrapped in the freezer for up to 7 days.

makes 12 ice pops

This is the story of how two unlikely flavor partners are brought together in an ice pop mold and find out that they get along quite swimmingly. Coffee, meet fig. Fig, meet coffee. Enjoy your delicious friendship.

sweet coffee &
FRESH FIG POPS

- 2 **cups warm strong coffee**
- ⅔ **cup sweetened condensed milk**
- ¼ **cup half-and-half**
- ¼ **teaspoon freshly grated nutmeg**
- 6 **fresh figs, stemmed and thinly sliced**

1. In a medium bowl, combine the coffee, sweetened condensed milk, half-and-half, and nutmeg. Pour almost all of the mixture into ice pop molds, filling them about three-quarters full. Add about 4 fig slices to each mold and top off with more liquid. Insert sticks and freeze until frozen through, about 6 hours.

2. To remove the ice pops, put each mold in warm water for 30 seconds. Gently but firmly tug at the stick of each ice pop to remove the pop. Wrap the pops individually in plastic bags and store in the freezer. The ice pops will keep well wrapped in the freezer for up to 7 days.

makes 8 ice pops

Sometimes all you need is frozen chocolate pudding on a stick. Honor that feeling. Embrace it. Be the person with chocolate-stained lips. We understand—and we're slightly jealous.

creamy
MILK CHOCOLATE POPS

2 cups whole milk

6 ounces milk chocolate, coarsely chopped

2 tablespoons sugar

1 tablespoon unsweetened natural or Dutch-processed cocoa powder

¼ teaspoon salt

Pinch of cayenne pepper (optional)

2 teaspoons pure vanilla extract

1. In a medium saucepan set over low heat, combine the milk, chocolate, sugar, cocoa powder, and salt. Cook, whisking, until the chocolate is melted, about 6 minutes. Remove the pan from the heat. Whisk in the cayenne, if using, and vanilla extract.

2. Pour the mixture into ice pop molds. Insert sticks and freeze until frozen through, about 6 hours.

3. To remove the pops, put each mold in warm water for 30 seconds. Gently but firmly tug at the stick of each ice pop to remove the pop. Wrap the pops individually in plastic bags and store in the freezer. The ice pops will keep well wrapped in the freezer for up to 7 days.

makes 12 ice pops

Some feelings speak to me in milkshake form. This particular milkshake feels just like a Saturday afternoon with my grandfather. It's not that my grandfather and I would lounge on porches drinking peach milkshakes—but we sure *could* have, because my grandfather was the only man I knew to actually drink milkshakes.

This big summery milkshake is over-the-top. It's sweet, *so* peachy, and has a hint of tang from buttermilk. Perfect for unbearable summer days. Perfect for good Grandpa memories.

peach & buttermilk
MILKSHAKE

1 pint vanilla ice cream

1 pint peach sorbet

1 cup cold buttermilk (add more if you'd like a thinner consistency)

1 cup chopped fresh peaches (canned will do in a pinch)

2 teaspoons pure vanilla extract

Pinch of salt

⅓ cup crumbled graham crackers, for serving

1. In a blender, combine the ice cream, sorbet, and buttermilk. Blend until smooth. Add the peaches, vanilla, and salt. Blend well.

2. Divide the milkshake among 6 glasses, sprinkle with the graham cracker crumbs, and serve immediately. This milkshake is best served with a fat straw or tall spoon.

serves 6

ACKNOWLEDGMENTS

Over the nearly two years it took to complete this book, a really cool thing happened. This book went from my mind, through my taste buds, in and out of my kitchen, onto pretty plates, into hungry bellies, through the camera lens, into words and computer documents and e-mails, into design, and then into your hands and kitchens. This book has become the work of so many people. It would be only a shell without their heartfelt participation.

Thank you to my agent, Kari Stuart, and to Ashley Phillips, Ashley Tucker, and all the people at Clarkson Potter for shaping this book word by word and picture by picture into something so beautiful!

Thank you, Mom, Dad, and Lauren for helping me test and brainstorm recipes. Thank you for participating in conversations about butter proportions and for helping me look over these pages when I was like, "aaaaaahhhhhhhh!!!" I'm so fortunate to be in a family with you!

Thank you, Hilton Carter, for eating your way through these recipes. Your partnership and encouragement make my life awesome.

Thank you to my maj, Tracy Shutterbean. Your morning text messages and constant encouragement are everything. It's such a blessing to be your friend.

Thank you, Michael Friedman for your constant support, vision, and friendship. Thanks, also, for all of the cat pictures.

Thank you, Jon Melendez for helping me shoot each and every image in this cookbook. It was vision work even among the spilled cocktails and melting ice cream.

Thank you to Disregarden for beautiful kitchen props. Thank you to Dishwish for the beautiful vintage plates featured in this book.

Thank you to my friends Kristin Guy, Matt Armendariz, Gaby Dalkin, and Catherine McCord for your friendship and feedback and support.

Thank you, Whitney Adams for being the girl with the right wine and words and love. I adore you.

Thank you to the Sundays with Joy ladies, who tirelessly tested these recipes with me!

Thank you to the readers of Joy the Baker. You inspire me every day. I love that we're in the world together. No matter how near or far, we bake with the same heart and that feels really special.

INDEX